ORGANIZATIONAL COMMUNICATION

A LIFESPAN APPROACH

FIRST EDITION

ORGANIZATIONAL COMMUNICATION

A LIFESPAN APPROACH

Michael W. Kramer

UNIVERSITY OF OKLAHOMA

Ryan S. Bisel

UNIVERSITY OF OKLAHOMA

New York   Oxford

OXFORD UNIVERSITY PRESS

Oxford University Press is a department of the University of Oxford.
It furthers the University's objective of excellence in research, scholarship,
and education by publishing worldwide. Oxford is a registered trade mark
of Oxford University Press in the UK and certain other countries.

Published in the United States of America by Oxford University Press
198 Madison Avenue, New York, NY 10016, United States of America.

Library of Congress Cataloging-in-Publication Data

Names: Kramer, Michael W., author. | Bisel, Ryan S., author.
Title: Organizational communication : a lifespan approach / Michael W.
    Kramer, University of Oklahoma, Ryan S. Bisel, University of Oklahoma.
Description: First edition. | New York, NY : Oxford University Press, [2017]
Identifiers: LCCN 2016019664 | ISBN 9780190606268
Subjects: LCSH: Communication in organizations.
Classification: LCC HD30.3 .K7125 2017 | DDC 658.4/5--dc23 LC record available
at https://lccn.loc.gov/2016019664

9 8 7 6 5 4 3 2 1

Printed by LSC Communications, Inc., United States of America

Dedicated to Students

BRIEF CONTENTS

CONTENTS

② Communication and Anticipatory Socialization   30

4 Communication and Management Theory

6 Communication and Organizational Culture

8   Communication and Leadership   209

9   Communication and Decision-Making   239

12 Communication and Work-Nonwork Issues 314

15 Communication During Organizational Exit 396

PREFACE

The inspiration to write this textbook was the result of a number of factors. Perhaps, at its most basic, the textbook I (Michael) used for many years was out of print. It was time to select a new one. That started me on a path of exploring options and conversations. Ryan and I began talking about organizational communication textbooks and imagining what a textbook could be. We discovered we had a number of common goals for a textbook. First, we wanted a textbook that included many of the major concepts and theories of organizational communication but one that had an applied focus and taught specific communication practices so that students could easily connect what they were reading about to their current and future organizational experiences. Second, we wanted it to integrate ethical issues throughout the book rather than examining ethics in just one chapter (or none). Third, we were both dedicated to telling the story of organizational communication as its own domain of study instead of merely adding organizational communication on to management concepts. Finally, we wanted to broaden the topic of the "organization" in organizational communication to include public organizations, family-operated organizations, and nonprofit organizations in addition to the more traditional focus on large for-profit businesses.

As a result, the chapters in the book contain a number of unique characteristics. Each chapter begins with a brief scenario or case study that is used throughout the chapter to make it easy to apply the concepts and theories to a specific example. The scenarios include organizations that range from traditional for-profit businesses, such as big box department stores and banks, to small family-owned businesses, social agencies, and public libraries. The individuals in the scenarios have androgynous names in an effort to reduce gender stereotypes. Each chapter includes ethical issue boxes to help students and instructors explore potential ethical issues related to the chapter's topics. Each chapter includes communication challenges that allow instructors and students to consider some of the practical issues related to applying the communication concepts in the chapter. Each chapter also includes a section applying the concepts to nonprofit and volunteer settings.

In addition to more common chapters regarding communication channels, organizational culture, leadership, decision making, power, and conflict (among others), the book also offers a number of unique chapters that we believe will help students better understand their past, present, and future organizational experiences. For example, in Chapter 2, we explore how our experiences influence our choices about careers and places to work (Chapter 2: "Communication and Anticipatory Socialization"). Most of our students are currently experiencing these issues in their lives, whether they are traditional college-aged students or nontraditional students finishing degrees. In another chapter, we explore the experience of being an organizational newcomer (Chapter 3: "Communication and Organizational Encounter"). Most of our students are preparing to enter new career-oriented jobs where these concepts will be particularly relevant. In Chapter 12, we explore work-life balance issues (Chapter 12: "Communication and Work-Nonwork Issues"). The popular press tells us that millennials are particularly concerned with these issues but so are students who are working full-time while trying to finish their college degrees. In the final chapter, we explore leaving organizations (Chapter 15: "Communication During Organizational Exit"). Although retirement is a long way off for most of our students, they are preparing to leave their university and current jobs. As a result, this chapter will be beneficial to them as well as they consider how they will exit their current organizations.

We want to thank a few people specifically for the resulting book you are reading. We want to thank Toni Magyar and the rest of the people at Oxford University Press for making this book a reality. We want to thank the reviewers who gave us feedback on the proposal and earlier drafts, both those listed in the following and those who choose to remain anonymous. We want to thank the students from Michael's Fall 2015 and Spring 2016 Organizational Communication classes who pre-tested earlier drafts of the book in PDF format and provided valuable feedback. We would like to think that we benefitted more from their feedback than they benefitted from receiving a free textbook. We want to thank Carla Kramer who proofread all of the chapters for us during the revision process. We also want to thank the various family members, friends, and students who shared work experiences with us that gave us the material to make the scenarios realistic.

We dedicate the book to students because it is our hope that the arrangement and content of the book will benefit them, not just in their organizational communication class but throughout their lives as well. We hope that they will be able to use what they learn from this book in their future organizational experiences whether it be in their careers or as volunteers.

Michael W. Kramer
Ryan S. Bisel

ACKNOWLEDGMENTS

Our sincere thanks are extended to reviewers of this text. They include the following:

Mohammad A. Auwal, *California State University–Los Angeles*

Carol-Lynn Bower, *Arizona State University*

Stephanie Dailey, *Texas State University*

Karl Babij, *DeSales University*

Jennie Donohue, *Marist College*

Kenny Embry, *Saint Leo University*

Michelle Fetherston, *Marquette University/ University of Wisconsin–Milwaukee*

Robin Frkal, *Northeastern University/ Assumption College*

Jeremy Fyke, *Belmont University*

Angela N. Gist, *University of Kansas*

LaKresha Graham, *Rockhurst University*

Meredith Harrigan, *State University of New York at Geneseo*

Jenna Haugen, *University of Kentucky/ University of Louisville*

Carole Isom-Barnes, *Queens University of Charlotte*

Lorelle B. Jabs, *Seattle Pacific University*

Ed Kellerman, *University of Florida*

William Kelvin, *Kent State University*

Lucyann Kerry, *Chadron State College*

Kathleen Krone, *University of Nebraska*

Holly Kruse, *Rogers State University*

David Lapakko, *Augsburg College*

Jaesub Lee, *University of Houston*

Patricia J. Lehman, *Goshen College*

Marla Lowenthal, *University of San Francisco*

Theresa MacNeil, *Florida Southern College*

Vernon Miller, *Michigan State University*

Michael P. Pagano, *Fairfield University*

Sarah Riforgiate, *Kansas State University*

Gary Shulman, *Miami University*

Frances Smith, *Murray State University*

Kimberly Smith, *University of Central Florida*

Brandy Stamper, *University of North Carolina at Charlotte*

Michael A. Stefanone, *University at Buffalo*

Heather L. Walter, *The University of Akron*

ABOUT THE AUTHORS

Michael W. Kramer (PhD, University of Texas) is Professor and Chair of the Department of Communication at the University of Oklahoma. He has received multiple teaching awards while teaching organizational and group communication to undergraduate and graduate students for over 30 years at three institutions. His organizational research primarily focuses on employee transitions as part of the assimilation/socialization process such as newcomer entry, transfers, exit, and corporate mergers. His group research focuses on decision making, membership, and leadership. He has used a range of qualitative and quantitative research methods from structural equation modeling to ethnography. He has published over 50 articles in refereed journals such as *Communication Monographs*, *Human Communication Research*, *Journal of Applied Communication Research*, *Management Communication Quarterly*, *Leadership Quarterly*, and *Small Group Research*, among others. He has written books on uncertainty management and socialization, and recently has coedited three books on volunteers and nonprofit organizations. He and his wife enjoy attending theater performances. He also enjoys performing on stage from time to time. He has been running long enough that he is often a top finisher in local races against the few other runners left in his age group.

Ryan S. Bisel (PhD, University of Kansas) is an Associate Professor of Organizational Communication at the University of Oklahoma. His research interests include leadership communication, organizational culture change, and behavioral ethics. Bisel and his colleagues have developed original organizational communication concepts such as the hierarchical mum effect, the workers' moral mum effect, ethical sensegiving, supervisor moral talk contagion, and organizational moral learning. Bisel's research is published in communication and management journals such as *Management Communication Quarterly*, *Communication Theory*, *International Journal of Business Communication*, *Western Journal of Communication*, *Leadership Quarterly*, *Small Group Research*, and *Human Relations*. Bisel has also worked as a speaker, trainer, and process consultant for organizations such as the Kansas Health Foundation, Douglas County Visiting Nurses Association, and National Weather Association. Bisel enjoys playing guitar, eating great foods, spending time with his wife, and playing "ninjas" with his two young children.

CHAPTER 1

Introduction

As a part-time employee while attending a nearby university, Shane has worked the morning shift from 9:00 a.m. to 12:00 p.m. three or four mornings a week at the local public library for over a year. Shane has always walked in the door between 8:55 and 9:00 a.m. even if it meant sitting in the parking lot checking emails to arrive exactly on time. Recently, the branch manager sent out the following memo to employees:

> **To:**   All employees
> **From:** Pat Morris, Branch Manager
> **Date:** February 25
> **RE:**   Work Policy

> *I have noticed recently that a few of our employees are arriving just in time to begin their shift. This results in rushing around at the last minute. It can create problems for those who are ready to leave because their replacement is not ready to begin. In the end, our service to our customers is less professional than it should be.*
>
> *As a reminder, we expect employees to arrive 15 minutes prior to their start time so that they can be ready to start on time. This will result in improved relationships with other workers, better service to our customers, and a more professional atmosphere overall.*

The full-time employees, who were salaried, appreciated this reminder of the library's "policy." They all arrived early anyway and were sometimes stuck waiting for a part-time employee to arrive when they were ready to leave. Shane and the other part-time employees privately complained to each other about this new policy. They did not think that they needed any time to prepare; they were ready to work when they arrived. In addition, expecting them to come in 15 minutes early seemed unfair because they were not paid for that extra time.

In the end, the part-time employees did start coming to work earlier because they did not want to risk losing their jobs. They came in earlier, although not always 15 minutes early. The branch manager heard that the full-time employees were pleased with the result and noticed that customers seemed to receive better service because of it.

Most people who have worked in the United States can probably relate to this story. If they have not had a direct personal experience like it, they perhaps know someone who has, or can imagine it happening based on their own work experiences.

Organizational communication is the study of situations like this and many more. Because we spend most of our lives involved in organizations, including schools, sports teams, workplaces, and volunteer organizations, a better understanding of organizational communication can assist us in navigating those organizational experiences. Knowledge of organizational communication makes it easier to understand and make sense of our organizational experiences and can make them more positive.

· · · · ·

Defining Communication

To begin studying organizational communication, it is important to first define *communication*. There are about as many different definitions of communication as there are textbooks. We consider three definitions as representative of those definitions.

Information Transfer

Early definitions of communication were based on information transfer models (see Figure 1.1). At the most basic level, these models suggested that one person, the sender, has an idea. The sender encodes the idea into a message, which is then sent through a channel (e.g., speech, written memo, text message) to a receiver who decodes the message and hopefully understands it as the sender intended (e.g., Shannon & Weaver, 1949). In this approach, *noise* is interference that results in less than perfect transmission of the intended message. This interference could include physical noise, such as background music or traffic noise that makes it difficult to hear, or psychological noise, such as biases and misperceptions that interfere with an accurate understanding of the message. Later, scholars recognized that information transfer is a cyclical process of sending and receiving messages through feedback (e.g., Schramm, 1954). The focus of study from this perspective is on the sender and factors that result in more or less accurate transmission of ideas from the sender to others. An information transfer model essentially defines communication as the process of transferring information or ideas

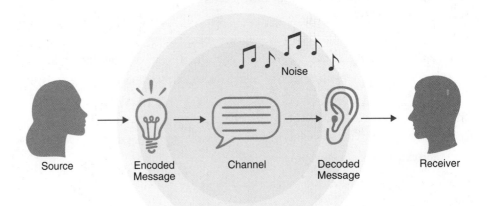

Figure 1.1. A Typical Information Transfer Model of Communication

from one person to another person or group through verbal and nonverbal behavior. Many individuals and organizations implicitly function with this understanding of communication.

Shared Meaning

A second way of defining communication focuses on the meaning that is assigned to communication messages and particularly if there is shared meaning among the people involved (e.g., Putnam, 1982). Whereas the transfer model emphasized the senders' role, a shared meaning definition focuses attention on the receiver. This approach also recognizes that meaning can be assigned to unintended messages. This is particularly critical in understanding nonverbal communication. If a supervisor has crossed arms while listening to a group of employees, they may conclude that the supervisor is opposed to their ideas. The supervisor may simply have been cold during that encounter, but because the employees shared an understanding of the crossed arms, they responded based on the meaning they assigned. The focus of the study of communication is on the process by which employees agreed that the supervisor is against their idea. So a shared meaning definition studies communication as the process by which individuals come to share an understanding of verbal and nonverbal communication.

Transactional Meaning Creation

A third way of defining communication looks at it as an interactive process: meaning is created in the communication transaction involving both parties or through the dialogue between the communicators. There really is no longer a clearly defined sender and receiver because both parties serve both roles as they interact. Through dialogue and interaction, the parties involved create meaning. The combination of messages produced, perception of those messages, resulting messages, and context all contribute to meaning (e.g., Gerbner, 1956). A transactional process definition of communication emphasizes that communication is the process by which individuals assign meaning in a communicative situation through mutual interaction and influence. In this way, meaning is co-created and there are no distinctions between senders and receivers.

Applying the Three Definitions of Communication

A public relations mishap illustrates the differences between these three definitions of communication. A few years ago, an investment firm known for being frugal sent out its monthly employee newsletter with a picture of a vanilla bottle on the cover and a headline boasting its values as "pure vanilla." The intended message was that just like vanilla ice cream is a reliable, no-thrills flavor of ice cream, their company was a reliable, no-thrills company that investors could trust. Despite this intent, minority employees of the company were upset by the message because it suggested that the company focused on white employees to the exclusion of others.

1 Information Transfer

An information transfer definition of communication would conclude that the message was unsuccessful or ineffective because the intended meaning was not transferred to the audience. It might blame the problem on insensitivity on the part of the sender, inadequate definitions of what plain vanilla means, or on the societal context that created noise for some receivers.

2 Shared Meaning

A shared meaning definition of communication would focus on the fact that shared meaning was not achieved and that there were instead subgroups that developed different shared meanings. One subgroup may have accepted the intended message that the company was simple and basic, whereas another ascribed an alternative meaning of exclusive hiring and promotion. Shared meaning occurred in clusters of employees based on the meaning they associated with "vanilla."

3 Transactional Process

A transactional process definition would look at how the meaning was created during the transaction between organizational members over time. So in this case, the writers of the newsletter, those people who liked the message, and those who were offended by it would communicate with each other until an understanding of the message was developed. This understanding might conclude that the message was not intended to be offensive but was potentially offensive because it was naively conceived without considering differences in the intended audiences' backgrounds. The understanding might simply be that we agree to disagree on the message's meaning. Whatever the final understanding of the message turned out to be was developed during the transaction between parties.

Interestingly, regardless of which definition of communication is used, the analysis leads to the same overall need: Additional communication is needed to correct the problems created by the ineffective communication that occurred.

Working Definition

So what definition should we use? Instead of defining communication in one way, we are going to focus on two definitions: one for effective and one for ineffective communication. Effective communication occurs when the senders and receivers reach an understanding in response to intentional verbal or nonverbal messages. Effective communication allows people to coordinate their actions and manage their relationships. Ineffective communication occurs when a lack of understanding happens as a result of intended and unintended verbal or nonverbal behavior. Ineffective communication inhibits participants' ability to coordinate activities and manage relationships. Note that understanding in these definitions does not necessarily mean shared meaning, although it could. For example, a supervisor and subordinate may not have the same understanding of what it means that the supervisor has "an open door policy" and still be able to work together and maintain their relationship.

Defining effective and ineffective communication in this way allows us to consider situations like the opening case study about Shane, the library worker, from more than one perspective. The memo could be considered effective because the entire library staff shared some understanding in that they all knew they were expected to arrive early for their shifts. It also allows us to consider how the memo may have been ineffective because some individuals (mostly full-time) assigned a positive meaning to it, whereas others (mostly part-time) assigned a negative meaning to it. The communication was simultaneously effective by getting employees to arrive early and ineffective in that it negatively affected the part-timers' morale.

Do you think Mimo's ice cream labeling of their Columbian products is offensive?

Defining Organizations

For studying organizational communication, it is important to recognize that there are three primary meanings for the term *organization* based on different assumptions. Organizations can be understood legally, communicatively, and socially (Drumheller, 2004).

A Legal Definition of Organizations

The legal definition of organizations views organizations based on recognizing them as entities with the same sorts of rights, privileges, and obligations as people (Brummer, 1991). This definition recognizes organizations as entities that buy and sell property, sign contracts, produce profits and losses on which they are obligated to pay taxes (unless they have nonprofit status in the United States), and must comply with the nation's legal system. From this perspective, it is fairly easy to determine who are the members of organizations as employees as well as who are not, although when organizations rely on volunteers and allow employees to work from home as tele-commuters, the membership boundaries become less clear. The use of this definition is sometimes criticized for implicitly characterizing organizations as impersonal containers that exist apart from people; it suggests that people enter and leave pre-existing organizations that have clearly defined physical boundaries (Smith & Turner, 1995).

A Communicative Definition of Organizations

A communicative definition of organizations views them as being created and maintained through communication. In its purest form, this definition asserts that organizations are constituted and exist only through communication (e.g., Taylor, Cooren, Giroux, & Robichaud, 1996). This idea might seem counterintuitive at first, but relationships and social structures that we eventually come to call *organizations* require communication at every turn. In fact, organizations are created and maintained in at least four kinds of messaging.

First, activity coordination—working interdependently with others to complete tasks—requires individuals to communicate to get work done. Second, self-structuring—discussing and deciding how roles and responsibilities will be divided—requires communication for planning and the creation of policies. Third, membership negotiation—determining who belongs and who does not belong to the group—requires communication, such as what happens during hiring and firing. Finally, institutional positioning—representing the organizations' image to those who are not members—requires messaging such as advertising, marketing, and public relations (McPhee & Zaug, 2000).

From the communicative definition of organization, the legal entity of the organization only exists as it is constituted through communication. In other words, a physical building is not an organization; through communication it becomes constituted as part of the organizing activities of the people who identify as an organization. From this perspective, it is more difficult to determine which people are or are not members of the communicatively created organization. For example, the CEO's spouse may serve an important role in the organization without being an employee. The technology team located in the building but employed by another company likely blurs the organizational boundary when the technology team is referred to as "our team."

A Social Definition of Organizations

A social definition of organization focuses on the social responsibilities of organizations and the expectations that they be responsible and responsive to the public. Because organizations have become an increasing complex part of our social system as we have moved from an agrarian society to an urban/suburban one, concern over institutional responsibility has increased. As a result of these growing expectations, organizations have needed to create a unique sense of identity or self for the organization in relationship to the community, its citizens, and other institutions (Cheney & Christensen, 2001). In part due to the distrust of organizations after various scandals such as the Watergate Scandal, the collapse of Enron, and the banking crisis of 2008, many organizations have embraced the corporate social responsibility movement to demonstrate that they are concerned about people in their communities, are guided by ethical principles, and are concerned about more than their bottom line (Pompper, 2013). Through community involvement and support for employee volunteering, organizational leaders strive to demonstrate that they value the relationship between their organizations and their various stakeholders—and not just profits. Although from this perspective it may also be easy to determine technically who the organizational members are, organizational members are simply some of the important stakeholders to consider. Community members who follow the organization through social media are also stakeholders. A social definition of organizations involves looking broadly at all the stakeholders to understand the organization and its context.

Having explained three different ways of defining organizations, it is important to recognize that most of the time we use these different definitions interchangeably. These definitional distinctions are often of more interest to organizational scholars interacting with each other than to people living and operating in organizations. Employees of an organization, regardless of its size, are likely aware of its legal status and recognize that it is accountable to the legal system. They also recognize that it is only through their communication interactions that the organization continues to function and be productive. They are likely concerned about how it is perceived by various community stakeholders, including stockholders if it is publicly traded, the local government who may provide tax incentives for job creation, citizens in the surrounding area who are concerned about how their quality of life may be impacted by the company's waste products, and a variety of others. Volunteers in nonprofit organizations are similarly aware of the importance of these factors. So although we easily understand the term organization, we frequently use a mixture of these three definitions.

The Complexity of Defining Communication in Organizations

Organizational communication is effective and ineffective communication that occurs between people involved in formal and informal organizations. The focus of much of this book is on creating effective communication that helps individuals and organizations accomplish goals by creating shared meaning rather than misunderstanding. Not surprisingly, even this two-prong definition of communication fails to completely capture the broader process of communication in organizational settings.

Strategic Ambiguity

All three definitions of communication in the previous section assume that clarity of meaning resulting in shared understanding is a desirable and achievable goal. Research by Eric Eisenberg (1984) suggests that strategic ambiguity, in which meaning is deliberately not clear, can serve an important communicative function in organizational settings. Eisenberg's study of the strategic use of ambiguity suggests that it has five possible positive outcomes.

First, ambiguity can be used strategically to create *unified diversity*. Unified diversity exists when different people have different understandings of the same words or ideas but think that they are in agreement. A common example of this is the mission statement of most organizations. For example, many state universities have a mission statement that says the university stands for excellence in teaching, research, and service. Students, professors, administrators, parents, and state legislatures may all endorse this mission statement but actually understand it quite differently. To students and parents, excellence in service may mean having good food service and recreational facilities on campus. Faculty members may think it means having effective committees to address faculty governance. State legislators often consider university outreach programs, such as agricultural education or nutrition and health programs to the community as important service. The different groups often have different ideas about what excellence in research means and how much time and money should be spent on it. So despite each group having a different understanding of the ambiguous mission statement, they all endorse the mission statement and create the impression of unity despite diverse thinking. A clearly worded mission statement, by contrast, would create problems for the organization, as different groups may be unwilling to support the mission statement or the organization because they do not agree with its specific focus. Due to these issues, most mission statements are strategically ambiguous.

Another value of strategic ambiguity is that is allows for *adaptability to change*. A very specific goal can be difficult to change, whereas an ambiguous one is easier to change. Eisenberg points out that the ocean liner industry first changed its mission from travel to entertainment when air travel replaced sea travel as a form of transportation. Although initially this meant providing fine dining and a relaxed atmosphere for vacationers headed to exotic places, this ambiguous goal has allowed the industry to add amenities to their boats from zip lines and surfing pools to casinos and Broadway shows; and they even offer trips to nowhere, ones that simply go out to sea and return. All of these changes were possible without having to change the industry's mission due to the strategic ambiguity of the mission. Similarly, an organization committed to providing excellent customer service can change how it provides that service without having to change its values.

On a more personal level, the use of strategic ambiguity can help *maintain relationships*. Although we often state that we want people to be honest, we frequently use strategic ambiguity to avoid complete honesty and save face for ourselves or others. Many of us have thanked someone for an unwanted gift by stating that it was "unique" or "unexpected" rather than giving our true evaluation of it. In organizational settings, we may describe a coworker's impractical idea as "creative" or "full of possibilities" while guiding the discussion toward a more practical alternative. In both instances, strategic ambiguity allows us to maintain our relationship with the other person when a more honest comment would likely strain the relationship.

People in power can often *maintain power* through the use of strategic ambiguity. If a supervisor creates a clearly stated policy that anyone who is late three times in one month will be fired, the supervisor loses the ability to make decisions about particular employees; the policy determines the outcome instead of the supervisor. A clear policy means that if the best employee is late three times in a month for any reason, that employee gets fired. An ambiguous policy that says "after three absences in a month, an employee may be subject to dismissal" maintains the power of the supervisor who can enforce it rigidly on poor performing employees but be more forgiving of the better employees.

Strategic Ambiguity

The concept of strategic ambiguity creates ethical issues. That is, when is the use of strategic ambiguity really a deliberate attempt to mislead someone else? For example, if the supervisor says "as soon as possible" but really means "I'm not going to address this problem unless I have to," that appears to be misleading or lying. If it means it could take a few weeks, but it will get done, that seems like strategic ambiguity. How do we distinguish between the ethical use of strategic ambiguity and the unethical behavior of lying, deception, or plain old "bullshit"?

Finally, an ambiguous statement may allow for *plausible deniability* at a later time. A commitment to address the problem "as quickly as possible" allows a supervisor to deny a subordinate's interpretation that "I expected this to be addressed by the end of the month." Of course, this can work both ways. A subordinate can also make ambiguous promises and deny the supervisor's interpretation as well.

The idea that strategic ambiguity is a form of effective organizational communication challenges most of our definitions of communication because it suggests that transferring information clearly or creating actual shared meaning are not always the appropriate goal for a communicator. A competent communicator may need to use ambiguity strategically to create coordinated activities and maintain relationships while being clear at other times.

Nonverbal Communication

Nonverbal communication occurs when individuals assign meaning to the behaviors and actions of others. These actions can include intentional actions like pointing to something to make meaning clearer or unintentional actions such as when a group assigns meaning to the fact that a person sat at another table instead of joining them. Among other behaviors, it includes facial expressions, eye contact, vocal cues, gestures, touching, posture/stance, and physical appearance. It also includes the use of physical objects such as clothing, artifacts, and the placement of fixed and semifixed features. At times, people assign meaning to these as nonverbal behaviors.

Nonverbal communication adds complexity to all communication contexts, but it has some unique characteristics in organizational settings. Steele (1973) identified three important communication messages conveyed nonverbally in organization settings: security, symbolic identification (status), and social contact. Although these are conceptually distinct, they often overlap or work in conjunction with each other.

Security can be communicated by a variety of physical attributes in an organization. For example, an office building may be arranged with individual offices or cubicles. An office provides more security and privacy than a cubicle, but even a cubicle provides a greater sense of security than an open office. Some organizations have security guards or entrance systems where individuals must have a badge to access a building or floor. In some courtrooms, individuals pass through airport-like security to gain access, whereas retail stores and restaurants are accessible to anyone and offer little security to their employees. The workspace arrangements and any security systems in an organization communicate a particular sense of security for people.

Symbolic identification or status is communicated nonverbally in many ways in organizations. People with higher status typically wear more expensive clothes, have private offices, and sit at the head of the table. Those with the lowest status typically may share work space and wear uniforms. Technology may be a status symbol as well. Having the latest, most expensive, and smallest computer likely suggests higher status than having a dated desktop computer. Organizations literally spend millions of dollars making sure that they communicate status correctly through the physical layout and artifacts in the organization such as the size of cubicles and the height of the dividing walls. A large computer company spent thousands of dollars assessing the quality of the artwork in employees' offices at their regional headquarters to make sure that they had the correct number and quality of art for their particular status.

Finally, *social contact* is encouraged or discouraged through the arrangement of fixed or semifixed features. A person who always stays behind the desk communicates a different desire for social contact than a person who comes around the desk, shakes hands, and sits with visitors. Eye contact and posture can also encourage or discourage social contact. In many organizations today, access to someone can encourage or discourage social contact. For example, if a person must first talk to an administrative assistant to gain permission to talk to a department manager, this discourages communication by limiting access. Alternatively, if the manager has an email account that anyone can access, the unlimited access encourages communication.

What are the security and social contact advantages and disadvantages to the workplaces shown here?

Because these three characteristics often work together, they can create communication challenges for organizational members. The same factors that communicate security and status often discourage social contact, and those that promote social contact reduce security. So having separate offices with doors communicates security and status but discourages interactions. By contrast, having cubicles encourages more social contact but provides limited privacy or sense of security. Balancing these various nonverbal cues may not be difficult in a small business where everyone knows everyone, but in a large organization, balancing them can be challenging. If high-ranking officers are located on the top floors of the building, it communicates their security and status but discourages social contact and communication. This very common arrangement makes it challenging for high-status individuals to keep in touch with rank-and-file employees. What might be more remarkable is when someone manages to maintain open communication across the levels of an organization despite the physical barriers to open communication.

Applying the Three Nonverbal Criteria

In many banks, the CEO is located on the top floor in a large office suite with lots of windows. It takes getting past the top floor security guard and the office manager to see the CEO. Once inside, the office has three possible "meeting places." The CEO can sit behind the desk in a large, comfortable chair while the visitors sit in smaller, office-style chairs. The CEO can also meet visitors at a round table where everyone has the same seating. Finally, there is a very comfortable area that is much like a living room with a couple of couches and a coffee table. These arrangements communicate a great deal nonverbally.

① Security

The location of the office communicates a great deal of security for the CEO because it takes a substantial effort to visit the CEO. A visitor must take the elevator to the appropriate floor and then convince the security guard and the office manager that it is acceptable to see the CEO.

② Symbolic Identification

Status is clearly communicated in many ways. The size and location of the office and the view from the many windows in it symbolically identify the CEO as important. The expensive furnishings also indicate status. A comparison of these nonverbal cues to a teller's small space with a stool to sit on make the status difference between the two clear.

③ Social Contact

Certainly the security that the office offers also limits social contact. However, it is also possible for the CEO to manage social contact for those who do visit. Meeting at the desk maintains distance between the CEO and visitors, most likely discouraging long visits. Meeting at the table reduces distance and creates a working relation between the CEO and visitors. Although the visit might be longer, it will focus on getting work done. Finally, if the CEO and visitors meet in the living room area, it suggests that they have a closer, more social relationship. The visitors might stay for quite some time and chat about many topics, not all of which are work related.

Ambiguity and nonverbal communication are just two factors that make defining effective and ineffective communication both interesting and challenging in organizational settings. The rest of this book concerns many other communication issues that make organizational communication fascinating and complex. Before we introduce those issues, it is important to expose you to the different perspectives scholars use to study organizational communication.

Office Design

The head of a volunteer organization wants to maintain open communication with the employees and volunteers but also needs to maintain a stylish office to meet with community leaders and officials from other organizations. The office must not be too lavish so that donors do not think that their money is being wasted. Technology has also created options that were unavailable until recently. Consider the ways to arrange physical attributes of the organization and office to communicate the intended messages. How can all of these goals be accomplished?

Perspectives on Organizational Communication

If you have ever discussed a piece of modern art with other people, you likely found that they had significantly different perspectives on it. Where one person sees an interesting combination of shape and color, another might see an abstract representation of some person or idea, and a third person might see something so simple that a child could reproduce it and wonder why it is in a museum at all. Similarly, we do not all look at organizations in the same way. We each have certain ideas or assumptions that influence how we view organizations. These assumptions influence not only what we see in organizations but also how we evaluate them.

Scholars have spent a great deal of effort attempting to identify different research perspectives (Deetz, 2001; Krone, Jablin, & Putnam, 1987; Putnam, 1982). Rather than introducing every perspective that scholars have identified, we are going to focus on three main perspectives: post-positivist, interpretive, and critical (Corman, 2000).

A Post-Positivist Perspective

The post-positive perspective to studying organizational communication is the oldest perspective. It grew out of what was initially called a functional or positivist perspective. Researchers who embrace this perspective view reality as an objective phenomenon and perceive that their role as researchers is to measure and examine organizations objectively much like scientists conducting experiments (Putnam, 1982). Functionalists initially viewed organizations as machines that did not change. Over time, they recognized that organizations are less like machines and more like living organisms that change and adapt to their environment, but they continued to view their role as that of scientists objectively dissecting an organization to understand the reality of how it worked. By understanding how the organization worked, researchers hoped to suggest ways to improve its functioning and efficiency.

The researcher might examine how many resources were purchased by the organization, how many employees were used in producing the final product, and whether the process was efficient. Focusing on communication, the researcher would measure how often supervisors interacted with their subordinates to determine if a certain amount of communication resulted in greater efficiency. If the organization recently adopted a teamwork philosophy, the researcher might compare the output under the former hierarchical structure to the output under the new team structure to see if the changes in communication channels from hierarchical, top-down communication to lateral communication resulted in a more efficient and effective organization.

Post-positivists differ from early functionalists in a number of important ways (Miller, 2000). First, although like functionalists, post-positivists largely accept that reality has an objective existence apart from researchers, they recognize that their efforts as researchers are not objective and that efforts to observe reality are always tainted by certain theoretical assumptions or personal biases of the researcher. Post-positivists try to maintain as objective a stance as possible in trying to measure concepts and establish cause–effect relationships, but they recognize that in choosing to focus on measuring a particular concept and seeing if it is related to a particular outcome, they are actually creating perceptions of reality through their subjective choices; those perceptions of reality do not represent an objective reality. For example, choosing to measure the frequency of supervisor to subordinate interaction—as opposed to the frequency of peer-to-peer communication–is a subjective choice. Examining how each affects company profits rather than employee turnover is also a subjective choice.

Second, whereas many researchers using a functional perspective focused on the bottom line of profit, post-positivists are likely to have a broader understanding of organizational effectiveness that includes outcomes such as employee satisfaction and identification with the organization, retention of employees, or a positive public image, among others. Whereas functionalists tended to maintain distance from human perceptions, feelings, and attitudes, post-positivists frequently explore the subjective and human side of organizations.

There are likely few pure functionalists currently studying organizational communication who believe that they are completely objective and that their measurements of various concepts and attitudes do not involve some level of subjectivity, but even with their changed perspective, post-positivists share some commonalities with functionalists. Like functionalists, researchers who embrace the post-positivist perspective typically use quantitative measures. Quantitative methods allow researchers to measure characteristics of the organization and its communication process and then look for statistical relationships between those measures. Typically, researchers begin with a theory or framework and then conduct a study to test the accuracy of its predictions. They often view their approaches as more scientific than other approaches because they try to remain objective and impersonal. Of course, the selection of a theoretical perspective and the decision to use quantitative measures are subjective choices. If they measure the quality of supervisor communication and its relationship to job satisfaction, the post-positivists know that their measurement of quality is not objective; however, they attempt to measure it in a valid and reliable manner so that others can replicate the study. The objective part of the process is the application of the statistical analyses conducted once the other research decisions have been made, but even those statistical tests are based on assumptions that do not have an objective reality.

An Interpretive Perspective

An interpretive approach to the study of organizational communication emerged in the 1970s and early 1980s as an alternative to the functional/positivist approaches. An interpretive scholar is not concerned with maintaining objectivity and does not focus on organizational efficiency. Instead, interpretive researchers focus on the subjective meaning that individuals assign to their organizational experiences. This approach focuses on communication as the process of symbolic interaction that creates meaning or understanding about organizational experiences for its members (Putnam, 1982). Interpretive scholars recognize the importance of understanding the subjective meaning of experiences and that there are multiple subjective meanings assigned to events by different individuals.

It is important to note that interpretive researchers do not adopt a relativistic perspective. A relativistic perspective suggests that any interpretation is acceptable because meaning is completely subjective. Interpretive researchers reject the idea that any one claim is as good as the next and that there is no way to establish knowledge claims (Cheney, 2000). For the interpretive researcher, there must be some level of intersubjective, or shared meaning, in which multiple individuals agree on the "reality" of the situation based on their communication interactions (Weick, 1995). This means that the researcher does not accept any single individual's subjective meaning but seeks to discover some level of agreement within a group of individuals.

For example, if the researcher is trying to understand the relationships of a team manager to the team, and the first team member interviewed says the manager is terrible, the researcher does not stop there. Instead, the researcher does additional interviews to establish if that is an appropriate representation of the intersubjective reality of the team. The next team member says the manager is great, and then others point out mostly positive characteristics of the manger and only a few negative ones related to handling personality conflicts in the team. Based on this information, the researcher then uses the collected evidence to conclude that the team manager is largely effective but fails to address some personality conflicts in the team. However, even though there is intersubjective agreement that this is an accurate description of the team, that "reality" is not some objective truth simply because of the agreement.

Interpretive scholars typically use qualitative research methods to systematically collect and analyze data to find the shared meanings of organizational members. Instead of relying on survey responses to measure concepts, interpretive scholars are interested in various communication "texts" or data. The data may include examination of actual written texts, documents, or artifacts of the organization such as annual reports, company slogans, or website information. The data that are studied quite often are interviews of organizational members, but they can also include notes taken while observing in the organization, recordings of dialogue among organizational members, and often both verbal and nonverbal behaviors.

To gain an understanding of the shared meaning, interpretive scholars typically say that they start with the data and then develop theory and understanding based on their analysis of it. Through careful, systematic data analysis, the researcher gains an understanding of how participants make sense of their lived experience (Weick, 1995). However, because it is impossible to approach a study without some preconceived notions of what is important or interesting to examine, interpretive scholars do not claim to be unbiased. Often the interpretive scholar will show the individuals who are the focus of the study a copy of their interpretation to check to make sure that they have accurately described the shared meaning of their experience. This process, known as "member checking," is just one of several methods interpretive researchers can use to establish the appropriateness of their interpretations (Creswell, 2007).

Most scholars and individuals using this perspective view organizations as cultures rather than as machines or organisms. An organization's culture has a set of expectations (norms), values, and beliefs that are shared among the organizational members; the culture is developed over time through communication (Pacanowsky & O'Donnell-Trujillo, 1983). Interpretive researchers gain an appreciation of the culture through their analysis of data and strive to represent the culture accurately as understood by organizational members.

A Critical Perspective

The critical perspective views organizations as systems of economic and political exploitation in which individuals in positions of power or influence use that power in ways that benefit themselves over other organizational members (Putnam, 1982). Critical scholars see organizations as places where power issues result in some groups being privileged while other groups are dominated or oppressed (Deetz, 2001). The system of domination and oppression is created through organizational communication. For example, the hierarchical structure that exists in most organizations creates a system in which the communication from those at the top of the organization generates an inequitable system in which their voices and decisions control those lower in the organization. Then those at the top of the organization decide that the profits of the organization should be funneled into high salaries for executives and modest ones for rank-and-file employees. Those who work with and cooperate with those in power receive disproportionate benefits compared to those who do not. In organizations dominated by white male executives, the result is often that women and minorities are excluded from those benefits.

Critical scholars may use a wide range of methods to support their critique of organizations as places of oppression, including those of the post-positive and the interpretive scholars. For example, the concept of the glass ceiling is the idea that certain groups, typically women or minorities, can only get close enough to see the people in high power positions in an organization but cannot actually obtain those positions for themselves. This concept has been explored using quantitative methods to show that women are underrepresented and underpaid in high-ranking positions as well as to examine what caused the problem and how to solve it across organizational types (Ragins, Townsend, & Mattis, 1998). Other scholars have used interviews to provide insights into the dynamics that contribute to gender disparity for women even in an industry increasingly dominated by women such as public relations (Wrigley, 2002). Other critical scholars have analyzed organizational texts or oral legends to show how these stories help those in powerful positions, like CEOs, maintain their power while keeping those near the bottom of the organization controlled through self-serving organizational rules (Mumby, 1987). This freedom to use whatever method can be used to critique an organization has advantages and does not align clearly with an objective or subjective view of reality.

Critical scholars face a number of criticisms themselves. Critical scholars like to position themselves as being marginalized in the field of organizational communication, much like the individuals they study, and then offer critiques of the dominant perspectives from that position. Given how frequently this type of research is published, however, it is difficult for critical scholars to continue to argue that they are marginalized (Mumby, 2000). In a somewhat related critique, it has been suggested that in providing a critique of others, critical scholars are themselves becoming dominant and elitist when they attempt to impose their perspective on others (Deetz, 2001).

Critical scholarship has also been criticized for failing to offer viable solutions to their negative evaluations. For example, one study criticizes an organization for promoting healthy lifestyles, including offering an on-site gym and exercise classes along with smoking cessation and time management classes (Zoller, 2003). The analysis concludes that these programs primarily serve the managerial goal of developing efficient employees without recognizing that the work the organization requires contributes to the unhealthy behaviors and stress of employees. At the same time, these programs marginalize those who are out of shape or continue to smoke, according to the critique. By pointing out these concerns, the study provides valuable insight into unintended negative consequences these programs have for some individuals. The study, however, failed to recognize the potential life-saving benefits to the employees of being healthier as a result of the programs and did not suggest a way in which the company can promote good health among its employees that benefits them as well as the company. Instead, it emphasizes that employees can resist the hegemonic efforts of the management.

Applying the Three Organizational Perspectives

To reinforce the distinctions between the three perspectives, in this section, we reconsider the opening scenario about the memo to library employees from each perspective. Not surprisingly, researchers see different issues in the organization due to their perspectives.

➊ The Post-Positivist Perspective

A post-positivist researcher would primarily focus on the effectiveness of the communication in the memo. The researcher would note that the branch manager, Pat, recognized a problem that was negatively affecting the organization and sent out a memo to correct the problem. A post-positivist researcher could evaluate the memo to see if its clarification of expectation had a positive effect on the organization. It seems that the memo was clear and the employees understood the new expectation that they should not arrive at the last minute for their shifts. The researcher could use a relatively objective measurement of how often employees arrived more than 10 minutes early during a 2-week time period both before and after the memo was sent. The results of the study could establish a cause–effect relationship to evaluate the memo's effectiveness.

A post-positivist researcher might also explore employee attitudes surrounding the memo by measuring the pre- and post-memo satisfaction of employees. The researcher exploring satisfaction is examining subjective attitudes using quantitative measures in an effort to be as objective as possible. The study might find that full-time employees were more satisfied after the memo because it made their work easier and the customers benefitted as well. The part-time employees likely would be less satisfied after the memo because it imposed on their time. If the researcher conducted a longitudinal study, it would be possible to determine if the memo had a long-term effect both on the number of employees coming to work early and on their satisfaction, or if their behaviors and attitudes reverted back to pre-memo levels over time. The researcher maintains a fairly objective stance by allowing the data collected to determine the conclusions rather than letting personal biases or expectations determine the findings.

➋ The Interpretive Perspective

An interpretive perspective would focus on meaning in the scenario. The researcher would likely notice that meaning has changed at the library over time. Based on interviews and observation, the researcher might discover that prior to the memo, part-time employees thought that the norm of arriving on time to start was all it took to be effective employees. By contrast, the full-time employees, including Pat, thought all along that arriving early was an appropriate expectation for professionals. After the memo, there was a shared understanding that the library valued employees who arrive early rather than at the last minute.

Despite this intersubjective understanding of the memo, the interpretive researcher would likely notice that there seem to be two subgroups in the library, each with their own understanding of the policy. The full-time employees thought that arriving early demonstrated professionalism and courtesy to other employees and customers. The part-time employees thought the expectation to arrive early was unfair. In addition, they also seemed to expect that voicing their concerns was not going to be productive and therefore did not share their viewpoint with Pat or the full-time employees. As a result, the two groups continued to exist with a different, shared understanding of the organization's policy.

A strictly interpretive scholar might be comfortable having identified how the communication process resulted in a shared meaning concerning what to do in response to the memo but resulted in different meanings in the two subgroups of employees at the library. Some scholars would want to suggest ways to communicate to create a mutual understanding for the whole organization without indicating which meaning is preferable. If they try to improve the organization by creating a more universal shared meaning, they are taking on some of the characteristics of a post-positivist scholar.

③ The Critical Perspective

A critical researcher would want to identify areas of oppression in the library. As a result, the researcher would likely identify part-time employees as being oppressed in this situation in several ways. First, they are essentially being required to be at work for 15 minutes without being paid. This policy benefits the organization and its customers, but overlooks hardships it creates for part-time employees. These part-time employees may be coming straight from class or another part-time job where arriving on time is the best that they can manage. Second, the part-time employees appear to be cut off from the lines of influence in the organization. Apparently through their complaints, the full-time employees were able to convince Pat to create a new expectation for part-time employees, a policy that had no ill effect on them. The part-time employees apparently were unable to voice their opinions about the new policy or were unwilling to do so because they feared that they might lose their jobs. The critical researcher would suggest that communication channels marginalize the part-time employees and limit their voice in creating a policy that would benefit them.

This brief analysis of the library memo scenario illustrates why it is important to recognize the perspective of the researcher. By approaching the situation from different perspectives, the researchers focus on different issues and draw different conclusions.

Other Perspectives

There are a variety of other perspectives that scholars and individuals take in examining organizations. For example, a psychological perspective explores more of the cognitive and psychological processes that result in communication practices in organizations (Krone et al., 1987). Using this perspective to explore the scenario, a scholar would focus more on why Pat decided to send out the memo at this time and perhaps why the part-time employees chose not to voice their dissatisfaction with the new expectations. A psychological perspective provides greater insight into the thought processes of individuals as they make communication choices.

There is no single feminist perspective on organizational communication, but feminist perspectives can be considered particular forms of the critical perspective. Scholars have identified these five different feminist perspectives (Ashcraft, 2014).

1. *Liberal feminism* focuses primarily on creating equal opportunities for women and treating women and men equally. It is concerned with reducing pay discrepancies, creating opportunities for advancement, and similar issues.

2. *Cultural feminism* disagrees with the focus on sameness in liberal feminism. Instead, it considers how women are different than men and how standards created for evaluating men are inappropriate for evaluating women.

3. *Standpoint feminism* emphasizes not only that men and women are different, but that women are different from each other. Due to race, socioeconomic status, and other life factors, the individual experiences of women need to be examined instead of treating them as a homogenous group.

4. *Radical-post-structuralist feminism* rejects the notion that it is possible to repair the current social system to create equality. Instead it considers current

institutions based on masculine principles to be irrevocably repressive and state that women must develop alternatives to these systems.

5. *Postmodern feminism* considers gender a social construction. As such, the focus then becomes on how communication creates our understanding of the differences and sameness of gender.

What all these feminist perspectives have in common is a primary focus on how women in particular are disadvantaged in organizations. A researcher examining the scenario from a feminist perspective might explore if the women make up a proportionally higher percentage of part-time employees than full-time employees, whether there are a disproportionate number of men in higher level positions, or whether the part-time employees are single women. Of course, due to societal norms, in the library setting, women are likely to be overrepresented compared to the general population in all of the employment categories and to hold most of the leadership positions. As a result, a feminist perspective might explore why a disproportionate number of women choose careers in low-paying jobs such as library work, whereas a disproportionate number of men pursue high-paying careers in engineering and computer science. More recently, scholars in the feminist tradition have broadened their concerns to include individuals besides women who are marginalized in organizations, bringing them closer to critical scholars in general.

Finally, a dialogic approach is one of the most recently developed perspectives on organizational communication. A dialogic perspective is a postmodern perspective that views organization experience as very local, emergent, and filled with dissensus rather than consensus (Deetz, 2001). The communication interaction and dialogue shapes the organizational experience, but the experience is constantly changing and being renegotiated. A dialogic perspective applied to the opening scenario would focus on the disagreement between the part-time and full-time employees and explore how their views have already changed and then study how they continue to change in the future. For example, the part-time employees may resist the policy by gradually testing it by coming in a few minutes closer to the start of their shift until the new expectations no longer exist and the employees continue as they did before. This gradual shift could create a new understanding of organizational policy in the memo as unimportant. Of course, if a new memo is sent out addressing the issue again, the meaning is again renegotiated. So the dialogic perspective is less likely to see the stability of the interpretive perspective while focusing on the meaning that people assign to the changing reality they face.

Application to Different Types of Organizations

The scenario and examples so far have all involved employees working in for-profit business or government agencies. Because about 25% of the U.S. adult population volunteers in any given year (Bureau of Labor Statistics, 2014c), a textbook of organizational communication should at least minimally address the ways in which the issues raised are similar or different for volunteers in nonprofit organizations. We plan to do much more of this in future chapters. For this chapter, we do not see any real differences. People working in and studying volunteers in nonprofit organizations use the same range of communication definitions and scholarly perspectives that we presented. Instead, we provide a helpful review of the chapter's many concepts by considering a food bank.

For example, a local food bank may want to improve its visibility in the community to increase donations. Applying an information-exchange understanding of communication, it may distribute information via its website and social media to make the community aware of its financial needs. Alternatively, based on a shared-meaning definition of communication, it may want to understand what people in the community think of it using focus groups or by soliciting replies through social media. Using a transactional understanding of communication, they may attempt to interact with the community members to gain an understanding of the food bank that is a mixture of the image they would like to have in the community and the way the community currently perceives it.

Issues of strategic ambiguity face the food bank leaders. If their guidelines for distribution are too strict, they may turn away people who are needy; or if they are too lenient, people may take advantage of them. If the media discovers either of these problems and does a story on it, they may have trouble maintaining their relationship with donors. Strategic ambiguity may help them create unified diversity among various stakeholders.

The local food bank could also be studied from a legal, communicative, or social definition of the organization. Given that it is a nonprofit organization, the social definition with an emphasis on community service would probably be the focus. Such a focus would emphasize its contribution to alleviating hunger and economic inequity in the community. The legal definition would focus on its nonprofit status and its ability to bring in resources like food and volunteers and distribute them in an economical manner. The communicative definition would focus on how it is only through the ongoing communication of its board of directors, paid employees, and volunteers that the organization continues to exist. For example, if it cannot recruit enough volunteers, it will cease to exist because it can no longer function.

Scholars could study the food bank from a post-positivist, interpretive, or critical perspective. A post-positivist perspective could focus on whether the communication between paid staff, volunteers, and food bank recipients is effective and efficient. An interpretive perspective could focus on what it means to individuals to be volunteers at the food bank, such as giving back to the community or helping eliminating poverty. A critical/interpretive perspective could explore the social situations that lead to some individuals having so many resources that they can afford to volunteer instead of work whereas other people need assistance to meet basic needs like food and shelter. So the range of perspectives can be used to study volunteers in nonprofit organizations as well as they can be used to study government agencies and business.

Preview of the Book

In the rest of the book, we use these fundamental concepts for the study of organizational communication to examine particular aspects of organizational communication. The order of the chapters is based on a lifespan perspective. This means that the chapters are organized around the intersection of an individual's career and organizations. As such, we build on an assimilation model of organizational communication, which views organizational experiences as consisting of four phases over time as illustrated in Figure 1.2:

1. *Anticipatory Socialization* refers to the experiences prior to joining an organization including deciding on the type of work or volunteering that a person is interested in doing (anticipatory role socialization) and selecting an

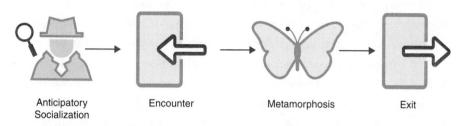

Anticipatory Socialization | Encounter | Metamorphosis | Exit

Figure 1.2. An Assimilation Model of Organizational Communication

organization in which to perform those activities (anticipatory organizational socialization).

2. *Encounter or Entry* describes the experiences of organizational newcomers as they initially assume a position in the organization and interact to learn about their roles and the organizational culture.

3. *Metamorphosis* represents the experiences of being a full-fledged organizational member including adjusting to various individual and organizational changes that occur over time.

4. *Exit* represents the process of leaving the organization at some point (Jablin, 1987, 2001; Kramer, 2010).

The process of assimilation is always an interactive process in which individuals negotiate their roles at the intersection of the organization's efforts to influence them to fill its needs (socialization) and the individual's efforts to change the organization to meet his/her needs (individualization). The role-negotiation process is ongoing throughout the time an individual participates in an organization. Although the model looks quite linear, the phases are not as distinct as the image suggests and individuals may move back and forth between phases or experience one or more phases simultaneously (Kramer, 2010).

Based on the assimilation model, in Chapter 2, we examine communication during anticipatory socialization, the time prior to selecting a career occupation or activity. In Chapter 3, we examine the encounter phase with a focus on joining an organization after completing formal education. In Chapter 15, we explore the process of leaving an organization voluntarily or involuntarily. In the chapters between them (4–14), we examine aspects of organizational communication that are experienced throughout the time spent within an organization, such as management theories, communication networks, organizational culture, and work-life balance issues. This assimilation framework should help provide a way to make sense of the various topics.

A lifespan perspective builds on this basic assimilation model but recognizes some of the realities of the modern workplace. Whereas this model works well for exploring participation in one organization, it does not take into account the fact that most people change jobs frequently and change careers as well. Lifetime employment is perceived to have been a common experience for past generations. Although it probably never was very common, it certainly is uncommon now. Few individuals work in the same organization for their entire career. It is difficult to find reliable statistics on this, but suggestions that people change jobs a dozen times and careers at least three times are frequently repeated. So although the chapters are organized around a career in a single organization, the discussion in the chapters will include implications for career changes as well, when appropriate.

The chapters themselves are structured to address particular issues that people in organizations face. So, for example, in the chapter on anticipatory socialization (Chapter 2), we address the problem of how individuals and organizations effectively bring about good individual-organization fit. In the chapter on exit (Chapter 15), we address the problem of employee turnover in organizations. We hope that this focus on addressing organizational communication problems will make the application of the principles and theories more apparent and relevant to you.

Summary

In this chapter, we introduced you to the study of organizational communication. We examined three different definitions of communication: information exchange, shared meaning, and transactional communication. We considered three different definitions of organizations: legal, communicative, and social. Then we looked at how strategic ambiguity and nonverbal messages make effective organizational communication a complex concept. We then discussed how people approach the study of organizational communication mainly from three different perspectives or assumptions: a post-positivist perspective that focuses on effective and efficient communication, an interpretive perspective that focuses on shared meaning and organizational culture, and a critical perspective that focuses on how privilege and oppression are created through communication systems within organizations. In the following chapters, we use these concepts and perspectives to address organizational communication issues in employment and voluntary settings using an assimilation framework to organize the chapters while focusing on a lifespan perspective on careers.

CHAPTER 2

Communication and Anticipatory Socialization

With a police officer and science teacher for parents, Chris sometimes got conflicting messages about attending college. However, Chris's teachers were clear; they were adamant about the importance of going to college to develop intellectual skills and have a successful career. Because standardized test scores indicated a strong aptitude in science, Chris wondered if it was possible to get a college degree that combined science and police work to please both parents and teachers. With all the crime scene investigation (CSI) programs on TV, Chris was considering enrolling in a bachelor's degree program in science that could lead to a career in a police department or Homeland Security. Chris's friends thought such a career would be interesting work. One of them, whose father worked in a nearby lab that processed drug tests for local employers, helped Chris get an internship for the summer. By the end of the summer, Chris was not sure that a CSI career was such a great idea. During the internship, there had been so many repetitive tasks that the job got boring, all the work had to be done so precisely, and there were all the test tubes to wash and equipment to maintain. It did not come close to matching the glamorous work of solving crimes shown on TV. Chris thought that maybe there were better career paths to pursue.

· · · · ·

Anticipatory socialization describes the period of time before an individual joins an organization. Anticipatory socialization involves communication processes that lead to two important decisions. Anticipatory *role* socialization explains how our communication experiences shape our decisions about the roles or careers we will assume in organizations, including work roles (i.e., jobs) or voluntary roles, as well as our more general attitudes about work. The opening scenario about Chris introduces many of the ideas we discuss about that process. Anticipatory *organizational* socialization examines how our communication experiences shape our decisions about which organizations to join or not join. A scenario about Jamie deciding on a job presented later in the chapter helps us explore that process.

We include this chapter because when we join an organization, we have expectations about many things, such as what we will do (i.e., what our job will be), what the organization is like (e.g., this is supposed to be an exciting place to work), what kinds of communication we will experience with our supervisor and coworkers (e.g., how frequently we will interact and how friendly those interactions will be), and other factors. During the process of choosing roles to pursue and organizations to join, we develop expectations for what our organizational experiences will or should be like. Those expectations influence our organizational experiences because when we join an organization, we compare our experiences to our expectations. Often when we do this, we experience unmet expectations. We often anticipate the future will be better or different than what we experience. Each of us can probably recall when we have gone to a movie with high expectations for the film based on the trailer, the reviews, and our friends' comments, only to be disappointed when the movie fails to meet those lofty expectations. In a similar manner, many people experience unmet expectations when they join organizations. Their experience in the organization is not what they expected based on the organization's reputations, what they heard about working there, and the information they received during their interview. A common reason people leave organizations after a short period of time is that they experience unmet expectations (Wanous, Poland, Premack, & Davis, 1992). In this chapter, we explore how people develop expectations for their organizational experiences as they make choices about jobs, careers, and organizations to join. In the remaining chapters in the book, we explore those organizational experiences.

Anticipatory Role Socialization

The study of anticipatory role socialization focuses attention on how communication experiences beginning early in life, and continuing throughout our lives, influence our choices about the positions and careers we pursue as employees or volunteers. Most research focuses on how we make choices about paid jobs, but we also look at how we develop expectations for voluntary roles. Scholars generally agreed there are five primary information sources that influence our occupational choices: family, education, peers, previous experience, and the media (Jablin, 2001; Kramer, 2010). We consider each of these separately.

Family

Communication with family members has a major influence on individuals' attitudes toward work, the career aspirations and choices they make, and their work expectations.

Although other family members, including siblings and extended family members, influence our expectations about work, communication with parents receives the most emphasis. Parents begin influencing their children's work attitudes at an early age in the way they treat work or chores in the home (Goodnow, 1988). Some parents protect their children from "work," believing children should be allowed to play, whereas others begin with simple "chores," such as picking up toys or making beds, and then move toward more complex chores over time. Some parents set up a pattern of work for pay by assigning chores to children in exchange for an allowance. In other families, particularly rural communities, chores are simply part of the responsibility of being a family member. It is not unusual for work to be divided in ways that reinforce gender stereotypes in which boys do outside work, like mowing lawns, whereas girls do inside work, like cooking and cleaning. Other families do not make such distinctions in assigning work. We begin developing attitudes about work from this these early interactions with our parents.

Parents' conversations about their work influence their children's attitudes toward future work. When children hear their parents complain about their supervisors and unfair practices at work, those children are more likely to grow up expecting that they will need to be suspicious of management (Levine & Hoffner, 2006). Conversely, if parents speak positively about work and encourage their children to pursue fulfilling work and careers, children tend to develop positive attitudes about future work (Langellier & Peterson, 2006). Overall, research suggests that parents talk more negatively than positively about their work (Levine & Hoffner, 2006).

Parents often influence their children's specific career aspirations, although sometimes the influence is different than intended. Parents may communicate to their children a desire for them to pursue careers similar to their own, or they may encourage their children to pursue alternative careers. In a study of the ways blue collar families talk about work, Lucas (2011a,b) found that the career aspiration messages of these families were not always consistent or obvious. On one hand, the members of the blue-collar families did not question the idea of social class or that some kinds of white-collar work tends to be more lucrative and prestigious. Lucas labeled this way of talking "The American Dream Discourse" in which upward mobility in socioeconomic status is possible through hard work. At the same time, however, the members of the blue-collar families disparage white-collar managerial work as less honorable, admirable, or masculine than their own physically taxing labor. Lucas labeled that way of talking "The Working Class Promise Discourse." These mixed messages emphasize different

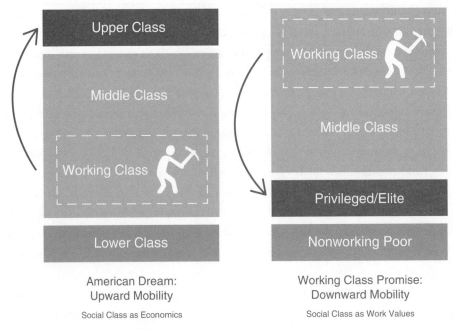

| American Dream: Upward Mobility | Working Class Promise: Downward Mobility |
| Social Class as Economics | Social Class as Work Values |

Figure 2.1. Incompatibility of the American Dream and Working Class Promise Discourse. A move from the working class to the middle or upper classes is viewed as upward mobility by the American Dream discourse and downward mobility by the Working Class Promise discourse.

goals (social class vs. work ethic) and may produce confusion for children of blue-collar families. These messages could make children's upward socioeconomic mobility seem undesirable. For these children, a move "up" in socioeconomic status as an adult may mean to be associated with the target of disparaging messages about doing less-than-honorable or less-than-masculine work (see Figure 2.1). It is likely that parents in many occupations, whether they are teachers, lawyers, or salespersons, send mixed messages about whether their children should follow their career path or pursue another career.

Finally, parents often provide realistic insight into future jobs if their children follow into similar careers. Because parents have insider information about their career and workplace, they can provide children with information that helps them have realistic expectations for the same type of work. Those realistic insights can be communicated during casual dinner conversations or they may be explicit conversations about their futures. Gibson and Papa (2000) found that parents and other family members gave explicit information to children considering joining them in working in the town's major factory. They told the children that they did not want to be embarrassed by them failing to meet the factory's norms for harsh, physical work. These norms included working through illnesses to avoid letting coworkers down. This information made it easier for the children to succeed in the factory setting. Similarly, parents in occupations, whether they are medical professionals, religious leaders, truck drivers, or journalists, can communicate valuable insider information to their children who enter similar careers.

Education

For many people, the education system provided them with their first organizational experiences. In addition to teaching basic skills like reading, writing, and mathematics, schools serve as an important socializing mechanism in other ways. In schools, students learn that they need to follow rules, take directions from adults other than their parents, and complete activities and assignments in a satisfactory and timely manner to succeed (Jablin, 2001; Wentzel & Looney, 2007). They also learn to sit still, which can be quite problematic for students who like physical activity. This general socializing role of schools is somewhat humorously immortalized in the book, *All I Really Need to Know I Learned in Kindergarten* (Fulghum, 1986). In general, students learn from their interactions with school personnel that it is important to be socially responsible, cooperative, and responsive to group goals (Wentzel & Looney, 2007).

In addition to the general socialization accomplished by schools, many adults report that a specific teacher influenced their career choices (Moore, 1969). This is perhaps a teacher who inspired them to pursue a specific career either because they were inspired by course content or by the teacher's previous work experiences. For many others who do not make such a claim, the education system still has a strong influence on occupational choices and expectations.

For example, students learn a great deal about their likes and dislikes through the courses they take. At the college level, this process involves selecting a major that prepares them for future jobs and careers. Research by Malgwi, Howe, and Burnaby (2005) suggests that men and women choose their majors based on different criteria. They found that both men and women rated interest in the subject equally as the most important factor. Men rated level of pay in the field, potential for career advancement, and potential for job opportunities as significantly more important than women. Women rated aptitude or skill in the subject and related subjects in high school as more important than men. These differences likely lead to different choices of majors.

Realistic Expectations

You are the advisor to a student who struggles in the classroom. The student's grades are generally in the C range. The student wants to pursue a career in some type of medical occupation. How do you communicate opportunity and realistic expectations to the student? Does it make any difference if the student is a high school student rather than a college student?

Unfortunately, the positive outcomes of the school system of exposing students to various career choices are not always accomplished equally across different groups of students. Interests are partially shaped by cultural reinforcement and not predetermined biologically. Particularly in the past, the education system too often failed to create equal opportunities for students and instead reinforced social, gendered, racial, and ethnic stereotypes by steering students from certain demographics or low socioeconomic status into vocational training while pushing those of greater means to college (Campbell, 1969). This communication pattern led to counselors recommending that Malcolm X not go to college to study law, despite being extremely skilled at argumentation. Although as a society, we have made many improvements in this area over the last few decades, economic disparities still make attending college difficult if not unobtainable to some young people. The patterns of enrollment suggest that the education system still may unintentionally discourage young women from entering science, technology, engineering, and mathematics (STEM) disciplines (Myers, Jahn, Gailliard, & Stoltzfus, 2011), although differences in how men and women chose majors may explain some of the disparity because STEM disciplines are typically associated with higher paying jobs.

Students also may learn more than just specific career skills through their education. Through presentation of different occupations, they learn that different communication styles are associated with different careers. For example, professionals and educators are presented as more receptive and responsive to communication than skilled or unskilled workers (Jablin, 1985). They also may learn the attitudes that are associated with their future career. For example, a longitudinal study of nursing students by Reutter, Field, Campbell, and Day (1997) found that first-year students learned many of the basic skills and norms of the profession. As they advanced in the program they developed more advanced skills, but they also developed a more realistic understanding of their chosen career and learned attitudes, such as confidence and independence, that they needed to succeed. Other majors that lead to fairly specific careers likely also socialize students into the job skills and attitudes appropriate for their future careers. More general majors that do not lead to specific occupations, such as communication or psychology, focus more on general skills like critical thinking, problem solving, and communication skills rather than specific job skills and attitudes.

The role of education in socialization does not end when someone reaches their mid-20s. More and more, adults with work experience return to school to enhance career opportunities. These adult learners or nontraditional students may seek to finish a degree they started previously or add an advanced degree to improve their opportunities for advancement or for making career changes. People who make career changes may either stop working to attend school or finish a degree before making a switch (Tan & Kramer, 2012). The availability of degree completion programs in the evenings, on weekends, and online make these opportunities more accessible than in the past.

Peers

Growing up, peers provide individuals with career information that supplements the information their family and the educational system provide. Peers share information about their work experiences, even if those experiences are just part-time jobs, and discuss the careers of their parents and other adult acquaintances (Jablin, 2001). So one peer may share what it is like to work in a franchise store that has store managers, regional managers, and corporate headquarters, whereas another may talk about what it is like to work in a small, family-owned business. Similarly, when peers talk about how much their parents or neighbors like or dislike their jobs, that information can influence the future choices of their friends. For example, they may hear that government jobs offer very stable employment and benefits but have an excessive amount of bureaucratic rules. The information shared by peers may encourage or discourage their friends from pursuing work in certain careers or organizations.

In addition, peers also provide information that evaluates the careers an individual is considering (Myers et al., 2011). It is likely that many of you reading this text received positive reactions from your friends about your decision to attend college and perhaps concerning the particular university you attend. Peers can also affirm that a particular major or occupation seems to fit you particularly well or that they cannot see you doing a particular type of work (Peterson & Peters, 1983). These are some of the important ways peers influence the career choices and aspirations of each other.

Peers also provide experiences for working together that can carry over to expectations for peer relationships in the workplace. Working together in the classroom, playing together on sports teams, or joining clubs like Scouts or 4-H provide individuals with experiences that are similar to workplace peers. Individuals learn about developing friendships, competing against others, and managing conflict (Jablin, 2001). So, for example, if while growing up you constantly interacted with teammates on sports teams or peers in 4-H—who were highly competitive and focused on individual awards and accomplishments even at the expense of the success of others—you may have similar expectations for peer relationships in the workplace. By contrast, if your peers were very supportive and focused on accomplishing group goals, you likely have different expectations. How peers interacted with teachers or coaches may also create expectations for the workplace. If your peers confided in one another but kept secrets from your teachers, you may grow up expecting to do the same in your peer and supervisor relationships at work (Kramer, 2010).

Later on in careers, peers provide information for individuals considering job and career changes. For example, Tan and Kramer (2012) found that individuals considering career changes often consulted with their peers for information and advice. Sometimes those peers had information about an alternative career. In other cases, they confirmed the individual's desire to make changes by making derogatory remarks about the person's current job or company. In some instances, they provided support for the person to pursue their interests and even mentioned wishing they had the courage to do the same. In these ways, peers helped job switchers make their decisions to change jobs and careers.

Previous Experience

Early examinations of anticipatory socialization only explored how part-time work during adolescence and young adulthood influenced career choices and aspirations. These studies supported several conclusions (Jablin, 2001). In general, studies revealed that the specific job skills of these part-time jobs, often in food service and retail sales, did not transfer well to future careers. However, skills such as the ability to communicate and work with peers and supervisors did apply to future jobs, even if there was

Comparing Workplaces

You were pleased to be able to hire someone with previous experience who did the same type of work in a different company. Now that person says regularly, "Well, in my previous position, we. . . ." How do you communicate that you welcome new ideas and are willing to make changes but also communicate that constantly comparing the two workplaces is alienating some of the veteran employees who take great pride in their company?

often limited communication with supervisors. According to this research, if you work or worked as a server in food service, you likely learned some important social skills about how to communicate with customers, how to cooperate with peers, and how to interact with a supervisor. Those communication skills will likely assist you more in your future careers than job-specific task skills.

An exception to this pattern of learning communication skills but limited job skills through part-time employment occurs when a person works in a job closely related to his/her career aspirations. Someone who wants to be an event planner may secure part-time work for a catering service. In this case, the part-time work experiences may directly transfer to a career in event planning. Of course, the person may or may not pursue that career based on what is learned from the part-time experience and depending on whether the time pressure of coordinating the details of the event at a particular time and place is perceived as unduly stressful or invigorating.

Because lifetime employment in one company or even one type of work is no longer common, more recent examinations of anticipatory socialization focused on how previous organizational experiences influence people's experiences of joining new organizations rather than part-time employment. Many organizational newcomers bring previous, extra full-time work experiences or volunteer organizational experiences that influence their expectations for participation in the new organization (Kramer, 2010). So, for example, when an individual starts a second, third, or fourth career in midlife, the experiences in the earlier careers are rich sources of work-related expectations for the individual. These expectations might concern communication with peers and supervisors, organizational culture, or opportunities for further career growth and development. These previous experiences can even influence postretirement participation in organizations such as in volunteering (Chinn & Barbour, 2013). Even though volunteering is not paid work, previous organizational and work experiences acquired during volunteering still influence work-related expectations. A retired volunteer working for Habitat for Humanity probably expects the work to be organized by some project manager and that individual job responsibilities will be clearly stated. The volunteer will be dissatisfied if there is a lot of standing around with nothing to do.

Media

Media, in all of its many forms—from books to television programs to movies to news and social media—also affect many individuals' career choices and aspirations. Although these are not likely as influential as the previous sources, they can be important, sometimes subtle, sources of information that influence organizational expectations.

Two types of books seem to be particularly worth considering. An analysis of children's books found that they actually contain many messages about what to expect as members of organizations (Ingersoll & Adams, 1992). The researchers found that books generally portray and promote passive organizational roles in which individuals do repetitive work, follow directions from others, and are required to fit in rather than rock the boat. When problems occur, these children's stories show them being resolved through rationality rather than feelings, usually with the assistance of some authority figure who steps in to solve them. The books also frequently reinforce gendered occupational stereotypes for men and women.

Adults also read books that present a particular narrative about how organizations do or ought to work. An analysis of self-help books, such as Steven Covey's popular *7 Habits of Highly Effective People*, found that books like these tend to promote career advancement through self-management to adapt to the organizational norms and expectations and achieve success (Carlone, 2001). So these books for children and adults tend to both discourage readers from departing from organizational norms (as might be common of innovators and entrepreneurs) and encourage people to conform to organizational routines and practices to be rewarded.

Other media convey different anticipatory role information. For example, on the positive side, television programs and movies introduce people to a variety careers that they would not be aware of from their parents, education, and peers (Hoffner, Levine, & Toohey, 2008). This includes not only the jobs performed by main characters in programs. It also includes the occupations of guest characters who may work in more varied occupations. Unfortunately, the media overrepresent a number of occupations, such as medical careers and various law enforcement and legal occupations compared to the percentages of the workforce, and often misrepresent the nature of many of those jobs significantly (Signorielli, 2009). For example, many lawyers never appear in a courtroom, and many police officers never fire their weapons, but a television watcher would not know that from media depictions. Fortunately, although adolescents reported being interested in certain careers based on their depictions in movies and television, most recognized that the career depictions were unrealistic (Myers et al., 2011). Overall, although adolescents are often attracted to the idealized jobs of their favorite characters, their work values are generally influenced more by their parents than media (Hoffner et al., 2008).

There are many studies that find that media tend to reinforce various gender stereotypes. Content analyses of popular media reveal that men tend to be portrayed in more diverse and higher-status occupations than women (Signorielli, 2009). Furthermore, men are more often the main character. Even when women are main characters, they are often portrayed in stereotypical roles by being more caring, emotional, and social, whereas men are presented as more task-oriented and action-oriented (Nathanson, Wilson, McGee, & Sebastian, 2002). A casual examination of current programs and movies suggests that there have been slight changes in these patterns over time and in the representation of different races, ethnicities, and nationalities.

Application

In the opening scenario, the influence of all five sources of anticipatory role socialization are apparent. Chris's initial career goals were strongly influenced by both parents' occupations. They both apparently spoke positively about their careers so that Chris had a positive attitude about work in general and about police work and teaching. An aptitude in science and supportive teachers led Chris to aspire to attend college and pursue a major leading to an occupation in the sciences. Television seemed to have influenced Chris to consider a career as a CSI as a way to combine the careers of both parents. Chris's peers supported that idea. One even helped Chris get an internship in a science lab. When working in a lab proved to be tedious, that previous experience led to consideration of other careers. Because most students change majors more than once during college, it is likely that Chris will change majors again; but that choice will have been influenced by all five sources: family, education, peers, previous experience, and the media.

The "Real Job" Colloquialism

Another way of examining the collective influence of anticipatory role socialization is to explore the meaning of a phrase nearly everyone has heard or used at some point: the colloquialism, "a real job." A study of the meaning of the phrase suggests that college students associate the phrase with a number of characteristics (Clair, 1996). In particular, college students reported considering a real job one that involves being paid, receiving benefits, using one's education, and working a fairly standard workweek while also being enjoyable. Participants described "not a real job" as part-time, seasonal, or voluntary, and occurring in an organization that is poorly managed or mistreats its employees. Of course, this conceptualization is highly personalized and changes. Students mentioned that when they were in high school, they considered working at a fast-food restaurant or in retail sales a real job because it was not babysitting or working within the home. As college students, they no longer considered working in one of these "McJobs" a real job, particularly after graduating from college. Some students recognized an inconsistency in their conceptualization of a real job because they might be working in some capacity that they did not consider a real job, such as part-time retail sales, but that people doing the same work next to them were working what they

ETHICAL ISSUE

Deconstructing Our Labels

Describing some jobs as "real" implies others are unworthy of consideration or less than real. However, work can be a great source of feelings of dignity, social belongingness, and life enrichment regardless of the type of work. Many nonprofits and social-service organizations leverage those aspects of work in therapeutic ways to benefit disadvantaged and recovering individuals. How might describing some jobs accomplished by these individuals as not "real jobs" undermine the jobs' potential to make a positive difference? What does the saying "real job" imply about our culture's assumptions regarding the purpose of work? Are those assumptions related to our socioeconomic class or status? How does the meaning of this phrase change in the context of emerging global economies?

considered real jobs. So although the colloquialism, a real job, likely summarizes anticipatory role socialization, the meaning is not necessarily shared across the working population. Its meaning for an individual likely provides insight into that person's attitude toward work and volunteer roles at a given point in time. The real job colloquialism is a good example of how the study of organizational communication is not only about studying communication *in* organizational settings but also includes the study of communication *about* organizations.

In the scenario, based on the summer internship experience, Chris does not seem to have concluded that being a lab assistant is not a real job. There are multiple organizations with similar jobs that are repetitive and require precision that are almost universally considered real jobs. Chris only seems to have discovered that a desirable job has different characteristics than what the internship offers.

Anticipatory Role Socialization for Volunteers

In any given year, 25% to 30% of the adult population in the United States is involved in some sort of volunteer role (Bureau of Labor Statistics, 2014c). These volunteers spend an average of 4 to 5 hours per week accomplishing voluntary work (Hooghe, 2003). They participate in a range of organizations, with religious organizations being the most common (33.2%); followed by educational or youth service-related activities such as volunteering at school or coaching a youth team (25.7%); and then social or community service organizations such as Habitat for Humanity or working at a crisis center (14.3%; Bureau of Labor Statistics, 2011). These numbers suggest volunteering is common and important to volunteers. Yet, the numbers also suggest that most working adults are not involved in volunteer roles in a particular year, and some are perhaps rarely if ever involved during their lifetimes. Differences in anticipatory role socialization for volunteering likely helps to explain these findings.

Communication during anticipatory role socialization influences volunteers' roles much like it does work roles. For example, a study of community choir volunteers found that nearly all of them were involved with music in their families, schools, or churches prior to joining the community choir (Kramer, 2011a). In recent years, many secondary schools and universities have begun encouraging students to volunteer in the future by requiring service learning education in which they are required to volunteer for community organizations. It remains unclear whether the strategy actually results in increases in future volunteering (Botero, Fediuk, & Sies, 2013). After a flood in 2012, media coverage and social media interactions between peers and even strangers resulted in large numbers of volunteers joining in the disaster clean up (McDonald, Creber, Sun, & Sonn, 2015). This research suggests that families, education systems, peers, previous organizational experiences, and media all potentially influence motivations and expectations about volunteering.

There seem to be two main differences in anticipatory role socialization for volunteering versus paid work. First, volunteering is generally defined as work done out of free will or choice that benefits others and does not involve receiving pay (Lewis, 2013). Based on these characteristics, some volunteers may not consider volunteering a real job because it does not involve pay, even though they may consider it doing *real work*. Volunteers may also wonder whether others view their work as constituting a real job, which may cause them concern about whether volunteering lacks prestige compared with other kinds of work. Second, anticipatory role socialization for volunteer roles typically suggests that a volunteer role is less critical than a work or family role. As a result, when there are conflicts between various roles, the volunteer role is often the first role to be eliminated (Kramer, 2011a). This suggests that most volunteers perceive their volunteer roles as more transitory than paid-work roles.

Summary of Anticipatory Role Socialization

In this section, we discussed how individuals make job and career choices based on their communication experiences with family members, the education system, peers, previous organizational experiences, and media. Collectively, these sources influence our attitudes toward work and what we consider a real job. These same influences affect attitudes toward volunteering. Communication during anticipatory role socialization is an important part of understanding organizational communication because it is through these interactions that people develop attitudes toward work and volunteering. These attitudes drive expectations for what organizational experiences will be like and become the backdrop on which organizational experiences will be understood. The expectations created by anticipatory socialization messages shape whether and how organizational experiences will be perceived as fulfilling our job and career aspirations.

Anticipatory Organizational Socialization

The second part of anticipatory socialization is anticipatory *organizational* socialization. This process focuses on how people choose which organization to join. It is divided into two areas of discussion: the recruitment and reconnaissance process and the selection process. Both processes are concerned with the issue of person to job fit.

Person-Job Fit

The concept of person-job fit (P-J) concerns the management goal of finding the right employee to fill an open position. P-J involves matching the attributes and personality of the person to the characteristics and requirements of the job situation (Caldwell & O'Reilly, 1990). From a management perspective, having the right person in the right position improves the efficiency and productivity of a unit, whereas having the wrong person leads to problems. Research indicates consistently that good P-J fit also results in positive employee work attitudes and job performance (Caldwell & O'Reilly, 1990).

Although the P-J approach spurred a significant amount of research that generally supports the premise that P-J contributes in a positive way to employee outcomes, more recent research distinguished between P-J and person-organization fit (P-O). Whereas P-J focuses on a match between the employee and the job requirements, P-O concerns a match between the employee and the organization's values and beliefs (Lauver & Kristof-Brown, 2001) or, in other words, the organizational culture. Although the two fit concepts are related, they are distinct and have different effects on employees. Research demonstrates that both P-J and P-O are positively related to job satisfaction and negatively related to intention to quit. Whereas both P-J and P-O contribute equally to job satisfaction, P-O contributes the most to reducing the intention to quit, as well as to various positive behaviors such as helping and cooperating with others and volunteering for extra duties (Lauver & Kristof-Brown, 2001).

Although not always stated explicitly, either P-J or P-O or both are typically considered in organizations' recruitment and selection process. When an organization's recruitment and selection process favors a concern for P-J, then there is an assumption that new members will learn the job quickly and adjust to the organizational culture over time. When an organization's recruitment and selection process favors a concern for P-O fit, then there is an assumption at play that new members can be taught the specifics of a job that they do not know; but if they do not fit into the organizational culture, they may not be satisfied and committed to the organization and be more inclined to leave.

Although fit is generally perceived as a management concern, it should be a concern of job candidates as well. As potential employees consider accepting a job offer, they should likely consider whether there is a good P-J and P-O rather than accepting a job simply because it pays well. There need not be a perfect match, but finding good P-J and P-O will likely lead to a more satisfying organizational experience.

. . . . .

As a college senior, Jamie signed up with the campus job placement center to be able to participate in on-campus interviews. These interviews involved signing up for 30-minute slots with campus recruiters and felt something like speed dating. Jamie knew to do some research on each company before the interviews, an easy task with the Internet. In the first interview, the recruiter who was from the human resources department seemed un-prepared, asked questions that were answered on Jamie's résumé, and seemed to have made a decision about Jamie's suitability for the company after just the first couple min-utes. By contrast, the second interview felt like a conversation between peers. They each asked and answered questions throughout. The recruiter had actually worked in the posi-tion for which Jamie was applying and provided good information on the job and the company. Jamie hoped that a job opportunity would come from the interview, but ex-pected it would take more than two interviews to land a dream job, or at least a good one.

. . . . .

Recruitment

Anticipatory organizational socialization involves the interaction between the organi-zations' efforts to recruit qualified people to fill open positions and the applicants' ef-forts to find positions in organizations. From the organization's perspective, improving the recruitment process involves considering three factors: (a) objectives, (b) strategies, and (c) activities (Breaugh & Starke, 2000). The recruitment objectives include more than just getting good applicants. Recruiting also involves determining how many po-sitions need filling, how diverse and large of an applicant pool is desired, and so forth. These objectives then affect the organization's recruitment strategies. Strategies include determining where to advertise positions to attract the desired applicants and whether to focus on the details of the specific job or on the image of the organization. Finally, the recruitment activities include when and where the recruitment activities and interviews will occur.

There are numerous strategies for recruiting. A partial list of places to advertise or post jobs includes company websites, general job sites like Monster Jobs (www.monster .com), trade magazines, and local newspapers. Other recruitment strategies include participating in community job fairs or campus job fairs and placement centers at some universities where interviews are conducted. Another common strategy is to use temporary employment agencies such as Kelly Services (http://www.kellyservices.com/ Global/Home/) or Express Employment Professionals (http://www.expresspros.com/). Some temporary agencies even specialize in particular types of occupations. Using temporary employment agencies offers both organizations and potential employees the opportunity to test each other out for fit prior to making any long-term commitment. Organizations also use a variety of social media to target potential employees including blogs, Wikis, podcasting, employer marketing videos, and text messaging (Joos, 2008). By the time you read this, there will likely be additional forms of technology used by recruiters.

For organizations, the most preferred recruitment source is one not mentioned so far: referrals from current employees. Although the results of research are not entirely consistent, in general, employees hired due to referrals or networking through current employees are more satisfied and have lower turnover rates than employees gained through other methods (Ryan & Tippins, 2004). This pattern is likely due to the fact that current employees serve as good judges for P-J and/or P-O fit. Satisfied employees are unlikely to recommend someone for employment who they think will not be a good coworker or who will not fit into the organization.

For individuals looking for work, networking through people they know is generally the most useful source for job leads. A highly cited study found that individuals had the most success finding jobs through the weak ties in their communication networks (Granovetter, 1973). Weak ties are not the people in individuals' networks with whom they regularly communicate, such as close friends, family members, or coworkers in the same department. Weak ties are distant acquaintances in one's communication network, characterized by limited contact, such as is typical of interactions with a neighbor of parents or a friend of a coworker or a second cousin. Where close friends and family often have access to the same information, these weak ties can often contribute different information that more likely leads to a job. In the modern world, it might be tempting to assume that job searches are most commonly conducted solely online or through networking sources like LinkedIn; yet the use of weak ties and interpersonal connections remains a prominent aspect of job searching.

In the scenario, the organizations using the campus job placement center have presumably determined how many positions they need to fill. They most likely have already exhausted their internal referrals and based on their previous experiences believe that by conducting preliminary interviews at this particular university, they will find the potential employees they need to fill their needs. Similarly, Jamie has apparently determined that interviewing through the placement center will present appropriate job opportunities for graduating students instead of, or in addition to, relying on a networking strategy to find a job. Having made a connection through the job placement center, the representative from the organization and Jamie proceed to the next step, the selection process.

Selection Process

Résumés and Cover Letters. Résumés and cover letters are one of the most important forms of communication during the selection process. Applicants use these documents to present a particular image of themselves, and organizational personnel use these documents to make decisions concerning who to interview (or not!). There is general agreement among scholars and practitioners that applicants should include contact information, education, work experience, activities/awards, and references. Applicants should write descriptions of previous work in the active voice. If they include a goal or objective, it should appear in only one of the two documents. There are literally hundreds of thousands of websites that purport to give out correct advice on what to include or exclude from these documents and how to format them. Some offer this information for free, whereas others charge a fee to assist job searchers. Job placement centers offer similar assistance. The problem with most of this advice is that it assumes that there is a best format or style that "guarantees" applicants jobs or at least greatly increase their chances. Although it is worthwhile to consult sources like these for guidance, being well qualified and having a weak-tie referral go a lot further in getting a job than the format of the résumé.

Research on résumés and cover letters offers similar advice to these websites while also raising some important concerns. For example, having work or education experience related to the job, providing concrete examples of accomplishments, examples of positive customer or client feedback, along with showing an interest in career development are associated with more positive evaluations of these documents (Knouse, 1994). Recent graduates with limited work experience are more likely to receive interviews when they (a) have relevant course work and accomplishments (which can include voluntary as well as paid experiences), (b) state specific instead of vague objectives, and (c) have high grade point averages (Thoms, McMasters, Roberts, & Dombkowski, 1999).

Unfortunately, research also indicates that the information in these job application documents leads to certain biases in the selection process. For example, married individuals have been found to be rated more positively than unmarried ones (Oliphant & Alexander, 1982). Because certain jobs tend to be perceived to fit stereotypes for men and women, applicants who fit the same-gender type (e.g., women applying for an elementary teaching position or men applying for manufacturing supervisor) are often rated more highly (Muchinsky & Harris, 1977). Although much of this research is dated, it seems likely that these and other similar biases based on race, ethnicity, nationality, or religious affiliation remain today. This probably means that applicants are not treated equally in the selection process even based on written materials.

Although applicants have control over the information that they present in their résumés and cover letters, it is important to realize that recruiters may also have access other information about them. Recruiters may search Facebook or other social media for additional information about applicants, although there are various legal and ethical issues involved in making decisions using information gathered in this way (Smith & Kidder, 2010). For example, it may be possible to gain information through social media that leads to biases in hiring or the information may be inaccurate. Regardless, savvy applicants will make sure that their social media messages are congruent with the image they want to project to potential employers.

Screening Interviews. A great deal of what we know about the interview process itself is based on studies conducted during on-campus screening interviews conducted by large companies at colleges and universities. These interviews serve multiple purposes (Miller & Buzzanell, 1996). Not only are organizations attempting to find good applicants via interviews, but they are also doing public relations work and image management simultaneously, as recruiters try to create a positive impression with applicants who are hired and those who are not. At the same time, applicants are attempting to gain information to help them decide if they want to accept a job, if offered.

Because there is a great deal of research on screening interviews, what follows are some of the major findings summarized elsewhere (e.g., Harris, 1989; Jablin, 2001). It is important to realize that interviewers and applicants have different perceptions of desirable communication behaviors during the interview in terms of the amount of talkativeness, listening, and questioning. That said, applicants who display high nonverbal immediacy are rated more positively. *Nonverbal immediacy* refers to behaviors that create a sense of psychological nearness with another. These behaviors include smiling, good posture, facing the interviewer and leaning slightly toward him or her, and responding with backchannel affirmations such as "uh-huh" or "yes" at appropriate times to convey agreement with the interviewer. Applicants are rated higher if they talk more, elaborate on their answers, and are assertive in emphasizing their positive traits and provide stories or examples to support the points that they make.

One of the more important findings is that individuals who are involved in more response-response conversations versus question-response interrogations generally are favored by interviewers. This finding suggests that the ideal interview does not necessarily unfold as a pattern in which the interviewer asks a series of questions and the applicant answers and vice versa. Instead, the most successful interviews unfold more like a conversation between peers or equals. Unfortunately, there is often a tension during the interview as the interviewer attempts to get the applicant to talk more and the applicant attempts to get the interviewer to provide more information (Engler-Parish & Millar, 1989).

There are some less positive findings as well. Interviewers tend to make their decisions very early in the interview, but unfortunately, they also often do most of the talking during the opening minutes of the interviews. Applicants do not tend to want to accept offers if their only source of information is an organizational recruiter, but they do trust people who previously held the job for which they are applying and believe that those individuals provide more realistic information than someone from the human resource department.

There are literally dozens of other studies and findings in the research, but those highlighted here emphasize the importance of effective communication during interviews. Research suggests applicants who display communication competency through fluent speech, appropriate content, and organized ideas receive positive evaluations and are more likely to receive second interviews and/or job offers.

Interviews remain an extremely common strategy for evaluating potential members. Organizations use interviews so regularly because predicting whether an applicant will be skillful at the tasks required by the job is not the only issue of concern.

Improving Interviews

It might surprise you to learn that employment interviews do not tend to be very successful at predicting whether an applicant will be competent in the job. This is because many interviewers ask leading, closed-ended questions such as "Are you comfortable giving customer service?" The success of interviews can be improved if the interview includes behavioral and hypothetical questions. A behavioral question might be "Can you tell me about a time you dealt with a difficult customer?" A hypothetical question might be "What would you do if a customer accused you of being rude?" Ideally, interviewers should work to get interviewees to answer questions about behavior, real experience or imagined. When you are interviewed, how could you try to answer a closed-ended question as if it were a behavioral question so that you can include an example from your education or experience?

Interviews are an opportunity to explore whether applicants are likeable, interpersonally attractive, and well mannered. In short, interviews are a means of evaluating potential members' communication skills.

In the scenario, Jamie seems to have experienced two extremes in the two screening interviews. In the first interview, the interviewer seemed to have quickly determined Jamie was not a good fit for the job opening, and so the interview developed into a question-and-answer period that left both participants dissatisfied. The recruiter is unlikely to want to hire Jamie, who is unlikely to want to accept the job, unless there are no other options. By contrast, in the second interview, Jamie was able to display strong communication skills and there was a give-and-take conversation, which makes it more likely the recruiter will offer a second interview and/or job. The fact that the recruiter also served in the position previously makes it more likely that Jamie will accept a second interview and job in this company if it is offered.

Follow-up or Second Interviews

Because high school and college students are often hired on the spot or after one interview and a background check or drug test, many have some experience with interviews that resemble initial screening interviews described in the previous section; but they often have no experience with follow-up interviews. Once an applicant makes it through the screening interview, the second interview or on-site interview is quite different in at least four ways:

1. Instead of occurring on campus or at a job fair, second interviews occur at the job site or multiple sites while the organization is in operation.

2. Instead of 30 minutes, follow-up interviews often take all day or more than one day, particularly if the position is more advanced or for an individual changing jobs from one company or career to another.

3. Instead of two people being involved, job candidates meet with multiple individuals and/or groups.

4. Instead of a predictable pattern with fairly standard questions, follow-up interviews with multiple people over an extended period of time are much more unpredictable and fluid. (Miller & Buzzanell, 1996)

These follow-up interviews have a number of advantages for the organization and the applicant (Kramer, 2010). For the organization, multiple representatives have opportunities to interact with the applicant allowing for a more thorough assessment of P-J and P-O fit. Various organizational members can also provide additional image-enhancing messages to attempt to recruit a candidate successfully who may have multiple offers, especially if they are seeking an advanced position or are a particularly strong applicant. The applicant has the opportunity to gain large amounts of information, not only during the numerous interviews but also from observing the organization at work and seeing how people seem to feel while they are at work.

Follow-up interviews also have a number of potential pitfalls for both parties. The U.S. Equal Employment Opportunity Commission (EEOC) is charged with making sure that applicants are not discriminated against in the hiring process based on a person's race, color, religion, marital status, or sex—including pregnancy, national origin, age, disability, or genetic information (U.S. Equal Employment Opportunity Commission, 2015). It is illegal to ask questions about many of these topics on applications or during interviews. There are various websites that list examples of such illegal questions. Although it is relatively easy to avoid illegal questions during highly structured screening interviews, it is not so easy to manage this issue during follow-up interviews on site that include many informal conversations during lunch or while walking from one interview to another. Conversations that are quite natural in those settings under other circumstances, such as talking about marital status, can actually violate EEOC guidelines depending on whether the organizational representative brings up the topic or requests that the applicant provide such information or whether the applicant simply mentions marital status during a conversation.

Overall, follow-up interviews or on-site interviews are common during the hiring process at larger organizations. They provide the organization and the applicant additional opportunity to determine if there is a P-J and P-O fit. More often than not, follow-up interviews lead to job offers. Only when the organization brings in three or more candidates to select the best candidate for a high-status job or highly selective position are the odds not necessarily any better.

Realistic Job Previews

As mentioned in the introduction to this chapter, it is not uncommon for new employees to experience unmet expectations that lead to high turnover rates (Wanous et al., 1992). It is not difficult to see why this happens. Family members and teachers typically encourage young men and women to have high expectations for their jobs. During the recruitment process, organizations are involved in image enhancement as they attempt to attract the best candidates. The combination of optimistic socialization messaging and strong impression management by organizations during recruitment and selection can often lead to job applicants' unrealistic expectations. These unrealistic expectations can be about abstract concepts like whether an organization has a positive work environment or many opportunities for advancement as well as objective issues such as the number of work hours required by a job, its salary, and the quality of benefits

ETHICAL ISSUE

Inappropriate Interview Questions

During an onsite interview, Jamie is asked a number of illegal questions by different parties. Jamie is very interested in the position but also is concerned that people seem unaware that it is inappropriate to ask about marital status or religious affiliation, even if it is during a lunch conversation. Should Jamie report this problem to someone in the organization? Does the decision to report differ based on whether Jamie wants to accept the job?

enjoyed by members. To address this concern, scholars proposed that the recruitment process should include realistic job previews (RJPs).

RJPs provide the applicant with the positive and attractive aspects of a future job and place of employment *as well as* information about some of the less attractive or mundane aspects of the job in their recruitment messages. By providing this more balanced or more realistic job preview, new employees will not experience as many unmet expectations. So for example, if a social work applicant is told during the interview process that there is a fair amount of boring paperwork to do, but that it is just part of the job that needs to be done to provide the kind of caring support to clients that makes the job attractive, when the new employee finds out that there really is a lot of paperwork, it will not be as big of a surprise and will be less likely to lead to dissatisfaction and turnover.

Research supports the conclusion that RJPs have positive outcomes for new employees. An analysis of 40 studies using RJPs found that that they were related to more accurate initial job expectations, higher job performance, and lower rates of turnover among new hires (Phillips, 1998). Given these findings, one might wonder why more organizations do not use RJPs. If all organizations were doing RJPs, none of them would be at a disadvantage. The fear is that an organization will lose some of its top prospects if they provide an RJP and their competition does not. There is some evidence to support this fear because more applicants drop out of the hiring process after RJPs (Premack & Wanous, 1985).

Given an organization's potential reluctance to provide RJPs, it may be up to applicants to find ways to gain information that will provide more realistic job expectations.

COMMUNICATION CHALLENGE

The New Technology of the Job Search

Websites like Monster.com have not necessarily replaced the importance of weak ties for most individual job seekers. However, websites like Glassdoor.com give employees an opportunity to rate and comment on their organizations. These messages from current and former organizational members can provide job seekers an opportunity to hear about positive and negative aspects of an organization and job prior to accepting. How should you weigh the information from these websites in comparison to interview information during anticipatory socialization?

A number of these have been mentioned already in this chapter. Parents, friends, or acquaintances who work in the career or organization provide more realistic information about the jobs. Organizational members who held the position previously are trusted to provide more accurate information during initial screening interviews. The opportunities to gain more realistic information about the job and organization are readily available to applicants during follow-up and all-day interviews by asking appropriate questions about what people like and dislike about their jobs and the company. There are also a number of websites that provide open forums for people to discuss the positive *and negative* aspects of working for a particular company (e.g., see glassdoor.com). An applicant can gain a more realistic job preview by consulting sources like these.

Anticipatory Organizational Socialization for Volunteers

Anticipatory organizational socialization for volunteers is quite similar in that it involves recruiting potential volunteers and then selecting ones and assigning tasks to them. There are a few important differences: Whereas nationally, employees across organizations turn over at an annual rate of 3% to 4% (Bureau of Labor Statistics, 2014a), turnover for volunteers is significantly higher at annual rates of 20% to 40% (Corporation for National and Community Service, 2014). This high turnover rate is largely due to volunteers generally placing work and family commitments ahead of their volunteer roles such that when they experience conflict, they tend to temporarily or permanently resign from their volunteer roles (Kramer, 2011b). This high turnover rate has a number of important implications for organizations relying on volunteers.

First, the high turnover means that these organizations are often in a perpetual recruitment process due to the constant need for new volunteers. This is a situation that only a few businesses regularly face (e.g., fast-food restaurants). As a result, volunteer-based organizations often cannot be very selective and tend to accept nearly every prospective volunteer to fill their many vacancies. There are exceptions to this, of course. These dynamics means that volunteers often have more control in the selection process because they can choose not to volunteer without experiencing any negative consequences, like loss of pay. As a result, the volunteer recruiter has the very challenging task of making the volunteer role and the organization appealing to the potential volunteer.

The constant recruiting also means that the selection process is typically less formal. Most volunteers do not submit résumés. Interviews, if they occur at all, are often informal activities. Again, there are exceptions for volunteer positions that require specific or unique skills. Overall, the selection process is more often a matter of informing volunteers about the organization and their roles rather than a selection process.

Summary of Anticipatory Organizational Socialization

It is during anticipatory organizational socialization that a prospective employee or volunteer makes contact with a potential organization. During recruitment and reconnaissance, the organization and individual exchange information to find out if there is a good fit between them. Then during the selection process, the organizational representatives and prospective members actively exchange information during initial and follow-up interviews. Effective communication increases the likelihood that an invitation to join will be offered and accepted. The degree to which the information exchanged is realistic increases the chances that the employee or volunteer will remain in the organization for a longer period of time.

1. Anticipatory Organizational Socialization

2. Recruitment

3. Selection Process

4. -Follow interviews

4.

Communication and Organizational Encounter

Jordan was surprised by how quickly the first weeks of the new job as a bank teller had gone. During the first week, all of the new tellers went through a week of training together in an office building downtown. After an opening session on the bank's history and values, they were trained on their job duties beginning with the simplest and most common transactions, such as managing deposits and cashing checks, and gradually working on more complicated ones like making a cashier's check and managing business deposits. There were always very precise procedures to follow for each type of transaction, and at each step of the way, there were tests on those procedures, which Jordan and the rest of the trainees passed easily. At lunch breaks, the trainees talked to each other about what brought them to the job and their interests, but because they knew they were likely to be assigned to different branches throughout the city, they did not make a lot of effort to become friends unless they happened to have common interests. The training seemed slow and pretty dull, but Jordan found the section on loss prevention much more interesting. Loss-prevention training included how to respond in the rare event of an armed robbery, but focused mostly on spotting counterfeit bills, bogus checks, and customers who might be potential victims of fraud. On Friday, after passing the last test, they were given their branch assignments for Monday.

When Jordan began working at the West Branch, there were a number of surprises. First, the training emphasized very exact procedures for every transaction, such as asking all customers for their IDs before dispensing cash, and Jordan felt compelled to follow the procedures carefully at first, but observed that most other tellers did not do this. When on Friday, an experienced teller asked Jordan to lunch, they talked about the formal training and the practices at their branch. The experienced teller assured Jordan that there were really only certain procedures that had to be followed so precisely—mostly related to transactions over $10,000 or with customers whose accounts were red-flagged in the system due to past problems such as overdrafts. After gaining those insights, the next week Jordan was able to work much more quickly and keep up with the other tellers by not being so rigid in following the rules. So far, there had been no problems from taking the same shortcuts Jordan observed the experienced tellers taking. There was one thing the experienced tellers couldn't help with, though; Jordan did not expect how tiring it was to stand most of the day. New shoes were a must.

. . . . .

Being an organizational newcomer is a common experience throughout life. We are new employees multiple times in our lives when we change jobs. In fact, the U.S. Department of Labor estimates that before the age of 48, working adults will change jobs nearly 12 times—with nearly half of those job changes occurring after age 25 (Bureau of Labor Statistics, 2014b). Furthermore, these statistics do not account for the times we are newcomers to volunteer positions, homeowners' associations, or faith communities, to name just a few of the other kinds of organizations that we join throughout our lives. In this chapter, we explore the experience of being newcomers. First, we present uncertainty management theory (UMT) to provide a theoretical framework for understanding newcomers' experiences. Then, we examine the communication experiences of newcomers' orientation and training, followed by an examination of the important issue of how newcomers gain information to understand and negotiate their roles. Finally, we explore a number of important outcomes of the newcomer experience, before considering the newcomer experience in volunteer organizations.

Uncertainty Management Theory

Newcomers experience a great deal of uncertainty during the encounter phase as they face new work, new supervisors, and new coworkers—all in a new organization. Scholars have created a wide range of typologies that identify various topics newcomers seek to learn. These topics have been reduced to a parsimonious list of four topics that seem to summarize these typologies (Kramer, 2010). First, newcomers experience *task-related uncertainties*. Newcomers experience uncertainty about what their job actually entails, whether there are specific procedures or norms for doing the tasks, and how they will be evaluated for doing their jobs. Second, newcomers experience *relational uncertainties*. Newcomers tend to be unsure about how to relate to their peers, supervisors, and other organizational members. Not only are they unsure of how to interact with others to complete their work, but they are also uncertain about how to interact with others socially as friends. They also experience relational uncertainties about people throughout the organization as well as with customers or clients and suppliers if they interact with them as well. Third, newcomers experience *uncertainty about the broader organization.* They do not know its culture or norms. There may be specific language and stories that are unique to the culture that they have trouble understanding. Fourth, they experience *uncertainty about the power relationships* in the organization. Some people are more influential in an organization than others. The power in an organization may or may not be reflected in people's titles, such that newcomers must determine who really is influential rather than who should be influential or thinks they are influential. Given these issues, newcomers must reduce or manage their uncertainties to adapt to their new situations. Newcomers reduce or manage those uncertainties through communication.

In the bank teller scenario, Jordan is uncertain about the exact norms for the teller job because the training sessions presented one set of expectations, and there seem to be a different set of norms at the West Branch. This inconsistency makes it unclear what it takes to get a positive evaluation as a teller. After lunch with the experienced teller, Jordan must determine the type of relationships to have with this particular coworker, as well as other peers and the teller supervisor; it may be a career booster to befriend this person or it might be a career killer. Jordan must also learn more about the general culture of the organization. Understanding the culture includes determining whether the bank's focus on good customer service means being friendly or being quick. Understanding the organization includes learning who the important people in the organization are regardless of their titles. It will be a gradual process by which Jordan reduces uncertainty about all of these topics.

UMT suggests a number of basic principles about how people respond to uncertainty. Originally an interpersonal communication theory (Berger & Calabrese, 1975), the initial premise of uncertainty reduction theory was that the experience of uncertainty in meeting someone new is uncomfortable. Faced with that dissonance, individuals will seek information through communication with the other person to reduce their uncertainty. Then, as they reduce their uncertainty, they will increase their liking or affect for the other person. Of course, from experience we all know that sometimes the more we know about a person, the less we like them. Not surprising, interpersonal scholars later confirmed that *gaining* additional information about another person can *increase* uncertainty and lead to a decrease in liking or even termination of the relationship (Planalp & Honeycutt, 1985). Applying these basic ideas to the experiences of organizational newcomers suggests that faced with the many uncertainties in their new situation, they will seek information to reduce their uncertainty. It certainly is possible that the increase in information will cause them to like their jobs more; it is also possible that the additional information will cause the newcomers to become less satisfied with their positions, depending on whether there is good or poor person-organization (P-O) or person-job (P-J) fit.

UMT suggests that the process of managing uncertainty is more complicated than these basic ideas of uncertainty reduction. UMT indicates that two main additions to the basic premises of uncertainty reduction are needed (Kramer, 2004a). First, individuals often manage their uncertainty through cognitive processes without seeking information or communicating with others. For example, based on previous experiences in other organizations, when faced with uncertainty concerning how to accomplish a task in their work, newcomers may simply assume that what they did in the previous organization will be appropriate in the new one. They also may simply imagine what they think their new supervisor would tell them. In either case, they have reduced their uncertainty, but they may or may not be correct. Second, due to competing motives, individuals often do not seek information actively. Especially for organizational newcomers with previous work experiences, the need for impression management—to make a good impression on others—may cause them to avoid asking for the information to avoid appearing incompetent. As a result, according to UMT, an individual's goal is not always to reduce uncertainty but more generally to *manage* that uncertainty so that it does not create problems. Managing uncertainty may include accepting or tolerating uncertainty in some cases and seeking information in other instances.

In the bank teller scenario, UMT suggests that after being assigned to the West Branch, Jordan will often manage uncertainty by trying to figure out tasks alone based on previous experience and the week of training newcomers received rather than seeking information every time when faced with uncertainty. In addition, to appear competent, it seems like Jordan was reluctant to ask for the information that could clarify how the practices and procedures at the branch were different than the training.

Newcomer Socialization Through Orientation and Training

Organizational management and veteran employees are generally aware of the uncertainty newcomers experience and the discomfort that uncertainty can cause. As a result, most organizations have some sort of orientation or training program to assist

The police academy is a specific type of training and socialization that is long and detailed.

newcomers in managing their uncertainty as part of the encounter phase of the socialization process. In some cases, this is a very elaborate, consciously designed program, like the week of training Jordan received in the bank teller scenario, the extensive training at Disney World, police academies, or boot camp in the military. In other cases, the orientation and training is quite brief and informally designed, such as when volunteers are quickly told how to do their jobs and left on their own to figure out the rest. Instead of viewing each training and orientation program as unique, work by two scholars, Van Maanen and Schein (1979), provide a useful typology of strategies for understanding and comparing the socialization of newcomers. Their work suggests six dimensions and three important outcomes.

Socialization Strategies

Van Maanen and Schein (1979) indicate that the socialization processes of training and orientation generally vary on six dimensions. Those dimensions can be grouped into three general areas: context, patterns, and goal (see Table 3.1). We describe each of these briefly.

TABLE 3.1 Socialization Strategies

General Issue	Institutional Strategies	Individual Strategies
Contextual factors	Group socialization	Individual socialization
	Formal socialization	Informal socialization
	Serial socialization	Disjunctive socialization
Patterns	Sequential socialization	Random socialization
	Fixed socialization	Variable socialization
Goal	Divestiture	Investiture

The context in which socialization occurs during orientation and training involves three dimensions. The first two dimensions are often related. The first dimension, *group socialization versus individual socialization*, refers to whether newcomers are put through orientation collectively as a group or experience it separately one by one as individuals. *Formal versus informal socialization* refers to whether newcomers are trained away from the work site where they can practice or receive their training on the job in situations where what they do has consequences for the organization or its customers. Any combination of these two dimensions is possible, although some are more common. It is not unusual for organizations to combine formal and group socialization to provide information about the history and culture of the organization and its benefits programs. Sometimes this kind of information is even presented through videos. Formal, group training away from the actual work allows the organization to make sure newcomers have mastered their job before they begin actually doing it. There are numerous occupations where it is preferable that newcomers practice and learn away from the actual site of work so that mistakes have limited consequences, whether it be police officers, surgeons, auto mechanics, or computer technicians.

Informal, individual socialization is also a common combination, especially in smaller organizations. Smaller organizations often only hire one or two employees at a time, usually when the need to fill a position is urgent. As a result, it is not worth the time and expense to develop a formal training program. Instead, newcomers are put to work immediately and trained on the job. They learn their jobs individually as they go along through their work days.

Although larger organizations who hire multiple employees at a time use formal, group socialization because it allows for all the newcomers to receive the same information consistently, this initial socialization is often followed by informal, individual socialization in which newcomers learn their specific task within their department one-on-one as they do their actual work. This pattern describes the socialization process in the bank teller scenario. Jordan first received formal, group socialization in a facility away from the bank branches where they could practice while learning; and then they received informal, individual training as the other tellers explained how tasks were done at that particular branch.

The third contextual dimension of the socialization process during initial training and orientation concerns the availability of role models or mentors for newcomers. In *serial socialization*, a role model or mentor is available to help newcomers learn their jobs. The role model or mentor is often someone who currently or previously served in the same position. Any newcomer trained by a predecessor or a supervisor who used to be in the same position experiences this type of socialization. In *disjunctive socialization*, newcomers have to learn on their own. Disjunctive socialization might occur when their predecessors left the organization and are not available or because the position is newly created such that no one knows exactly how the job should be done. For example, a telecommunications firm was so impressed with a recent graduate that they created a position so that they could hire her. Because the position was new, she experienced disjunctive socialization as she developed the job requirements and procedures of her own job. In the bank teller scenario, Jordan experiences serial socialization because there are a variety of experienced tellers who serve as role models for how to do the job.

The next two dimensions concern the pattern of training. In *sequential socialization*, newcomers are taught information and tasks in a particular order, perhaps based on difficulty. In *random socialization*, newcomers are taught information and tasks without any concern for sequence; instead, newcomers are taught according to when the topic happens to seem relevant. Sequential socialization can be particularly beneficial if each skill builds on the previous skill, but random socialization has the advantage that newcomers learn the information or skill when it is important to them rather than forgetting it because it was not important at the time they were taught. In *fixed socialization*, newcomers know exactly how long it will take to complete a particular type of training. For example, they may know they will spend a week learning and practicing a particular skill before moving on to another one. In *variable socialization*, newcomers are not told how long any particular part of the process may take. They may move on to learning another skill as soon as they master the current one whether it takes them a day or a week.

These two strategies may also affect career advancement opportunities and not just the initial newcomer socialization of learning about the job and organization. In some organizations, there is a particular order of jobs and a particular amount of time in each job that a person must follow to advance. For example, in one organization, a person may need to spend 6 months in each of the four areas of the business before being promoted to a supervisory position. In another organization, a person may not need to have experience in all the departments and can be promoted to a supervisory position in as short or long a period of time as it takes.

In the bank teller scenario, there is a mixture of these strategies. The bank tellers initially experienced sequential, fixed socialization. They learned their job skills in a particular order based on the commonness and difficulty of the transactions, and they knew exactly how long the initial training would take prior to being assigned to a branch. Jordan is now experiencing random socialization because new skills are learned when or if the particular activity comes up, and there is no set schedule as to when a teller might be promoted to a teller supervisor, let alone how long it might take to become a manager or a bank officer.

The final strategies really concern the overall goal of the socialization processes. *Divestiture socialization* seeks to "deny and strip away certain personal characteristics of the recruit"; by contrast, *investiture socialization* seeks "to ratify and document the viability and usefulness of those personal characteristics they bring with them to the organization" (Van Maanen & Schein, 1979, p. 250). Perhaps the most obvious example of divestiture socialization is the military in which the organization uses a very harsh orientation program—boot camp—to strip away many of the personal expressions of uniqueness of newcomers. The organization reinforces its divestiture goal nonverbally by having all the recruits wear the same uniforms, have the same haircuts, and sleep in the same barracks. The opposite end of the spectrum would likely be an organization such as Google, which appears to want new employees to bring all of their unique characteristics and new ideas into the organization. Most organizations, even the military and Google, are actually some mixture of these two strategies. In the bank teller scenario, the bank management wants to strip away any personal idiosyncratic ways of conducting transactions and wants newcomers to follow very specific procedures, but they likely want people like Jordan to use their own personalities to interact with customers in a way that reflects their own style, within limits.

Compare the military barracks on the left with the Google UK office on the right. What are the signs of divestiture and investiture socialization captured here?

Socialization Strategy Outcomes

The choice of strategies has a number of important outcomes for newcomers. Research by a number of scholars suggest that the strategies can be divided into two broad categories: institutional strategies, which communicate to newcomers that they should adapt to the organization; and individual strategies, which communicate that the organization accepts the newcomers and is even willing to adjust and adapt to them (Ashforth & Saks, 1996; Jones, 1986). Table 3.1 divides the six dimensions according to these two dimensions. The institutional strategies reduce uncertainty for newcomers by communicating clear expectations; the individual strategies create more uncertainty by allowing the newcomers to experiment more in their roles. The results of these studies also support the basic premise of UMT because employees who experience the institutional strategies experience more role clarity, are more committed to the organization, and are generally more satisfied than those who experience the individual strategies.

It is important to note that not all scholars agree with the classifications in Table 3.1. The original article argues that having fixed socialization allows the individual the security to explore ideas and approaches without fear of failure because there is a fixed time to learn each step (Van Maanen & Schein, 1979). The work of other scholars argues that having a fixed socialization process instead reduces the motivation to be creative or innovative because there are no rewards for doing so. The results of studies support the idea that a fixed time frame reduces innovation (Ashforth & Saks, 1996; Jones,

ETHICAL ISSUE

Mixed Messages

It is common for an organization's formal, institutional training messages to sometimes conflict with the actual work practices of organizational members. In many of these situations, training materials are not up-to-date with ongoing changes. What are the implications of newcomers experiencing these mixed messages so early in their encounter socialization? What is the organization's ethical responsibility to manage and update training information? Who specifically is responsible for drawing attention to the problem? Who specifically is responsible for keeping materials updated? Does the cost of constantly updating material matter?

1986). It is likely that individual factors, such as an individual's personality, and contextual factors, such as the size of the organization and its industry, influence the outcome.

Part of the reason that the strategies may have different effects than hypothesized is that it is also important to account for the content communicated during the socialization and not just the strategy used (Hart & Miller, 2005). For example, formal group training could include messages about how much the organization values innovation and expects newcomers to bring their new ideas into the organization. Likewise, informal individual training from a mentor could emphasize that everyone is expected to comply with rules, which is the only way to succeed in the organization. In addition, newcomers receive many socialization messages informally from established members at social and recreational activities (Hart & Miller, 2005). When the strategies and various messages are mixed or contradictory, it likely leads to increases in uncertainty for newcomers.

Beyond these two general outcomes, Van Maanen and Schein (1979) suggest that the combination of strategies result in particular types of organizational roles. Schein (1968) suggested four main role orientations are outcomes of the socialization process. Newcomers who simply accept the values and practices of the organization assume *custodial, caretaker,* or *team member roles.* These individuals primarily conform to or comply with the organization either to reduce uncertainty or because of a particularly good P-O fit. This role response is associated with institutional strategies. Other newcomers become *content innovators.* These individuals generally conform to the values and practices of the organization but look for opportunities to improve their work situation and the organization. These innovations are along the lines of improving efficiencies and work conditions. *Role innovators* go a step further and actually look for ways to change their roles to better suit their interests and needs. This might include changing job responsibilities and expectations. *Rebels* reject the values and practices of the organization. Rebels also are likely to leave either because they are asked to do so or of their own accord due to their dissatisfaction with the organization.

In the bank teller scenario, the bank uses institutional socialization strategies for the initial orientation and training. This strategy to newcomer socialization likely results in most of the tellers assuming custodial roles and conforming to the organization. Because banking is a highly regulated industry, it is important that employees conform to standard operating procedures. However, because after the first week, the tellers experience individualized strategies, they appear also become content innovators as they figure out various shortcuts that make their work easier while still supporting the mission and values of the organization. The tellers may also become role innovators. For example, Jordan may ask for additional responsibilities and duties in an effort to make work more interesting and so may become the new teller trainer for the branch as a result, even though the position never existed before.

Newcomers and Communication Exchange

In the previous section, we emphasized how experienced members of the organization design training and orientation to assist newcomers in managing their uncertainty. This approach treats newcomers as passive receivers of information who are socialized by the experienced members. In reality, newcomers and established organizational members are both active participants in the communication process of exchanging information to manage their uncertainty. Throughout their careers, as they have new and different experiences, organizational members need information to manage their uncertainty. For example, in addition to experiencing uncertainty in their new jobs during the encounter phase, newcomers create uncertainty for established members who must learn about their new colleague and make adjustments (Gallagher & Sias, 2009).

Information Seeking

As suggested by UMT, seeking information is one way for organizational newcomers and established members to manage uncertainty. When we think of information seeking, we likely think of going to someone and asking them a question, or these days, think of going to some online source to search for more information. Miller and Jablin (1991) identified seven different strategies newcomers employ to seek information about their organization (see Table 3.2).

The first strategy, *overt questions*, is one that has already been mentioned. If a newcomer is uncertain about how the supervisor wants something done, an individual can go to the source of uncertainty, the supervisor, and simply ask a question. Using this approach in the scenario, Jordan could simply have asked the teller supervisor, "How do I handle a third-party check? I can't remember." Asking questions is the most direct way of seeking information. However, because of competing motives like impression management, newcomers are often reluctant to use this approach. Some newcomers may be concerned that asking a question implies they are incompetent and therefore

TABLE 3.2 Information-Seeking Strategies

Strategy	Definition	Example
Overt questions	Ask the source of uncertainty for information.	How would you want me to do this job?
Indirect questions	Make a statement that implies a question.	In my old job, we did this job this way.
Disguising conversation	Talk about a topic in hopes of gaining information.	One of the interesting things about this job is getting a chance to....
Third-party inquiry	Instead of questioning the source of uncertainty, ask someone else.	So what do you think our supervisor would want me to do in this situation?
Observation	Consciously observe someone to gain specific information.	An employee watches coworkers to see if they cut corners or follow standard operating procedures.
Surveillance	Be alert for information in general.	An employee happens to notice that everyone wears casual clothes on Fridays.
Testing	Intentionally break a norm to gain information.	An employee takes an extra 10 minutes for lunch to see what happens.
Consult documents	Read organizational manuals or electronic documents.	An employee finds the employee handbook online to look for a policy statement.

does not make the right impression. There are many indirect ways Jordan could seek information to avoid this concern.

Instead of asking an overt question, an individual may use an *indirect question*. In this approach, the person avoids asking a direct question but instead makes a statement that suggests a question. It is possible that Jordan used this approach during lunch with the experienced teller by saying, "I just can't seem to figure out how to get transactions done as quickly as the rest of you." This is a noninterrogative statement, but Jordan would probably hope that the experienced teller would treat it more as a question and provide some advice on how to work more quickly by not following all of the steps prescribed in the training. Because this is not a direct inquiry, the other teller is not obligated to provide information but could volunteer information about not needing to ask for IDs most of the time.

Another less direct approach is *disguising conversations* in which the newcomer talks about a topic in the hope of receiving additional information from conversational partners. For example, during lunch with the experienced teller, Jordan may have deliberately started talking about the training they both went through and then focused the conversation to the very precise procedures they were taught. A discussion of the training would allow the experienced teller to provide Jordan with information about when it was not necessary to follow procedures.

Another alternative to direct inquiry to the source of uncertainty is to use *third-party inquiries*. In this approach, instead of asking the person who is the source of uncertainty a question, the individual asks someone else for information. During lunch with the experienced teller, Jordan may have asked about how flexible the teller supervisor was about following procedures instead of asking the teller supervisor directly. The experienced teller can then reduce Jordan's uncertainty about the supervisor by explaining which procedures are flexible and which are not.

Two similar information-seeking strategies are *observation* and *surveillance*. Both do not involve any communication like the previous strategies. Observing involves watching others for specific information to manage a particular issue of uncertainty, whereas surveillance involves a more general attending to what is happening with the hope of perhaps gaining some insight into the workplace. In the scenario, Jordan was using one of these two strategies in noticing that other tellers were not asking for ID cards like the training said should be done. Although these two approaches avoid any impression management concerns because they can be done unobtrusively, they also do not necessarily provide enough information to manage uncertainty. Jordan observed a clear difference between the training and practice, but that did not provide information on which behavior was the most appropriate. Jordan still needed additional information.

The final strategy that Miller and Jablin (1991) identified was *testing*. In testing, the individual either accidentally or deliberately breaks some perceived procedure or norm to see what the reaction is. If there are no consequences, then the individual might try to violate the norm more severely to discover what is and is not acceptable or results in consequences. Instead of seeking information from the experienced teller, Jordan could have tried first not asking for IDs for small transactions under $50, then for medium-sized transactions. If no one seemed to care, Jordan could finally attempted a large transaction of over $1,000 without asking for an ID. If the teller supervisor only reprimanded Jordan for transactions over $1,000, that would reduce uncertainty about the norm for requesting IDs on transactions.

One additional way to seek information is by *searching organizational documents*, including printed manuals and books, or more likely now electronic sources or texts. Searching organizational documents is somewhat similar to third-party inquiry in that it does not rely on another person to provide the information. In the scenario, after seeing the other tellers not asking for IDs, Jordan might have consulted the online training manual to determine the correct procedure. In this case, however, Jordan might have been even more confused after seeking information because it would confirm that the other tellers were not following procedure.

One final way that organizational members gain information is by *receiving unsolicited information*. This is not an information-seeking strategy because colleagues provide information without being asked or without the subtle indirect approaches. They simply volunteer information that may assist in managing uncertainty. Studies have shown that newcomers who receive unsolicited information from their colleagues generally adjust to their new positions more effectively because they have a better understanding of their jobs and are more satisfied (e.g., Morrison, 1993). What is not clear from such studies is why some newcomers are given more information than others. It could be characteristics of the newcomers or of the established employees or some combination of the two. Jordan may be fortunate to have the experienced teller offer valuable information in the future.

Information Sources

It is important to mention that newcomers can seek information from a multitude of sources. In a summary of a variety of typologies concerning sources, Kramer (2010) identified four main types of sources: (a) *workgroup sources*, including peers, supervisors, and subordinates; (b) *other organizational sources,* including staff or administrative

COMMUNICATION CHALLENGE

Trusted Colleague

Savvy newcomers employ several means of helping themselves understand the norms and practices of their new organization. The faster and more completely newcomers understand what is expected of them, the more adeptly they are able to perform their role (or the more quickly they can decide to exit the organization, in certain cases). One strategy for seeking information is to identify and befriend a successful veteran member of the organization who can be trusted with "stupid questions." This general form of third-party inquiry can be helpful in reducing or managing uncertainties but also in managing impressions of competence with one's new supervisor and peers. What are the advantages and risks of this approach?

personnel and senior colleagues or mentors, as well as individuals throughout the organization; (c) *impersonal sources*, including employee handbooks and organizational websites, as well as media and Internet stories about the organization; and (d) *external sources*, including suppliers, customers, or clients, along with family and friends. It may seem odd to include family and friends as sources of information for managing uncertainty. In the same way that family and peers provide career advice as part of anticipatory role socialization, they can provide information to assist someone on the job. That assistance may be very task-related, such as how to do a particular job, or it could be about broader issues such as how to get along with a difficult colleague. Overall, there are many sources of information for managing uncertainty. In the bank teller scenario, Jordan seems to have only made limited use of the available sources of information even during the training period and so far has relied primarily on one experienced teller for information. Expanding the sources would likely assist Jordan in reducing uncertainty about this new job and organization.

Information Giving

Most research on newcomers and the encounter phase has focused on information going from the organization and the established members to the newcomer. As the discussion of the definition of communication in Chapter 1 indicates, a one-way information transfer definition of communication fails to capture the complexity of organizational communication. To include some of the complexity of communication, we need to consider how newcomers give information and are involved in the transactional creation of meaning. Minimally, because newcomers are sources of uncertainty for established organizational members (Gallagher & Sias, 2009), newcomers become sources of information for established organizational members in much the same ways that incumbents are sources of information for the newcomers. Newcomers may provide information in response to the various direct and indirect information requests, they may model behaviors that the incumbents observe and imitate, or they may simply provide unsolicited information to established employees (Kramer, Callister, & Turban, 1995).

In addition to addressing uncertainty the veterans experience from having to get to know newcomers, newcomers may also have work-related information that would be valuable for the veterans based on the training they received. For example, in one case study, researchers observed how new firefighters received more recent and up-to-date training about fire science that differed from what veteran firefighters learned years ago. Unfortunately, when the newcomers provided that information through modeling and explanation, veteran firefighters were not receptive to the new information and even mocked and ridiculed one newcomer for his firefighting technique, despite the fact that the technique was appropriate (Minei & Bisel, 2013). The newcomers' knowledge was threatening to the veteran firefighters and triggered their hostility. In the scenario, it is possible that Jordan was taught a new approach to processing transactions that the established tellers should imitate, but it appears that they prefer their routine. In other instances, newcomers may provide established employees with new ideas that are welcome.

Communication Exchange

Information seeking and information giving interact during the communication exchanges as part of the role negotiation process. Role negotiation refers to the social process that newcomers face in needing to figure out what their work role responsibilities will be and how those duties will be performed (Jablin, 2001). Many of the general role responsibilities are negotiated during anticipatory organizational socialization as a newcomer accepts a position in the organization, but many specific details are negotiated after organizational entry. The negotiation process for newcomers is typically viewed as some variation on five steps that include role-sending from the established members and role-making by the newcomer (Katz & Kahn, 1978). First, the organizational members have role expectations for themselves and others. Second, those role expectations are communicated to the newcomer. Third, the newcomer interprets those expectations combining them with the self-expectations he or she has. Fourth, the newcomer enacts the role, thereby communicating a particular understanding of the role. Then, the enacted role provides feedback to the established members on how the role is being performed, which affects their new expectations for the newcomer as the process repeats itself. It is through this communication exchange process of negotiating the role that the newcomer and the other organizational members reduce their uncertainty for each other.

In the bank teller scenario, the general role of all the bank tellers is established during the hiring process and the week of orientation and training. When the tellers arrive at their assigned branch, the role negotiation process continues. Jordan is in the process of negotiating a role at the West Branch. The initial role expectations for strictly following procedures were communicated during the week of training. After the experienced teller communicates that it is okay to not follow the procedures so carefully, Jordan enacts a more relaxed role and no longer follows all of the procedures to increase efficiency. The established tellers and the teller supervisor communicate acceptance of those new behaviors, or perhaps communicate different expectations if their expectations have not been interpreted correctly, as the role negotiation process continues. If Jordan excels and is considered for additional responsibilities and a promotion, role negotiations will again be obvious as the uncertainty of change is addressed.

Encounter Outcomes

There are a number of important outcomes of the encounter phase for newcomers. Three of these are considered here: (a) boundary passages, (b) differences between expectations and experiences, and (c) general adaptation.

Boundary Passages

It is often valuable to think of organizations in terms of boundary passages. *Boundary passages* are psychological or socially constructed boundaries that separate social spheres and groups of individuals. These boundaries are not physical, but because they are such a common part of our way of describing organizations, they are worth considering. There are three primary boundary passages in organizations: functional, hierarchical, and inclusionary (Van Maanen & Schein, 1979). During the encounter phase, newcomers experience all three.

Functional Boundaries. Most organizations are divided into different departments or functions. There are certain boundaries between those departments. Banks are typically divided into internal departments and external departments. Internal departments include accounting, processing, information technology, and so forth. External departments include tellers, customer service representatives, investment services, and others. As customers, we are rarely aware of the internal departments because of the functional boundaries. Figure 3.1 might represent some of the functional boundaries in the departments of a typical, small bank branch. There may only be one person in some departments. Although there are no physical barriers—so people in the different departments talk to each other—there are clear distinctions or boundaries between the departments. Each department has its own work or functions to complete.

Figure 3.1. Functional Boundaries in a Typical Bank Branch

In the scenario, Jordan is assigned to the teller department. Tellers do not give out loans and investment advisors do not cash checks. There may be language differences between departments such that tellers may not understand what a loan officer or investment advisor is talking about to a customer. Employees can cross these boundaries through job changes. Tellers may cross functional boundaries if they are promoted or transferred to another department. In the scenario, Jordan may eventually take a position in customer service opening accounts and dealing with customer account problems and no longer do window transactions.

Hierarchical Boundaries. Hierarchical boundaries have to do with rank or status in the organization. When we joke about climbing the corporate ladder, we are referring to hierarchical boundaries. Figure 3.2 might represent the hierarchical boundaries of the same hypothetical bank branch. As entry-level employees, tellers are at the bottom of the pyramid and the branch manager is at the top, although the branch manager may be middle management in the hierarchy of the entire bank. Some departments are considered higher status than others. For example, the loan department is considered higher status than customer service. Even if there is no official hierarchical difference

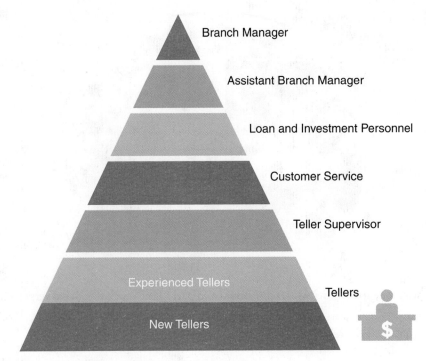

Figure 3.2. Hierarchical Boundaries in a Typical Bank Branch

between the loan department and investment services, it is likely that some employees perceive one to be of higher status than the other. Not all of the hierarchical boundaries are by formal title. As Figure 3.2 suggests, tellers are informally divided into beginning and advanced tellers although there are no official differences. An employee can move in status over time. As a new teller, Jordan is at the lowest level of the branch and looks (up) to the experienced tellers for help even though their titles and responsibilities are technically the same. As new tellers are hired, Jordan will pass the informal hierarchical boundary. A promotion to customer service representative would represent a formal hierarchical boundary passage.

Inclusionary Boundaries. Whereas functional and hierarchical boundaries are often delineated clearly in organizational documents, inclusionary boundaries are generally not so clear. Inclusionary boundaries "concern the social fabric or interpersonal domain of organizational life" and whether a person is on the periphery of the organization or at the center (Van Maanen & Schein, 1979). Another way of thinking of

Vocabulary of Hierarchy

The talk of the workplace tends to apply vertical metaphors to hierarchical boundaries and can be heard in common phrases such as "climbing the ladder" or describing others in the hierarchy as "above" or "below" us. Consider also the term "superior." Many of us would be quite uncomfortable describing ourselves as "inferior" to our boss, even though the term is the antonym of superior. These vertical metaphors in the common talk of organizational members can shape ways of thinking, often without us even realizing it. How might those ways of speaking and thinking cloud our judgment about individuals' intrinsic value and potential contribution to the organization?

this would be to consider who is influential and part of the decision makers versus who is more on the fringe or edge of the group. Figure 3.3 illustrates this idea for the same hypothetical bank branch. New tellers cross one inclusionary boundary when they complete their training, but likely remain on the periphery until they demonstrate that they are competent and reliable coworkers. They cross an inclusionary boundary when they are accepted by established employees. In the scenario, when the experienced teller suggests lunch together, Jordan moves from the very edge of the organization to closer to being accepted. Exchanging insider information about how they do not follow all of the procedures strictly further indicates an inclusionary boundary passage. It will likely be some time before Jordan becomes part of the center of the branch, most likely after also passing some hierarchical and/or functional boundaries as well.

Presenting the boundaries separately is convenient and easy to follow in a small organization such as a family-owned business or a single location of a large company that only has a few employees. It becomes quite complicated to draw a figure that represents the complexity of the three boundaries in a large organization. For example, the bank branch is part of a large bank with multiple branches and headquarters. Each branch represents a functional boundary; but the departments, like the loan departments, cross branch boundaries, as they often work together. To illustrate the relationships of all of the boundaries simultaneously would be challenging, but it can still be useful to think of the three types of boundaries. In the scenario, if Jordan moves to the corporate headquarters after becoming an assistant manager, it will indicate crossing functional boundaries from

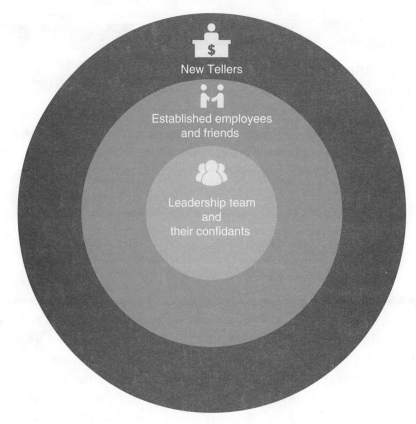

New Tellers

Established employees
and friends

Leadership team
and
their confidants

Figure 3.3.   Inclusionary Boundaries in a Typical Bank Branch

branch to headquarters; hierarchical boundaries by moving in status; and likely inclusionary boundaries by being closer to the leadership team of the bank. At the same time, Jordan may seem to be on the periphery of the company headquarters in terms of social relationships and at the bottom of its hierarchy in some particular department.

During the encounter phase, newcomers cross the first boundary by joining the organization. Individuals then experience the three types of boundaries as they change relationships and positions throughout their time in the organization.

Differences between Expectations and Experiences

In Chapter 2, we discussed providing newcomers with realistic job previews to prevent them from experiencing unmet expectations that lead to turnover. In this section, we explore some of the unmet expectations and discrepancies that newcomers often experience that can lead to turnover.

Being a newcomer involves letting go of a previous role in another organization and taking on a new role in a new organization. It is the comparison of the old role to the new role that creates awareness of differences. For young people entering the workforce for the first time, there are often significant differences between their roles as students and their workplace roles. Students sometimes have trouble letting go of the habits and behaviors that were acceptable in a high school or college setting and adapting to the norms of the workplace (Louis, 1980). For example, college students are typically accountable for attending class around 15 hours a week and have flexible and self-determined schedules in which to accomplish their responsibilities, such as studying, working part-time in many cases, as well as maintaining a social life. Moving from this setting to one in which they must be at work for 40 plus hours a week beginning at 8:00 a.m. under the watchful accountability of a supervisor can be a challenging adjustment for some. Besides these kinds of issues facing students entering the workforce for the first time, there are other differences between expectations and experiences for experienced employees changing jobs throughout their careers. These discrepancies can be divided into three categories: changes, contrasts, and surprises (Louis, 1980).

Changes are differences that can be known objectively by the newcomer and established employees prior to the encounter phase. For example, newcomers know the job title and description they will have, that they will be part of a new organization working in a new location with a new address and phone number, and what their work schedule will be, including how many hours and days they will be expected to work. Moving from working 8 hours a day for 5 days a week to working 10 hours a day for 4 days a week is an objectively known change. Newcomers and established colleagues are aware of most of these differences whether they are in comparison to being a student or a previous job. Because these differences are known in advance and understood, these objective differences are unlikely to cause any particularly strong reaction for newcomers. In the scenario, Jordan and the rest of the bank employees knew about a number of objective changes; Jordan would now be working for West Branch of the bank as a full-time teller, for example.

Contrasts are differences that are more subjective and usually only known by the newcomer. Some of these contrasts are known in advance, but others may only be noticed once the newcomer begins working. For example, only the newcomer may be aware of some of the differences in the informal dress code in the new workplace compared to a previous job because the established employees have lived with a definition of "business casual" for a long time; their definition may be different than the newcomer expected. These contrasts likely differ from newcomer to newcomer because they have different frames of reference. In the scenario, Jordan experienced a contrast between the training program and the practice at the branch. Other newcomers may not have experienced the same contrast because the branch they worked in did follow the procedures very closely. In Jordan's case, the other tellers may not have been aware of the contrast unless they experienced the same discrepancy as new tellers at the branch.

Surprises are also subjective differences between previous experiences and expectations and the newcomer's experience. Surprises differ from changes and contrasts in that they evoke a strong emotional response. The emotion-evoking surprises may be due to differences in the job or organization and may have been partially known ahead of time or may emerge as important unexpectedly. For example, a newcomer assigned to an office without a window, a fairly objective difference, may not realize until working for the first week without one that having a window is very important. This relatively small matter may actually cause a significant emotional response in the newcomer who never realized how important having an office window was. Other surprises occur when the reaction to differences is incorrectly anticipated. A newcomer might expect to enjoy working in a tall building only to discover that the negative reaction to waiting for elevators outweigh the pleasure derived from the view. In the scenario, Jordan did not anticipate the strong, negative effect of standing for hours during the workweek. Fortunately, purchasing new shoes may solve this surprise. In other cases, the surprises an individual experiences can lead to job turnover if the response is severe and negative. For example, if a bank teller who is used to interacting with people on a regular basis is promoted to a position in accounting that requires little or no interaction with customers and long hours of creating reports, the emotional reaction to the discrepancies may cause the person to look for another job either within the same bank or at another business.

It is important to note that not all differences are negative like the examples so far. For example, a newcomer may discover that colleagues are much more supportive in the new position than expected. This positive difference could result in a strong positive emotional response for the newcomer and more commitment to stay in the organization. It is also important to realize that throughout a career, even within the same organization, as someone switches jobs and crosses organizational boundaries, there will continue to be differences between expectations and experiences.

General Newcomer Adaptation

During their organizational encounter, newcomers face a great deal of uncertainty and often experience differences between their expectations generated by their communication activities and their organizational experiences. Through orientation and training programs and exchanging information with experienced organizational members, they gradually gain information to manage their uncertainty. Research shows consistently that when newcomers gain information, it helps them manage their uncertainty so that they understand their work and organization, which in turn helps them adapt in positive ways to their new positions. For example, a combination of socialization tactics and information seeking results in newcomers who have more clarity about their roles, more commitment to their organizations, and more satisfaction with their jobs (Mignerey, Rubin, & Gorden, 1995). Proactive information seeking and role negotiations had similar positive effects for newcomers' self-reported performance and satisfaction (Ashford & Black, 1996). Newcomers are more effective in their roles over the first 3 years of their careers when they gain information about the history of the organization, learn the language of the organization, develop relationships with others, and master their job tasks (Chao, O'Leary-Kelly, Wolf, Klein, & Gardner, 1994).

Whereas newcomer research in the past has focused primarily on managing uncertainty for improving role clarity and job satisfaction while reducing turnover, scholars have begun to also examine organization identification as an important outcome of the socialization process. According to social identity theory, an individual's self-concept includes two important identities: (a) a personal identity consisting of various individual traits such as physical features, cognitive abilities, psychological characteristics, and interests; and (b) a social identity consisting of claiming membership in various groups, organizations, and societies (Ashforth & Mael, 1989). Claiming membership with a particular group or organization means that an individual accepts its values and attitudes and feels a personal connection to its successes and failures. In addition, identification with one group or organization often involves disassociation from another group or organization (Scott, 2007). For example, if as a student you identify with your university, you are claiming its values and practices. At the same time, you likely disparage other universities in your state or athletic conference. Of course, it is possible to attend a university or work for an organization and not identify with it. However, research suggests that a common outcome from the socialization process is identification with the organization. From interacting positively with coworkers and supervisors, negotiating appropriate job duties, and gaining an understanding of the organization, newcomers can experience higher job satisfaction and identification with the organization (Gailliard, Myers, & Seibold, 2010). Together, these results indicate that the experiences individuals have during organizational encounter can result in significant outcomes for their futures in the organization.

In the scenario, it is probably too early to determine if Jordan's experiences during the encounter phase will have a positive or negative effect. The unexpected differences between the training and the reality of the West Branch could create a negative response. Alternatively, the differences might be perceived positively because it is a relief to know that it is not critical to follow every policy exactly. The positive relationship with the experienced teller clarifying expectations could provide Jordan with the information needed to manage uncertainty and lead to a positive career in the organization and perhaps identify with this particular bank. Jordan may even begin to talk negatively about the other banks in town if the identification is strong.

Newcomers in Volunteer Organizations

Although there are important differences between volunteers and employees, many of the concepts discussed so far apply to volunteers as well. For example, volunteers face the same sorts of uncertainty that employees do, as they must learn about their tasks, develop relationships with others, and gain information about the culture of the organization (McComb, 1995). Some organizations, such a botanical garden and disaster aid group, have extensive training programs for volunteers (Iverson, 2013) that represent the institutionalized strategies of socialization. Others have very informal, individualized orientations that leave people learning "by the seat of their pants" as board members (Castor & Jiter, 2013). Volunteers seek and exchange information with various colleagues who may be paid employees or volunteers to manage their uncertainty. Volunteers often identify with the organization and its mission.

One common difference for many volunteers is that their status as a newcomer or volunteer may not be as clearly defined as it is for employees. Individuals may participate in a nonprofit group or organization on more than one occasion and not consider themselves volunteers or members, whereas the established volunteers may think of them that way (Kramer, 2011a). This can create uncertainty for the organizational leaders, its current members, and the new volunteer as they negotiate a particular role in the organization.

Summary

Being a newcomer is a common experience, not just at the beginning of a career but throughout a lifespan. Newcomers experience a great deal of uncertainty as they must learn their tasks, create relationships with others, and learn the organization's culture. Organizations generally attempt to help newcomers manage their uncertainty through orientation and training programs that vary from formal, structured programs to informal, unstructured activities offered on an as-needed basis. The socialization process that an organization uses for its newcomers can influence whether they take on custodial or innovative roles. By seeking various types of information from a variety of sources inside and outside the organization, the newcomers actively manage their uncertainty. During the encounter phase, the newcomers cross boundary passages and experience a number of differences between expectations and the reality of the new organization. The severity of the differences and the success in managing uncertainty affect the newcomer's adjustment to the organization and future participation in it.

In the next chapters of the book, we provide a deeper examination of the characteristics of the organization the newcomer has joined. Whereas in this chapter, we mentioned the topics of relationship with others and organization culture as important parts of the newcomers' information needs, in the next chapters, we look at those topics and many others in greater detail.

CHAPTER 4

Communication and Management Theory

Waiting for the annual recognition ceremony, Kendall reflected on a 25-year career at Computers International (CI). While still attending college, Kendall worked in the company's warehouse part-time. The work was repetitive and simple, and conditions were strenuous because employees needed to prepare and ship a large volume of orders during their shift to avoid being reprimanded by management. Breaks were carefully timed, and supervisors rarely interacted with the employees unless it was to correct a problem. Kendall knew that if it was not for the good pay, most employees would have found work elsewhere.

After graduation, Kendall took a position in the external sales department (not to be confused with incoming phone sales in the call center). The sales people certainly had a lot more flexibility as they called potential customers and traveled within their region. They all had specific quotas to reach each month, but management adjusted those numbers depending on the territory and time of year. This reduced direct competition among the sales staff so that they could maintain positive relationships. The supervisors talked to the sales staff when they were in the office to confirm work was going well and to see if they needed assistance. Sometimes Kendall thought the supervisors were genuinely concerned for them, but at other times it seemed as if they were simply doing their jobs and had little real concern for personnel unless the goals were not being met.

After attending college at night and on weekends to earn a degree in computer programming, Kendall was able to move to the product development division, a much smaller part of CI. The division was divided into teams that worked on separate projects. The teams had a mixture of personnel from artists to engineers. Kendall enjoyed the way the team had nearly complete control over the product development process. They decided the features for the product and details down to the colors of the packaging. There was an approval process, and the team was accountable for producing a new product within a certain amount of time, but they were also rewarded collectively for beating deadlines and creating profitable products.

A few years ago, Kendall got promoted to an upper management position. Work changed from producing, selling, or creating a product to supervising other personnel and motivating them to meet organizational goals. The annual review process changed too. Instead of being given goals, Kendall got to establish personal goals for the next 6 months and determine the steps needed to achieve them. If it required additional training or attending seminars, CI paid for it. At the end of the 6 months, a higher level manager sat with Kendall as they evaluated whether the goals were met and then established new ones for the next 6 months.

So here Kendall was, receiving recognition for 25 years of service. It was hard to predict how different the coming years might be.

. . . . .

Every organization has a management philosophy or practice. Sometimes, upper management decides and announces explicitly that it is adopting a particular approach. For example, the Saturn Division of General Motors announced in the 1980s that it was going to use a teamwork approach to manufacture cars. In many other organizations, a management approach may have been used implicitly for years, even decades, without anyone articulating aloud the assumptions behind their approach to managing their employees. In many organizations, the management approach evolved out of previous experiences of the founders and in responses to organizational changes like growth or external issues like competition.

Part of the uncertainty facing organizational newcomers is figuring out "how things are done around here." An important part of that learning process is understanding the management approach or philosophy that is at play in a particular organization—even when that philosophy is not articulated overtly. These management approaches and philosophies are often called "theories," but they are not theories like uncertainty management theory or other social science theories we present in this book. They are more like guidelines that represent how people think work relationships should be accomplished. The proponents of these different approaches think that if management follows these principles, they will see improvements in their organization.

In this chapter, we explore the main management theories that have been developed by organizational practitioners and scholars over the last 100 years. Having an understanding of the classical, human relations, human resource, and teamwork approaches to management will enable you to understand an organization's management practices that you have already experienced or will in the future; and they can provide you with options if you become an entrepreneur, executive, owner, or operator of an organization in the future. We present these four approaches in the historical order in which they were developed or became popular. Each of these management theories continues to influence the way organizations manage employees to this day.

Classical Management Theory

Context

By the beginning of the 1900s, people were leaving rural communities and migrating toward urban centers in large numbers to take the growing number of jobs in factories and warehouses. These jobs generally involved repetitive work and required few skills or ones that were easily learned. It was a time of major increases in productivity, but it was also often a time of deplorable work and housing conditions as well. What is now called classical management theory came of age in the context of improving production in areas such as mining and manufacturing as owners tried to improve efficiency. Three writers in particular are usually credited with developing classical management theory: Frederick Taylor, Henri Fayol, and Max Weber. Although there are some important differences between these three theorists, they share some deep commonalities with respect to their underlying assumptions about how organizations should work. McGregor's Theory X provides a good summary of the classical management approach.

Frederick Taylor's Classical Management Theory

Taylor was primarily concerned with increasing productivity by increasing the efficiency of workers, especially in steel manufacturing. Taylor (1923) observed what he called *systematic soldiering*, a communication process in which veteran workers would influence newcomers to slow down their work output to levels more manageable by all. In other words, veteran workers would socialize newcomers to slow down and match their rate of work so as to not raise expectations of output to an unsustainable or more difficult level for all workers. Although Taylor did not recognize it as such, the identification of systematic soldiering is an example of how organizational communication was recognized early on as important to understanding workplace experiences. Observing systematic soldiering led Taylor to search for scientific means of knowing how much work should be accomplishable so that standards could be set accordingly. The scientific means Taylor employed often involved what are now called "time and motion studies."

In a time and motion study, a manager or expert watches a worker to determine how to minimize the amount of physical movement and time required to accomplish each aspect of the task to maximize efficiency. This might include designing the workspace to reduce the number of physical steps it took to complete a task or determining the appropriate stance and posture to maximize effort. Taylor (1923) summarized his ideas in four principles of management:

1. Managers should develop a science for each person's work. In other words, managers should determine the best way to do each job instead of relying on tradition or the rule of thumb of veteran workers. Taylor was convinced that every job could be streamlined through the application of science.

2. Managers should select and train workers scientifically. Some individuals are better suited for certain jobs than others, making it important to select people suited for the job and then train them in the science of their work.

3. Managers should gain cooperation of workers to ensure that the work is done according to the scientific principles. This involved communicating clearly to workers and compensating workers in relationship to their productivity.

4. Managers should divide the work between managers and workers. This division of labor meant that managers are responsible for organizing and designing the work and workers are responsible for doing what they are told by managers.

Taylor's principles of management may seem fairly appropriate, and in many ways they are. There is merit to all four of them. We would not criticize an organization for developing ways to work efficiently and having a well-trained person in the right job. These are positive goals for many for-profit or nonprofit organizations (NPOs) alike.

However, rather than accept Taylor's ideas uncritically, it is valuable to look at how Taylor expected to communicate with employees to gain their cooperation. In his book, he describes how he gained cooperation from a worker, Schmidt, of Pennsylvania Dutch ancestry, whose job was to lift and move pig iron, blocks of partially processed iron ore, at the plant. Schmidt moved 12½ tons of pig iron a day, but scientific study demonstrated that a worker could actually move 47 tons a day if trained properly. Taylor described the following conversation as gaining cooperation from Schmidt:

"Schmidt, are you a high priced man? . . ."

"Vell, I don't know vat you mean."

"Oh, come now. . . . What I want to find out is whether you are a high-priced man or one of these cheap fellows here. What I want to find out is whether you want to earn $1.85 a day or whether you are satisfied with $1.15. . . ."

"Did I want $1.85 a day? Vas dot a high-priced man? Vell, yes, I was a high-priced man."

"Oh, you're aggravating me. Of course you want $1.85 a day—everyone wants it! You know perfectly well that has very little to do with your being a high-priced man. For goodness'

sake, answer my questions, and don't waste any more of my time. . . . You see that pile
of pig iron? . . . Well if you are a high-priced man, you will load that pig iron on that
car to-morrow for $1.85.

"Vell—did I got $1.85 for loading dot pig iron on dot car to-morrow?"

"Yes of course you do, and you get $1.85 for loading a pile like that every day right through the
year. That is what a high-priced man does. . . ."

"Well, den I vas a high-priced man."

"Now, hold on, hold on. You know just as well as I do that a high-priced man has to do exactly
as he's told from morning till night. You have seen this man before, haven't you?

"No, I never saw him."

"Well if you are a high priced man, you will do exactly as this man tells you to-morrow from
morning till night. When he tells you to pick up a pig and walk, you pick it up and you
walk, and when he tells you to sit down and rest, you sit down. . . . And what's more,
no back talk. . . . Do you understand that?" (Taylor, 1923, pp. 44–46)

Taylor admits that this interaction would be "rather rough talk" for more skilled or intelligent workers but appropriate for many employees who are "mentally sluggish" (Taylor, 1923, p. 46). Fortunately, most of the organizations that use a form of classical management today have improved on their communication skills considerably, but they still follow Taylor's four principles.

This conversation demonstrates a couple of other characteristics that are typical practices of classic management theory. From this example, it is clear that communication is largely considered a one-way transmission process from management (thought to be "thinkers") to workers (thought to be "doers"). The manager or expert tells the employee what to do and the employee does it and is not expected to provide any feedback ("back talk") to management. Finally, it demonstrates that classical management theory believes that employees are primarily motivated by money. During the conversation, the employee's motivation for complying is based entirely on gaining additional compensation.

From a critical perspective, it is also apparent that the communication is highly manipulative so as to assist management more than employees. The manager does not share information openly but rather holds back information and forces the employee to guess at what he has in mind. He presents information only when it will assist management in achieving its goals. Although the wages in the 1920s are probably shocking to us today, what is more important to consider is that the manager is offering the worker a 60% increase in pay to motivate him to follow directives from management that will result in almost a 400% increase in output. This improved worker efficiency likely means that the number of employees in the company can be reduced—an outcome that again benefits management. Not surprising, as scientific management took hold, there were frequent layoffs at factories, and the rise of unions and worker unrest were common employee responses.

Looking at these issues more broadly, it is important to note that Taylor believed strongly that if scientific management was adopted, there would be an overall increase in wealth and productivity that would benefit everyone—workers and management alike. As Taylor predicted, throughout the 20th century, the overall wealth and productivity of the nation did improve. That of course did not necessarily benefit the specific employee who lost a job due to increased efficiency.

Henri Fayol's General Management Theory

Henri Fayol is the second person generally associated with classical management theory. Although some of his principles clearly overlapped with Taylor, Fayol was less concerned with increasing productivity through micropractices and instead focused on organizing the organizations. He focused on issues of organizational structure and management. Fayol (1949) espoused these 14 principles of management:

1. *Division of labor*: Each person should have one and only one job to increase productivity by reducing effort. This is consistent with assembly line work, but was applied to other work as well.

2. *Authority and responsibility*: Like Taylor, Fayol thought that those in authority should give orders and expect workers to comply. Authority involved responsibility, which came with the position but could be enhanced by personal characteristics.

3. *Discipline*: Mangers should have clear and fair policies that include sanctions for noncompliance.

4. *Unity of command*: Each employee should receive directions from only one manager to eliminate confusion and contradictory directives.

5. *Unity of direction*: There should be one head of the plan to coordinate action toward one unified goal or objective. Within an organization, unity of direction might be accomplished by placing functional areas together in the same unit (e.g., facilities management, financial services) under the supervision of one officeholder.

6. *Subordination of individual interests*: The interests of the organization (i.e., the interests of upper management) are more important than those of any individual and are achieved by example and constant supervision.

7. *Remuneration*: Employees should be paid fairly in response to the work they do taking into account the type of work and the productivity of the individual worker.

8. *Centralization*: Whether decision-making should be centralized or decentralized depends on the circumstances of the organization such as its size and the quality of the manager.

9. *Scalar chain*: Related to the unity of command, a clear hierarchy with clear lines of communication should exist from level to level of decision-making authority. However, there can be horizontal communication if peers and their supervisors are in agreement. If they are not in agreement, the communication should follow the chain of command.

10. *Order*: There should be a place for every material object in the organization, and each employee should also have a designated place in the organizational structure.

11. *Equity*: Employees should be treated well, with kindness and justice, but this does not preclude being forceful or stern with them; everyone receives similar treatment.

12. *Stability in tenure*: To maintain a stable organization, employees should be retained once they demonstrate competence in performing their job after an adequate period of training. Personnel instability creates problems for the organization, although some turnover is natural.

13. *Initiative*: The ability to plan and execute the plan are important skills.

14. *Esprit de corps*: Management should promote a sense of unity, harmony, and cohesion. This includes avoiding the abuse of or excessive use of written communication when giving orders or dealing with other business matters. Written communication can lead to misunderstanding when a face-to-face conversation can clear up such confusions.

In these 14 principles, Fayol departed from how classical management is generally presented by being more flexible than most. For example, most descriptions of classical management theory favor centralization of decisions and would insist on following the chain of command rather than allowing exceptions to those principles. It is likely that it was assumed that management and not the rank-and-file employees would be the ones showing initiative.

Communication and Span of Control

Span of control refers to the number of subordinates managed by a single supervisor. Although many factors affect the ideal span of control within an organization, modern organizational communication scholars tend to recommend that span of control not exceed nine subordinates regularly. Why? Most individuals can maintain five to nine items in their short-term working memory. When the number of subordinates exceeds these limits, information overload is likely to follow. There are many exceptions to this general rule; for example, when subordinates are highly self-managed, the span of control can be larger because the supervisor does not need to remember as much or check in with these subordinates as often. What organizational contexts might allow for a larger span of control? What contexts might require an even smaller span of control?

Fayol did reinforce a number of general principles of classical management. Again, it is clear that a transmission model of communication is being promoted, which has a top-down focus with manager giving orders to workers via the chain of command. Workers still appear largely to be motivated by pay and job stability. They are expected to follow directions for the most part. In another slight departure from others, Fayol's focus on esprit de corps suggests more concern for employees than Taylor; however, the goal still seems largely to improve productivity for the benefit of management. Again, there remains an assumption in Fayol's writing that managers are thinkers and workers are doers.

Weber's Bureaucratic Theory

Max Weber is the third writer most commonly identified as a classical management theorist. His focus clearly overlaps with Taylor and Fayol, yet there are differences. Weber's writing considered especially large organizations; he saw the need for them to work in machine-like precision, and he focused his writing on administrative workers rather than production workers like Taylor. He used the term *bureaucracy* as the focus of his work. Bureaucracy refers to a system of management established through policy crafting. Policies are those rules we write down that prescribe how work should be governed. Weber emphasized 10 main principles:

1. Employees are only subject to the authority of the management concerning their official obligations.
2. Employees should be organized into a clear hierarchical system of offices or authority.
3. Work should be clearly defined by rules and separated among workers based on competence.
4. Employees enter freely into their contractual relationships.
5. Employees are appointed to positions based on technical qualification.
6. They receive fixed salaries according to rank in the hierarchy.
7. The workplace should be their primary occupation.
8. The workplace should be a career with promotion opportunities according to achievement and/or seniority.
9. The employee is not an owner.
10. The employee is subject to strict, systematic discipline and control. (Weber, 1924/1978)

Conceptual overlap with Taylor and Fayol is apparent. All three writers agree that employees should have clearly defined, specific jobs. They agree on the importance of employees having technical skills. They all stress the importance of financial benefits in keeping employees motivated. There is also a sense in all three that management makes the rules and decisions and simply communicates those policies, rules, and practices to the employees. Then management enforces the rules as it controls the employees.

Weber is unique, however, in his focus on the need for impersonal contractual relationships. He supported the idea that having clear rules and duties eliminated bias and unfair treatment of people within an organization as well as those served by the organization. In his ideal version of bureaucracy, the organization runs efficiently because workers are skilled at their jobs; and everyone is treated in an unbiased manner because the rules and regulations are clear; and everyone is subject to strict discipline and control by those rules. It is important to recognize that although the term bureaucracy probably has a negative connotation in the 21st century, Weber's conceptualization was positive in that the bureaucratic ideal enhanced the transparency, fairness, and justice of organizations because decisions were made in reference to preestablished policy and not managements' whim. Weber did, however, predict that bureaucracies could become so steeped in policy that rapid adjustment to new needs and situations would be

difficult. He termed that possibility the *iron cage* of bureaucracy. Perhaps the negative connotations the term has for many today was predicted accurately by Weber himself.

Douglas McGregor's Theory X

The basic similarities of classical management theory are recapped by what McGregor calls Theory X management (McGregor, 1957). McGregor reasoned that managers had assumptions about human nature and that managers express those assumptions in their communication with workers. If a manager's worldview suggests that workers are inherently lazy, then we would expect a different quality of supervisor communication from that manager than from one who assumes workers are inherently creative and motivated to work. McGregor summarizes the Theory X manager's assumptions about human nature with the following characteristics:

1. Management is responsible for organizing and directing people and resources to achieve economic goals.
2. Management must direct people by controlling, directing, and modifying their efforts to meet organizational needs.
3. Management must persuade, reward, punish, and control employees or they would be passive and unproductive.
4. Employees are generally not very smart, dislike work and responsibility, and lack ambition; they are self-centered, indifferent to organizational needs, and resistant to change.

McGregor admits that applying these principles in a harsh manner—through coercion, tight control and supervision, and threats—results in an antagonistic resistance to management, militant unionism, and efforts by employees to sabotage management objections; but too soft of an approach leads to employees taking advantage of the organization (McGregor, 1957). Clearly, if these ideals accurately represented a manager's assumptions about human nature (especially the preceding point 4), then strict, authoritarian management communication is sure to flow from those assumptions.

Classical Management Today

Given the changes in society over the last 100 years, it might seem likely that classical management would no longer be used. Certainly its harshest approaches are more common in developing countries, whereas a softer approach has evolved in more developed economies. Despite this, many organizations still have vestiges of classical management in them, particularly in work settings that require repetitive work. In the opening scenario, the shipping portion of CI exhibited many of the characteristics of classical management. For example, expectations for the repetitive tasks of employees are carefully detailed by management, which maintains fairly impersonal relationships as it enforces those expectations on everyone. Employees are not involved in any decision-making, and they are not expected to provide input and feedback. It is worth noting that Kendall's focus at that time on making money was consistent with how classical managers view employee motivation. But this hypothetical scenario occurs in organizations across the United States. A documentary called *Amazon Rising*, aired by CNBC on June 29, 2014, suggests that many of the management practices and

expectations in the Amazon warehouses are consistent with classical management theory (available at https://www.youtube.com/watch?v=llA3-K_VpS0). For example, employees are carefully monitored and give specific allotments of time to complete tasks; those who do not meet those expectations consistently are fired by the company. Not surprisingly, the employees comment that the pay is good, but the work conditions are difficult. Other companies have similar practices.

Human Relations Management

Context

By the middle of the 20th century, the workplace was changing in significant ways. During World War II, women in the United States joined what had previously been a predominately male workforce in large numbers. This transition was made famous through the iconic "Rosie the Riveter," a representative of the patriotic work of women during the war. After the war ended, many women remained in the work force.

After WWII, a number of studies were published that challenged classical management approaches. These studies, known as the *Hawthorne studies*, were conducted in a large factory in a suburb of Chicago—a factory that opened in the early 1900s and operated until the early 1980s. The factory produced electronic equipment, such as telephones, switches, and circuit boards. The Hawthorne studies were actually conducted by researchers who were devoted to the ideas of classical management; however, their observations at the Hawthorne Works factory changed their thinking.

Hawthorne Studies

Because of their belief in classical management, the researchers conducted a series of studies to determine how to maximize employee productivity under the leadership of Fritz Roethlisberger (1947). In the *Illumination Studies*, the researchers attempted to determine the optimal lighting needed to maximize workers' productivity. The researchers began the study by recording the output of workers; then, they varied the lighting. Their initial results were promising. When they increased the lighting, productivity increased. The researchers increased lighting more and productivity when up again. Then, the researchers decided to reduce the lighting as a means of verifying their initial findings that more illumination was associated with great employee productivity.

To the researchers' surprise, productivity increased again when lighting was dimmed. Curiously, the researchers tried again; this time, they simply replaced lightbulbs with the same wattage bulbs. Workers commented on the improvement, although their productivity did not change. Only when lighting was reduced so much that workers could not see well enough to do their jobs did productivity finally go down. These results did not coincide with their expectations; the results indicated that employee output was unrelated to the lighting.

In the *Relay Assembly Experiments*, the researchers conducted an extensive study of a group of women over 2 years. In those experiments, the researchers manipulated the number of breaks, the length of breaks, the food eaten during the breaks, and the length of the workday. Furthermore, the researchers also studied the female workers' nonwork activities, such as the number of hours of sleep the night before or 2 nights before. Again, results were inconsistent with the idea that any of these single variables could influence productivity. There was no relationship between the changes in the work environment and actual output of the workers. When researchers restored work conditions to the original conditions, work productivity remained high.

It took these researchers steeped in classical management theory some time to interpret the meaning of their results. Eventually, they determined that the workers changed their productivity because they realized someone was paying attention to them. The workers knew that they were the subjects of the researchers' experiments. The Hawthorne researchers attributed the high output to their own presence and the social attention paid to the workers in all the conditions. The phenomenon is generally called "the Hawthorne effect." It is the idea that people will behave differently if they know someone is paying attention to them and they are being watched. Although the Hawthorne effect is generally temporary—over time, people tend to revert back to their normal behaviors—this idea has been a worry not only of management, but also for social scientists who are concerned that participants in research change their behaviors in ways that will please them.

The researchers also decided to expand beyond observing workers performing tasks, and so they conducted follow-up interviews of the relay-assembly women. The interviews provided important additional information. During the experiments, the workers were consulted about possible changes; in some cases, but not all, their input resulted in alterations in the researchers' plans. From the interviews, it became clear that this change in the customary relationship between management and workers made workers feel treated as human beings rather than objects. The opportunity to talk

Are Happy Workers Productive Workers?

The human relations theorists' work might be read as supporting the "common sense" adage that "happy workers are productive workers." More than 70 years of rigorous organizational studies have failed to find that association consistently. We can easily imagine many happy workers who do little work and are happy because of that arrangement. Likewise, many unhappy and downtrodden workers are quite productive! The issue of what motivates workers to high productivity is much more complex than the common saying implies. How should a manager communicate to maintain the appropriate balance of satisfaction and productivity?

to someone about their concerns improved their morale and productivity. It is important to note that the researchers were not management, but workers thought of them as authority figures nonetheless.

The *Bank Wiring Room Experiments* yielded some additional findings. Accepting the classical management assumption that employees are motivated primarily by financial incentives, the researchers tried various changes in compensating employees, such as paying per piece rather than hourly wages. Productivity actually went down with the individual incentives, apparently due to workers' suspicion of management. In addition, *group* productivity tended to be the same even when *individual* productivity changed. So, if one worker was ill and working slowly, other workers seemed to pick up the slack, resulting in about the same total output for the group. There was also pressure on slow workers to work faster and for rate-busters to slow down. The most liked employees were the ones closest to the group average.

The researchers had less trouble interpreting these findings, probably in part because of the previous studies. It was clear that there were social forces among workers that were at least as important to them as management's goals or their own personal financial gains. People gain security through a combination of being socially accepted and recognized by their work associates; money is not the only form of recognition that is important to them. Although there are critics of these interpretations of results, together the findings from the Hawthorne studies supported that idea that people resent being treated like objects or merely as cogs in a machine. Rather, workers respond positively to attention from management and are influenced by group norms. These lessons led to the development of what is typically called Human Relations Management, which became popular in the decades following WWII.

There are several principles that are common to the human relations approach to management. Roethlisberger (1947) suggested a number of these in his writing:

1. Employees are motivated by their social relationships with managers and coworkers in addition to financial concerns.

2. When managers communicate with their workers and accept input from them, it improves their morale and productivity.

3. Managers need to listen to their employees talk about what is important to them to understand their concerns.

4. Effective managers use persuasion to gain compliance and control rather than coercion. To accomplish this often involves addressing the sentiments and concerns of the workers while expressing facts rather than personal sentiments.

Other human relations scholars similarly emphasize that managers need to maintain friendly relationships with workers by listening to their concerns, although decisions are still made by management (Mayo, 1946). This suggests the importance of recognizing workers' social needs and giving them a sense of inclusion and participation.

Human Relations Management Today

It would not be surprising if many readers of this textbook can think of a job they have had in which the managers seemed to be using a human relations approach. In the CI scenario, Kendall experienced this sort of management on the sales force. The managers of the sales employees maintained positive relations with their workforce and accepted input from them. The sales people knew management could compare their productivity to others and yet maintained positive relationships with each other despite the possible competition between them. Kendall was motivated, in part, due to these positive relations and in part due to financial incentives. There are a wide range of organizations that use human relations principles as their primary management style, particularly in service work rather than manufacturing work, such as retail sales and the hospitality industry—including restaurants, motels, and vacation destinations.

A human relations approach certainly seems like an important improvement from classical management studies. A critical scholar, however, might view this approach as a clandestine method of control. The managers are simply using a new tool—social relationships—to achieve management goals, which benefit upper management more than employees. The illusion of participation in decisions while management still maintains control of the decisions manipulates employees into being more productive for the benefit of management without actually giving them any additional personal benefits other than feeling good about themselves. It is likely that this critique is not universally applicable. Some organizations using a human relations approach likely do use human relations principles simply as a way to achieve organizational goals, whereas others are truly concerned about their employees as much or more than their bottom line. In either case, it seems likely that the work conditions are often more positive in organizations using a human relations approach instead of a classical management approach.

Human Resource Management

Context

Although some of the principles and practices of a human resource management approach have been around for many years, human resource management really became prominent in the United States in the 1970s and 1980s. A number of factors contributed to this trend. First, the economy in the United States was shifting from a manufacturing to a service-based economy as factories began to close or move overseas where labor costs were cheaper. Second, during this era, protests against the Vietnam War and the

ETHICAL ISSUE

Humans as Resources

Organizational communication scholar Charles Conrad (2011) asks us to think carefully about the use of the label "resource" as it gets applied to human beings in workplace settings. Organizations leverage a number of resources to accomplish goals. Technologies capital, facilities, and raw materials are just a few resources some organizations use. What is the ethical implication of attributing a metaphor of "resource" to describe human beings? In what ways are human beings unlike a resource?

antiestablishment attitude that was often associated with them meant that those entering workforce tended to be less loyal to organizations than U.S. workers once were. Third, increasing job opportunities—although not continuous due to recessions—gave employees more mobility to change jobs and careers. Whereas in previous generations it was not uncommon for someone to grow up, live, and die in the same community, people in the United States moved and switched organizations much more often. In an effort to address these problems, organizations attempted to develop and support their employees more instead of taking them for granted. One visible indicator of this change was the shift from personnel offices, which simply kept track of employees, to human resources offices, which helped employees find opportunities to develop and grow *within* the organization. The name, "human resources," is a way of thinking about employees *as* resources. From the human resource management philosophy, human beings are the organization's greatest resource or asset because human beings are the source of innovative and creative problem-solving. In other words, the human resource philosophy values human beings for their potential to provide cognitive contributions, such as new ideas. Yet, gathering cognitive contributions from employees is quite difficult for management to standardize in bureaucratic ways.

Some Roots of Human Resource Management: McGregor's Theory Y

Although written well before the human resource management approach became common toward the last quarter of the 20th century, McGregor's Theory Y summarized many of the characteristics of the approach. You may recall that McGregor's Theory X described the association between managers' assumptions about human nature (i.e., humans are lazy and avoid work) and how these kinds of assumptions shape managers' communication with subordinates. McGregor also proposed Theory Y to classify dramatically different assumptions than Theory X managers did. The most important difference is that Theory Y managers view employees as intrinsically motivated to accomplish goals. Theory Y managers assume that workers are not passive individuals, motivated only by money; they are motivated by their internal needs. In turn, Theory Y managers' assumptions about human nature shape their communication with subordinates.

According to McGregor, employees' drive to accomplish goals can be described by Maslow's (1954) hierarchy of needs. Those needs include (a) physiological needs, such as food, clothing, and shelter; (b) safety needs including an orderly, safe, predictable environment free of unmanageable or dangerous situations; (c) social needs including friendships and acceptance; (d) ego needs such as achievement, recognition, and status; and (e) self-actualization needs, the feeling of self-fulfillment and achieving ones potential. In general, the lower level needs must be addressed or fulfilled before the higher level needs provide motivation. However, Maslow emphasized that although often presented as "if this hierarchy were a fixed order, it is not nearly so rigid" (Maslow, 1954, p. 98). For a variety of reasons, the needs may occur in different orders or simultaneously for individuals. Classical management only addresses physiological and safety needs with its focus on economic rewards, and the human relations approach only adds social needs to the mix. According to Theory Y and the human resource approach, effective management recognizes the importance of the higher level ego and self-fulfillment needs of employees in motivating employees. As a result, according to MacGregor's Theory Y, managers need to practice these four principles:

1. Management needs to decentralize and delegate control to employees. This allows employees the freedom to assume responsibility, direct their own activities, and satisfy their ego and self-fulfillment needs.

2. Management needs to provide opportunities for job enlargement. Although much easier to do in many office jobs and professions, it applies equally to factory work where employees can be given responsibilities to meet their more advanced needs.

3. Management needs to practice participatory decision-making so that employees have a voice in decisions to satisfy their advanced needs.

4. Performance evaluation needs to move away from the typical economic rewards or punishments of classical management to allowing employees to develop their own targets or objectives and conduct self-evaluations. This process allows them to be responsible for their own planning and appraisal, which will meet their higher level needs.

Principles of Human Resource Management

As human resource management became more common, scholars attempted to define more specifically the principles and communication practices involved. As they did so, they also began to test whether these principles and practices impact organizational performance. This post-positivist emphasis linking the practices to outcomes is often referred to as strategic human resource management. Research suggests that there are seven dominant characteristics of human resource management (Delery & Doty, 1996):

1. Training opportunities: Not only do new employees receive training for their jobs, but established ones periodically receive training to assist them in their careers.

2. Participation: Employees are asked their opinions and are able to make real decisions that influence their work. They have a voice in what happens in their work environment.

3. Employment security: Employees can expect that they can continue to work for the company as long as they want (assuming competence) and that the organization would attempt to avoid layoffs even in challenging economic times.

4. Job descriptions: Jobs are clearly defined and up-to-date so employees know their responsibilities.

5. Results-oriented appraisal: Appraisals include clear performance objectives and objective measures to reduce the potential for biased appraisals.

6. Internal career opportunities: There are clear and multiple career paths in the company; supervisors know their subordinates' aspirations.

7. Profit/stock sharing: Employees are eligible for bonuses and company shares.

These seven characteristics are not only common in the United States but also internationally. A study of Chinese firms confirmed the same seven factors (Akhtar, Ding, & Ge, 2008). Of course, not all human resource organizations use all seven of these characteristics in equal amounts. For example, profit sharing is probably more unusual than some of the other characteristics. The main principles of involving participatory decision-making and open communication about jobs and appraisals are more universal.

It is important to notice that although these principles may initially seem to have something in common with a human relations approach to management, they really are quite different. In a human resource management approach, employees are treated as having internal motivation beyond money and social relations, and they are involved in decision-making, not just asked for their opinions to created positive relationships between management and employees. Part of the problem, however, is that many organizations may say that they use human resource management when they actually use some sort of hybrid management approach that combines elements of both of these.

Human Resource Management Today

There is little doubt that human resource management is common at least in name and often in practice in the United States today. This is particularly true in many large companies that employ skilled and educated workers. A human resources approach is not necessarily used equally across an organization. In the CI scenario, Kendall and the upper level managers experience a human resource approach. They were involved in developing their own goals so that they could grow and develop in their careers. They were involved in decision-making about their own careers as well as other decisions at their level, but human resource approaches were not apparent in other parts of the organization.

A number of large organizations boast openly about their human resource approach. For example, Google describes this about their organization:

> We strive to maintain the open culture often associated with startups, in which everyone is a hands-on contributor and feels comfortable sharing ideas and opinions. In our weekly all-hands ("TGIF") meetings—not to mention over email or in the cafe—Googlers ask questions directly to Larry, Sergey and other execs about any number of company issues. Our offices and cafes are designed to encourage interactions between Googlers within and across teams, and to spark conversation about work as well as play. (http://www.google.com/about/company/facts/culture/)

Notice how this description suggests many of the characteristics of the human resource approach. Google holds meetings where everyone can express ideas as part of making decisions, and there is open, multidirectional communication. The images on the Google website suggest employees work collaboratively and have fun in the process.

Walmart also communicates that they use human resource principles. According to their website:

> We look to our HR associates to motivate and empower our 2.2 million associates, working to ensure that every single member of our team feels uniquely fulfilled, challenged and capable of successfully accomplishing his or her role in our day-to-day operations. (http://careers.walmart.com/career-areas/corporate/human-resources/)

Elsewhere they boast that their jobs are "Real Opportunities" so that if you start as an associate (entry-level store job), you receive training and development opportunities,

Motivation at Despair, Inc.

Entire organizations have emerged with the purpose of satirizing management's insincere use of motivational strategies like asking employees for their input without really intending to make changes—as may be common of human relations approaches. Despair, Inc., is one such organization. The organization creates humorous posters, shirts, mugs, and other office supplies that mock sayings of the workplace. We recommend looking at despair.com. Here is an example of one such mock poster:

What truths about managerial communication might be embedded in this and other critiques? What role does such humor play in shaping supervisor-subordinate relationships in organizations?

management training, a lifelong learning program, and stock purchase plan with a company match (http://careers.walmart.com/about-us/working-here/). These messages include many of the principles of human resource management from fulfilling needs to profit sharing.

There are probably thousands of small businesses, mid-sized companies, and corporations that claim they practice human resource management. The degree to which those claims are an accurate description of their actual approach to management and management communication can be assessed in whether and how managements' messages align (or fail to align) with their practices.

Teamwork or Theory Z Management

Context

In the later part of the 20th century, U.S. companies were concerned about international competition, initially from Japan, but eventually from other countries—and, more recently, from China. As the global economy became driven more by global interconnections, organizations looked for new approaches to take advantage of the creativity of their employees. With a strong influence, especially from Japanese approaches to management, this led to the development of a teamwork approach to management, also sometimes associated with labels such as self-managed teams or Theory Z. Due to the success of its economy at that time, many of the ideas were adapted from the practices of Japanese companies.

ETHICAL ISSUE

Top-Level Management and Organizing for the Short Term?

Theory Z advocates that we structure organizations to reduce incentivizing workers to achieve short-term gains at the expense of long-term prudence. To achieve those ends, employees in team-based management organizations are often constrained from the possibility of quick promotion. However, many Fortune 500 firms in the United States have no such requirement of top-level executives and officers. In fact, for many Fortune 500 executives who own stock in their own organization, short-term gains (like those created by downsizing or moving jobs overseas) can result in huge personal financial benefits. What responsibility do board of directors and stockholders have in keeping upper management and employees focused on long-term goals?

Principles of Teamwork

A commitment to a teamwork approach to management involves more than simply grouping people together and calling each collective a "team." The teamwork approach to management also involves much more than giving lip service to the idea that we are all part of the same team. A commitment to team management involves more.

To begin, as a precursor to successful teamwork, it is important that the organization have a strong culture or set of values that are shared among employees. The organization should seem more like a tribe, clan, or a culturally homogenous group than a bureaucratic hierarchy of employees pursuing individual goals (Ouchi & Price, 1978). This shared set of values and goals is needed so that when teams are given the opportunity to make decisions, those decisions will be consistent with the broader goals and objectives of the organization.

A number of other characteristics seem to describe organizations committed to teamwork. The organizations need to promote long-term rather than short-term employment, gradual rather than rapid evaluation and promotion, consensual decision-making based on holistic rather than individual decisions based on individual concerns, and employee responsibility (Ouchi & Price, 1978).

Taken together, these practices set the stage for teams within the organization to make decisions that are not focused on individual rewards. For example, when there is guaranteed long-term employment and no opportunity for rapid promotion, employees should focus on decisions for the long-term benefit of the organization; they know that they are not going to get a quick promotion from some decision that made them look good in the short term but are detrimental to the organization in the long term when they will still be employed.

When a teamwork approach to management is applied comprehensively, teams are empowered and become self-managed. Team members assume a collective responsibility for the decisions and actions while keeping them consistent with the organizational values. There are six primary principles that are needed for groups of people to become self-managed teams (Chansler, Swamidass, & Cammann, 2003; Kirkman & Rosen, 1999):

1. Team members should have an understanding of the work process. It is not sufficient for them to understand their individual job; they must understand the flow of work in the organization to make appropriate decisions.

2. Team members should experience collective autonomy. They should experience freedom, independence, and discretion as a team. This may mean giving up some of their individual autonomy to the group.

3. Team members should have the ability to make important decisions. They must have a sense that their decisions have an impact on the organization and its stakeholders such as customers or clients.

4. Team members make decisions through consensus. Taking the time to communicate until the team reaches consensus increases team members' commitment to its decisions.

5. Team members should have control over resources. Team members need to manage physical resources needed to complete their tasks, but they also should manage the hiring and firing of personnel; without that control, they are not self-managing.

6. Rewards should be team based rather than individually based. Team rewards encourage decisions for the collective good rather than that at the level of individual reward.

When teams are given the sort of responsibility and authority to become self-managed, there tend to be a variety of positive outcomes—including increased team productivity, improved morale, satisfaction, trust, and commitment. There also seem to be a number of characteristics that develop in the communication within the teams. Salas, Sims, and Burke (2005) identified five important characteristics of teamwork approaches:

1. Team leaders became decision facilitators instead of decision makers. Instead of the group expecting the leader to solve problems, the leader assisted the group in developing their collective solution.

2. Team members developed mutual performance monitoring. Instead of a supervisor monitoring the team, team members monitored each other and gave each other feedback.

3. Team members practiced backup behavior. They assisted each other on tasks working together or used their slack time to assist others with work overloads.

4. Team members developed the ability to adapt. Through collective pooling of resources, they were able to adjust to unexpected events, develop alternative plans, and carry out a new plan.

5. Team members develop a team orientation rather than an individual orientation. This can include improving individual performance for the benefit of the team performance.

It is easy to see the potential positive outcomes of a teamwork approach to management. These characteristics all point to improved communication among team members. Research suggests that there are positive organizational outcomes and improved interaction within the group making up the team resulting from implementing teamwork management in some settings.

Teamwork and Concertive Control

There is also a potential dark side of self-managed, team-based organizing. These general ideas seem particularly well-suited for a collectivistic culture like Japan but may be more challenging to implement in an individualistic culture like the United States (Hofstede, 1980). Because teamwork depends on a "clan mentality" of shared values and beliefs, a teamwork approach to organizing can be hostile to alternative perspectives and resistant to newcomers, especially those who are culturally different (Ouchi & Price, 1978). Taken to the extreme, close-mindedness can make teamwork organizations less likely to adapt to changes in the environment.

A less obvious outcome of teamwork approaches to management that may be problematic arises from the consequences of shifting control from explicit managerial dominance to implicit teamwork pressures. Particularly in classical management, and to a lesser degree in human relations and human resources approaches, management controls employees through supervisors who attempt to motivate and monitor them. In Weber's (1924/1978) concept of bureaucracy, the control largely shifts to rules and regulations rather than the supervisor, although supervisors must make sure rules are being followed in a fair and unbiased manner. Under teamwork management, the control shifts to a large degree to the team, as it collectively makes decisions and manages resources based on company values. As noted previously, this often includes team members developing mutual performance monitoring (Salas et al., 2005). In other words, in self-managed work teams, team members observe and manage one another. The teams also make decisions by consensus (Chansler et al., 2003). From management's perspective, teamwork reduces the need for the direct supervision typical of classical management approaches because peer coworkers monitor one another. Furthermore, many teamwork approaches are predicated on managers' beliefs that teams are especially creative, such that teamwork approaches seem to be in concert with much of the human resources philosophy—although, in reality, teams are not necessarily more creative than individuals (see Allen & Hecht, 2004). On the other hand, however, these activities create pressure on individuals to conform to peer norms. The importance of peer pressure on productivity was noted as far back as the bank wire experiments in the Hawthorne studies where peers enforced productivity norms for those who worked too fast or too slow (Roethlisberger, 1947).

Barker (1993) studied the implementation of teamwork in an electronics firm and eventually focused on the issue of peer pressure as a form of what he termed "*concertive control*." Concertive control is a form of implicit, team-based, value consensus that disciplines team members to conform to team-based norms. Essentially, Barker argues that having an entire team monitoring work behavior creates an even stronger form of control than previous management approaches. He provides compelling evidence to support the claim that the concertive control of peers creates harsh controls that surpass authoritative control or bureaucratic control.

When teamwork was implemented at the firm, there was initial confusion, but gradually employees adapted and felt increased morale; and the team-based approach increased organizational output and productivity. Over time, as the teams continued to enact the organization's values through teamwork, it meant that they put intense pressure on individuals to meet productivity norms, even if it meant working overtime and canceling other plans. For example, in one case, most of the 11 team members agreed to work overtime without any complaints, although one had to delay after-work plans. The team allowed the one who could not stay due to her daughter's activities to leave only if

ETHICAL ISSUE

Is Control Ethical?

Control is a central concern of organizational studies. To coordinate individuals' actions to achieve collective goals seems to require some degree of control. Edwards (1981) characterized systems of control in terms of how organizations routinized the directing of work tasks, evaluated work accomplished, and rewarded and disciplined workers. Nearly every imaginable organization has some pattern or routine for conducting these essential features of control. However, control takes on a negative connotation in many areas of society. Is organizational control necessarily unethical? Is bureaucratic or concertive control more ethical?

she agreed to stay late the next time to make up for missing. It is not clear if management would have been able to enforce this type of behavior, but peers clearly did.

Over time, the team enacted more specific and rigid rules. Barker (1993) was completely surprised one day when he saw a chart on the wall of all the team members that recorded any "occurrences" for all to see. Occurrences could be as minor as being 5 minutes tardy to a team meeting. The team apparently decided to use this approach to enforce norms it adopted collectively. It seems unlikely that management would have considered such a public and potentially humiliating plan unless it practiced a harsh version of classical management. Morale in the team decreased over time, as team members felt increasingly trapped by the norms they imposed on themselves.

Concertive control has been studied in other settings such as the Grameen bank in Bangladesh (Papa, Auwal, & Singhal, 1997). In that case, organizational members identified so strongly with the organizational goal of loaning money to help poor people start businesses that loan officers went to extreme lengths to maintain their 99% loan recovery rate, even if it meant personal sacrifices. Of course, it seems unlikely that concertive control will develop in every organization that adopts a teamwork philosophy. However, when a homogenous clan mentality develops, based on adherence and identification with organizational shared values and beliefs, the rise of concertive control remains possible. Interestingly, the organizational values that inform concertive control are not typically developed through participatory, teamwork decision-making but are instigated by top management and communicated down to employees. In Barker's (1993) study, the employees were not consulted about converting to teamwork, although they were informed about the upcoming change, and they did not help develop the organizational values; those changes and values were imposed on them by management with the rationale that it was vital for the survival of the company and their jobs.

Teamwork Management Today

It might seem that self-managed teamwork is best suited for certain kinds of creative activities, such as research divisions or advertising firms. For example, in the case scenario of CI, Kendall experienced teamwork management while in the product development division. In that division, teams were empowered to be self-managed. Although goals were set by management and there was some approval process, the teams worked independently, made important decisions, and managed their resources collectively. Teamwork has been applied to many other types of organizations. Scholars studied teamwork in a range of organizational settings such as a Harley Davidson plant (Chansler et al., 2003), electronics firms (Barker, 1993), forestland firefighters (Glaser, 1994), textile manufacturing, high-tech manufacturing, and insurance (Kirkman & Rosen, 1999). So although management sometimes uses language such as "we are a team" to try to create cohesion and compliance while practicing top-down decision-making, real teamwork management will likely continue to be common as organizations learn to capitalize on the advantage afforded by the creativity of their personnel in the global economy.

Management Approaches to Volunteers

Like for-profit businesses and government agencies, organizations that rely heavily on volunteers to do the work of the organization have to adopt a management approach that is either consciously selected or developed over time based on previous experiences or through trial and error. The management approach has to take into account the unique characteristics of relying on volunteers. Volunteers clearly are different than employees because they do not "work" out of a desire for economic gain but for some other prosocial motive that often benefits others more than themselves. People tend to volunteer for one of these six reasons:

1. *Values*: The volunteers believe that the organization has values consistent with their own.
2. *Personal growth*: The volunteers hope to learn new information or skills.
3. *Enhancement of self*: The volunteers hope to feel important or better about themselves by volunteering and helping others.
4. *Social belongingness*: The volunteers want to initiate and develop friendships.
5. *Career-related benefits*: The volunteers hope to make contacts or explore options that may lead to future career benefits.
6. *Protection of self*: The volunteers relieve guilt over their good fortune or escape from personal problems by volunteering (Clary et al., 1998).

Comparing this list to Maslow's hierarchy of needs suggests that the needs that drive volunteers are primarily in the categories of social needs, ego needs, and self-actualization needs.

Considering volunteers' motives suggests some possibilities for selecting an appropriate management approach for working with volunteers. It might seem like nothing

Communicating to Reduce Volunteer Turnover

Although happy workers are not necessarily productive workers, happy workers (and happy volunteers) do tend to stay with their organizations. Research confirms that workers' job satisfaction is negatively associated with their intentions to leave the organization. Many organizations that depend on volunteer workforces (like churches and other nonprofits) might gravitate toward a human relations approach to management because a friendly, social, and affirming approach to management, endorsed by human relations, may facilitate volunteer workers' satisfaction and keep them from leaving. What strategies can a manager of volunteers employ to communicate a friendly, open approach to management while achieving important outcomes?

from a classical management theory would be appropriate, given the lack of economic motivation that drives volunteers; however, some volunteers perform simple repetitive tasks and like to show up and be told what to do. So principles of division of labor and directive communication from classical management may be appropriate at times. The social needs of volunteers could be met through a human relations approach, or the personal growth and career benefit needs could be addressed through a human resource approach. Teamwork might also be appropriate at times, such as building homes for Habitat for Humanity (Hale & James, 2013). Certain volunteer activities, such as community theater productions, likely succeed when the director/producer assumes a collaborative teamwork approach; but other directors who use a classical or human relations approach also achieve success (Kramer, 2006a). Because volunteers for any particular organization likely have a mixture of motivations, it seems management approaches for working with volunteers likely needs to be a mixture of approaches.

It does seem likely that volunteers can be driven away by a poorly chosen management approach. A rigid, bureaucratic, and impersonal management approach is likely to demotivate volunteers by failing to meet their social acceptance and belongingness needs. At the same time, organizing them into self-managed teams may leave them floundering such that they quit because they are unable to see that they are meeting their needs for growth and enhancement.

Finally, it is also important to consider that volunteers can sometimes organize and manage themselves without the need for management, hierarchy, or formal organization. For example, after a natural disaster caused by flooding, potential volunteers became frustrated with the slow movement of NPO bureaucracy and government agencies to provide them with opportunities to serve. Volunteers used social media to converge on flooded areas and began working on their own (McDonald, Creber, Sun, & Sonn, 2015). These temporary, self-managed teams likely satisfied the needs of the volunteers to express their values and fulfill many of their other prosocial needs.

Applying the Three Organizational Perspectives to Management Theory

It might be easy to confuse management theories with the researcher perspectives introduced in Chapter 1. For example, there are some similarities between a post-positivist emphasis on organizational efficiency through communication and a classical management emphasis on worker efficiency. However, the post-positivist perspective is a researcher approach to studying organizations (that can be applied to any organization); the classical management theory is an approach to managing that is used by some organizations. To reinforce the distinctions between the three researcher perspectives and the four management approaches, in this section, we consider how each researcher perspective would examine each of the management theories as demonstrated in the opening scenario about Kendall's career at CI. Essentially, the researcher—guided by a specific perspective—would approach organizations the same, regardless of the organization's dominant management theory.

The Post-Positivist Perspective

Post-positivist researchers primarily focus on the effectiveness of a management theory in a particular organization and tend to use quantitative methods to measure communication and its various organizational outcomes. For example, in a business run on classical management principles, such as the shipping department of CI, researchers could seek to determine if the focus on downward communication and decision-making at the top results in an efficiently run shipping process. If the business was using a human relations approach, such as the sales department in the scenario, researchers could try to determine if opening up lines of communication to the sales staff to fill their social needs would, in turn, improve their productivity and morale. For a business run on human resource management principles, such as the upper management of CI, researchers might instead want to know if the time and money spent on developing employees and involving employees in decision-making was useful in reduced turnover and more effective supervision of departments. If the business was using teamwork, such as the product development division in CI, researchers could try to determine if teams with better internal communication perform better than teams that lack effective internal communication. In each case, the researchers might also try to determine if an alternative management approach would be more effective than the one currently in use.

The Interpretive Perspective

By contrast, the interpretive perspective focuses on the meaning that employees assign to the messages they receive from management. Most likely through interviews, the researchers would try to gain an understanding of the employees' understanding of working in organizations run by each of the types of management theories. In a classically run business like the shipping department of CI, researchers may find that employees interpret the messages from management as indicating that they are "cogs in a large machine" who must work efficiently because "they are replaceable." If the human relations approach is viewed as sincere, researchers may discover that employees in the sales department of CI talk about how managers communicate that their input is valued and that they are treated like family members. If the employees view the approach as manipulative, researchers may find them describing management as putting on a façade of caring and that communicating concerns to management is pointless. In an organization run on human resource management principles such as upper management in CI, the researcher might find employees talking about being valued employees who are encouraged to learn new skills and enroll in training and education programs. In a teamwork environment, the team members in the product development area of CI may describe how management has empowered them to make decisions and rewards them collectively for their successes.

The Critical Perspective

Critical researchers want to identify areas of oppression in the organization. From a critical perspective, regardless of the management theory, some individuals are being marginalized, whereas others are advantaged. In an organization operating under classical management theory such as the shipping department of CI, it would be easy to see that the employees near the bottom of the organizational chart, mainly those involved in the physical labor of shipping products, are being oppressed because they are excluded from important organizational communication channels and decisions. They have little opportunity to communicate to change their work environment and receive only a small portion of the rewards that their work produces compared to what upper management receives. A critical scholar would focus on the manipulative nature of communication in the human relations management approach as practiced in the sales department of CI. They would note how the appearance of participation creates an illusion of influence through upward communication when decisions are actually made primarily for the benefit of owners, and decisions on sales quotas are determined by upper management. In an organization run by human resource management principles similar to upper management in CI, the critical scholar might focus on how the messages that encourage employees to use their spare time to gain additional training and education fail to mention that this means the employees are "working" longer hours for no pay as they attend evening classes and weekend seminars; and that in the end, their increased training assists the organization more than them as individuals. In a teamwork setting such as the product development division of CI, the critical scholar might notice that by communicating the values and goals for the teams, but delegating responsibility to the teams, upper management is causing team members to bear more responsibility and work, which benefits management without compensating the teams proportionally. If concertive control occurs in the teamwork setting, the critical scholar would try to determine which employees are being controlled by their peers.

As these descriptions indicate, a scholar or researcher can choose any particular lens to examine any organization, regardless of its management theory. By choosing a particular lens, the researcher focuses on certain aspects of an organization while omitting other perspectives.

Summary

In this chapter, we examined the characteristics of four main management theories that have been advocated over the last 100+ years in the United States. Classical management theory focused on impersonal relationships and directive communication while considering employees to be motivated by money. Human relations approaches recognized the importance of social relations. As a result, management listened to employees while maintaining control over decision-making. In human resource approaches, the needs of employees to achieve individual goals led to involving employees in making decisions that affect them and providing opportunities for development and advancement. In a teamwork approach, the focus became on empowering teams with decision-making authority and responsibility. This sometimes resulted in peers creating strong, concertive control over one another.

In the discussion, we suggested that organizations adopt one of these four approaches, either consciously or accidentally, and then enact it consistently organization wide. This is an oversimplification of how organizations are run. As the scenario about CI suggests, different management approaches may be used in different parts of a single organization. Entry level employees may experience one management approach, whereas more experienced employees have a different experience. Realistically, many organizations use combinations of these approaches. However, being aware of the different theories of management provides you with a better understanding of your experiences and helps make you aware of the options you will have if you become a member of a management team in the future. You will need to determine your assumptions about your employees and the appropriate management practices to use to meet personal ethics and organizational goals.

CHAPTER 5

Communication Channels and Structures

Although pleased to be promoted to the electronics department manager at a big box department store, there was still plenty for MJ to learn through its official and unofficial communication channels about how work was done at the store. Parts of it were pretty easy. MJ knew a lot about reporting to an immediate supervisor. As an assistant department manager in electronics, MJ learned how to report to managers. Assistant managers were told to report good news and bad news and to keep department managers informed. From talking to each other when their managers weren't around, however, they learned to focus on the positive. They also learned to omit reporting minor issues but to include any problems that were big enough that the manager would likely find out anyway. They needed to make sure their managers heard of any problems from them first, not other employees.

It wasn't always clear to the assistant managers whether their department managers reported all the information from them to the assistant store managers or what information got reported up to the store manager and then the district manager and so on. What to report up the chain of command used to be the department manager's problem, but now it was MJ's problem—at least as far as reporting to the assistant store manager was concerned.

Directing the full-time and part-time employees in the electronics department was something MJ was used to from being its assistant manager. This involved setting up work schedules and reminding employees of what they needed to accomplish during their shifts. MJ tried to maintain positive relationships with everyone in the department through regular interactions and small talk. The full-time employees usually didn't require much supervision. They generally worked hard and often gave suggestions that could be used to improve the way the department operated. MJ could tell that they talked to each other to arrive at creative ideas for the benefit of the department. On the other hand, it could take a lot of time dealing with all of the part-time employees whose suggestions usually amounted to trying to get a better schedule for themselves. Sometimes MJ simply had to tell them what to do—no ifs, ands, or buts.

MJ had yet to figure out how to communicate with other department managers who attended the same meetings conducted by the store manager, or more often an assistant store manager. It wasn't unusual for MJ to have to work with one of the managers of an adjoining department after the meetings. There always seemed to be tasks that required them to coordinate with one another, particularly during seasonal changeovers of displays.

Fortunately, MJ still had friendly relationships with the other assistant department managers who had not yet been promoted. They would get together almost every week after the store closed for a bite to eat and a few drinks. They didn't always talk about work, but they usually did.

MJ became particularly reliant on talking to Dakota, the assistant manager of the men and children's department. Dakota worked at the store longer and seemed to know all of the important people including the store manager and the front office employees who were not involved in the direct sales part of the operations. If MJ was worried about a shipment arriving on time, Dakota knew who to call.

Recently the company's management decided to do more to address the health and safety of employees. To accomplish that goal, MJ's store manager organized two different committees. One was designated for educating employees about ways to improve their health. The other was supposed to organize activities like a volleyball team in the local recreational league to promote healthy behaviors. Each committee had members from all levels and various departments. MJ volunteered for the activities committee and, as a result, met some of the people Dakota talked about. This meant that MJ could go directly to some of them, if necessary, in the future.

· · · · ·

As mentioned in Chapter 1, many organizational communication scholars argue that organizations exist *in* communication; they do not exist outside of communication behaviors (Taylor, Cooren, Giroux, & Robichaud, 1996). In other words, from one perspective, we can think of organizations *as* communication. Instead of exploring the theoretical implications of that approach, in this chapter, we examine the communication that occurs that creates and maintains the organization. After the introduction, the chapter is divided into two sections. In the first section, we explain a traditional approach to studying the way communication channels are "expected" to work in organizations. As such, we focus primarily on formal downward, upward, lateral/horizontal, and integrative communication channels or structures while also exploring the importance of informal or grapevine communication. Then, in the second part of the chapter, we take an alternative perspective on organizational communication—the communication network perspective—which focuses on the communication channels that actually emerge and develop over time rather than considering the way communication was designed and prescribed to occur.

As we consider communication channels from either the traditional or network approaches, it is important to recognize not only the *directions* that communication moves throughout organizations but also its *content*. A wide range of content topics are communicated throughout a typical organization. Although it is possible to identify other ones, scholars identified five primary topics (Monge & Eisenberg, 1987; Tichy, 1981). Importantly, the content of a single message can have multiple and overlapping goals.

Production or *task communication* is probably the communication that comes to mind immediately. Task communication includes any communication related to producing the organization's output, whether it is a product or a service or even a public image. Task communication involves content such as giving directions, providing feedback, or making reports. We know that new employees and volunteers depend on this type of information to reduce their uncertainty about what their job duties are, how to perform those tasks, and how they will be evaluated; but task information is important to established organizational members as well (Kramer, 2010; McComb, 1995). For example, managers and upper management need task information in the form of reports and feedback from subordinates to make quality decisions and do their jobs well.

Maintenance or *authority communication* has to do with establishing and maintaining the chain of command or hierarchy in the organization. It is often important to know who is responsible for reporting to whom, who is responsible for making certain decisions, or whom to contact when there are problems. Maintaining these communication channels is not particularly time consuming in most organizations, but knowing them and being able to use them is an important part of keeping everyone informed about the structure of the organization.

Social or *relational communication* develops and maintains personal relationships and friendships in the organization. Although employees may focus on their tasks, most are concerned with developing social relationships with some of their coworkers as well. Newcomers must find their place in the social fabric of the organization to feel included, but social relations are important to established employees as well. People sometimes stay in organizations as much as a result of their social relationships as for their interest or commitment to their jobs.

Innovation communication involves discussions of new ideas and approaches, particularly ones that solve organizational problems. Whereas nearly everyone is involved in task and social communication, because many employees assume custodial roles, innovation communication generally involves a small number of people in most organizations (Albrecht & Hall, 1991). These people might be considered the movers and shakers in the organization because they promote change and innovation through their communication.

Some scholars, particularly critical scholars, focus primarily on organizations as political systems. The *political and influence communication* involves discussions about or by the people who have the actual power or influence in an organization. The influential people are not necessarily those who have influence according to the organizational chart but are those who actually have the ability to make or influence decisions. So an assistant manager may have more influence than a manager because the manager listens to the assistant and so do subordinates and managers in other departments. People talk about and identify those who are "really" influential; furthermore, influential people talk to each other.

Although these different content areas have been presented as if they are separate and mutually exclusive topics, a single conversation can cover a range of topics. For example, in the opening scenario, MJ's conversations with Dakota are focused on task communication, but they include elements of political communication because Dakota knows whom to talk to get things done, and the two of them developed a friendship as well (i.e., social communication). So although these content areas are frequently blended together in conversations, recognizing the differences can be valuable in understanding the communication that creates and maintains the organization and the relationships between people.

Traditional Communication Channels and Structures

A traditional approach to understanding communication channels in organizations is based on the formalized organization structure, sometimes called the organizational chart. For example, Figure 5.1 represents a partial organizational chart for the retail store in the opening scenario (some departments are not included, such as shipping and receiving). The chart defines the chain of command or lines of authority so that everyone knows who reports to whom; it also defines the official channels for lateral (i.e., peer-to-peer) communication. Organizational charts suggest three primary communication channels: downward, upward, and lateral or horizontal; but it recognizes that a fourth channel, informal, occurs outside of these formal lines of communication, which we describe in the next section.

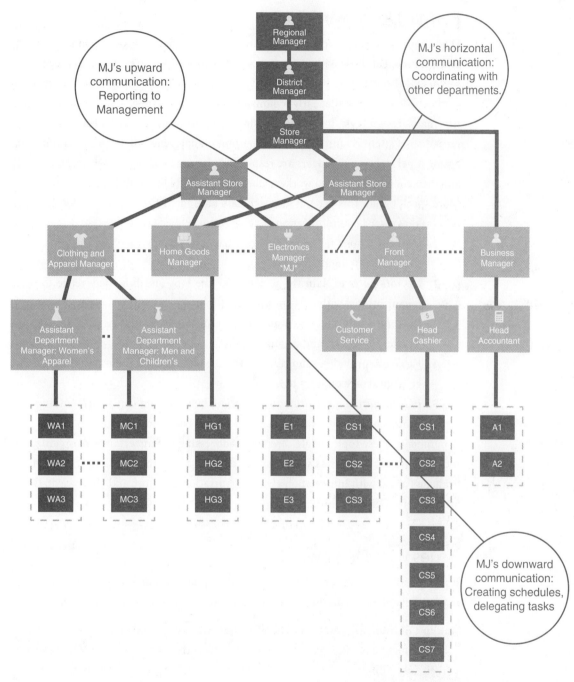

Figure 5.1. Formal Organizational Chart

Formal Downward Communication

Downward communication originates with those higher in organizational authority and is directed at those with less organizational authority. For example, in the opening scenario, MJ participated in downward communication by giving subordinates their work schedules. Given that early organizational scholars were generally used to a scientific management style, it is not surprising that downward communication received a great deal of attention initially, which continues today. After all, from a scientific management perspective, managers are responsible for organizing and designing the work and then communicating to workers who are responsible for following their directives. More specific than this general idea, scholars have identified at least five types of important downward communication (Katz & Kahn, 1978; Sias, 2009):

1. *Job instructions* tell subordinates what task or jobs they need to do and the process for doing them.
2. *Job rationales* explain the purpose for the jobs and how they relate to other organizational activities and goals.
3. *Procedure and practice information* provides explanation of organizational policies, practices, and norms.
4. *Feedback* provides subordinates with evaluations of their performance and gives guidance on ways to improve.
5. *Indoctrination or culture information* helps create an understanding and commitment to the values, beliefs, and goals of the organization.

A number of these topics relate directly to addressing the uncertainty of organization members on such topics as what tasks to do, how to do them, and how they will be evaluated along with information about organizational culture and "how we do things around here" (Kramer, 2010).

Issues with Downward Communication

It is impossible to consider all of the potential issues with downward communication in a brief chapter. Yet, among those identified are these three important ones:

Amount of Information. One issue with downward communication is providing the "correct" *amount* of information. Supervisors report that they provide more information to their subordinates than subordinates perceive receiving; consequently, subordinates often report receiving less information than they need (Jablin, 1979). This concern suggests a need for more downward communication. At the same time, employees often report suffering from information overload (Edmunds & Morris, 2000). Information overload is not a new problem but has increased, as the use of email and other electronic messaging has increased making it easy to send a lot of information, to a large number of recipients, at any time. The increase in information volume makes it more difficult for individuals to separate useful from unimportant information. This problem suggests the need for less downward communication. Avoiding sending too little *or* too much information makes managing the amount and content of downward communication challenging.

Nature of Feedback. Performance feedback can focus on the positive by finding behaviors to praise, or feedback can focus on the negative by finding behaviors to criticize. The difference in effects is striking: positive feedback is associated with positive commitment, intrinsic motivation, and increases in organizational citizenship behaviors (i.e., voluntary behaviors that benefit the organization); negative feedback is associated with defensive feelings, counterproductive behaviors, and increased intentions to turnover (Belschak & Den Hartog, 2009; Downs, Johnson, & Barge, 1984). However, negative feedback is an extremely potent source of communication that can result in improvement and learning for employees. Finding the balance between giving positive and negative feedback is challenging. Unfortunately, managers frequently fail to provide any sort of feedback, or they have a tendency to focus on the negative unless they make a conscious effort to provide positive feedback.

Information Distribution. Given the importance of downward communication, it is important to determine whether communication is actually distributed throughout the organization as expected. An influential study suggests that it often is not distributed, at least not when it relies on oral communication (Davis, 1968). In the study conducted at a manufacturing plant, two messages—one concerning parking (a new lot opening) and one concerning layoffs (within 30 days)—were given by upper management to the next-in-line managers with directives to pass the information down through the chain of command to the next four organizational levels. The researcher then later determined whether the message was distributed to all of the employees at the different organizational levels. Although both messages achieved 100% saturation through the top two layers of hierarchy, only 38% of the next level, and only 15% of the bottom level, of the organization learned the parking information. For the layoff information, the numbers were much better, 94% and 70% at the lower levels, respectively. Because there are many more employees at the lower levels of the hierarchy than at the top, these numbers meant that overall only 36% of the employees learned about the parking situation, but 83% of the employees learned the layoff information.

These results suggest a number of important ideas to consider in the 21st century. First, it is not surprising that the more urgent, job-implication message received wider distribution than the rather trivial parking message. Layoffs could mean employees will be out of work and their livelihoods affected. Managers need to keep in mind that the importance of the message affects how likely people are to relay messages down the chain of command. Second, given the study relied only on oral communication due to when it was conducted, we might suspect that electronic messaging solved some but not all of this problem for at least two reasons: First, there still are many employees who do not sit at desks or have regular access to computers who may not be reached by electronic messages. For example, most of the retail sales and warehouse-based employees at the department store in the opening scenario are not able to access email during their work time and would have little motivation to do so when they are not at work. There are many other similar situations in organizations. Another concern is that providing the message electronically does not mean that it is necessarily read, particularly when individuals receive multiple, lengthy messages from the same source. Information overload can create as many problems as lack of distribution of information can create. It would be valuable to determine in what contexts and with which employees has the use of electronic messages made the situation any different.

Formal Upward Communication

Perhaps in response to the human relations movement discussed in Chapter 4 and the growing awareness that listening to subordinates is important, a second focus on communication channels has been on upward communication. Upward communication originates with individuals who are lower in organizational authority and moves up the chain of command. For example, in the opening scenario, upward communication occurred when MJ listened to the ideas from the full-time employees and implemented them to improve the department. Upward communication serves at least these four important purposes (Katz & Kahn, 1978; Sias, 2009):

1. *Job performance reports* provide managers with information about how individuals or units are producing.

2. *Task procedures* communicate to managers the procedures subordinates use to accomplish tasks.

3. *Problem reports* to managers identify issues that are inhibiting an individual or other organizational members from accomplishing individual or organizational goals.

4. *Policy responses and feedback* communicate to management subordinates' positive or negative reactions and perceptions of organizational policies and practices, especially when they involve changes.

In addition to these, in organizations that use a human relations or human resource approach to management, upward communication provides either *input into decision-making* or *participation in decision-making*. Upward communication can be a way to *obtain creative ideas* from employees that can be turned into practice. Unfortunately, "suggestion boxes" as the most common form of suggestions systems have a bad name in many organizations. Employees rarely submit ideas because they believe their suggestions will be ignored. The Dustin comic strip makes fun of suggestion boxes by

showing one with no slot or another as a paper shredder. At one state agency we visited, the wooden suggestion box was filled with dead bugs and spider webs—implying the box was rarely, if ever, inspected by management for suggestions.

Yet, when actually used, suggestion systems can be successful and provide positive outcomes to companies and employees. A study of four organizations with successful systems found that most had a decentralized system of submitting ideas, had a committee or panel of experts to evaluate ideas (rather than an immediate manager), dedicated substantial resources to implementing positive suggestions, and most provided economic rewards to originators of ideas that saved the organization money (Van Dijk & Van Den Ende, 2002). Having a strong upward communication system is crucial to healthy organizational functioning because subordinates and frontline workers often know about the most critical challenges that face the organization as it is operating in the moment. Getting bad news to flow up the chain of command allows effective managers to identify problems while those problems are small and resolvable.

Issues with Upward Communication

There certainly are more than four issues related to upward communication, but these four have received specific attention.

COMMUNICATION CHALLENGE

Technology Application for Suggestions Boxes

Getting good ideas from employees is big business. Great ideas can mean high employee satisfaction, the potential for market advantages when good ideas shape goods and services, and the potential to curb unethical behavior while it remains small and resolvable. Yet in certain situations, employees want to know their suggestions are anonymous to avoid retribution from management or other coworkers. Because of the potential value of anonymous, upward communication, websites offer services to mask identifying information. A few examples include sites such as suggestionbox.com, boxwire.com, and freesuggestionbox.com. How could your university, club, or current employer improve its suggestion system?

Lack of Receptivity. It is not uncommon for subordinates to feel that their supervisors talk about being receptive to them and having an open door policy when they are actually not receptive to information, particularly negative information. Rather than a claim of an open door policy, subordinates are more likely to voice their ideas when their managers are perceived as demonstrating openness and they feel that it is safe for them to communicate without fear of retribution (Detert & Burris, 2007). Employees often fear being fired if they point out unethical company practices. Even though laws have been passed to protect whistleblowers, the financial burden and career consequences of seeking restitution under the law remains a deterrent to providing strong negative information upward. Fear of retribution is a particularly strong deterrent from communicating negative information upward, but employees also report keeping silent with negative feedback when they (a) construct their supervisor as ultimately responsible, (b) construct themselves as not knowledgeable enough, or (c) predict their supervisor will not take action (Bisel & Arterburn, 2012).

Power Differentials. Upward communication involves communicating information to someone who has more power or influence in the organization. Often the person has the ability to fire or promote. This power differential intimidates many individuals.

COMMUNICATION CHALLENGE

Dealing with the Normal Alteration of Upward Communication

The normal alteration of upward messaging by politeness and impression management can skew managers' understanding of what is happening in their organization to the organization's detriment. Jeffrey Kassing (2011) recommends a host of ideas for shaping organizational culture in ways that encourage forthright and candid upward messaging. Kassing recommends managers' ordinary, day-to-day communication include regular invitations of disagreement from subordinates and regular scrutiny of positive feedback. These two management communication strategies should help create the expectation that upward negative feedback is desired by management and that management will not be receptive to ingratiation attempts. How can you live out these principles without creating hurt feelings?

As a result, subordinates are less likely to provide accurate information, especially negative information, to a manager who has power over the subordinate's career advancement opportunities or when the subordinate has high career aspirations (Jablin, 1979). In a study by Ploeger, Kelley, and Bisel (2011), participants were randomly assigned to deny an unethical business request from their boss, a coworker, or a subordinate. The researchers then coded those denials and detected significantly more politeness and equivocation in the denial messaging when participants were assigned to respond to a boss rather than a subordinate. Thus, power differentials even shape how employees discuss their ethical concerns.

Upward "Distortion." Partly due to fear of retribution and the normal rules of impression management in ordinary talk, subordinates tend to shape their upward communication. At times, without even realizing it, upward communication can be especially skewed or filtered toward reporting only positive news, or using polite or ambiguous language to soften the harsh-sounding nature of negative feedback. Subordinates are particularly likely to remain silent or soften bad news if they do not trust their supervisors (Jablin, 1979). New managers often experience the sensation that friends and coworkers treat or speak to them differently once promoted to a higher position of organizational authority. Mirroring the findings regarding downward communication, subordinates perceive that they communicate more information than managers perceive they receive. This dynamic can result in managers perceiving that the information they receive is limited or filtered. Information can be shaped at each level, as it travels up the chain of command.

Self-promotion or Ingratiation. It is important to provide performance reports and to be visible to managers to receive appropriate evaluations and promotion opportunities in an organization; simply doing a job well is not enough. For example, subordinates who are more assertive and reason with their supervisors are viewed as having stronger interpersonal skills, which is associated with being evaluated as promotable (Wayne, Liden, Graf, & Ferris, 1997). However, excessive self-promotion is generally perceived negatively and even perceived as brown-nosing. Ingratiation is evaluated negatively when it is perceived by others primarily as self-interest without concern for coworkers, done instead of work, and excessive (Hall & Valde, 1995). The challenge for the individual is to do enough self-promotion to be noticed and appreciated and not so much as to be perceived as brown-nosing.

Horizontal or Lateral Communication

Horizontal or lateral communication involves communication between peers or people of equal or nearly equal status in the organizational hierarchy. Lateral communication includes within-group communication, such as two coworkers in a department talking to each other. It also includes between-group communication, such as when managers of two departments meet to talk about working together on a common problem. For example, in the opening scenario, MJ could tell that the full-time workers talked to each other to originate innovative ideas for improving the department. MJ was also involved in interdepartmental horizontal communication when talking to managers of other departments. Among its many uses, horizontal communication serves these primary functions (Katz & Kahn, 1978; Sias, 2009):

1. *Information sharing* occurs as coworkers share their knowledge about the organization and its norms and culture, including their perceptions of management, which supplements information from downward communication channels.

2. *Task coordination communication* helps address issues of interdependence and control between people within a department or between departments or units, such as when one person or department relies on someone else to complete part of a task before being able to work on it.

3. *Problem-solving communication* addresses mutual problems or concerns within or between units, which can lead to innovative ideas and change.

4. *Employee growth, development, and mentoring* occurs as coworkers learn new job skills from each other that goes beyond what they learn through formal organizational programs.

5. *Social support and relationship communication* focuses on building and maintaining interpersonal relationships between coworkers that create the social environment of the workplace.

By serving these functions, horizontal communication addresses much of the uncertainty that organizational members experience. This includes information about organizational politics and culture as well as relationship development.

Issues with Lateral Communication

Competition. Peers often compete with each other for salary increases and promotions. Departments compete for resources including money to hire additional employees or purchase other resources that will make their job easier. This competition can cause individuals to limit their horizontal communication because information is an important resource.

Specialization. A common problem with horizontal communication between units can be the result of knowledge and task specialization. Specialization in knowledge and tasks can be a barrier to lateral communication because it often involves the development of unique vocabulary and language used to communicate. Departments often have *group restricted codes* or language that they use. These are communication shortcuts that help them quickly and efficiently do their jobs within the department but that may sound like a foreign language to those outside the department. Many people are puzzled by the language of the Information Technology (IT) department of their organization with its highly technical jargon. So not only does the specialized work that IT people do separate them from other departments, but their specialized language creates communication barriers that can inhibit their ability to aid people in other departments that they are supposed to serve.

Territoriality. Departments are often competing with each other for limited organizational resources. Territoriality can include physical resources including actual space, but often has to do with claiming responsibilities and functions in part because other resources are associated with them. We recall when a new building was going up on campus and different departments were embroiled in conflict trying to lay claim to certain classrooms or offices for their own department. Ultimately, a higher level administrator intervened so that a very small department did not commandeer most of the building for its use. Similarly, gaining some new responsibility can be a way to increase the size and importance of a department. For example, if a university department can increase the number of required courses all students on campus must take in their department, they can then ask for more faculty and space to meet the increased workload; those increases usually come at the expense of other departments. Circumstances like this incentivize unit-to-unit communication within organizations to be competitive, hostile, and territorial in many organizations.

Lack of Incentive. Although people will certainly engage in horizontal communication to develop social relationships without any additional incentive than their own social needs, they will not necessarily cooperate in other areas due to a lack of incentive. An excellent example of this occurred in a national department store chain (Papa,

Daniels, & Spiker, 2008). Local stores would not assist each other when one store was short on merchandise even when another store had excess inventory. The lack of cooperation was largely because store managers were rewarded only on the basis of the performance of their individual store. When the company began giving bonuses based on district-wide sales, store managers began cooperating with each other because it increased sales across the district—which, in turn, benefited everyone. In many organizations there are no incentives to communicate and cooperate, or there may be incentives *not* to communicate and cooperate, between units.

Informal Communication

Informal communication is an inevitable part of organizational communication. It is probably the most common channel of organizational communication, accounting for perhaps 70% of communication in organizations (Crampton, Hodge, & Mishra, 1998). Informal communication, often called "grapevine" communication, does not follow the channels of the formal organizational chart but instead travels from person to person based on personal relationships and contacts. Of course, it is virtually unimaginable that in the context of an organization larger than three or four persons that an employee, manager, or entire organizational system could be successful in navigating their workplace relationships and get all work accomplished if they *only* follow formal channels, making informal communication a necessity.

In the opening scenario, MJ participates in a great deal of informal communication by talking to other assistant managers both before and after being promoted to manager of the electronics department. Dakota's interactions with MJ were also informal because they did not have any direct reporting responsibilities. MJ's informal communication occurred at work when other managers were not around as the assistant managers talked to each other about what to report and not report. It also occurred during their informal gatherings after work that were largely social interactions but at times included work-related issues. Informal communication provides a lot of the same information as some of the other channels, but does so in an unofficial or informal manner. Informal communication seems to address three primary functions (Crampton et al., 1998; Hellweg, 1987).

1. *Satisfying social and personal interests* is the most common reason for informal communication, as individuals create friendships, provide social and emotional support, and discuss topics of mutual interest through their interactions.

2. *Addressing gaps in formal communication* is an important use of informal communication because it helps employees reduce the uncertainty they experience from a lack of information through formal channels.

3. *Managing a threatening and insecure environment* is another way that informal communication helps employees to gather information to help them deal with problems and concerns they perceive, particularly when they do not trust formal communication from management.

These are some of the basic functions of informal communication. A number of important characteristics of informal communication have been identified in an extensive summary of studies (Hellweg, 1987) and supplemented by a later examination of managers' perceptions of informal communication (Crampton et al., 1998). These characteristics raise important issues.

Issues with Informal Communication

Accuracy. The name "grapevine" suggests that the information shared informally might be unreliable, although downward and upward information flows can also be quite inaccurate and distorted for myriad reasons. Most scholarship estimates that informal organizational communication is 75% to 90% accurate. It is hard to know if this is better or worse than the accuracy of formal information. Anyone who has attended a meeting only to be told something quite different about what happened by another participant might think 90% accuracy was quite good. However, because employees are often more likely to believe informal than formal information, the 10% that is inaccurate or incomplete can have significant negative results.

Speed. Informal communication tends to move much faster through a network of relationships than formal communication. Because people do not have to wait for formal permission or an announcement to pass along information, they can immediately share information with others. The proliferation of electronic media has made speed an even more important issue. In the case of emergencies or important information, the increased speed that technological media afford can be advantageous. In the case of incomplete information, speed can be problematic because that incorrect information can be rapidly distributed through personal interactions, text messages, and social media. Unfortunately, an initial attention-getting rumor or falsehood is more likely to be remembered than the message correcting that information.

Mid-Level Employee Participation. Initially it was thought that lower status employees and staff personnel, such as receptionists and administrative assistants, were the primary participants in informal communication. It turns out that managers use the grapevine just as frequently; in fact, mid-level employees are the most involved in the grapevine. Those at the top or bottom of the organization are more isolated from the informal communication. Most people absorb the information but do not repeat the information to others. It remains to be determined if the increase in electronic communication has changed these patterns.

Accountability. When informal communication consisted primarily of face-to-face interaction in hallways and around water coolers, there was little accountability for informal communication because it was usually difficult or impossible to trace the message, especially rumors, back to its initial source. Damage resulting from misinformation and gossip could not be attributed to anyone in particular. With the increased use of electronic communication, including social media, to relay informal communication, it may be easier to trace the message to a source, but that still does not repair any damage that may have occurred.

The Competence Network. Perhaps grapevine communication seems like a hindrance to organizational functioning. That is not necessarily the case. Organizations have members at nearly all levels that hold key memories, ideas, skills, or influence that can help get work done, especially in a time of crisis. These "go-to" people are highly competent at their jobs and are looked to by others when complex and urgent challenges arise. At these times, the informal channels of communication with these "go-to" members can make all the difference, even though communicating and coordinating with them is not outlined by the formal organizational chart.

Integrative Communication Structures

The formal communication channels discussed so far are defined by an organizational chart, although the organizational chart does not include informal communication. Organizations also use a number of other structures to integrate communication across departments and levels. Three commonly used ones are committees, quality circles, and project teams.

Committees. Many organizations use committees to integrate organizational activities. These include *standing committees*, which address a certain topic or issue on an ongoing basis, such as an employee welfare committee. Membership rotates on and off as members from different sectors and levels of the organization participate. Other committees are *ad hoc committees* (Latin for *to or for this*). These committees meet for a limited time period to accomplish some specific task or goal. In the opening scenario, MJ has been assigned to a committee to address health and safety issues for the organization. The membership came from across the organization, so the ad hoc committee has the potential to integrate communication across the organization on health and safety issues as well as on other issues. Whether this ad hoc committee will eventually turn into a standing committee remains to be seen.

Quality Circles. A particular type of integrated committee that received some scholarly and popular attention during the 1980s, quality circles were created with individuals across departments, divisions, and hierarchical levels. Their task was to find ways to improve the quality of the output of the organization whether it was a product or a service. Initially, quality circles were viewed positively, and research focuses on characteristics of quality circles that were more successful in having improvements adopted by the organization and in increasing satisfaction of members (Griffin & Wayne, 1984). Interest dropped in quality circles when research showed that the attitudes, behaviors, and effectiveness of a plant using quality circles went up temporarily but then returned to previous levels—the same as a plant not using quality circles (Griffin, 1988). This is reminiscent of the Hawthorne effect (see Chapter 4). The quality circles had an influence because someone was paying attention; but after the novelty of the process faded, it no longer had an effect.

Although the use of quality circles to integrate communication has generally disappeared, some of the ideas behind them continued to be relevant as organizations adopted a total quality management (TQM) approach (Powell, 1995). Organizations using TQM focus on project-based teamwork and team-based problem solving, with teams empowered to communicate openly in both horizontal and vertical directions across the formal organization structure. The approach created a more relaxed hierarchy. There are many other characteristics of TQM, such as benchmarking against measurable goals, increased training, flexibility, and focus on process improvement. Overall, implementation of TQM likely increases integrative communication in an organization.

Project Teams. Another integrative structure used by many organizations is project teams. This approach is used by many different divisions or companies including research and development organizations, engineering firms, product development divisions, and public relations firms. The essence of project teams is to integrate across departments by having individuals from different departments being assigned to teams typically to produce some new product or outcome. When practiced consistently and systematically, it creates what can be called a "matrix organization" like the one depicted in Figure 5.2. In a matrix structure, there is a project leader, and people from various departments are assigned to a given project. Figure 5.2 illustrates the case of a public relations firm. The firm has a hierarchy of account supervisors and executives and separate departments of staff associates, art, digital/social media, and interns. Each project team then has a senior account supervisor, an account executive, and then representatives from the other departments. Individuals serve on multiple client accounts simultaneously. This structure produced integrative communication across departments and across the hierarchy of the organization. The issues with integrative communication are similar to those of horizontal communication described earlier.

Limitations of Traditional Communication Channels Approach

Two limitations seem particularly problematic in the traditional communication channels approach to understanding organizational communication. First, researchers and practitioners who use this approach rely on a very narrow definition of communication. They seem to limit their understanding of communication to *information transfer*. There is a sense that communication means transferring information from person to

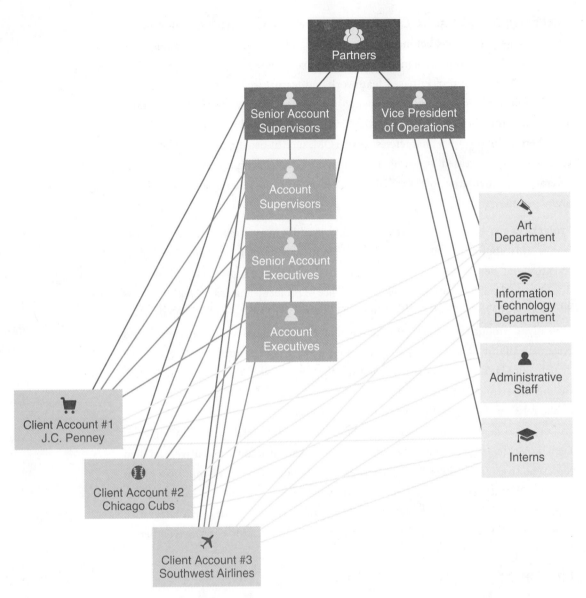

Figure 5.2. Matrix Structure Public Relations Organization

person whether it is downward, upward, lateral, informal, or integrative. There is limited consideration of communication as a process of creating shared meaning or of communication as a transactional process. Second, this approach assumes that actual organizational communication patterns are closely related to the preplanned and prescribed directions indicated by organizational charts and structures, with the exception of informal communication. There is strong evidence that this is frequently not the case. In the next section, we address this concern in particular.

Communication Networks

In the first half of this chapter, we focused on communication channels in relation to organizational charts, with the exception of informal communication. Although valuable and easily understood, such an approach often fails to provide an accurate picture of how communication actually flows in many organizations, particularly given that as much as 70% of communication is informal (Crampton et al., 1998). A communication network approach provides an alternative approach to explore the way communication occurs in an organization. The organizational chart prescribes who should communicate with whom, whereas a network analysis describes the communication links that actually emerge in practice without making a distinction between formal or informal channels.

In addition, whereas organizations only have one chart prescribing how communication should flow, a network approach does not assume a single communication network exists but allows for the possibility that multiple communication networks can emerge across time. Recall that communication concerns a variety of topics such as task, authority, social, innovation, and influence. Organizations often have different but overlapping communication networks for each of these areas, and different people may have different roles in these different content areas. For example, a person who is very prominent in the social network of the organization may not be prominent in the political/influence network. Alternatively, a person who controls resources may be an important member of the task network of the organization but not have a role in its social network. So whereas people typically only have one role on the organization chart, they can have different roles in multiple communication networks. For example, in the opening scenario, MJ had a network of former assistant managers that includes a mixture of task and social communication. MJ's linkage with Dakota was more of a political or influence network. It is not unusual for an organizational member to have different contacts, or networks, for achieving different communication goals.

Because a network approach attempts to examine who actually communicates with whom in an organization, this may or may not have a strong relationship to the organizational chart. For example, there is a strong link between proximity and the frequency of communication (Allen, 1970). When coworkers work near each other, they are more likely to communicate. As a result, communication networks may be quite different than organizational charts, simply based on where people are physically located. In addition, we would not expect that the social communication network would follow the organizational chart very closely because social relationships are often created due to factors other than organizational roles, such as common interests or personal similarities. The political or innovation networks may follow patterns that are quite different than the formal organizational structure, as informal influence and power—who knows whom—may be more important than a particular job title on the organizational chart. Of course, in some organizations, especially small ones, there may be a great deal of similarities between communication networks and organizational charts. The informal communication in an organization likely has a strong relationship to the social network of the organization.

In the following, we first examine how to collect network data. Then we discuss the kinds of information or characteristics a network analysis describes; and finally, we discuss a few specific studies based on network analysis.

Collecting Network Data

There are a wide variety of ways to collect data for a network analysis. We consider four of the most commonly identified approaches (Albrecht & Ropp, 1982). Historically, the most common way of collecting network data is the *recall method* in which people are asked to self-report who they communicate with in an organization or social system. A wide variety of prompts are used to do this. The most basic prompts ask people to report "Who have you communicated with in the last week in this organization?" In an effort to aid individuals in recalling more complete information, some prompts might ask about specific content, such as, "Who do you talk to in a typical week to get your job done," or "Who do you talk to about social activities?" In another attempt to improve recall, sometimes individuals are provided with a list of all the organization's employees and asked to identify "how often have you communicated with the following organizational members in the last week?" This way individuals put check marks or numbers for frequency of communication without having to recall everyone by memory. This approach might also include columns for different topics such as task, social, and so forth, to assist individuals in providing a more accurate record.

Probably the second most common method of collecting network data today is through *unobtrusive data collection*. Given the recent issues related to the accusations of the National Security Agency spying unlawfully on American citizens, you probably realize your email and phone records are recorded and stored and can be searched. From examining their electronic records, many organizations can determine the phone number or email address that every person in their organization contacted through the company email account or company phone—if they wanted to do so. This information provides an accurate picture of active communication linkages among individuals. It is possible to explore the content of the emails, but generally not the phone calls. Recently, researchers have also used Facebook links as a way to examine networks. A network analysis can be conducted on the linkages between people based on any sort of electronic media.

A less common approach of data collection involves *direct observation* or *naturalistic observations*. In this approach, an observer watches the organization at work in its natural patterns and records key communication interactions including the time, length, and setting of the interaction. This strategy might be particularly valuable in gathering data in a small office or business, as it would provide a record of actual interactions as they occurred without relying on individuals' memory of their interactions.

A final approach that can be used is *nondirective interviews*. In this approach, organizational members are interviewed about the work they do and the people they talk to as they go about their workday and so forth. Then the interview data are analyzed to identify network linkages. For example, the individual may imply the existence of a task network link by discussing how he or she received work assignments or filed reports. The same person may identify social links by talking about going out to lunch or chatting in the parking lot after work.

In considering each of these approaches, there are certain advantages and problems related to each for issues like ease of collection or accuracy and comprehensiveness of the data. As a result, Albrecht and Ropp (1982) encourage researchers to use more than one data collection method to gain a more comprehensive picture of the organizational networks.

The four approaches discussed so far are all considered communication or *interaction networks*. These are the approaches most often used by communication scholars who are interested in the communication linkages between individuals. Scholars have also investigated patterns of relationships based on other factors. *Reputational networks* get at perceptions of who is influential, as identified by other organizational members, whereas decision networks examine who was present during important organizational decisions (Tichy, 1981). Instead of focusing on who talks to whom how often, these approaches examine networks in terms of who is perceived as influential or which individuals are most involved in decision-making activities. These types of network analyses provide a different perspective on an organization than the interaction analyses.

Characteristics of Networks

There are a variety of statistical packages designed to analyze network data and create graphic representations of social links. Most of these programs produce network diagrams or sociograms, although it is possible to produce sociograms by hand for small organizations. Figure 5.3 is an example of a network diagram for MJ's big box department store in the chapter-opening case. The complexity of the programs in conducting the analysis and producing a sociogram and various important statistics is beyond our interests here. Instead, we focus on some of the characteristics of networks that are typically identified through network analysis. These characteristics can be explored at the linkage, individual, group, or organizational level of analysis (Tichy, 1981).

Linkage Characteristics. The basic unit of a network analysis is a link or linkage. There are three main characteristics of the linkage of interest: reciprocity, intensity, and multiplexity (Monge & Eisenberg, 1987; Tichy, 1981).

Reciprocity considers whether the relationships are symmetrical or asymmetrical (although some scholars make distinctions between reciprocity and symmetry). Lack of reciprocity occurs particularly when using recall data. Some people will report communicating with another individual who does not report communicating back. In addition, there may be a lack of symmetry as some people may send information to more people than they report receiving. For example, a manager may send email or voicemail messages to many more individuals than individuals who reply to the messages, creating asymmetrical relationships. Reciprocity is not always important to consider. Sometimes, network analysis simply assumes reciprocity, particularly in recall data. However, when it comes to influence or innovation networks, it may be important to consider if the communication is asymmetrical because it may indicate that influence or ideas are flowing only in one direction.

Intensity refers to the strength of the linkage. Because frequency data is most often used in network analysis, the general assumption is that the more frequent the

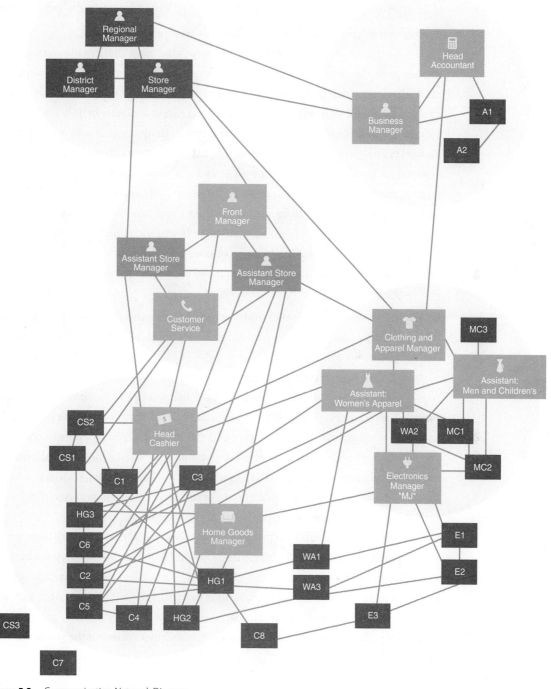

Figure 5.3. Communication Network Diagram

interactions, the stronger the link—in terms of information shared and resources exchanged. It would be possible to consider intensity based on importance as well. The point is that in actual practice, not all linkages are equally important.

The concept of *uniplexity* versus *multiplexity* is the most challenging characteristic of linkages to understand. Recall that an organization has multiple communication networks—task, social, and so forth—which may overlap or operate somewhat separately. A uniplex link is one that occurs between two individuals in only one network; a multiplex link is one that occurs between two individuals in two or more kinds of networks. For example, in the scenario, MJ has task network linkages to all the other department managers because they all attend the same meetings. Most of these are uniplex linkages (i.e., *only* task-related relationships). MJ and Dakota have a multiplex relationship because they exchange information about tasks and political or influence issues in the company. It is likely that they also have a social network link, as they occasionally have lunch together because of their friendship in addition to their work relationship.

Individual Roles. A network analysis helps to identify a number of roles that individuals may have in a network. The first three roles are considered positive; the last two are probably cause for concern.

Stars are well-connected individuals in a network. They have connections to many members. In addition, most of those links are likely reciprocal and many are multiplexed. They have a central role in the communication network because people communicate to them on a variety of topics and vice versa. Of course, a person could be a star in one network and not in others. For example, a star in the political/influence network might not be a member of the social network because people want to be careful to keep a safe distance to avoid creating problems with someone who is so important. In Figure 5.3, the head cashier is one of the network stars.

Liaisons are individuals who link two clusters or groups in the network together but are not particularly identified with either group. In Figure 5.3, WA1 is a liaison between women's apparel, home goods, and electronics. An assistant store manager should probably serve as a liaison between various departments, but other people may also serve in this role. *Bridge Links* are similar to liaisons in that they link two groups in the network together. Unlike liaisons, they are active members of one of the groups and not of the other. Normally it takes two bridge links to make a connection. In Figure 5.3, the home goods manager and the electronics manager serve as bridge links between different parts of the store.

All three of these roles—stars, liaisons, and bridge links—serve important functions in the organizational network. Without them, communication would likely not flow through much of the organization. If managers are not in one of these three roles, it is probably critical that they know who is and have communication links to them.

Two related roles should be a concern. An *isolate* is someone with very few or no links in the network. An *isolate pair* is a set of two individuals linked to each other but not to anyone else. It is unlikely that there is anyone in an organization who never communicates to someone else, but when issues such as reciprocity and intensity (frequency and strength) are taken into account, there are individuals in these isolate roles. In Figure 5.3, CS3 and C7 are isolates. Their lack of connection to others suggests that they are not integrated into the communication system of the organization. This often means that they are more likely to leave the organization.

COMMUNICATION CHALLENGE

Reducing Employee Turnover by Cultivating Network Density

Communication scholar Thomas Feeley and colleagues (Feeley, Moon, Kozey, & Slowe, 2010) proposed and confirmed the Erosion Model of Employee Turnover. The authors demonstrated that when employees are highly interconnected with others in their workplace, they have much more access and opportunity to receive social support from coworkers when work is difficult or stressful. That social support, in turn, helps employees cope with job strain and reduces employees' turnover. The model's label "Erosion" invokes the metaphor that those on the outskirts of the network, with few connections, are more likely to erode away, or leave the organization. How might a manager use this insight to reduce employee or volunteer turnover? How might a manager be able to encourage newcomers to achieve high connectedness rapidly?

Group-Level Characteristics. It is common for sociograms to reveal clusters of individuals who communicate a great deal with each other but have limited interaction with other parts of the network. Some of these are easily identified. In Figure 5.3, circles have been drawn around some of the more apparent groups. What identifies them as groups is the high number of internal links to other group members as compared to the rather limited linkages outside the group. A *clique* is a group that maintains its linkages over time and most likely has many multiplex linkages as well. This could be a group of people who work within the same general area (task network), who are always thinking of ways to improve the organization (innovation network), and who also socialize outside of work (social network). In the opening scenario, MJ seems to be part of a clique with other former or current department assistant managers. Even though some of them have been promoted, like MJ, and others have not, they still communicate with each other regularly and even get together occasionally.

A *coalition* is different than a clique in that it is a temporary group. In the opening scenario, MJ is part of an assigned coalition, the ad hoc committee to promote health and safety among employees. When this committee has finished its work, they will likely discontinue their frequent communication to each other, such that the group will no longer exist. Other cliques may form without support from management. For example, a group of employees may gradually form because they want to pressure management into providing improved lighting in the parking lot or create a smoke-free work environment. They will likely form a coalition to work together until they achieve their goal or decide that the goal is unobtainable. When they no longer communicate, they will cease to be a coalition.

Organizational or System-Level Characteristics. There are a large number of network characteristics that can be examined at the organizational level. These include its size or its openness/connectedness to networks in other organizations. Three structural characteristics are frequently examined.

Density or *connectedness* refers to the ratio of the number of links compared to the number of possible links. If everyone in the network is connected to everyone else, something that might happen in a small organization but not in many larger ones, its density would equal one. Density can also be measured at the group level. In Figure 5.3, the group in the lower left corner is more densely connected than the group on the lower right side. Density is an important network measure because it is likely associated with shared understanding. The more connected the organization is, the more likely they have the same information and the same understanding, although that is not always the case.

Somewhat similar to connectedness is *reachability*. This has to do with the average number of links it takes individuals to connect to others in the network. The lower the number of links, the more connected everyone is. If the network looks more like an assembly line than a conference table, it takes a lot of effort for information to flow to everyone. Given how information often does not reach organizational saturation if it has to go through many links, a high reachability score could be problematic.

Finally, *stability* refers to how consistent the linkages in the network are over time. The more stable and predictable the network, the easier it is to disperse information along the linkages that work consistently. In an unstable network with frequent changes, it would be difficult to determine who the stars and coalitions are.

Impact of Communication Networks

Although being able to identify network characteristics might be somewhat interesting, it is more important to be able to determine some ways to apply that information. There have been hundreds of studies of communication networks. What follows are just a few that show the importance of paying attention to communication networks.

Studies of decision-making groups have consistently shown the importance of network configurations at the group level (e.g., Brown & Miller, 2000). Groups that have a highly centralized network structure are particularly good at handling simple, routine decisions and actions. Group members funnel their information to one network star, who completes work or makes decisions efficiently. By contrast, when problems are more complex and involve unusual circumstances, a highly connected network performs better. The ability to interact with everyone allows for more creative and thoughtful deliberations needed to work on complex issues. Not surprisingly, groups recognize the unequal participation in the more centralized groups but may not be concerned due to its beneficial efficiency on simple tasks.

A study of bank tellers explored the impact of being a communication network isolate and likely made a difference in how banks are physically designed (McLaughlin & Cheatham, 1977). In the 1970s, the drive-up or outside tellers in many banks were located in drive-in work stations that looked a lot like tollbooths. The outside tellers worked individually and the customers drove to the booth and interacted with the teller inside through a sliding window or tray. One such bank was having trouble with chronic dissatisfaction in their outside tellers, but not their inside tellers. This puzzled them because both sets of tellers had the same policies, the same pay, the same supervisor; and yet the outside tellers had significantly less positive attitudes toward those factors than inside tellers and higher turnover rates. The difference in communication networks explained the problem. The outside tellers were isolates in the communication network, especially in the social network. They simply were physically unable to have casual interactions with other tellers. The lack of participation in a social network led to dissatisfaction in general with their jobs. Outside tollbooth-like work stations are probably long gone, replaced with pneumatic tubes that whisk your transactions back and forth to a group of tellers who are able to chat and socialize with each other. In many bank branches now, it is impossible to distinguish between inside and outside tellers because they help each other based on customer load. There are no longer network isolates.

A study of employees in a plant explored the importance of network involvement on workers' satisfaction and performance (Marshall & Stohl, 1993). In the study, employees indicated the size of their communication network (number of contacts) and their number of strong links to supervisors—essentially a measure of their connection to the authority or political networks. The results of the study indicated that high levels of involvement in the communication networks for employees were related to their satisfaction and performance as rated by their supervisors. They also found that having strong connections to their managers, a form of empowerment, was also associated with satisfaction and performance. Together this indicates that communication network involvement, and particularly connection to those in authority or a political communication network, matters.

The influence of communication networks is also studied at the organizational level, that is, between organizations rather than just between individuals within organizations. One way organizations link to each other is through interlocking directorates in which individuals serve as board members for multiple corporations. A number of benefits have been identified from these network linkages (Mizruchi, 1996). These board member linkages increase perceptions of the legitimacy of the organizations because important people serve on their boards. In addition, through their interactions, board members can monitor their environment and share information to reduce their uncertainty about their business environment. Individual board members also benefit by developing social relations across organizations that can lead to career advancement as well.

These are just a few of the studies using network analysis out of hundreds that have been conducted. They provide just a sample of some of the ways that understanding the communication network of an organization, instead of focusing on the formal channels, can provide important insights into how communication operates in organizations.

Limitations of Network Analysis

Like the traditional communication channel approach to studying organizational communication, network analysis is also limited due to its strong tendency to assume a communication transmission concept of the process. If any two people or two organizations are connected, it is assumed that information transfers between them. There is little consideration of interpretive or transactional definitions of communication. There are exceptions, of course.

Nonprofit Organizations and Volunteers

Nonprofit organizations (NPOs) often have a formal structure or a chain of command for their paid employees that works quite similarly to the model presented earlier in the chapter with upward, downward, and horizontal communication and informal communication. What makes nonprofits that rely on volunteers different from businesses and government agencies is that there may be little or no formal communication structure for volunteers, who frequently are the largest part of the organization. Still, formal communication channels do function even if no formal chart exists to clarify how communication to volunteers should flow. The results and issues for volunteers are similar to communication to lower level employees in businesses and government agencies.

Like employees, volunteers are influenced by formal downward communication. For example, volunteers in an organization that sponsored running clubs, for unemployed individuals to help them improve their self-image, were consistently reminded to avoid getting too close to clients because of the potential dangers; volunteers complied with this policy because the rationale given seemed compelling (Wojno, 2013). In another study, volunteers responded positively to the training and directives they received when they joined as zoo volunteers and were quite satisfied with their custodial roles, but they responded negatively when the zoo management reduced their roles and responsibilities later on (Kramer & Danielson, 2016). These research findings indicate the importance of formal communication for volunteers.

Network analysis has been used in a variety of ways to study NPOs and volunteers. A recent study of volunteer members of a Korean church found some important relationships between individuals' positions in the network and a number of important outcomes for the volunteers' experiences (Lee, 2014). Korean immigrants who had been in the United States longer and who had a larger network of contacts also tended to have more diverse networks that included more non-Korean individuals. In addition, those individuals who had more diverse network linkages to non-Koreans were also more likely to be conscious of cultural differences in their community and were more willing to adapt to them. Those with less diverse linkages tended to be less willing to adapt to their multicultural setting. In this way, network analysis demonstrates the importance of network linkages on the cultural adaptation of the voluntary members of this nonprofit/religious organization.

At the organizational level, network analysis indicates the importance of links between NPOs. NPOs link together frequently due to similar goals and in an effort to gain the economic resources that they need (Shumate & Contactor, 2014). For example, two NPOs may collaborate to apply for government grants because they are more likely to succeed, or the funding agency may even require collaboration across organizations. One of the common ways that NPOs maintain network linkages is through individuals who serve as board members in multiple NPOs, similar to the idea of interlocking directorates for businesses discussed previously. NPOs with more network linkages are more likely to maintain formal collaborative agreements that assist both organizations in reaching their goals (Guo & Acar, 2005).

Because volunteers have a different relationship to organizations and different goals and motives than employees, communication channels and networks function somewhat differently with them than they do with employees. However, the research indicates the value of using both approaches to better understand the role of communication in NPOs involving volunteers.

Summary

In this chapter, we provide a description of some of the ways communication operates in organizations. Formal channels of communication are important components in the way organizations operate. Downward communication provides directives and feedback to employees; however, there are issues related to how much information to provide without providing too much, making the feedback effective, and distributing the information adequately throughout the organization. Upward communication can be an important source of information to managers about how well the organization is running, but subordinates often filter the negative information out due to power differentials or focus on ingratiation to gain favors. Lateral communication serves important coordination and employee development functions but is often hampered by territoriality and competition. Through informal communication, the most common form of organizational communication, individuals develop relationships and address concerns that formal communication fails to address; however, its quickness, lack of accountability, and occasional inaccuracies can create problems. Organizations also create other methods of communication through committees and project teams that lead to integration across levels and departments.

As an alternative to studying formal communication based on organizational charts, network analysis focuses on who actually communicates formally or informally rather than who is supposed to communicate. Results identify characteristics of linkages between individuals, roles individuals hold, groups that form, and organization-wide networks. Results indicate that network activities affect employee satisfaction and retention and how groups make decisions. An understanding of the combination of formal communication structures, informal communication, and communication networks provides a more comprehensive understanding of how communication functions to create and maintain organizations.

Communication and Organizational Culture

Jeremy and Michelle had been married for 7 years, and both disliked their jobs when they decided to quit and open their own restaurant. They defied the odds for small business success and, 20 years later, were facing some important decisions. When they began, they did all the work themselves: cooking, serving, ordering supplies, and keeping the financial records. It took long hours, but once the business started to do well, they quickly hired some of their extended family members. Customers were often regulars who enjoyed the relaxed and friendly atmosphere. When they ran out of relatives to hire, Jeremy and Michelle hired a cook. This allowed Jeremy to become the business manager: ordering supplies, doing the payroll, arranging for advertising, paying the bills—all the behind-the-scenes work that needed to be done. He still helped out in the restaurant if needed, but he did not miss the cooking. Michelle managed the personnel and customer service part of the operation from the start. She made the hiring and firing decisions, although both were rare. Between their three children, who were old enough to work, and other relatives, about half of the employees were family. The half who were not family generally seemed to like the small, close-knit relationships everyone had. Family and nonfamily employees tended to remain with the restaurant, and turnover was rare. Those employees that left usually mentioned a lack of opportunity for advancement in a family-owned business as a main reason. That reason was why they had to replace the cook about a year ago.

Unexpectedly, after that change in personnel, they witnessed a significant increase in business. Many new customers told the wait staff that they heard the food was better now and so they were trying it out and returning. At first, it was not uncommon for people to be waiting for tables at rush periods, such as Friday and Saturday evenings and Sunday brunch. Now, they often had people waiting during lunch and dinner. They had to reduce the personal attention they usually gave specific customers so that they could manage the tremendous volume of customers. Sometimes they wanted to rush some of their loyal customers out the door so they could have the table. They seemed to be facing a turning point. It seemed like they needed to open a new location. They found one on the other side of town and were discussing if their oldest child was ready to manage the new location with the assistance of one of their nieces.

· · · · ·

We know from experience that a family-owned restaurant, like the one just described, is not the same as a national chain restaurant, even if both of them are Italian restaurants, for example. One of the primary differences arises from their organizational cultures. In Chapter 1, we mentioned that interpretivist scholars view organizations as cultures. In Chapter 3, regarding the topic of organizational entry, we pointed out that learning about the organizational culture and adapting to it are important activities for organizational newcomers. In both cases, we left the concept of organizational culture relatively undefined. In this chapter, we address the topic of organizational culture more directly. We explore the concept of organizational culture, examine how organizational culture is developed and exhibited, consider more complex descriptions of organizational culture, and then explore ways to analyze an organization's culture.

Defining Organizational Culture

A wide range of definitions of organizational culture have been proposed by different scholars over the years. The commonalities in those definitions are highlighted in this definition: "Organizational culture is the set(s) of artifacts, values, and assumptions that emerge from the interactions of various members" (Keyton, 2005, p. 28). To understand the four components of culture in this definition, we consider each one separately.

Artifacts

An organization's artifacts are tangible, material representations of some aspect of the organization's culture. Culture can be manifested in a wide range of artifacts, including *individuals* who may embody heroes or villains, *language and stories* told to convey its past, *norms* that demonstrate appropriate behaviors, and *rituals* that represent important values of the organization (Pacanowsky & O'Donnell-Trujillo, 1983). These artifacts can be visible, such as a mission statement posted in the main office, the way cubicles are arranged, or a portrait of the organization's founder. They may be audible, such as coworkers telling the story of the organization's founder or a peer explaining "how we do things around here" to a newcomer. Often, artifacts combine sights and sounds, such as when an annual volunteer recognition dinner includes speeches about the volunteers and provides them with recognition certificates. The organization's artifacts give a feel for what is or is not important in the organization. Artifacts are important because they are the *visible* manifestation of the *invisible* culture. Values and assumptions—not artifacts—are invisible and powerful in influencing organizational members' behaviors and decisions. Every artifact contains within it certain values and assumptions. Learning to decipher the meaning of organizational artifacts—in accordance with organizational members' understandings—is the essence of deciphering an organization's culture.

Values

An organization's values are the key principles or attitudes that organizational members should ideally hold. These values guide members' behaviors and decision making. For example, if the organization values customer service, then employees should make decisions based on whether they improve customer service rather than based on how they affect company profits. Of course, at times an organization's values are in conflict with one another, which makes it challenging to make decisions that support multiple values. As a result, if the organization values supporting the community and providing a strong return to its investors, it may be difficult for an employee involved in community relations to determine how much financial support the company should give to sponsoring a 5K race designed to raise money for a worthy cause.

Assumptions

Assumptions are the taken for granted beliefs held by organizational members. These assumptions may have started out as stated values or they may never have actually been openly discussed. In either case, these assumptions have become so engrained, apparent, and obvious in the minds of organizational members that they no longer need to discuss them. Everyone simply knows or accepts that there is a certain way things are or should be done without questioning them. For example, if a newcomer asks why the company only recruits new employees from the state's large public university and never from the regional ones, and the established members cannot provide an explanation other than "that's just the way we do things around here," the newcomer inadvertently questioned an organizational assumption that may not have been considered for many years. That assumption has been driving its recruitment practice without conscious consideration by organizational members.

Interactions of Various Members

Ultimately, an organization's culture emerges from the communication interactions among its members. Through communication, members express their values and create artifacts that represent the culture. Interestingly, assumptions are rarely questioned or discussed because they are just accepted or understood. When organizational members do discuss assumptions, it is possible that an organization's culture may be reinforced or challenged. Although anyone can question an assumption, it is often newcomers who question assumptions that cause organizational members to reconsider their own assumptions. Keyton (2005) argued that *all* organizational members' interactions have the potential to reinforce or challenge culture (however slightly), even though we tend to think only of management's formal and official messaging as creating an organization's culture. We explain this point in greater detail in the following section.

Continuing the previous example of the organization's recruitment practices, through interactions between the newcomer and established members the management may reaffirm its stance by insisting that it only wants the best new employees; therefore, it should not recruit at the regional universities. Alternatively, hiring managers could reassess their practice and begin to recruit at other campuses as well. If this happens, it means that the organizational culture changed because the artifacts have changed (where organizational members recruit), the values have changed (recruiting decisions should be made on criteria other than the university attended), and a new assumption is in the process of being reproduced.

Structuration Theory and Culture

Structuration theory, based on the work of Anthony Giddens (e.g., Giddens, 1984), a sociologist, explains why an organization's culture is relatively stable and yet can and does change, even if slowly or in small ways. Structuration refers to the process by which a social system (like a society or an organization) produces and reproduces itself. Because the social system only exists when its members enact or participate in it, it must be continually reproduced or recreated regularly, essentially we might say, on a daily basis. Structuration theory was brought into the study of organizational communication by Scott Poole and his colleagues (Poole, Seibold, & McPhee, 1985). Think of structuration this way: An organization would cease to exist if no one returned to work the next day. Similarly, when work rules, policies, or practices are not produced and reproduced, they stop mattering and even stop existing. The system is structured or produced through the use of, what Giddens called, *rules* and *resources*. Rules and resources are guides for how to act, think, decide, and speak. Essentially, rules and resources are the patterns of behavior organizational members witnessed or learned in the past. Those past patterns form a recipe for what to do next in the here and now. By following various rules and norms, organizational members continually produce and reproduce the organization. Although considerably more complex in its more elaborated forms (and probably more confusing), the basic premises of structuration theory can be illustrated relatively easily.

To further illustrate these concepts, consider the family-owned restaurant presented in the opening scenario. This social system exists only because the owners and employees create or reproduce it every day. If they suddenly stopped coming to work, the building and supplies would exist as physical structures, but the social system of the company would no longer exist. When they arrive each day, the employees reproduce the family business by using the available resources—including the building, kitchen facilities, supplies, personnel, policies (however informal they may be), and so forth—to make the restaurant happen. Using typical business rules, they supply the customers with food in exchange for money, which they use to pay the personnel and purchase more supplies. The next day, the process repeats itself. Despite being produced or reproduced each day, the restaurant appears to be a stable, consistent social system with its own organizational culture.

According to structuration theory, the social system both constrains and enables its members. The system *constrains* them because there is a strong tendency to reproduce the same system with few changes or additions. We like to follow the recipes provided by the past; those recipes are predictable and reduce uncertainty. The system is also *enabling* because the system can be changed by the application of new or different rules and the acquisition of different resources. People like to follow patterns and recipes, but they always also have agency to make changes (however small); yet, in trying to accomplish something new, they often experience limitations because of the existing system.

Returning to the scenario, the family restaurant seemed to have remained unchanged for a long period of time after the initial startup; however, when the resources changed, the system changed. When the cook quit for opportunities elsewhere, the new one apparently made better tasting dishes–creating a change in resources. Then, more customers started coming, which resulted in additional financial resources. At the

The culture of the family restaurant discussed in this chapter depends on the people who work there carrying out their roles and communication as well as the physical environment and artifacts.

same time, the growth in customers created a problem because there was insufficient room to serve them. So although the owners and employees exercised agency, which resulted in more customers, they were also constrained by the limited size of their facility. The owners are considering exercising agency by choosing to use their added resources to expand to a new location. If they do, the new structure of two facilities should enable them to serve more customers; however, by having two locations, it will make it more difficult to maintain and operate the two as a single business, a new constraint.

In terms of organizational culture, structuration theory suggests that an organization's culture is created by applying the rules and resources of the system to reproduce the culture. The family-owned business example shows how the change in one resource,

Communicating a New Value

Bisel, Messersmith, and Keyton (2010) explained that the relationship between organizational communication and organizational culture is structurational: As organizational members communicate, they call organizational culture into being, which both enables and constrains the kinds of communication activities members will likely enact in the future. That insight suggests that the way to change organizational culture is to influence the way organizational members talk between and among one another. Imagine wanting to encourage a culture of gratitude in your organization. You could thank others personally, which will have some influence in shaping a new culture. However, your culture change attempts will be more influential if you can encourage expressions of gratitude between and among many organizational members. How might you encourage such messaging from others and its related organizational culture change? Can you think of another value that might be desirable and worth a strategic organizational culture change attempt?

the cook, resulted in changes in the organization's culture, its artifacts, and possibly its values as well. The norm had been to provide very personal attention to customers and let them take as long as they wanted to eat in a relaxed setting. Now the servers were providing more impersonal service and focusing on making room for the customers waiting in line rather than on satisfying those already seated. So the culture was changing from a relaxed, slow-paced, family restaurant to a more rushed and impersonal one that tried to serve more customers in less time.

Although the change in resources resulted in changes in the cultural norms and values, other aspects of the culture seem likely to remain unchanged during this structuration process of creating a two-location organization. For at least some employees, there seems to have been a sense of nepotism (i.e., favoritism granted to family) in which the owners, their relatives, and their children had special status and more opportunities for advancement. If the oldest child and a niece become managers of the new facility, that culture of nepotism will be produced and reproduced because the system is constrained by an apparent rule that favors promoting those with family connections. However, if two family members go to college in another state and the niece decides not to work for the family anymore, those changes in personnel resources will likely change the culture of nepotism whether the business expands to a new location or not.

Using structuration theory to consider organizational culture supports the position that an organization's culture is something it does or enacts, not something that it has (Pacanowsky & O'Donnell-Trujillo, 1983). It is only by acting and reproducing the culture that it exists. At the same time, structuration theory supports the position that an organizational culture is something that an organization has because existing rules and resources are used to reproduce the system.

Organizational Norms

Norms are an extremely important indicator of an organization's culture because they are artifacts that represent its values and assumptions. Norms are behavioral patterns of organizational members and suggest to members which behaviors are expected, obligatory, preferred, and/or prohibited (Shimanoff, 1992). An organization's set of norms reveal which member behaviors are appropriate (or inappropriate) expressions of the organization's values. It is important for organizational newcomers to learn organizational norms; however, because norms are assumed or understood and rarely discussed by experienced members, it may be difficult for experienced members to teach norms to newcomers until they are violated. Given the importance of norms, we explore them more thoroughly as manifestations of organizational culture.

Norms are related to rules—the terms are often used interchangeably—and different scholars make different distinctions between them (Shimanoff, 1980). In general, organizational rules are often an attempt to codify the organization's norms explicitly. In other cases, norms are not written into policies, but organizational members know the normative expectations implicitly because they witnessed patterns of behavior in their workplace. The relationship between rules and implicit norms can be complicated. For example, consider three organizations that have statements (i.e., rules) in their employee handbooks specifying that employees have 30 minutes for lunch. In one organization, everyone seems to follow this rule closely; employees even seem to make sure other people notice when they leave for lunch and when they return. In the second organization, employees generally follow this rule most days but also routinely take longer breaks with no real consequence unless they are gone for more than 60 minutes, in which case a supervisor may say something to them. In the third organization, on most days, individuals usually eat at their desks while working unless they have a "lunch meeting." If they have a lunch meeting, they often are gone for an hour and a half and justify this behavior based on working through lunch on other days. In each organization, the explicit rule is likely intended to be an explicit norm or expectation and is stated with little ambiguity. In practice, the implicit norms vary widely in the three organizations. Newcomers face the challenge of learning the rules and the norms and, if they differ, which of the two are more important to follow to fit into the organization's culture.

Types of Norms

Beyond this general understanding of norms, scholars identified specific types of significant organizational norms. Schein (1968) identified three types of organizational norms that members need to know: pivotal, relevant, and peripheral. *Pivotal norms*, as the name suggests, are behavioral patterns that must be closely followed to maintain membership in the organization. Some of these pivotal norms are actually stated explicitly as rules and policies. For example, being intoxicated at work and routinely missing work violate pivotal norms for most organizations. *Relevant norms* are behavioral patterns that are less likely to be written down, and violating them will not likely result in expulsion from the organization, but failure to follow them will likely limit an individual's success in the organization. For example, always submitting work at the last moment will not usually result in termination, but always submitting work early will likely increase opportunities for pay raises and promotions. *Peripheral norms* are behavioral patterns that are rarely written down and the least important to learn because the consequences for violating them are usually quite minor. For example, experienced employees may have a habit of sitting in the same seat at each department meeting. When a new person sits in someone else's seat, there may be some confused or negative responses, such as a joking comment about "taking my seat"; it is unlikely that there will be any other consequences.

Communication Norms

There are important *communication* norms in organizations, especially at the group level. Groups and organizations have norms about who, says what, to whom, when, through what channel, for what duration, by what decision procedure (Shimanoff, 1992). Consider how a typical executive board meeting of a nonprofit might be conducted. The chief executive opens the meeting by thanking everyone for attending and then takes a few minutes to discuss the state of the organization in general. Next, each board member reports on his/her specific area of responsibility. Inevitably, the only report that invokes much discussion is the treasurer's report because there is always a shortage of funds. During these financial discussions, the chief executive calls on people when they look as if they have something to ask or say, except for the one board member who asserts herself whenever she has a point to make without being called. Another board member never speaks unless he is asked a direct question. Some of these communication patterns are specific to individuals (who talks), others seem more general (short durations), and there is generally a procedure for determining who communicates next (the chief executive decides except for the one individual). Other groups and organizations have their own communication norms that may vary from very formal adherence to parliamentary rules of small group discussion to very relaxed discussions without an agenda.

The norms (and rules) of an organization are important indicators of its culture. By providing a sense of how people should behave and act, norms provide an indication of the important values of the organization. They also often exhibit some organizational assumptions.

Norm Development

Norms do not appear out of nowhere but are developed over time. A number of actions make certain behaviors potential resources for creating and reinforcing them as norms (Graham, 2003; Shimanoff, 1980). In particular, individuals bring some expectations about how to behave in an organization based on previous experiences. Behaviors are more likely to become norms when they are done early in a group's history or are enacted by high-status individuals. When these behaviors are repeated and reinforced as positive, or at least not rejected, they often become normative. Most norm development occurs without any explicit discussion. This pattern suggests that norms develop in a manner consistent with structuration theory such that past experiences and early experiences are used as rules and resources for reproducing those same patterns over time.

It is usually only when a norm is violated that any explicit discussion of it occurs. Explicit discussions of norms by a group can shape how they are understood. A study of a computer-mediated group found that when a general norm of "communicate regularly" was not being followed, the group made a more specific norm of "check email daily" (Graham, 2003). In this way, norms develop and change gradually, as the members practice agency by changing current norms that are not working adequately to create new norms in a process that seems to slowly move from general to more specific or more explicit norms over time.

Creating Conformity to Norms

Creating conformity to norms involves giving positive reinforcement to those who follow the norms, and more importantly involves providing negative sanctions for those who do not follow them. The pressure to conform to norms is not equal across norms or individuals. Some norms have a wider range of acceptable behavior than others, have varying degrees of acceptance, and are applied differently to people, usually based on status (Shaw, 1981). Interestingly, high-status individuals may be expected to follow certain norms more closely than other organizational members, particularly if the norms represent core values; simultaneously they also may be allowed to deviate on other more peripheral norms due to the important contributions they make to the group. For example, a leader of an environmental organization may be expected to follow the recycling practices of the group carefully and advocate on behalf of those practices as a role model to other members and the community; at the same time, the leader may be allowed to arrive late to board meetings, despite the inconvenience to others, because of the leader's overall contributions to the group. When the group does choose to sanction an individual for norm violations, the process is one of gradually increasing the pressure to conform.

According to observational studies conducted at the University of Minnesota, a group may initially delay any sanction of a member who does not conform to the norm to allow the person to self-correct (Bormann & Bormann, 1988). This observation indicates that much of norm enforcement occurs through self-monitoring in which individuals notice their behavior is inconsistent with others in the group or organization and then change to meet those normative patterns (Graham, 2003).

According to the Minnesota studies, when self-correction does not happen, the group may begin to address the issue by engaging in joking and humor with the norm violator. If that tactic fails to correct the behavior, the group may begin to deride and ridicule the person openly. Next, the group may attempt to persuade the individual to conform. Heated arguments may ensue if the deviant behavior continues. Finally, the group may isolate and reject the person. For example, the first time a member of a project team misses a deadline, the other members may not address it, hoping that the individual will be embarrassed enough by the situation to meet future deadlines. If the person misses a second deadline, other members may joke with the person about how they missed deadlines when they were in college, but outgrew that when they got "a real job." The humor may turn more to making fun of the person for having too many late night parties to meet deadlines. Then, they may actively try to convince the person to meet deadlines because of its negative affect on the work schedules of other team members and because it makes them all look bad to upper management when important deadlines are missed. These discussions could become quite heated if the individual continues to deny the behaviors' influence on others. Finally, if change is still not apparent, the team may no longer offer suggestions or assistance to help the person with work and may exclude the individual from lunches and assign work to others.

Norms are one of the most apparent artifacts of an organization's culture. They represent the values that are important to organizational members. They develop through a structuration process as behaviors become rules and resources for reproducing and reinforcing the values of the organization. In the restaurant scenario, employees seemed most conscious of the customer service norm; but other norms about work schedules, and who talks to the owner, were most likely present. Employees likely pressured each other to follow these norms too.

Three Approaches to Culture

So far in the discussion, we have treated organizational culture as if it is consistent across an entire organization. Although this is a valuable perspective, it likely does not provide a complete picture of the complexity of an organization's culture. In her book, Joann Martin (1992) presents three potential perspectives on organizational culture: an integrated perspective, a differentiated perspective, and a fragmented perspective. It is important to note that Martin does not advocate one perspective as more valuable than another. Each perspective simply focuses on different aspects of an organization's culture.

An Integrated Perspective

Martin's integrated perspective is essentially the perspective that has been presented so far and so we discuss it only briefly. An integrated perspective looks for an umbrella culture that unifies an organization's culture. It focuses on consensus and agreement. The goal of examining an organization's overarching culture is to find those artifacts, values, and assumptions that are common across organizational members.

A Differentiated Perspective

Martin's differentiated perspective recognizes that there are disagreements and differences that cause divisions within organizations, especially large ones. Instead of looking for what unifies an organization, the differentiated perspective examines these differences to see if they represent subcultures within the overarching culture. Some of what divides a unified culture occurs because of organizational structure and the responsibilities required of different organizational units. For example, the sales division and the research division in a large company are likely to have somewhat different values and practices because of the nature of the work that they do and the people with whom they must interact. Other consistently held differences among organizational subgroups may be the result of factors such as organizational status or demographic characteristics. Upper management and entry-level employees generally have different experiences and concerns that likely result in different values and practices as well. Whatever the cause of these differences, subcultures can differ from each other in important ways. At the same time, each subculture is really an integrated or unified culture of its own, with shared artifacts, values, and assumptions. These subcultures can be viewed as islands of consistency within the larger sea of the organization.

A Fragmented Perspective

Martin's third perspective, the fragmented perspective, is the most challenging to understand, in part because it may seem to be focused on something other than culture. Instead of focusing on the unifying set of values and beliefs of a subculture or overarching culture, the fragmented perspective examines the complexity of the culture as expressed through ambiguity and inconsistency. The fragmented perspective recognizes that certain aspects of a culture are interpreted in so many different ways that it is difficult to make sense of a singular cultural understanding. There is likely a lack of shared meaning or understanding about these issues. At best, there is temporary agreement, or a clearing in the jungle of ambiguity.

Applying Martin's Three Perspectives on Organizational Culture

To make the value of each of the perspectives clear, consider the scenario of the family-owned restaurant at the beginning of the chapter. According to Martin, using all three perspectives provides a better understanding of the organization and its culture.

An Integrated Perspective

There seem to be a number of important unifying aspects of the culture of the small business. Employees all know each other and seem loyal to the business as indicated by the low turnover of employees, whether they are family members or not. The business seems to have been built on a norm of providing good customer service. It has a relaxed, friendly atmosphere for employees and customers in which no one seems rushed. Taken together, this suggests a unified culture that values positive interpersonal relationships among employees and customers and promotes a relaxed social environment. This overarching culture then might be described as a close family business, not unlike many small businesses.

A Differentiated Perspective

There seem to be two dominant subcultures in the organization. The owner and employees who are family members likely view the organization differently than the other employees. Whereas the family members may think that if you work hard you can get ahead in the organization, other employees may view it as a culture in which there are few opportunities for advancement and that favoritism is given to family members in promotion decisions. The family members support their perspective by pointing to the success of the new cook, who is not a family member. The other employees consider the cook an anomaly (See Figure 6.1). They note that although everyone is treated fairly well, family members get most of the opportunities for advancement, such as managing the opening of a second location. It is also possible that there are further subcultures to explore. For example, subcultures may divide cook staff from servers.

A Fragmented Perspective

A fragmented perspective would explore the ambiguities and incongruities of the organization. For example, the story of Jeremy and Michele supports the American dream that you can get ahead through hard work; but for the employees of the organization, there really are

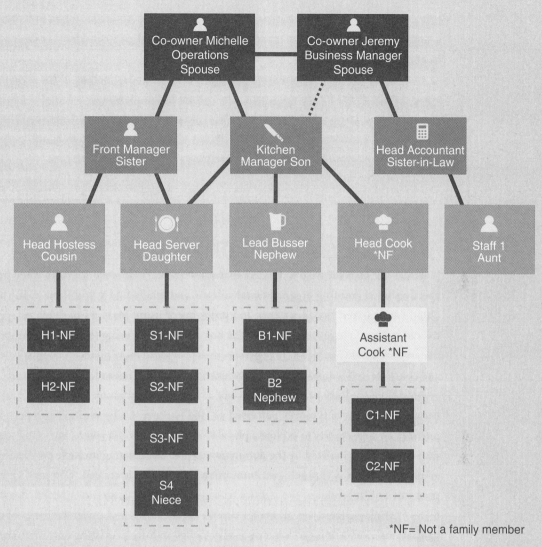

Figure 6.1. Organizational Structure for Family Owned Restaurant

few opportunities for more than mid-level, supervisory positions. Even though the possibility of expansion further supports the dream of success, the expansion will lead to additional profits and benefits for the owners while providing only minimal differences in opportunity or success for the rest of the employees. The incongruity between the restaurant being an opportunity for the owners to achieve the American dream and it being a land of limited opportunities for others is never really explicitly considered or discussed by anyone (see Figure 6.1).

Combining the three perspectives provides a broader understanding of the organizational culture of the family restaurant. The culture is simultaneously a friendly, relaxed place that values personal relationships; a place where family members and other employees have different experiences that support different views of the organization; and a place where there are contradictions between opportunity and a lack of opportunity.

A Critique of Applying the Three Perspectives

It should not be a surprise to readers that some scholars embrace Martin's three perspectives for examining organizational culture, and others find it problematic. Keyton (2014) summarized the advantages and problems of using Martin's multiple perspectives to study organizational culture. The first advantage of using the multiple perspective approach is that using all three perspectives provides a more nuanced, sophisticated, and complete understanding of the organizational culture. Second, the typical study of organizational culture prioritizes the voice of the dominant group in the organization because their view is typically perceived as "the" culture. Using multiple perspectives provides an opportunity to explore a plurality of viewpoints and voices, including some who may be marginalized by the dominant culture. Third, using multiple perspectives emphasizes that it is through communication that culture is created. Communication produces and reproduces the culture as suggested by structuration theory. Fourth, using multiple perspectives allows for diverse explanations and understandings of organizational events. It is no longer necessary to view culture as existing only when there is one shared meaning across the organization. Finally, Martin's approach helps to elevate the use of interpretive and critical approaches to studying organizations.

Keyton (2014) identified three problems with the multiple perspective approach to studying culture. First, the multiple perspective approach confuses what we know and how we know. It proposes a method to learn about the culture but essentially assumes that the three different aspects of culture exist. This creates a sort of self-fulfilling prophecy in which the finding of the different aspects of culture is predetermined by asking about them. Second, although claiming to be an interpretive approach, applying the multiple perspective approach suggests some level of objectivity, which is more consistent with a post-positivist approach. The approach suggests that the researcher can objectively differentiate between the three perspectives rather than allowing the meaning to come out of the examination of the culture. Third, the approach suggests that communication is the outcome of some preexisting meaning of the culture that existed prior to communication creating it rather than the meaning emerging through communication.

By choosing to consider all three perspectives, we can create the advantages in studying organizational culture identified previously. Alternatively, choosing not to use all three perspectives results in the creation of a different, more limited understanding of organizational culture. As a result, using all three perspectives seems to have more advantages for understanding organizational culture for organizational members.

Analyzing Organizational Culture

Research on organizational culture used a variety of methods. Although it has been studied using quantitative methods in a few instances, it is primarily studied using a variety of qualitative methods. In this section, we explain five qualitative methods that can be used to gain an understanding of an organization's culture: script analysis, ritual analysis, metaphor analysis, reflective comment analysis, and ethnography.

Script (or Narrative) Analysis

People are storytellers. Individuals express what is important to them—such as their values—through the stories or narratives they tell and retell. Although organizations think that their stories are unique, many of the stories express themes and values that address common concerns across organizations such as is the boss too big to follow the rules, can little people rise to the top of this organization, will I get fired because of what is happening to the organization, how will the boss react if I admit I made a mistake, and how will the organization deal with obstacles it faces (Martin, Feldman, Hatch, & Sitkin, 1983). Through narratives that address concerns like these, organizational members express their values and behaviors while at the same time trying to persuade other organizational members to adopt the same values and practices (Meyer,

1995). Whether the content of the stories actually occurred is not important; what is important is that people create and recreate the culture when they accept the stories as expressive of the way life really works around the organization.

A five-step script analysis provides a useful way to discover the values, beliefs, and behaviors that are part of an organization's culture:

1. Find a frequently repeated organizational story, myth, or legend.
2. Determine the communication network(s) on which the story is told (who tells the story to whom).
3. Consider if the story is about any rites or rituals or if telling the story is itself a ritual.
4. Identify any heroes or villains in the story.
5. Finally, identify the underlying values and behaviors the story indicates are expected in the organization.

To apply these steps, we begin by finding a frequently told story in one company that addresses the "Will I get fired?" concern:

> One industry was particularly hard-hit by economic difficulties in the late 1970's. Most companies responded by laying off large numbers of employees. One company had a long-standing policy of avoiding layoffs whenever possible. In order to keep their promise of job security, everyone in the company, even the president, took a 10% cut in pay. In return for the cut, employees were required to work only nine of every ten days. (Found in Martin et al., 1983)

For the second step, we consider the communication network on which the story is told. For example, if the story is primarily told by executives to lower level employees, its meaning might be somewhat specific because the purpose of telling the story would seem to be related to enhancing upper management's own self-image and reassuring anxious employees. Other employees might assign a different meaning to it based on their communication network. If it is told by coworkers to one another, that suggests employees have accepted the story as indicative of organizational values. In this case, the story appears to be told by experienced employees who helped avoid the layoffs to employees who joined the organization recently. This indicates that the experienced employees believe the story expresses important organizational values and practices that the newer employees should know.

For the third step, there is a clear ritual being addressed in the story. The ritual in this case is the use of layoffs to balance the bottom line for organizations during tough economic times. This occurs periodically in many workplaces. In 2008, widespread layoffs resulted from the economic recession and eventually led to an increase in the unemployment rate in the United States from 5% to 9.5%. The fact that this particular story addresses the layoff ritual with a different outcome makes the story particularly important as part of this organization's culture because it suggests that this organization handles layoffs differently than many organizations. In some instances there may also be a ritual to telling the story. For example, if the story is always told by the same person at new employee orientation, the ritual of when and how the story is told may also indicate the importance of the story to organizational members. There is no indication of a ritualistic telling of the story here.

For the fourth step, the economy is clearly the main villain, but executives at other companies who laid off employees are also likely considered villains for not protecting their employees. There is clearly one main hero in the story, the company president who decided that if everyone took a 10% cut, then they could avoid layoffs; he is also a hero for taking a 10% cut as well. However, beyond the president, other employees are also heroes for agreeing to sacrifice to protect each other's jobs rather than be greedy.

Based on the previous steps, there seem to be some important values and practices being espoused through this simple narrative. For the fifth and final step, the analysis suggests that management will support its key value of not laying off employees through creative thinking even in hard times. In addition, their organization values cooperation over self-interest; employees in this organization are expected to sacrifice for the common good of all employees. Overall, it seems that the organization values its employees more than profits.

Similar stories exist in other organizations, such as the story of the Malden Mills company whose CEO decided to continue to pay its employees while rebuilding a plant that was destroyed by fire (http://www.cbsnews.com/news/the-mensch-of-malden-mills/). To provide a broad understanding of an organization's culture using script analysis, a researcher should collect multiple stories and then examine how the collective analysis provides an understanding of the values, beliefs, and practices of the organization. This type of multistory research explored the culture of one university (Kramer & Berman, 2001) but could be conducted on any organization, large or small. From a structuration theory perspective, these organizational stories are artifacts that become resources, which can be used to reinforce specific values and behaviors over time as the organization's culture is recreated through the telling of the stories. The introduction of new stories has the potential for changing an organization's culture.

Ritual Analysis

A ritual analysis is quite similar to a script analysis but differs from it in a couple of important ways. A ritual analysis assumes that the common formal or informal rituals of an organization are indicative of its culture. Rituals are symbolic affairs that usually mark changes or turning points. The analysis includes four steps: (a) identify a ritual; (b) classify the ritual; (c) consider characteristics of the ritual, such as how or where it occurs and who is involved or excluded from the ritual; and (d) draw conclusions about the values and practices of the organization's culture.

In identifying a ritual, it is important to consider both formal and informal rituals. Formal rituals in organizations include activities such as graduations, work anniversary recognition ceremonies, annual picnics, and a host of others. Informal rituals might include personal rituals such as greeting everyone in the morning, going out for happy hour, or celebrating birthdays.

Rituals can generally be classified as one of six types (Trice & Beyer, 1984). *Rites of passage* indicate making important transitions indicative of success. These rites include being initiated or inducted into the organization, being promoted, or retiring. *Rites of degradation* are also transitions but indicative of failure. These rites include being demoted or moved laterally due to incompetence in a position. *Rites of enhancement* provide recognition for success but without necessarily including a transition. For example, receiving the employee of the month award or being recognized for 25 years of service recognizes accomplishments without providing any formal change in status. *Rites of renewal* are common in some organizations. These include rituals like company retreats, training and development programs that may be offered or mandated for employees and are designed to reinvigorate the employee. *Rites of conflict reduction* are activities designed to address conflict between two parties and often include negotiation. A common example is union negotiations in some organizations, but other grievance or appeal processes are also examples. *Rites of integration* bring people together usually for some sort of celebration. Company picnics, Christmas parties, and after-work happy hour breaks at a local eatery are all examples of these. It is important to recognize the type of ritual to understand its meaning for the culture of the organization.

In analyzing the ritual, it is important to consider how the ritual is observed and who is included or excluded in the activity. For example, if an organization chooses to include or exclude family and friends from an enhancement ritual, this sends different messages about work–life boundary norms. If a promotion is announced privately or via email rather than at a department meeting, it also has a different meaning. Conclusions are drawn as the final step of the four-step ritual analysis. For example, consider the description of an informal ritual:

> The social workers in this social service agency usually all get together at the same local restaurant for happy hour every Friday after work for an hour or two before they leave for the weekend. Managers are never invited. In fact, if someone is promoted to management, they usually come one last time to celebrate with their friends, but then no longer attend.

Classifying this ritual is relatively easy. This informal ritual is primarily an integration ritual for employees. It also becomes a rite of passage ritual occasionally when they celebrate someone's promotion. To understand the culture of the organization, it is important to note that managers are never included, even if they were former peers. It is also important to note that it occurs off-site and after work, which means that participants can discuss aspects of the organization in ways they cannot at work. It would likely take knowing a bit more about the characteristics of this ritual to understand what it says about the organizational culture. In particular, it would be important to know what they discuss that creates the camaraderie for participants. If happy hour is often a gripe session about management, the ritual suggests that the culture includes a somewhat adversarial separation of management from lower level employees. If they relax by sharing stories of the clients they serve and then discuss a lot of topics unrelated to work, the ritual should not be read as separating themselves from management.

Much like the script analysis, analyzing a number of rituals in an organization provides a better insight into the overall culture of the organization than an analysis of just one. But indicative of structuration theory, the repetition of the rituals recreates certain cultural values. The introduction of a new ritual can gradually change the culture, such as if managers in the organization started inviting the social workers to join them once a month for happy hour on Thursday, it would begin to create a somewhat different culture.

Metaphor Analysis

An alternative approach to discovering the culture of an organization is a metaphor analysis. Metaphors are comparisons of one phenomenon to another to provide insight into the meaning of the first. From this perspective, metaphors that individuals use to describe their workplace reveal the values, beliefs, and appropriate behaviors for the organization. Conducting a metaphor analysis generally involves four steps. First, the researcher usually interviews organizational members and has them talk about what it is like to work in their organization. As an alternative, the researcher could simply observe and listen as people talk about work. Second, the researcher identifies common or repetitive metaphorical language used to describe work. For example, there might be frequent references to "making a profit," "the bottom line," and "future growth." Someone might actually describe the workplace using a specific metaphor such as, "Working as a manager here is a lot like herding cats; everyone wants to go a different direction." The third step involves grouping the repetitive language and metaphors that were identified to see if there is a unifying theme represented. The last step is to draw conclusions about the culture of the organization.

Most readers have some idea of the image that Disney World tries to convey to the public through its advertising. The corporation wants people to think of Disney World as a fun place to take families for vacation. Smith and Eisenberg (1987) provided an example of a metaphor analysis based on their interviews of Disney managers and employees.

During the analysis, Smith and Eisenberg (1987) found repetitive language that supported two broad metaphors. For example, they found that that the Disney employees referred to themselves as "cast members" who wore "costumes" and maintained a particular appearance. Cast members followed "scripts" as they "performed" their "roles." The parking lot was referred to as the outer lobby with ticket booths referred to as the box office. Taken together, the researchers concluded that there was a root metaphor of "the Disney experience as drama." The researchers reported that none of the people they interviewed (cast members) ever used words like customers, uniforms, or amusement park to describe their workplace. This pattern of language seems to indicate how accepted or taken for granted this metaphor of performance was as part of the culture and its customer service emphasis to its "guests."

In their interviews, Smith and Eisenberg (1987) also found evidence of a second metaphor, which they identified as "the Disney Experience as Family." At first, participants described Disney as a friendly, wholesome place for family entertainment with the expectation that this language would improve employee–customer relations. However, by referring to everyone, including the CEO, on a first name basis and providing "Disneyland University" to offer career activities, there gradually developed a sense among employees that this was a paternalistic organization that took care of its family. Long-time employees eventually came to accept that management considered them

Enron's Metaphors

In early 2001, the Enron Corporation collapsed under the weight of its own unethical business dealings. The company's president and chief financial officer were indicted on accounting and securities fraud. The collapse of the organization devastated thousands of employees whose retirement plans were intertwined with the fate of the corporation. Professor Anna Turnage (2013) undertook a metaphor analysis of Enron's email messages sent to Enron's president as a means of understanding the organization's culture in which the unethical business deals were done. Prior to the management team's wrongdoings becoming known to the public, emails sent and received by organizational members contained machine and business metaphors that emphasized Enron's machine-like functionality and productivity. Later, after the top management's malfeasance became public, employees' metaphor usage with the president shifted to ethics and human body metaphors. Metaphors of machines were replaced with metaphors such as Enron is "morally bankrupt" and employees felt "slapped in the face." How might Enron's culture as a "machine" have encouraged its unethical business practices? What does the shifting metaphorical usage imply about Enron's culture as the wrongdoing became known to employees?

family members rather than employees. They talked about employee-to-employee relations using language like "brothers and sisters," "family-like," or "marriage" to describe the relationship of the employees to each other and management.

Faced with economic troubles at one point, management proposed a wage freeze and elimination of some benefits for future employees to improve the organization's economic position. The family metaphor may have exacerbated their negative experience of management's actions. Employees eventually went on strike for 22 days. According to Smith and Eisenberg (1987), after the strike ended, there continued to be tension between management and veteran employees over management's failure to "live out" the family metaphor in their decision-making. Interestingly, the employees still used family language to describe the conflict, only in an unkind way, saying that management "treated us like children." The original use of the family metaphor of Disney as family entertainment continues to this day.

Together, the two metaphors and how they changed over time provided an understanding of Disney's culture. Disney's culture values presenting a show or performance for the guests that provides them with family-friendly entertainment. That familial relationship does not extend to employees. Although it treats its employees relatively well, Disney is still a business that must make a profit.

Many organizations have used language that is consistent with some root metaphor. It is not unusual for other organizations to use the family metaphor, and it is not just in small, family-owned businesses. Sometimes when the metaphor seems particularly inappropriate, the employees resist the metaphor with comments like, "Yes, it's a family, just a dysfunctional one."

Reflective Comment Analysis

The reflective comment analysis method is an interesting, but seldom used, method of analyzing the culture of an organization. Instead of examining artifacts like stories and rituals, or language used in interviews to describe the workplace, this approach examines the decision-making of the organization to determine the values enacted by those decisions. The premise of this approach is that individuals will reflect their underlying values by providing explanations for their decisions. This approach involves three steps: (a) gathering decision-making comments, (b) identifying the criteria or decision-making premises used, and then (c) drawing conclusions about the values of the organization.

At least two different methods have been used to gather decision-making comments. One approach is to interview people and have them give accounts or explanations of how a group made their decisions (Cheney, 1983). The second approach is to record the actual decision making as it occurs (Geist & Chandler, 1984). There are issues related to both approaches. People giving accounts of decisions have the opportunity to justify that account in a way that frames the decision as following from prosocial or positive values, but it provides access to many different decisions. This approach could potentially include different individuals' accounts of the same decision to explore consistency among accounts. Recording the group as it makes the decision avoids the problem of individuals framing their account, but many decision makers will be reluctant to provide such access—and one particular decision may not represent the gamut of important values.

Once the decision-making comments are recorded and transcribed, the researcher then examines the text for instances in which decision rules or premises were expressed, whether the source of those rules are mentioned, and the other individuals to whom the decision makers plan to explain or justify their decisions (Geist & Chandler, 1984). Once these instances have been identified, they are examined for common themes that represent the organization's culture as enacted in its decision making.

A study using this approach examined the decision making of a psychiatric health-care organization making decisions about patients during weekly staff meetings (Geist & Chandler, 1984). The researchers found that ideas about good clinical practice gained support when they were consistent with the appropriate authority's opinion (such as a doctor's opinion). Also, groups supported decisions that could be defended to others, such as doctors, patients, and the family members. If an individual staff member did not like a decision because it seemed objectionable to them, that opinion did not influence the decision because it did not meet the standard.

In this case then, the decision-making demonstrated that the culture of the organization valued clinically or scientifically supported treatments rather than hunches or opinions. It also was one that valued being able to provide accounts to those in higher positions and family members. Values are expressed and enacted during the decision-making process, and it would be valuable to study several decisions to be more confident that the cultural values have been accurately identified.

Other organizations have different decision-making premises that express their values. For example, they may value customer service or supporting employee development. Although challenging to conduct, a reflective comment analysis provides a way to discover those values by examining the decision-making process.

Ethnography

Ethnography is a method of research for studying culture that was initially popular in the field of anthropology in the early 1900s. Anthropologists used this method of participant observation to study cultures, especially isolated cultures that were relatively unaffected by modern society. Ethnographers spent long periods of time living among the population of interest (e.g., the native tribe) before describing its culture.

An organizational scholar conducts an ethnography in much the same way by joining and becoming a member of the organization and then producing a document that describes the organization's culture. The goal is to gain an insider's perspective of the organization by communicating as one of its members and collecting other communication evidence such as written or electronic messages. Conducting an organizational ethnography generally involves four steps: (a) gaining access to join the organization,

(b) participating and observing in the organization and keeping field notes (a diary of sorts), (c) conducting interviews with members to gain a more accurate understanding of the lived experiences of members and/or collecting documents the organization produces, and (d) writing a description of the culture of the organization.

For example, I conducted an organizational ethnography to understand the culture of one nonprofit organization, a community theater (Kramer, 2002). I joined the community theater group by trying out for one of its productions. After being cast in a role, I gained permission from organizational members to conduct the study including the production staff, the cast, and the directors. In addition to participating and observing, I interviewed nearly all of the individuals involved. Then, based on my analysis of the data, I drew a number of conclusions about some of the unique characteristics of the organization's culture.

Because the production was essentially a temporary organization made up entirely of volunteers, its culture had a number of unique characteristics. One characteristic of the culture was the very public and frequent communication of positive feedback. In many organizational settings, feedback is infrequent (e.g., annual reviews) and private. However, in the community theater organization, the director praised participants frequently and immediately during and after rehearsals, usually in front of the rest of the cast. This public and frequent praise seemed important for achieving the organizational goals in a short time period.

Although there was tension between members' commitment to the production and their other life activities, a high level of commitment was expected of them. This was a temporary commitment, but for the duration of the production, members prioritized rehearsals and performances over paid work and family obligations, even if this meant missing work, neglecting home duties, or not having time for friends. Participants communicated this commitment to people outside the organization to explain their neglect of work, family, and friends, and disparaged those who did not make similar commitments.

Another unique aspect of the volunteer culture was its very fluid membership and roles. Despite the desire for strong temporary commitment to the production, individuals frequently left or joined the production, especially during the first weeks of rehearsal. This resulted in other participants changing roles or filling multiple roles to cover gaps left by someone's departure. There was a general attitude of "help wherever you can."

A final unique characteristic of the culture involved the frequent use of wordplay and joking during organizational interactions. This may not seem to be so unusual except that much of it used sexual innuendo that would likely be considered sexual harassment in other work or academic settings. In the community theater culture, this behavior was considered acceptable.

Overall, the culture of this particular volunteer organization included frequent verbal praise and playful banter between members that might be inappropriate in other contexts. It also included expectations of strong temporary commitment to the production over other work and family commitments, as well as flexibility and adaptability when some members failed to meet that commitment standard. This example of an ethnography of a temporary organization of volunteers illustrates how ethnography is a useful method for studying an organization's culture.

A Comparison of Five Methods of Cultural Analysis

Table 6.1 provides a comparison of the five methods of analyzing culture. It is important to note that each method uses slightly different data, and yet each leads to an understanding of the values and beliefs of the organization.

Because all five approaches can provide similar insights into the culture of an organization, it can be challenging to decide which research approach to use. The choice is likely determined by three primary factors: research focus, access, and time. The researcher's focus is an important factor in determining the method. If the researcher is primarily interested in decision-making criteria as an indication of the organization's values, then the reflective comment analysis is really the only appropriate way to do the study.

TABLE 6.1 A Comparison of Five Methods of Analyzing Organizational Culture

	Script Analysis	Ritual Analysis	Metaphor Analysis	Reflective Comment Analysis	Ethnography
Data or artifacts	Stories told including myths and legends	Formal ceremonies and informal routine activities	Interviews about work and organization	Decision-making records or accounts of decision making	Participant-observation field notes and interviews
Analysis	Identify networks Rites/rituals Heroes and/or villains	Classify ritual type and characteristics	Identify repeated language underlying metaphors	Identify decision criteria	Conduct systematic analysis of data
Conclusions	Values and beliefs	Values and beliefs	Values and beliefs	Values and beliefs	Values and beliefs

If the focus is on a broader concern about the general values and beliefs that guide behavior, then most of the approaches could work. Access can also be a factor. Obtaining permission to record decision-making meetings is quite challenging, but company documents that tell its stories and report on its ceremonies can often be accessed by anyone. Finally, time may be a factor. Conducting an ethnography is more time consuming than the other approaches, which also vary in the amount of time they require. Considering the research focus, access, and time should help the researcher decide on a method.

Applying Three Research Perspectives to Organizational Culture

Based on the information in Chapter 1, it should be apparent which perspective led to an emphasis on the study of organizational culture. However, all three perspectives have been used to examine organizational culture. To see how they each view culture differently, again consider the opening scenario of the family restaurant.

The Post-Positivist Perspective

Post-positivists generally view organizational culture as a tool for management. From this perspective, having a particular type of organizational culture is associated with positive outcomes. This approach was made popular by the best-selling book *In Search of Excellence* by Peters and Waterman (1982). The authors tried to identify characteristics of the cultures of successful organizations. Taking this approach to examine the family restaurant, the researcher would focus attention on whether hiring mostly family members and maintaining the relaxed, friendly atmosphere was positively associated with the organization's viability and profits. The fact that a change in cooks, rather than the maintenance of this friendly culture, led to a boost in sales would suggest that valuing the quality of the product rather than atmosphere may create a more effective organization.

The Interpretive Perspective

The study of organizational communication grew out of an interpretive perspective; thus, its focus would be on the shared meanings that exist in the organization. As noted earlier in the analysis, there appears to be a unified culture in which all the employees value commitment and relationships between owners and employees and between employees and customers. The culture is divided into two subcultures of family members and others employees, which creates some ambiguity about opportunity in the organization.

The Critical Perspective

The critical perspective would focus attention on areas of oppression within the organization. This approach would quickly focus on the issue of nepotism in the organization. For the critical scholar, nepotism in this organization creates unequal opportunities. Family members receive benefits, and the other employees are disadvantaged. The goal of the critical scholars would be to find ways to eliminate these discrepancies. This might involve communicating clear performance standards so that family members do not advance over more qualified non-family members. Selecting a non-family member as manager of the new restaurant would be one way to address this problem.

Which approach is more insightful? In the same way that Martin (1992) argues that applying three perspectives on organizational culture provides a more complete understanding of an organization's culture, examining the culture from the three different researcher perspectives provides different insights into the organization.

Summary

In this chapter, we define organizational culture as the values and assumptions of an organization as expressed through artifacts—such as norms, stories, and rituals—that create and recreate the organization through the structuration process. We then present a more complex approach to understanding organizational culture as containing integrated or unifying characteristics, differentiating characteristics that create subcultures, and ambiguous or fragmented characteristics that are difficult to interpret. We go on to describe five different approaches to analyzing an organization's culture: a script analysis, a ritual analysis, a metaphor analysis, a reflective comment analysis, and ethnography. In the final section, we demonstrate that although the study of organizational culture grew out of an interpretive perspective, it can be studied from a postpositivist and critical perspective as well.

CHAPTER 7

Communication with Organizational Members

In college, Taylor had not planned to work for a social welfare agency. The organization was a for-profit business but received most of its funding from reimbursements from the government for providing services to clients.

Taylor's choice turned out well for the most part. Helping clients get the services that they were eligible for could be very rewarding, such as when clients moved into new living quarters or received medical treatments they could not afford.

Work relationships were generally positive as well. Take, for example, the group of case workers Taylor worked with daily. Even though they varied in educational background and age, they got along well. Most of them helped each other with answers to questions about how to serve a client or how to manage the paperwork that always seemed to pile up. They supported each other as they dealt with the inevitable disappointment when clients failed to follow advice and got evicted or ended up in the hospital or jail. There were many times Taylor felt upset when things turned out poorly despite all the preparation and planning that was done.

Taylor had "lost it" only once at work and expressed angry emotions openly about a particularly difficult client, but that was in a private conversation with Morgan. The two of them became best friends over the past year. Even though they came to social work via different routes—Morgan majored in social work in college whereas Taylor was a communication major—they had a lot in common. They both played tennis and enjoyed hiking in the nearby national park.

Some case workers were more than just work colleagues. Taylor enjoyed the biweekly Friday after-work trips to try out different local restaurants. There were about 6 regulars each time, but often 10 or more. Mostly they had a good time eating, drinking, talking, and laughing. They felt free to gripe about clients, but they also discussed politics, the economy, national issues, and sometimes even their bosses.

There wasn't much to complain about regarding Taylor's case manager, Sydney. Sydney had an open door policy and seemed to mean it. When necessary, Taylor felt comfortable going in to discuss issues about a particular client or how to cut through red tape. During those talks, Sydney often gave positive feedback on how Taylor handled client cases and only occasionally offered suggestion for improving. Taylor recognized that Morgan had a closer relationship with Sydney. Sydney would consult with Morgan on decisions, and Taylor usually felt like it was better to have Morgan present ideas to Sydney that the case workers identified for improving "best practices." Sydney just seemed more open to suggestions if they came through Morgan.

As a result, Taylor counted on a former coworker, Pat, for career and personal advice instead of Sydney. Taylor could count on Pat, who was promoted to a manager in a different department, to know the real scoop on what was going on. Pat knew about job openings in the company before they were posted and helped Taylor plan out a career trajectory in the agency. Pat helped Taylor get the promotion that was happening next week. The bad part about the promotion was that it would be harder for Taylor to socialize with the other case workers.

There was one "difficult employee" that everyone tried to avoid. To put it lightly, Jamie was a force to be reckoned with, always aggressive, always willing to put someone down. When it came to Jamie, Taylor was glad to be moving to a different department.

· · · · ·

Interpersonal relationships are a major part of organizational membership. As mentioned in Chapter 3, during the encounter phase, newcomers face uncertainty about their relationships with supervisors, coworkers, and other work-related contacts such as customers and clients. This uncertainty includes not knowing how to interact to get work done as well as how to relate to others informally or socially. Interpersonal relationships are important initially but also throughout the duration of a person's involvement in an organization—be it is as an employee or a volunteer.

This scenario introduces many facets of organizational relationships that we address in this chapter. Developing positive relationships at work is an especially important part of the process of socialization for newcomers. Newcomers are unlikely to feel accepted in the organization or feel commitment to it until they have developed positive interpersonal relationships. But maintaining positive relationships is important throughout your lifespan of organizational experiences. It is often the positive interpersonal relationships that influence the decision to continue or discontinue participating in a particular organization. Many different types of organizational relationships need to be managed, such as supervisor to subordinate relationships, peer relationships, and mentoring relationships. In this chapter, we consider each of these important workplace relationships as well as the topic of emotion management in workplace interactions.

Supervisor–Subordinate Communication

The supervisor–subordinate relationship is often considered the most important interpersonal relationship by employees. In this chapter, we do not focus on the supervisor or manager as the leader of the department or division, which we discuss in the next chapter on leadership, but rather on the interpersonal relationship between the supervisor and various subordinates, that is, how they communicate and maintain their relationships with each other. The discussion of supervisor–subordinate communication is divided into three parts: average supervisor communication style, differentiated supervisor communication style, and the influence of supervisor–subordinate communication.

Average Supervisor Communication Style

Much of the research on supervisor–subordinate communication, especially the early research concerning it, assumed that supervisors communicated to all of their subordinates with an average style such that they treated all their subordinates quite similarly. The goal of the research was to describe supervisor–subordinate communication that was typical of effective supervisors as compared to ineffective ones or to identify or describe the communication style that supervisors should use with their subordinates. The very early research using this approach was summarized over 35 years ago (Jablin, 1979). That research was organized into the following areas. Additional research has been conducted in many of those areas since then, but not all.

Interaction Patterns. Supervisors spend between one-third and two-thirds of their time communicating face to face and electronically with subordinates. Much of that time is spent communicating job responsibilities, deadlines, and performance feedback to subordinates; but they also communicate about topics like sports and weather, and, less often, about personal topics like families. In general, perceptions of the interaction patterns between supervisor and subordinates are significantly different (Jablin, 1979). On average, supervisors perceive that they communicate with subordinates more frequently than their subordinates perceive they communicate with them. Similarly, on average, subordinates perceive that they communicate to their supervisors more frequently than their supervisors perceive they receive communication from subordinates.

Openness to Communication. Open supervisor–subordinate communication involves a willingness of both parties to be clear, candid, and honest in their communication.

Openness involves a willingness to listen as well as provide information. Open communication is often reciprocal. When supervisors listen and respond positively to messages from their subordinates, subordinates respond by providing more information to their supervisors. Alternatively, if supervisors reject, criticize, or avoid communication from their subordinates, subordinates will likely withhold information from supervisors. Overall, employees are more likely to communicate their ideas and disagreements openly when they have positive and trusting relationships with their supervisors (Kassing, 2009).

Upward Distortion. As was mentioned in Chapter 5 under issues with upward communication, communication to supervisors is often overly positive and tends to consist of softened negative information. Upward distortion is most likely to occur when subordinates do not trust the supervisor, when the supervisor has power over the subordinate's career advancement, and when the subordinate has high aspirations for advancement. In addition, supervisors sometimes discourage accurate upward information by responding negatively or even inadvertently punishing subordinates for providing negative but accurate information. When supervisors fail to cultivate trusting interpersonal relationships with subordinates and subsequently do not receive unequivocal corrective information and opinions from their subordinates, an entire organization's ability to learn and adapt can be hindered (Bisel, Messersmith, & Kelley, 2012).

Upward Influence. A number of studies have demonstrated that the amount of influence supervisors have with their supervisors has an influence on their supervisor–subordinate communication. In particular, subordinates tend to be more satisfied and more likely to communicate to supervisors who are perceived as having strong upward influence with their own supervisors. This so-called Pelz effect is particularly true for subordinates who also perceive their supervisors as supportive, although it has a more limited effect for subordinates who perceive their supervisors as unsupportive (Jablin, 1980). Some research suggests that there may be an upper limit to this pattern such that if a supervisor is perceived as having too much upward influence, this may encourage subordinates to reduce their communication (House, Filley, & Gujarati, 1971). Overall, there is generally a positive relationship between supervisors' upward influence and subordinates' satisfaction with their relationship.

Semantic Information Distance. *Semantic information distance* is the gap that can exist between how supervisors and subordinates attribute meaning to words, ideas, and events. When supervisors and subordinates share a similar understanding or perception

The Pelz Effect

The Pelz effect is the observation that subordinates are more open and satisfied with their boss when they perceive the boss is influential with his or her own boss (i.e., the boss's boss). That insight can be applied by supervisors who want to increase their subordinates' openness and satisfaction. How? Supervisors can tell the story of instances when they were influential with their own boss to their subordinates. Those quick stories can leave subordinates with the idea that "my boss is influential with my boss's boss." In turn, the Pelz effect, with its increased openness and satisfaction, will tend to follow. How can a supervisor achieve this goal without appearing to be bragging?

of their work duties, abilities, and company culture, there is very little semantic information distance, and subordinates tend to have higher morale. Unfortunately, often due to lack of effective communication, semantic information distance can be quite large, particularly when the communication is ambiguous. For example, suppose a supervisor tells subordinates to "do excellent work" on a project for an important customer. The supervisor merely wished to reinforce that they should do their usual high quality work. They may interpret that to mean that they should "spend whatever it takes" to achieve an outstanding final product. The supervisor may only discover the semantic information distance when the project comes in 25% over budget.

Effective versus Ineffective Supervisors. A great deal of research has attempted to distinguish between effective and ineffective supervisors. We summarize a few important findings here (Jablin, 1979). Effective supervisors communicate in such a way as to initiate structure that leads to completing tasks. They provide a strong sense that they are oriented toward their subordinates and concerned about their needs and feelings. More effective supervisors are communication minded. They enjoy talking with their subordinates, seek rather than avoid opportunities to communicate, and demonstrate immediacy by being willing and empathic listeners. In addition, they tend to ask or persuade their subordinates to do things rather than demand or tell them what to do. More effective supervisors pass on information to subordinates. They provide explanations and advance notices for changes that will affect the subordinates.

Feedback. A very important aspect of supervisor–subordinate communication is providing feedback. Unfortunately, supervisors are often reluctant to provide accurate feedback that includes positive and negative information, whereas subordinates tend to be reluctant to seek negative feedback and appraisal information (Sias, 2009). Supervisors who provide positive feedback and reinforcement tend to have better performing and more satisfied subordinates. By contrast, those who provide only negative and critical feedback are more likely to be perceived as ineffective. A cycle of positive performance and feedback tends to repeat itself, as does a cycle of poor performance and negative feedback. The challenge in being an effective supervisor involves providing the correct balance of positive feedback without overlooking problems so that employee performance can improve.

Systemic Factors. Because organizations have a variety of structures and technologies, it is difficult to provide generalizations about effective or ineffective supervisor–subordinate communication in all the variations that are possible. That said, it does seem that location in the hierarchy has in influence on supervisor–subordinate communication (Jablin, 1979). Those in higher level positions in an organization are more likely to develop open communication relationships with their subordinates and involve them in decision-making than those in lower level management or supervisory

COMMUNICATION CHALLENGE

"Living" versus "Having" an Open Door Policy

Organizational communication scholars recommend that supervisors "live" an open door policy and not merely "have" an open door policy. An open door policy refers to the idea that subordinates have a standing invitation to come and discuss issues with supervisors. When supervisors espouse having an open door policy but in practice are unavailable or hostile to subordinates who want to discuss issues, the espoused policy creates an expectation that is then violated by the practice. Thus, it is likely that having an open door policy and not practicing it creates more damage to supervisor–subordinate relationships than not having such a policy, although being welcoming in practice. What are some specific verbal and nonverbal communication messages that support or contradict an open door policy?

positions working with entry-level employees. This difference may in part be due to that fact that the job responsibilities of those in higher level positions require them to make more unique or unusual decisions, and thus, they ask their subordinates for their input more often. Those in lower level positions may primarily make routine decisions or enact the decision made by upper management and so have fewer reasons to consult their subordinates.

© 2004 Ted Goff

"I don't have time to write performance reviews, so I'll just criticize you in public from time to time."

Providing Feedback

Differentiated Supervisor Communication Style

Other research on supervisor–subordinate communication challenges the notion that supervisors treat subordinates similarly or equally. Instead, this research indicates that supervisors actually treat their subordinates differentially. This finding should not come as a surprise to most readers. We have all observed that supervisors seem to have certain employees that they trust more and interact with more than others. This is not to say that the other employees who are not the supervisor's favorite employee are necessarily treated poorly or inappropriately, just differently.

Originally called vertical dyad linking by George Graen and his research associates (Dansereau, Graen, & Haga, 1975), this approach to studying supervisor–subordinate communication has focused on describing how supervisors communicate and maintain different types of relationships with different groups of subordinates. Vertical dyad linkage later became known as leader–member exchange (LMX) theory and has resulted in a large body of research that has been summarized in a variety of places (e.g., Graen, 2003; Graen & Uhl-Bien, 1995). Depending on the researcher, differential supervisor–subordinate relationships are divided into two or three different types of relationships, which are described in the following.

Partnership Relationships. Partnership or in-group relationships, also known as high LMX relationships, describe the close, personal relationship that supervisors have with some of their subordinates (Graen & Uhl-Bien, 1995). In these relationships, supervisors share more information than in other relationships. Their communication includes task-related information, such as duties and responsibilities, and much more. In partnership relationships, the supervisor likely consults with the subordinate in decision-making, and they may work jointly on projects. The supervisor may give career advice and guidance, especially for a subordinate with career aspirations. The communication goes beyond work issues to most likely include more personal information about life away from work, and perhaps the pair may even socialize together on occasion. Subordinates in high LMX relationships with their supervisor tend to receive more trust, information, and promotional opportunities than low LMX subordinates.

A study of the communication in partnership relationships found specific communication patterns were common (Fairhurst & Chandler, 1989). During their conversations, both supervisors and subordinates felt comfortable interrupting one another. Subordinates felt comfortable trying to influence the decisions of supervisors, and supervisors offered support for the decisions that subordinates made in completing their work duties. Overall, there appeared to be little power distance between the supervisors and subordinates in these high LMX relationships. To an outsider, their conversations might appear to be between peers or friends rather than between supervisors and subordinates.

Overseer Relationships. By contrast, overseer or out-group relationships, also called low LMX relationships, describe the formal, relatively impersonal relationships supervisors have with another group of subordinates (Graen & Uhl-Bien, 1995). In overseer relationships, supervisors generally only share the information necessary for subordinates to do their jobs appropriately. They exchange information as necessary, but the supervisors do not take a personal interest in the subordinates. A supervisor in an overseer relationship may be unaware of the career aspirations of these subordinates and is unlikely to make subordinates aware of opportunities for advancement. Supervisors may share impersonal social information with outgroup subordinates, such as conversations about the weather or sports, but they are unlikely to socialize together other than at organizational functions.

A study of communication in overseer relationships found quite different patterns of communication than in partnership relationships (Fairhurst & Chandler, 1989). In overseer relationships, interactions tended to be brief, as the supervisor gave directives and the subordinate simply agreed. There was little give and take during the conversation. Overall, power distance was maintained, as the supervisor's decisions were not questioned and the subordinate did not interrupt during the short conversation.

Middle-Group Relationships. When a third group is included in studies of LMX, it is simply called the *middle group* and it is somewhere between the two extremes of the partnership and overseer relationships. A middle-group relationship would include more information exchange and more personal communication than an overseer relationship, but it would not be as personal as the partnership relationship. The subordinate is not likely to participate much in decision-making but may find that the supervisor does listen when approached because the power distance is somewhat ambiguous (Fairhurst & Chandler, 1989). Recent LMX research suggests that middle-group relationships might be short-lived, as supervisors tend to desire certainty in deciding how much they can expect to trust a particular subordinate. In other words, middle-group relationships might exist for a short time while supervisors assess whether to deem a particular subordinate as trustworthy or not and then make partnership or overseer relationships accordingly (Kelley & Bisel, 2014).

Relationship Development. An important question concerns why some individuals develop partnership relationships, whereas others develop overseer relationships. Two explanations are generally given. One explanation suggests that personal characteristics determine the likelihood of developing partnership relationships (Graen & Uhl-Bien, 1995). Subordinates who are dependable, competent, optimistic, and have a desire to experience growth in their work and career are more likely to develop partnership relationships. In addition, they generally have an internal locus of control and high self-efficacy, meaning that they believe they can and do control their situation rather than that they are controlled by it. In addition, they see the value in developing relationships with their supervisors and so put effort into developing mutual trust, respect, and obligation with their supervisors. Other personal similarities also seem to increase the likelihood of developing partnership relationships including having similar demographic characteristics, such as having lived in similar locations or attended the same schools, or having similar cognitive and decision-making skills.

The second explanation suggests that it simply takes time for partnership relationships to develop (Graen & Uhl-Bien, 1995). Newcomers will have a distant, overseer relationship with their supervisors initially because they are largely strangers and have not had the opportunity to develop trust. Over time, the supervisor may offer opportunities for the subordinate to demonstrate competence and build trust. As the supervisor and subordinate communicate more frequently, they discuss more topics and develop a more personal relationship. As a result, they will gradually develop a middle-group and then partnership relationship. A contrary view notices that some subordinates immediately develop partnership relationships, and some people never move beyond overseer relationships.

Both explanations seem to fail to consider the supervisor's role sufficiently. Supervisors who have more than a few subordinates to manage may simply lack the time to maintain the communication relationships necessary for a partnership relationship with everyone. In addition, supervisors may also have personal characteristics or preferences that result in them developing few partnership relationships to maintain their supervisory role.

Outcomes of Supervisor–Subordinate Communication

Because supervisor–subordinate communication is such an important part of organizational experiences, it is not surprising that it also has a significant influence on subordinate outcomes. According to the average supervisor style research, those subordinates with more open communication relationships with their supervisors and whose supervisors who are generally more effective are more satisfied, more productive, and have higher morale—and thus are less likely to leave their organization (Jablin, 1979; Sias, 2009). Similarly, subordinates in partnership relationships demonstrate more prosocial and extra-role activities on behalf of the organization (i.e., organizational citizenship behaviors) as well as have more positive attitudes about job climate, procedural justice in the organization, and their own sense of empowerment (Graen & Uhl-Bien, 1995). Overall, as the quality of the supervisor relationship improves, subordinates report receiving a greater quantity and a higher quality of information from their supervisors (Sias, 2005); and those in partnership relationships are more satisfied, more committed, and less likely to leave the organization. Furthermore, subordinates in high LMX relationship with their supervisors receive higher job performance evaluations and are more innovative and creative (Sias, 2009).

Summary of Supervisor–Subordinate Communication

In the social welfare agency scenario, from an average supervisor communication style perspective, it appears that Taylor and the other case workers have an open communication relationship with their supervisor, Sydney, who espouses and practices an open door policy. Sydney listens to them and seems to respond to their ideas positively, especially if Morgan presents those ideas. As a result, we would expect that there would be limited upward distortion of communication, except perhaps from a case worker who has high aspirations for advancement in the organization. There would be little semantic information difference in the understanding of the workplace, although the case workers and Sydney likely have different perceptions of how frequently each communicates with the other. Sydney seems to provide Taylor with a good mixture of mostly positive feedback with occasional suggestions for improvement; but because case workers are low in the organizational hierarchy, we would not expect they would be regularly involved in decision making with Sydney. Overall, the case workers would likely rate Sydney as an effective supervisor like Taylor seems to do and to be satisfied with their supervisor–subordinate relationship.

From a differentiated supervisor perspective, it appears that the supervisor, Sydney, has differential relationships with the case workers. Based on Taylor's observation, it appears that Madison and Sydney have a partnership relationship. They discuss issues in a way that influences decision making for the department. Taylor seems to have more of a middle-group relationship with Sydney. The two interact regularly, and it goes beyond just directives for getting work done; but Taylor does not seem to receive the kind of career advice and involvement in decision-making that Madison receives, perhaps indicating a middle-group relationship. Some of the case workers likely have overseer relationships, especially any new ones, because it may take time to develop middle-group and partnership relationships. Overall, we would expect to find that Taylor and the other case workers would be generally satisfied and that the department would generally be productive because "There wasn't much to complain about Taylor's case manager, Sydney."

Peer Communication

Peer or coworker communication may be almost as important as supervisor–subordinate communication because it is the type of communication that is most available and most common in organizations—to a large degree simply because employees generally have many more peers than supervisors (Reichers, 1987). So even though employees view their communication with their supervisors as more important than peer communication, they actually rely more on peers for information they need to do their jobs (Comer, 1991). Because peers often do similar work or have done the same job in the past, peers provide valuable information for completing work and relevant feedback. For newcomers in particular, peers can provide additional information about the unwritten rules and the organizational way of doing things that may not be included in orientation programs or in communication from the supervisor (Miller & Jablin, 1991).

Peer Social Support

In addition to task-related information, peers are an important source of social support. Employees routinely face a range of stressors in their work environment including uncertainty, role ambiguity, emotional labor, organizational politics, information overload and underload, conflict, and planned changes among others (Louis, 1980; Miller, Ellis, Zook, & Lyles, 1990). Peers can provide the kind of support that helps employees cope with stressors and reduce the negative effects of them. Research suggests peers provide three types of social support (Miller, Considine, & Garner, 2007).

1. *Instrumental support* provides tangible or physical assistance. This support might be in the form of providing materials or equipment needed to complete a job (e.g., access to the copier) or even assistance in completing a job (e.g., helping to finish a report).

2. *Informational support* provides insight and advice needed to manage uncertainty or ambiguity. This support might include information needed to complete a job (e.g., you can access that information on the company website) or advice on how to interact appropriately with another organizational member (e.g., here's how you need to approach our supervisor).

3. *Emotional support* provides sympathy and empathy in dealing with stress. This support might include providing a safe place for complaining and venting or providing consolation after something has gone poorly (e.g., a shoulder to cry on) or praise and approval when something has gone well (e.g., a party to celebrate a promotion).

Types of Peer Communication Relationships

Not all peer relationships are equal. Peer relationships vary on a continuum based on the depth of information exchanged and depth of support offered (Kram & Isabella, 1985). The most common and least intimate relationships are *information peers*. Information peers are characterized by fairly limited information exchange, mostly work related. There is little exchange of social support and limited self-disclosure of personal information as well. Newcomers in particular are likely to have mostly information peer relationships (Sias, 2009).

Collegial peers are more personal and intimate than information peers. Collegial peers provide some social support and exchange more information. They have moderate levels of trust and disclose some personal information with each other as a result. According to one study, it can take on average about a year before newcomers feel like they developed collegial peer relationships so that they are comfortable sharing personal information (Sias & Cahill, 1998).

Special or close peer relationships are the least common. These relationships are what might be called best friends or at least "almost" best friends. In addition to the kinds of information that information and collegial peers share, special peers have a higher level of trust such that they rarely keep secrets from one another and disclose intimate information that may or may not be work related. They provide candid feedback to each other and provide high levels of support and friendship to each other. These are the least common, in part, because it takes an average of 5 years to develop such deep peer relationships at work (Sias & Cahill, 1998).

Outcomes of Peer Communication

The kind of peer communication an employee has affects a number of important outcomes. For example, social support from peers helps mitigate or reduce work-related strain and stressors (Viswesvaran, Sanchez, & Fisher, 1999). Employees with higher percentages of collegial and special peer relationships receive more information in general, and the quality of the information is also higher than for employees with high levels of information peers (Sias, 2005). Other outcomes are not surprising. Employees who report that they are satisfied with the quality of their peer relationships are more satisfied with their jobs and their professional development and growth, more committed to their organizations, more motivated in their work, and less likely to leave (Sias, 2009). It is not uncommon to meet someone who stays in a job that they do not particularly like because they enjoy the people they work with and stay to maintain those relationships.

Workplace Friendships

Although partnership relationships between supervisors and subordinates and special peer relationships have elements of friendship in them, we want to consider how friendships develop in the workplace. Friendships are different than other workplace relationships. Whereas supervisor–subordinate relationships are mandatory and so are many peer relationships due to work interdependence, friendships are completely voluntary relationships (Sias, 2014). Although they may develop out of other formal relationships, workplace friendships can develop between individuals who have no work-related relationship as well. A friendship development model suggest that workplace friendship develops over four stages (Boyd & Taylor, 1998).

Stage 1 Friendship Potential: This stage involves meeting and finding out about potential commonalities for friendship. This can include similar attitudes, activities, demographic factors, and even physical proximity.

Stage 2 Exploration: This stage involves further exploration of commonalities and cautious self-disclosure to determine if there can be an equitable relationship that is mutually beneficial.

Stage 3 Casual Friend: This stage involves increased communication and liking. More self-disclosure occurs as the relationship seems to be positive, and the pair may begin to do some social activity together outside of work.

Stage 4 Close Friend: This stage involves a commitment to friendship. It includes mutual support and high levels of trust and self-disclosure and most likely more activity together.

Different factors seem to drive the movement from one stage to another—and many relationships do not move beyond the first two stages, and few move to the fourth stage (Sias, 2009). The initial movement toward friendship is driven primarily by perceptions of similarities and personality compatibility. If there seems little potential for friendship, even proximity may not be sufficient for the friendship to develop. Additional friendship development occurs as individuals work on shared tasks or projects and begin socializing outside of work, although there is still likely some tentativeness in the casual friendship. Movement toward the close friend stage often occurs after significant events at work or away from work. Conflict with a mutual supervisor or company policy or problems away from work such as a family illness or marital problems often cause individuals to develop close friendships as they provide support to each other. It may be difficult for intimate friendship relationships to develop in many work settings.

Summary of Peer and Friendship Relations

The importance of peer relationships and friendships is illustrated in the opening scenario about the social welfare agency. Taylor seems to have developed positive relationships with other case workers. They provide instrumental and information support to each other to help each other complete their work, and they provide emotional support and a buffer against job burnout as they commiserate about clients who disappoint them by failing to follow their advice. Most of the case workers seem to have collegial peer relationships in which they support one another. The six who socialize together regularly are probably casual friends or maybe close friends. It seems that Taylor and Madison have developed a special or close relationship that would be considered close friendship as well. If it lasts after Taylor moves to a new department, it indicates the close friendship is continuing without the benefit of close proximity. Overall, we would expect that the case workers and Taylor are generally satisfied with their peer relationships.

Interaction of Supervisor and Peer Communication

In the previous sections, we discussed supervisor–subordinate relationships and peer relationships as if they are separate and unrelated. Research suggests, however, that the nature of the communication in one type of relationship influences the communication in the other. To begin, coworkers are aware of the kind of relationships their peers have with their supervisors (Sias & Jablin, 1995). They recognize if one of them has a partnership relationship or an overseer relationship with the supervisor.

The type of LMX relationship individuals have with their supervisors affect their interpersonal communication with peers (Sias & Jablin, 1995). From a coworker's perspective, a peer with a high LMX or partnership relationship is somewhat comparable to a teacher's pet in that the individual has a closer relationship with the supervisor than others. According to research, peers respond differently depending on whether that closer relationship is perceived as earned and deserved or not. If the coworker is deemed to be deserving of the close relationship with the supervisor due to competent work, then peers recognize the person as having legitimate influence on the supervisor. Peers may funnel ideas to the person hoping to use that person as a conduit for influencing the supervisor to make changes that they would like to see.

In other cases, a high LMX partnership relationship may be viewed as undeserved. Sometimes the individual is seen as having used excessive ingratiation or brown-nosing to gain an insider relationship with the supervisor rather than hard work (see Chapter 4). When that is their perception, the peers will tend to have a negative attitude toward the person and as a result reduce their communication to that person. They are likely to have information, or, at best, collegial relationships with that person. This pattern of communication will have a tendency to isolate the peer for what others deem to be the undeserved insider relationship with a supervisor.

Coworkers may also recognize that a peer has an overseer or out-group relationship with their supervisor. Again, depending on whether they perceive the relationships as deserved or undeserved influences their communication with the peer. If peers decide the person does not deserve the out-group relationship and does competent and reliable work, then peers will see this as the supervisor treating their peer unfairly. In such a case, the peers often will communicate social support and commiserate with the person, showing solidarity and including the person in their work circle. The unfair treatment by the supervisor actually results in closer relationships among peers.

Alternatively, if the coworker seems to deserve the overseer relationship by being unreliable or incompetent and failing to make an effort to improve, peers will avoid communicating with the person because they will not want to be identified with a poor coworker by their supervisor. This situation results in person being isolated from peers.

Supervisor–subordinate communication can have a general effect on peer communication as well. If the supervisor is generally inconsiderate or ineffective, this problem will likely cause a decrease in communication to the supervisor and an increase in peer communication, which can actually result in them developing closer relationships (Sias, 2009).

Summary of Supervisor–Peer Relationship Interaction

In the scenario for the social welfare agency, Morgan is apparently viewed by coworkers as having earned a close relationship with their manager, Sydney. Morgan is recognized as being competent and hard working. As a result, Taylor and the other case workers communicated their ideas to Morgan, who then communicates them to Sydney. This approach seemed to be satisfactory to everyone because Sydney is more often influenced by Morgan than if one of the other case workers presents their ideas. Due to a deserved partnership relationship, Morgan is used as a conduit for communication to Sydney, the supervisor.

Mentor(ing) Communication

"*Mentoring* refers to a specific type of relationship in which the mentor functions as a type of 'guide' for the development and career advancement of the protégé/mentee"

(Sias, 2009, p. 29). The relationship is somewhat different than other organizational relationships in that it is often considered a one-way relationship in which the mentor assists the protégé. It is now recognized that the mentor can also gain certain benefits from being a mentor, and it has been found that assigning someone a mentoring position can provide benefits such as increased motivation and satisfaction for employees in middle to late career positions who have become stagnant (Rotondo & Perrewé, 2000). As a result, mentoring can potentially serve multiple goals: Mentoring can help facilitate the adjustment process for newcomers and help groom experienced employees for potential advancement (Jablin, 2001) while also providing benefits for the mentors as well.

In its initial conceptualization, the study of mentoring was limited to relationships between an advanced or experienced organizational member (the mentor) and a newer, less experienced member (the protégé/mentee) who were not in a direct work relationship with each other. In other words, the original theorizing on the topic defined a mentor as an experienced employee in *another department or division* rather than one in the direct line of command with the protégé. However, more recent research demonstrates that communication with direct supervisors and peers can, and often does, serve valuable mentoring functions (Kram & Isabella, 1985; Sias, 2009).

The functions of mentoring communication include introducing the protégé to important organizational members, providing career trajectory information, and identifying career development and advancement opportunities. The focus is on assisting the protégé's career and not on improving organizational productivity and outcomes (Sias, 2009). Given these functions, a supervisor or peer can easily mentor someone by

COMMUNICATION CHALLENGE

Mentoring Communication

If you have been an employee for some time in your current job or a volunteer for some time in a nonprofit organization, you have the potential to be a mentor for newcomers to the organizations. What are some specific communication actions you can take to help the newer person learn what you already know? When and where could you interact with the person to share this information? How do you avoid being a pushy, know-it-all who annoys the newcomer?

introducing them to other organizational members in their communication network, by providing project advice and opportunities to learn valuable skills, or by creating high visibility for the individual. Much of this mentoring behavior arises in partnership supervisor–subordinate relationship communication or in collegial and special peer relationships and not just through senior people outside of a person's chain of command.

Research has explored the influence of formal and informal mentoring programs. In formal mentoring programs, a new employee is officially assigned a mentor for a specific period of time. In such programs, usually some effort is made to match a volunteer mentor with a protégé who has some similarities with the mentor. For informal programs, new employees are encouraged to seek out and select a mentor of their own choosing, and the relationship lasts as long as the two parties find it satisfying. The results of mentoring studies are somewhat inconsistent. Informal mentoring generally seems to provide more benefits than formal mentoring, but both provide benefits compared to not having a mentor (Sias, 2009). Those benefits include greater understanding of organizational issues beyond their specific job and higher levels of satisfaction with their jobs.

Sometimes mentoring relationships can become dysfunctional, particularly when the mentor is too domineering or the protégé too submissive. For example, the mentor may coerce the protégé into working on personal projects that benefit the mentor and provide little visibility for the protégé. When the mentoring relationship becomes dysfunctional, it can result in deception and even sabotage as the protégé experiences lower self-esteem, decreased job satisfaction, and higher absenteeism and turnover (Sias, 2009). Fortunately, these negative effects appear to occur very infrequently compared to the benefits.

Summary of Mentoring

In the scenario of the social welfare agency, Taylor seems to benefit from mentoring behaviors from a number of organizational members and from an informal mentoring relationship. The other case workers provide Taylor with helpful information that could be considered mentoring, as does Sydney, the department manager. More importantly, a former colleague, Pat, who is now in another department, seems well connected in the organization and provides insights into how the organization works and identifies career advancement opportunities.

Upside Down Mentoring?

The 2015 movie, *The Intern*, puts an unusual twist on the idea of mentoring. In the movie, retired and widowed Ben (played by Robert DeNiro) takes an internship in a fast growing startup company to relieve boredom. The owner Jules (played by Anne Hathaway) is overwhelmed with the growth of the company. Eventually the intern becomes the mentor for the owner's work and personal life. Is this an unlikely scenario? No doubt. But it raises the question, can a lower level employee, like a newcomer, mentor a high ranking employee? What communication strategies should you use if you try to "mentor up?"

Ben mentors Jules

Emotion Management in Interpersonal Interactions

So far, we have discussed communication in organizational relationships as if it involves primarily reasoned and deliberative interactions in which people talk about ideas and choose whether to share information in a rather thoughtful, stoic manner. It is important to recognize that interactions also always involve an emotional component. Even a stoic interaction involves emotion. Emotions can range from very positive to neutral to very negative. Probably most of our interactions are in the neutral or unemotional range, perhaps slightly more positive than negative. As a result, we may not think about neutral as an emotional state. In this section, we consider the emotional component of interactions including what causes emotional experiences; what are some of the common emotions in organizational settings; and finally, what are the emotion management expectations for communication in our relationships in organizational settings.

The Nature of Emotions in Interactions

Emotions are a complex phenomenon that involve a mixture of cognitive and physiological factors. That is to say that the experience of emotion involves mental and physical responses. When we are upset with or offended by someone at work, we also experience the emotion physically, with an increased heart rate, for example.

Strong emotions can be triggered when individuals' expectations about a situation differ greatly from their actual experiences in that situation. Individuals bring many kinds of expectations to their organizational experiences. These expectations may include notions about demonstrating commitment, competence, and integrity in completing their work assignments; maintaining positive relationships with coworkers; and establishing appropriate boundaries between work and life (Carver & Scheier, 1990). The organization also sets various expectations for its members. Through the socialization process, it may set expectations for the types of emotions individuals should be expected to display. For example, flight attendants and Disney workers (cast members) are expected to display positive, friendly emotions while working despite circumstances (Hochschild, 1983; Van Maanen & Kunda, 1989). In addition, organizations set expectations for career advancement opportunities, supervisor and coworker relationships, and general behavioral norms as part of the organizational culture.

Events that exceed our expectations cause positive emotions. For example, if we receive an unexpected raise, we experience joy or happiness. When events fail to meet our expectations, we experience negative emotions. If coworkers fail to complete their part of a project on time, we experience anger or frustration. Strong emotions are often the result of discrepancies or differences between our expectations for achieving goals and the rate at which we actually achieve them. So if the expectation is that we will have a positive work environment and the work setting is unfriendly or stressful, we experience negative emotions because we are not achieving our goal at the desired rate.

In the opening scenario, Taylor experiences a number of emotions. The promotion going into effect next week provides a mixture of positive emotions from gaining status

The Moral "Signaling" Function of Emotions

Professor Vincent Waldron (2012) describes how emotions can serve an important "signaling function" or serve as an early warning for organizational members that plans or decisions may have the potential to cause harm or wrongdoing. When we feel flashes of emotions—such as guilt, embarrassment, or disgust—regarding organizational interactions, it may indicate that an authentic dialogue is needed about the ethical implications of what is happening in the here and now. Yet many notions of professionalism encourage individuals to suppress and regulate their strong emotions. How might the common practices of professionalism and emotion management influence the likelihood of discussing our moral emotions in the workplace?

and additional pay and negative ones because it will make maintaining interpersonal relationships harder. Taylor looked forward to leaving behind Jamie, whose aggressive behaviors created negative emotions for department coworkers by hindering their ability to maintain a positive work environment.

Types of Emotions

The experience of many kinds of emotions is integral to the experience of organizational membership. Research has identified five different types of emotions related to organizational membership (Miller et al., 2007). *Emotional labor* occurs when individuals express *in*authentic emotions as part of their work for the benefit of organizational goals. Emotional labor occurs when there is a mismatch between the organizationally sanctioned emotions employees are supposed to display and the emotions they are actually feeling. For example, employees involved in customer service are expected to perform emotional labor by acting in positive and upbeat ways as they interact with customers regardless of their personal feelings (Hochschild, 1983). Picture, for example, how flight attendants or restaurant servers tend to react to rude customers by smiling, remaining calm, and speaking politely. In the opposite direction, bill collectors are taught to present the right level of sympathy or sternness with clients, depending on their goals in collecting money. They must detach from their own personal feelings to convey the appropriate emotion (Rafaeli & Sutton, 1991). Emotional labor may be considered the least "natural" of work-related emotion because it often involves pretending to feel an emotion. Emotional labor can create a discrepancy between the organizational expectations to express certain emotions and the actual emotions the person is feeling during the interactions. As a case worker in the opening scenario, Taylor likely does some emotional labor by remaining upbeat and optimistic in dealing with clients, despite feeling pessimistic and disappointed at times.

Emotion work involves the emotions someone feels in response to the type of work they do as an organizational member. The type of work usually involves dealing with other people's emotions. This means that emotion work is the individual's genuine response to the work and the emotions of others. Emotion work is common in many occupations, particularly in the human services area. We typically consider emotion work the often unpleasant emotions associated with certain types of work, such as when a nurse or hospice worker feels empathy for a dying patient. Emotion work can be positive, too, such as when an advisor feels positive emotions along with the students who become excited about finally achieving their graduation goals. The emotions of the individuals being served create emotion work for the person helping them. Taylor and the other case workers appear to experience emotion work regularly as their clients succeed or fail in response to the advice and treatments they are given.

Emotion with work occurs in response to the day to day interactions with supervisors, peers, and other organizational members. Emotions with work are often based on whether the individual experiences movement toward their goals (positive emotions) or feel that they are hindered in achieving their goals (negative emotions) through their interactions with others (Carver & Scheier, 1990). For example, Taylor likely feels positive emotions about receiving a promotion with the help of a mentor, Pat. This assistance moved Taylor toward a career goal. Jamie, the abusive coworker that Taylor is happy to be leaving behind, is a hindrance to a positive work environment for everyone and so creates negative emotions for others.

Emotion at work considers emotions that may be experience while at work but are unrelated to work events. If you have ever had trouble concentrating on your work (or your college class) because of some event that occurred outside of work—such as finding out someone was in an accident or diagnosed with an illness—you experienced emotion at work that hindered your ability to do your work as well as you might normally. These emotions often violate personal expectations that an individual can separate their work and nonwork experiences. In the scenario, Taylor does not appear to experience any spillover emotion "at" work at this time.

Finally, *emotion toward work* is the general affect or emotion that a person has about the workplace. Some level of job satisfaction or dissatisfaction is perhaps the most common emotion toward work. An individual's level of job satisfaction represents some evaluation of whether the work experience is meeting or exceeding their expectations or not. Similarly, stress is an emotion toward work. A high level of stress indicates a discrepancy between an expectation of healthy, positive work environment and the actual experience. In the scenario, Taylor apparently has a positive emotion toward work because the choice to work there "has worked out well for the most part." As we discuss in Chapter 15 on organizational exit, emotion toward work is often assumed to be a major contributor to job turnover, but it is certainly not the only cause.

Emotion Management

As important as it is to understand the cause of emotions and the different types of emotions in the workplace, the challenge for the organizational member is *managing* the different types of emotions appropriately. In the case of emotional labor, the organization likely makes it clear what emotions employees are expected to display. For example, Disney Corporation makes it very clear that employees in its amusement parks are to display positive emotions regardless of whether the person is sweeping streets or performing on one of its rides or stages (Van Maanen & Kunda, 1989). They reinforce these norms during the selection process and training of new employees, as well as by having supervisors observe and evaluate employees on the job. Similarly, 911 operators and firefighters are taught to maintain a neutral, unaffected demeanor in their communication with the public, also a form of emotional labor; however, these kinds of employees are often more forthcoming about their emotions when interacting with each other away from the public (Scott & Myers, 2005; Shuler & Sypher, 2000). Unfortunately, the norms for displaying the other types of emotion at most workplaces are stated less clearly.

An important part of maintaining interpersonal relationships in organizations involves managing the *display of emotions*. There appears to be a general expectation of "professionalism" in the management of emotions in most workplaces (Kramer & Hess, 2002). Although the norms of professionalism are never clearly stated, they seem to involve a number of expectations. In general, professionalism means avoiding communicating negative emotions and instead primarily expressing a neutral or slightly positive demeanor. These ideas indicate that professionalism is largely performative in nature because professionalism is attributed to employees who are adept at regulating their emotions in their interactions with others. Even too much exuberance, a positive emotion, is often considered unprofessional if it is excessive, lasts too long, or occurs in front of others who are likely having different emotions. A professional response to being named "Employee of the Month" should be modest, especially because other employees may feel that they deserved the award. The problem with the norm of professionalism is that not everyone has the same understanding of what it means, as it is rarely discussed openly and directly in many occupations.

In the opening scenario, the case workers all seem to know to maintain a positive, professional demeanor while interacting with their clients. They save the expression of strong negative emotions for when they are away from work and clients as they griped about them to blow off steam. Taylor also apparently has some understanding of what it means to manage emotions in a professional manner in interactions with coworkers. Rather than expressing negative emotions in front of others, Taylor had only expressed genuine anger in response to a client privately in front of Morgan one time. Their friendship allowed for the private expression of emotion that would have been inappropriate to express to the client. Taylor avoided expressing those negative emotions in the workplace in general as part of being professional.

Volunteers and Interpersonal Relationships

The topics in this chapter can generally be applied to volunteers and nonprofit organizations without many adjustments. For example, volunteers have supervisor relationships that can vary in closeness from overseer to partnerships, and they have peer relationships that can vary from information to special. What likely makes these relationships different are volunteers' motives. A primary motive for volunteering is to develop relationships. For example, community theater members primarily volunteer for the opportunity to perform and meet other people (Kramer, 2005). Even though choir members join for various prosocial reasons initially, volunteers often continue for different reasons (Willems et al., 2012). It is not uncommon for volunteers to continue due to a desire to maintain their social relationships, even if they are not as satisfied with their volunteer work or the organization. This observation suggests that communication with volunteers may need to be more focused on social relationships than it is for employees if reducing volunteer turnover is a concern.

Volunteers may not need much mentoring communication like employees because either they are not typically motivated to advance in the organization or it is not a career for them. However, volunteers are sometimes motivated by learning new job skills and finding work opportunities (Clary & Snyder, 1999) and sometimes quit when there seems to be little opportunity to face new challenges or learn new ideas, techniques, or methods (Willems et al., 2012). Because retaining volunteers is often important, volunteer supervisors may need to identify volunteers motivated by opportunities to learn and then provide the volunteers with opportunities for growth and development of new skills.

Emotions are an important part of volunteer communication, although the five types of emotions related to organizational membership (Miller et al., 2007) may function somewhat differently. For example, volunteers are probably not faking emotions (emotion labor) for the profit of the organization, but they likely do present certain emotional behaviors due to role expectations and a desire to adhere to the ideal of professionalism even in a voluntary role. They can experience emotional responses (emotion work) to their activities including negative ones, for example, if they are hospice volunteers (Gilstrap & White, 2013) or positive ones if they are coaching a team that wins. They respond positively or negatively to their interactions with other volunteers and paid staff (emotion with work). Their volunteer efforts are likely influenced by their emotional responses to other work and life events (emotion at work). Whereas paid workers may go to work even when they experience emotions related to nonwork activities like family incidents, volunteers are probably more likely to cancel their volunteer activities when they experience strong emotions in their other life activities. Volunteers also have general levels of satisfaction or other emotional responses to their volunteering (emotions toward work).

The emotion management norms are likely different for volunteers than employees. Employees likely feel that they must present the appropriate "public" image of their organization. Because volunteers may feel more inclined to consider their volunteering "private," they may be more willing to break organizational rules or norms to fulfill their own rather than organizational expectations (Onyx, 2013). Particularly, human service volunteers may express emotions more freely, including touching clients to provide comfort, than would be expected by professional norms. These expressions of emotion may be considered unprofessional in other contexts.

Summary

In this chapter, we explored some of the important interpersonal relationships that are part of being an organizational member. We included descriptions of supervisor–subordinate communication, peer communication, friendships, and mentoring. In addition, we described the overall issue of emotions and emotion management as part of interacting professionally as an employee or volunteer. Of course, in many organizations, there are other interpersonal relationships that are important as well. For example, relationships to customers or clients are important for anyone in a service provider position. Other individuals must maintain positive relationships with vendors or suppliers who provide the resources needed for the organization to function. By focusing on supervisors, peers, and mentors, we hope to have provided many of the important concepts and principles that apply to the various organizational relationships that you must develop and maintain throughout your lifespan in organizations, both as an employee and as a volunteer.

CHAPTER 8

Communication and Leadership

JB found it very interesting consulting with three departments in the same organization at the same time, although sometimes it was confusing as well. The company developed computer systems to control manufacturing processes for other companies. What made it challenging consulting in all three departments was that the managers in each department had different ways of handling issues, which meant that JB had to remember to adapt to each of them. For example, Casey's department was responsible for shipping out and installing the final control systems. People often referred to Casey as a born leader. JB just saw Casey's approach to leadership as a very directive style of managing in which subordinates only did exactly what they were told to do and little else. The department was run very efficiently and they always completed work on time. JB always had to go through Casey for approval before working directly with any of the department members. By contrast, Shawn in the product research and development department had all experienced department members who knew what they were doing. Shawn had confidence in their skills and gave them a lot of freedom to make decisions on their own and so seemed to focus on maintaining positive relationships with them. As a result, JB could work directly with them. Shawn didn't mind finding out about problems after they were solved. In JB's mind, Harper, in the human resource department, was the ideal manager. Unlike Casey and Shawn, Harper seemed to adapt to the different department members rather than treating them all the same. With the newer employees, JB checked with Harper first because they seemed to need to know that their manager agreed with JB's suggestions. JB could work directly with more senior members because Harper expected them to use their judgement.

· · · · ·

Few recent college graduates are hired into organizational leadership positions right away. Your initial experiences will likely involve following the leadership of someone else, perhaps a supervisor or a team leader formally assigned to you or a coworker who serves as your informal leader as you begin. You will also likely have some communication experiences with the organizational leadership, owner, president, or chief executive officer (CEO). Perhaps you will watch a video of the CEO welcoming you into the organization or receive a paper or electronic welcoming message. You may receive occasional paper or electronic newsletters from that person.

As you progress in your career, you will gradually take on leadership roles. You will likely become a supervisor or team leader. You may gradually move into higher levels that involve increasingly larger leadership roles in that same organization. A more likely alternative is that your career will involve you moving from organization to organization. Eventually, after you acquire more formal working experience, you may assume various leadership roles, even as a newcomer to a different organization. Of course, you might decide to be an entrepreneur and start your own business, in which case you could be the organizational leader immediately.

In this chapter, we explore communication and leadership so that you have a better understanding of some of the many different ways you will experience leadership as an organizational member or when you are in a leadership position. The research on leadership is immense, and it is impossible to cover more than a small portion of it here. For conceptual simplicity, we divided the chapter broadly into two sections. In the first section, we examine managerial leadership or what some people might refer to as group leadership. Managerial or group leadership involves communicating and interacting directly with the people you lead on a regular basis. In the second section, we examine leadership at the organizational level. Except in small organizations, organizational leadership involves leading in a less direct and impersonal manner because it is simply not possible to communicate interactively and personally with a large number of organizational members. As such, organizational leadership involves different issues and skills than being a group or managerial leader.

Are these two categories mutually exclusive? Absolutely not! Managers often exhibit characteristics that we associate with organizational leadership, and organizational leaders have to manage groups of people that interact directly with them whether it is the management team or department heads. Does everyone make the distinctions between managerial and organizational leadership like we do? No, they don't. So although the line between managerial leadership and organizational leadership is blurry at times, it can at least be useful to discuss them separately initially to provide some clarity to the issues of leadership and leadership communication. Near the end of the chapter, we address the distinction between managerial and organizational leadership again.

Managerial or Group Leadership

The study of managerial leadership has been investigated from a variety of different approaches based on different sets of assumptions. We present these as leadership traits, management styles, situational leadership, contingency leadership, and external group leadership. We conclude the section by presenting dialectical theory as a way of integrating your understanding of these various approaches to managerial leadership.

Managerial Leadership as Traits

If you have ever heard someone say, "She's just a born leader," or "He just always seems to end up in a leadership role," you are talking to someone who implicitly accepts the assumptions of the trait approach to leadership. The trait approach assumes leaders have different characteristics or talents than non-leaders and assumes that people are born with certain traits or genes that make them effective leaders. There have been literally hundreds of studies that attempt to identify the characteristics of people who are leaders and try to distinguish them from non-leaders.

Two summaries of research conducted since the 1920s, much of it at Ohio State University, concluded that people who are in group leadership positions differ from those in non-leadership positions in the following ways (Kirkpatick & Locke, 1991; Stogdill, 1948):

1. They have greater cognitive abilities on average in terms of intelligence, verbal facility, alertness, and originality, although they are not necessarily exceptional or brilliant.
2. They have more ambition to achieve and excel, including motivation to take on leadership roles because they find leading satisfying.
3. They exhibit higher levels of responsibility, dependability, initiative, persistence, and self-confidence in making decisions.
4. They demonstrate higher levels of participation in their group including activity, sociability, cooperation, adaptability, and humor.
5. They demonstrate honesty and integrity such that their words and actions match; they are not deceitful, which means that they gain the trust of others,
6. They have knowledge of their business or work.
7. Given their roles, they are also perceived as having higher status in terms of popularity and socioeconomic status.

A more recent study asked people identified as effective group leaders to report what was important in leading groups (Galanes, 2003). They reported that effective group leaders were good at establishing the intention of the group, creating a positive group culture, monitoring and managing group interactions so that they were positive, and managing the task to keep the group focused. Group leaders also exhibited a number of personal characteristics such as humility and flexibility, and they were open and approachable and inspired confidence while modeling appropriate behaviors.

Although these studies suggest that group leaders possess certain characteristics or exhibit certain behaviors in greater amounts than non-leaders, there is no convincing evidence that certain traits make people into leaders. In fact, the authors of the first two articles have concluded the following: "A person does not become a leader by virtue of the possession of some combination of traits, but the pattern of personal characteristics of the leader must bear some relevant relationship to the characteristics, activities, and goals of the followers" (Stogdill, 1948, p. 64); and "traits only endow people with the potential for leadership" (Kirkpatick & Locke, 1991, p. 56). In other words, people with these characteristics do not all become group or organizational leaders. Social inequities such as racism, sexism, ageism, and religious discrimination—among others—are also potent factors that can limit individuals' opportunities to lead in certain workplace contexts.

Further, an examination of the characteristics and behaviors just listed suggests that most of them are learned or developed. Few, if any, of the descriptors are determined by birth. Through practice and positive reinforcement, most of the behaviors can be developed. Of course, you will still likely hear people say, "That person is a born leader," like people said about Casey in the shipping and installation department. Those explanations are not scientific, but are actually post hoc reasons or well-meaning (but inaccurate) compliments. The comment fails to recognize and appreciate the effort and work it takes for people to lead and acquire leadership skills.

Models of Management Styles

If you have heard someone say about a manager, "That's just the way he does things," or "She's very predictable," you are hearing someone describe leadership from a managerial style approach. This approach assumes that individual managers have a particular style that they favor and use as they manage workers. The goal of this approach is to identify an individual's preferred style of leadership. There are two particularly common typologies of management styles.

A common typology suggests leaders vary from autocratic to democratic to laissez-faire (Lewin & Lippett, 1953). The *autocratic manager* largely controls by setting the agenda and giving directives with limited, if any, input from group members who follow the directives. Communication is generally directive, with some feedback or reporting by group members. *Democratic leadership* involves the manager working with the group and making decisions collectively by democratic principles of discussion and majority rule. The leader communicates to guide the group toward making a decision but attempts to be almost a regular member of the group. *Laissez-faire management* is a form of delegating in which the leader allows the group to make decisions and do what they choose. The manager limits communication and provides little oversight or support.

The other most common typology developed by Robert Blake and Jane Mouton (1964) suggests managers vary on their concerns for organizational needs or task production and their concerns for human or social needs of the individual group members. Each of these two dimensions is then rated on a scale of 1 to 9 (See Figure 8.1). The management grid suggests five styles of managing:

1. *Impoverished Management* (1,1) has low concern for getting the job done and low concern for personal relationships. This approach has parallels to the laissez-faire manager except that it involves neglect rather than delegating. As a result, the employees may not feel motivated to act on their own.

2. *Country Club Management* (1,9) has low concern for getting the job done but high concern for personal relationships and needs. This type of manager is quite concerned about employees' needs and keeping them happy and satisfied but does not worry about meeting organizational goals and likely assumes those goals will be met if the employees are happy.

3. *Authority Compliance Management* (9,1) has a high concern for getting the job done and meeting organizational expectations but low concern for personal relationships. This type of manager has similarities to the autocratic leaders with a focus on giving directives to make sure that organizational goals are met even if it means creating some discord among employees.

4. *Middle-of-the-Road Management* (5,5) tries to balance a moderate concern for production with a moderate concern for relationships. The mixture may be satisfying to a large number of employees because it provides adequate productivity and moderate levels of employee morale.

5. *Team Management* (9,9) tries to maximize concern for meeting organizational goals and positive relationships. This approach involves interdependent and

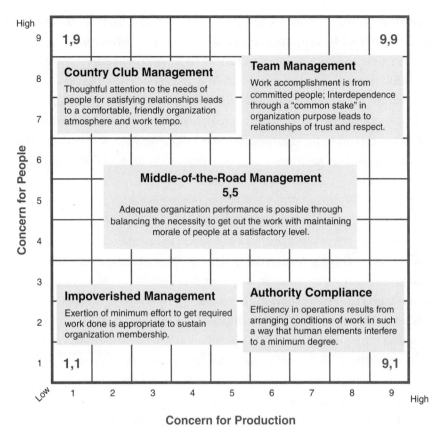

Figure 8.1. Blake and Mouton Managerial Leadership Grid

committed individuals working together for common goals and positive relationships.

The developers of this style model suggest that managers who use the middle-of-the-road and team-oriented approaches will have the most productive groups.

Research that has focused on team-oriented management conceptualizes the management style as a collaborative or shared leadership style and has identified conditions necessary for it to occur (Pearce & Conger, 2003; Perry, Pearce, & Sims, 1999). Those conditions include the manager framing situations in a way that group members feel empowered to make decisions to solve problems. Also, team-oriented managers communicate in such a way so as to minimize status differences and motivate group members to act rather than giving directives. Productivity is enhanced by integrated approaches.

The style approach seems to presume, somewhat idealistically, that a particular approach is effective across situations. For example, in the opening scenario, it seems that Casey in shipping and installation manages with an authority compliance style. By contrast, an educational theater director who prefers a collaborative style reports that it only works when the actors are mature and skilled enough to assume responsibility; as a result, he has to adapt his style (Kramer & Crespy, 2011). This suggests that there are situational factors that affect the effectiveness of a collaborative style, such as the readiness and competence of team members to assume responsibility for accomplishing tasks.

Situational Models of Managerial Leadership

Some scholars do not make a distinction between situational and contingency approaches to understanding managerial leadership. We make the distinction between them based on two different views of the situation or context in which the group management occurs and classify some of the models differently as a result. A situational approach to leadership focuses on the situation as a fixed or stable context and then indicates that the situation determines which leadership style will emerge as most appropriate or effective. "The situation just called for someone to take charge," or "Given the situation, the leader needed to be understanding," are comments that support a situational understanding of leadership in which the situation determines the appropriate style of managerial leadership to use. A situational approach directs our attention to the possibility that an autocratic style may be the most appropriate in certain situations but a laissez-faire style may be in another. According to one situational model, situations vary in terms of task structure, leader–member relationships, and position power (Fiedler, 1967). Task structure includes how routine and certain versus unpredictable and ambiguous the situation is. Leader–member relationships concern the degree of trust that members have with the manager in the situation. Position power concerns the authority associated with the position. These three interact in complicated ways.

In an effort to simplify the way these interact, we focus primarily on the task structure of the situation. Results suggest that a directive style of leadership fits situations that are particularly low or high in task structure. Michael Kramer experienced an example of low task structure while volunteering to create sandbag barriers along a river during flooding. The situation was very ambiguous and unpredictable, but the volunteers were eager to assist. As a result, we followed directives from anyone who would tell us what to do. In the end, a man operating an excavator machine that carried sandbags from the loading area to where they were needed directed the operation. He told people what to do and we did it because we trusted him and the situation seemed to call for his directive style. Directive leadership also seems to work effectively in highly structured and routine situations. For example, in an assembly line, there is little need to discuss what to do. A trusted and directive manager can keep the operation running by providing clear directives.

Many situations are between the extremes of the chaos of flooding and the structure of an assembly line. Those situations contain a mixture of certainty and ambiguity, routine and unpredictable situations. In those situations, a less directive, relationship-oriented leader who permits group members to have some control in the situation seems to be most effective. This situational description seems to characterize typical office and service industry work.

The key distinction for a situational view of managing is to see a particular style of leadership fitting (or not) with the situation. Matching the style to the situation leads to effectiveness. Task-oriented, directive managers seem to do well in either very structured or very unstructured situations. Relationship-oriented leaders are most effective in situations that are neither too structured nor too unstructured. In the opening scenario, Shawn in the product research and development department seems to recognize that department members are experienced enough to deal with the complexities of their job situation, and so a relationship-oriented style of management is appropriate.

Contingency Models of Managerial Leading

Whereas a situational approach to management assumes a stable context, a contingency model instead assumes that the situation changes over time and that the management style also needs to change over time. A statement such as, "Our manager is very flexible and adapts to different employees and situations very well," suggests a contingency model of managerial leading.

One such contingency model is the path-goal model, which explores various approaches managers should use to motivate subordinates in different situations (House, 1971, 1996). Those styles include directive, supportive, participative, and achievement-oriented behaviors. The first three are similar to styles previously discussed, whereas the last is setting challenging goals or striving for excellence rather than simply completing

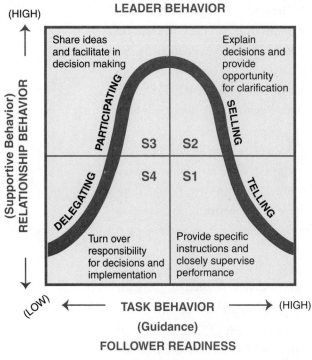

LEADER BEHAVIOR

(HIGH)

(Supportive Behavior)
RELATIONSHIP BEHAVIOR

Share ideas and facilitate in decision making	Explain decisions and provide opportunity for clarification
PARTICIPATING S3	S2 SELLING
DELEGATING S4	S1 TELLING
Turn over responsibility for decisions and implementation	Provide specific instructions and closely supervise performance

(LOW) ← **TASK BEHAVIOR** → (HIGH)
(Guidance)

FOLLOWER READINESS

HIGH	MODERATE		LOW
R4	R3	R2	R1
Able and willing or confident	Able but unwilling or insecure	Unable but willing or confident	Unable and unwilling or insecure

FOLLOWER DIRECTED   LEADER DIRECTED

Figure 8.2. Hersey and Blanchard Contingency Model of Managerial Leadership

work. The nature of the task and the nature of the followers help determine which style of management is most appropriate.

A model with similar contingencies to the path-goal model is the Hersey and Blanchard (1993) model (see Figure 8.2). Two factors related to followers' readiness determine the appropriate leadership style: their willingness and their ability. As those factors change, managers should change their leadership style. The two dimensions of the model are similar to previous ones: task and relational behaviors. Hersey and Blanchard have changed some of the names of the management styles over the years, but the essential factors have remained the same.

Starting in the lower right-hand corner (S1), if the group members are unable and unwilling (insecure) to try to perform the group's tasks, the managerial leader needs to adopt a telling or directive style of management that tells them how to complete the work with limited concern for relationships. Then (S2), as group members become more confident but still lack ability, the manager needs to adjust to a selling or coaching style to provide them with the additional training they need; the manager also needs to focus on building positive relationships with them to encourage them to develop further. Next (S3), as they become skilled and are less dependent on the manager for task leadership, the manager needs to adopt a participating or supporting style that motivates them to perform and allows them to share ideas and participate in decisions. The manager's focus becomes predominately about relationships, rather than tasks, as a means of encouraging additional effort. Finally (S4), as the group members become able and willing, then the manager can delegate decisions and allow the group members to work on their own because the manager no longer needs to attend much to tasks or relationships and simply may monitor progress. In a sense, delegating is similar to laissez-faire management style and is a goal of leading a highly developed and mature group.

One example of how the contingency model might work is in the relationship between a college advisor and college students (Waters, 2001). In many cases, incoming, first-year college students are uncertain of their major, unclear about graduation requirements, and unable to interact appropriately with the bureaucracy of the university. The advisor needs to adopt a directing style of leadership concerned with getting them enrolled in classes initially and be less concerned with developing relationships. By their sophomore year, students are more able to manage their own schedules but still need some direction to meet the requirements for their newly chosen major. As a result, the advisor can adopt a coaching style that can focus more on developing relationships with the students to understand their long-term goals while still making sure they are picking their major and enrolling in appropriate classes. By their junior years, students should be quite able to manage the bureaucracy and succeed in their classes, but they may need encouragement to finish the required courses and enroll on time so they do not miss classes they need. A supporting role for the advisor becomes appropriate based on a positive relationship the two have developed over time. Finally, as the students prepare to graduate, the advisor has little to do as they achieve their goals.

This example points out the important contribution of the contingency approach. It emphasizes how to adapt the management style to the changing situation as the group changes and develops maturity. It also illustrates one of the challenges in applying the contingency approach. The manager has to be sensitive to the changes in group members' readiness. Of course, it would be rare that every group member would be at the same level of development at the same time. This makes it difficult for a manager to determine the appropriate style to use. Some seniors still need to be directed and some first-year students are ready for delegating. In the opening scenario, Harper seems to use a contingency style of leadership by being fairly directive with new employees and applying a delegating style with the experienced ones.

External Communication Focus of Managers

All of the managerial leadership approaches so far have really focused on the interaction between managers and group members or subordinates. Missing from this focus is the idea that part of leading a group is also communicating between the group and other parts of the organization or environment. Research suggests that an important aspect of leading a group involves serving four important external roles (Ancona & Caldwell, 1992). The *ambassador role* involves keeping others in the organization aware of the group and its progress. In some ways, being an ambassador involves managing impressions of others to make sure that other organizational managers and leaders are aware of the group. The *task coordinator role* involves making sure that the group is able to gain resources and outputs with other groups so that they can accomplish their goals. Because groups or departments within an organization are interdependent, the manager needs to make sure those connections are maintained. The *scout role* involves being aware of information and opportunities in the organization or environment that can assist the group. For example, if there are new funding opportunities for the group within the organization or external to it, the manager can make the group aware of those opportunities. Finally, the *guard role* involves serving as a gatekeeper for the group so that it is not overloaded with unnecessary information or concerns. Different levels of these roles are associated with group success. High levels of ambassador and task coordinator role work are associated with successful outcomes, whereas extensive scouting can actually have a negative effect if the group keeps adapting and changing based on new information rather than completing its work.

Dialectical Theory and Managerial Leadership

Although there is no general theory that guided the research on managerial leadership, you have likely noticed some commonalities between several of the different models. In particular, a number of them have a task or goal orientation dimension and a social or relational dimension. Dialectical theory provides a theoretical approach to understanding these various approaches collectively.

Dialectical theory suggests that in many situations we face in groups or organizations, there are two seemingly opposite goals or options we have to strive to integrate. Dialectical theory holds that instead of viewing the opposites as dualistic choices in which a person must select one option over the other (e.g., choosing between being task or relationally focused), individuals instead simply must manage the two options simultaneously because both are important, valuable, and desirable (Baxter & Montgomery, 1996). So for example, a common dialectical tension in interpersonal relationships is between dependence and independence. We want to have close relationships (dependence) with

TABLE 8.1 Dialectical Tensions of Managerial Leadership

Dialectical Tensions of Managerial Leadership
Task and Off-Task (Relational) Focus
Directing and Facilitating
Process and Outcome
Structure and Flexibility
Talking and Listening
Internal Focus and External Focus

others—whether it be parents, friends, coworkers, or romantic partners—but we also want to maintain independence from them. Too much dependence or independence generally creates problems within the relationship. As a result, we try to balance the two opposites in most of our relationships.

Research indicates that there are a number of dialectical tensions that managerial leaders face (Galanes, 2009; McNamee & Peterson, 2014). Some of the more commonly identified tensions appear in Table 8.1. One important tension is between balancing an on-task focus with off-task diversions. Although clearly there must be some task focus, without some off-task focus on social relationships, many group members will become dissatisfied, and group outcomes will suffer as a result. Two of the tensions deal with the level of managerial control. These include tensions between directing and facilitating as well as communicating structure and maintaining flexibility. Managerial leadership can range from being autocratic by telling people what to do to simply assisting them in reaching their goals. Similarly, the manager establishes control by communicating a structure (e.g., goals, evaluation criteria, deadlines), but a lack of flexibility may inhibit consideration of creative options. Balancing control with delegating control is challenging. Directly related to communication, managerial leaders have to balance talking and listening. Too much of one or the other is generally dysfunctional. Finally, managers need to balance a focus on internal communication within the group and an external communication for creating connections between the group and others within the organization.

These tensions align well with some of the issues raised in the managerial leadership approaches discussed so far. A careful examination of many of the models presented makes it apparent that task versus relational concerns are common among them, even if not stated overtly. The tension over control emphasizes that different styles are more

African American Women Executives' Leadership Communication

Professor Patricia S. Parker (2001) interviewed African American women executives about their leadership practices in U.S. organizations that tended to be majority white and male-dominated organizations. The executives' descriptions of their leadership practices revealed that they worked to combine the apparently opposite strategies of being controlling and collaborating as well as direct and indirect. They were aware of a common belief that women leaders are supposed to be especially collaborative and participative. They found times when those approaches were useful; however, they also found a controlling and direct approach was warranted as a strategy for managing their positions as Black women leaders within dominant-culture organizations. Taken together, the executives described their leadership approach as attempting to negotiate the dialects of their leadership situations. What other underrepresented groups may face similar issues in leadership positions?

or less appropriate depending on the different contingencies that develop in a situation. The presence of multiple dialectical tensions probably implies that one approach to managerial leadership will not fit all leadership situations.

Dialectical theory, with its focus on the need to balance between two desirable but conflicting choices summarizes the complexity of managerial leadership well. Managerial leaders must negotiate the task with the social aspects of the group, control with flexibility and adaptations, and use internal and external communication, including speaking and listening. That negotiation requires a lot of skill to perform successfully.

Managerial Leadership and Volunteers

Managing volunteers has challenges that make it different from managing employees, primarily due to the differences in their motivations. Yet, it is not difficult to see how each of the different approaches discussed seems applicable to volunteers as well. Some managers of volunteers seem to take charge at work, at home, and in their volunteer roles, as if they were "born" to be leaders. Volunteer managers use the breadth of different styles identified, although an impoverished style would likely result in volunteers quitting or taking on managerial roles themselves. In one community theater group, that is exactly what happened when the designated leader failed to provide even minimal leadership. The actors and the rest of the production staff took over the leadership functions (Kramer, 2006b). Sometimes the situation, such as with flood-preparation volunteers, seems to demand a directive manager; however, often the situation requires a more relationship-oriented style, particularly because volunteers are often motivated by a desire to develop relationships (Clary & Snyder, 1999). Overall, this might suggest that a contingency approach to managing is most appropriate, as the manager of volunteers needs to adapt to the situation and the volunteers while balancing the various dialectical tensions that exist in the situation, including the internal versus external focus.

Summary of Managerial Leadership

There are a plethora of models of managerial leadership that have been suggested and studied over the last century. We covered only some of the prominent ones here. The ones presented illustrate many of the major ways managerial leadership has been studied. As such, they provide you with a general understanding of some of the general traits managers may possess, some of the different styles managers may use, some of the ways that the situation may determine an appropriate managerial leadership style, and some of the ways that leadership style may change and adapt to the changing context. Dialectical theory helps to identify some of the important issues implicit in each of the approaches, balancing task and relationship concerns, providing structure and flexibility, and an internal or external focus. This survey of managerial leadership gives you a good sense of the issues involved in being a manager or team leader.

Organizational Leadership

In the second section of this chapter, we focus on organizational leadership, or leadership from the person or people near the top of the hierarchy who have responsibilities for leading either the whole organization or some large unit within a larger organization. Whether the organization has 50 people or 50,000 people, whether it is a large for-profit business or a small community organization, the people responsible for guiding the organization exhibit behaviors and skills that are, at times, different from those of managerial leaders in part because organizational leaders have a much greater potential for influencing the culture of the organization. A number of different explanations of organizational leadership have been developed over the years. We focus on four relatively common ones: charismatic leadership, visionary leadership, transformational leadership, and institutional leadership. Then we examine framing theory as a way of integrating some of the communication characteristics that are common to these different types of leaders.

Charismatic Leadership

Charismatic leadership has been approached from a variety of perspectives including sociological, psychological, political, behavioral, attributional, and communication approaches (Hackman & Johnson, 2000). Rather than try to discuss all of these variations with their overlapping and sometimes contradictory perspectives, we present one approach thoroughly as representative of the notion of charismatic leadership. In a study comparing two social movement organizations, Harrison Trice and Janice Beyer (1986) identified five general characteristics of charismatic leaders. We discuss each characteristic individually.

First, charismatic leaders typically have a number of *personal characteristics*. These include, among others, self-confidence, effective communication skills, belief in their own morality, and a need to influence others. It is the communication skills and self-confidence that we perhaps most often associate with commonly identified charismatic leaders of the past century such as Martin Luther King Jr. and John F. Kennedy. However, it seems equally important that charismatic leaders believe that their moral views are correct and that they have a desire to influence others to accept those beliefs. Their beliefs and need to influence seem to provide the motivation for them to speak up confidently as charismatic leaders.

Next, charismatic leaders orient their influence of others toward solving some problem, crisis, or a *felt wrong,* something that seems to need to be changed. For social movement organizations, there is usually some perceived injustice that needs to be addressed, be it a health issue, poverty issue, or equality issue. For business or nonprofit organizations, the problem may be the lack of quality products or services that need to be filled.

It is not just enough to want to solve some problem or issue. The charismatic leader also needs to achieve some *early success* in attempting to address that issue. For a social movement organization, success might include improving the lives of a small number of people with the expectation of improving more lives in the future. In a business on nonprofit organization, it might include initial success with selling the product or service.

Based on the success, the charismatic leader needs to *develop loyal followers*. These might be active members of the social movement organization, loyal employees for a business, or loyal volunteers for the nonprofit organization. These loyal followers help to provide the critical mass of people and effort it takes for additional success. They also tend to recruit other like-minded individuals to their organization to continue to address the issue.

Finally, according to Trice and Beyer (1986), the charismatic leader needs to be involved in the *routinization of leadership.* Routinization simply means "to make routine." Charismatic leaders work to make two aspects of their leadership routine. First, the charismatic leader tries to assign and delegate routine organizational matters to someone else. Second, the charismatic leader tries to develop a routine of ceremonial rites or rituals to make addressing the problem a routine part of the organization's ordinary work.

Hopefully, you are already thinking of some past or current examples of charismatic organizational leaders of social movements and businesses who exhibit many or all of these five characteristics. One example you probably have not considered is Mary Kay Ash, the founder of Mary Kay Cosmetics. Her story can be found in her biography (Ash, 2008), online at a variety of locations by searching for her full name, or in news stories particularly around the time of her death. Mary Kay exhibited all five characteristics of a charismatic leader described here.

Mary Kay had the personal characteristics of a charismatic leader. She was a confident, dynamic speaker who believed in her slogan, "God first, family second, career third," and her leadership principle of "praise people for success." She addressed the important economic and social issue of limited career opportunities for women when she began the company in 1963. She wanted to create a new business in which women could maintain rich family lives as well as high-paying successful careers. She had early success starting the business with just $5,000, and generating, in turn, $200,000 in revenue in the first year. She developed loyal followers quickly, and the company grew from 11 salespeople initially to over 750,000 worldwide now. She was also effective in routinization. Her son, Richard Rogers, served as the cofounder, chairman, and CEO of Mary Kay.

This freed Mary Kay to make inspirational speeches to the workforce. There are numerous rituals involved in the local Mary Kay meetings, many involving giving out awards based on levels of sales to praise people for success, including the pink Cadillac for the highest achievers. These rituals are so routinized in the organization that they have continued even after her death.

Mary Kay Ash giving one of her inspirational speeches to delegates. Ash is known for my inspirational quotes like this one: "throw out the words 'If I can,' 'I hope,' and 'maybe,' and replace them with 'I can, I will, I must.'"

Visionary Leadership

Visionary leadership is a second well-developed conceptualization of organizational leadership. There are many different conceptualizations of the meaning of an organizational vision. A study of over 300 business executives suggests that there are a wide range of visions for their organizations that differ in focus on factors such as purpose, response to environment, conservativism, ease of articulation, or being action-oriented (Larwood, Falbe, Kriger, & Miesing, 1995). Scholars have also developed a wide range of conceptualizations of vision and visionary leadership. Again, we present one of the more developed conceptualizations of visionary leadership, that of Warren Bennis and Burt Nanus as representative of others.

To begin, Warren Bennis and Burt Nanus (2007) make a clear distinction between managers and leaders, although they indicate that both are important for organizational success. For Bennis and Nanus, managing involves taking responsibility for accomplishing certain actions, whereas leadership involves influencing and guiding the direction of those actions. This distinction is similar to the way we differentiated between managerial and organizational leadership. Next, visionary leadership involves five principles according to Bennis and Nanus (2007). We discuss each separately.

First, the visionary leader must *create a vision*. This vision is some idea of the desired end state or goal that the organization should be striving to achieve. The vision creates a focus for the organization that invites and motivates others to want to achieve it.

A strong vision creates a willingness to expend physical, spiritual, and emotion energy to achieve it. Visions are not simplistic goals like making a large profit but are more transcendent and ideological in nature. For a business, a vision is more likely related to developing innovative new products and services. For a nonprofit, the vision might be to provide some new or more effective service to help community members. The vision needs to be more than just a goal because it must also inspire.

Next, the visionary leader *communicates the vision effectively.* If the vision is not communicated effectively to other organizational members, or potential organizational members, then it will not provide a focus or be motivating. The vision will simply be lost. Effective communication may have to do with the use of meaningful metaphors, stories, and other framing devices, as well as effective delivery through various media choices from face-to-face to multimedia presentations. Effective communication creates meaning for the audience that allows them to understand and accept the vision.

The visionary leader must be able to *develop trust through positioning.* This concept might best be understood as a sort of political savviness that allows the visionary leader to be perceived as credible and trustworthy to the important stakeholders. Those individuals may be internal to the organization, the employees, or volunteers, but it also includes individuals outside the organization. For-profit business leaders need to gain the trust of external stakeholders such as suppliers and investors as well as governmental bodies and community members. Nonprofit leaders need to gain trust of the community, funding agencies, and potential volunteers. When the stakeholders trust the visionary leader, it becomes possible to move ahead toward accomplishing the vision.

Finally, the visionary leader must practice *self-management* or *positive self-regard.* Self-management includes a number of factors. It includes self-awareness of strengths and weaknesses. The visionary leader focuses on developing strengths and determining how to apply the strengths while compensating for weaknesses to meet the organizational needs. It also involves treating others with respect and empowering them to assume responsibility and make decisions. When successful, the focus of organizational members should be on achieving the vision and not on the visionary leader.

Again, hopefully you are thinking of some individuals you believe are visionary leaders. We present one pair of visionary leaders as an example of this concept. A visit to the Ben & Jerry's website confirms that they are visionary leaders. Their vision is clearly stated and communicated in their values. Those values include creating fantastic ice cream for its own sake; practicing sustainable growth, which includes being

From a renovated gas station in Burlington, Vermont, to far-off places with names we sometimes mispronounce, the journey that began in 1978 with 2 guys and the ice cream business they built is as legendary as the ice cream is euphoric.

environmentally conscious; and being innovative in making the world a better place. They create trust with their stakeholders by buying locally from small producers and purchasing fair-trade ingredients internationally (i.e., products produced in developing countries by companies that pay appropriate wages and protect the rights of employees). They demonstrate their commitment to support social justice and environmental issues. Although their names are on the cartons, the focus of the website, the employees, and the customers seems to be on the product and the mission and not on the leaders themselves. When Michael Kramer had the opportunity to hear the two speak to an audience, it reinforced his perception that they also practiced self-management in that they balanced each other's strengths and weaknesses in running the organization.

In their talk, they provided an example that demonstrated how they practiced their vision. That example is explained on their website (http://www.benjerry.com/greyston). The chocolate brownies used in some of their ice cream flavors are baked at the Greyston Bakery in Yonkers, New York. The bakery hires and trains employees who have been incarcerated, homeless, or substance abusers to give them opportunities to work, no questions asked. Profits from the Greyston bakery help provide child care, housing, and other benefits to low-income members of the community. This example illustrates clearly how the vision of the leaders, Ben and Jerry, are being achieved by the organization they started.

Transformational (versus Transactional) Leadership

Charismatic and visionary leadership often, but not always, involves founding an organization with the leader helping to shape the organization's culture as it develops and grows. When an individual replaces a previous leader, that person could be become a visionary leader who takes the organization in new directions. However, individuals who produce that type of change in an organization are more often called transformational leaders. Transformational leadership involves a leader changing an organization's culture.

As with the previous types of organizational leadership, there are a wide variety of descriptions of the characteristics of transformational leadership including factors such as being creative, demonstrating interactive and effective communication, creating a vision, empowering others, and being passionate (Hackman & Johnson, 2000). All of the different descriptions agree that being a transformational leader is different than being a transactional leader. Transactional leaders maintain the status quo and provide rewards for high performers and corrective action for poor performers. They lead by rewarding and punishing others in a process of quid pro quo (this for that). By contrast, transformational leaders provide a sense of vision or mission and build relationships that inspire and motivate others to make large changes (Bass, 1990). This conceptual difference is consistent with our distinction between managerial (transactional) leadership and organizational (transformational) leadership.

Identifying the characteristics of transformational leadership is not the same as explaining the process of being a transformational leader. Here we present the process model of Noel Tichy and David Ulrich (1984) to explain how transformational change is accomplished through leadership. We explain each step briefly.

The first two steps in the process are nearly identical to what visionary leaders do. The transformational leader needs to first create a vision for a new organization and then communicate the vision effectively to create initial commitment to change. It is sometimes suggested that the characteristics of charismatic leadership also come into play during this part of the process by identifying a problem that needs to be addressed to make the new vision seem essential to adopt.

Transactional leaders then need to convert their new vision into reality through a three-step process of change. The first step involves ending the old ways of doing things, the previous organizational norms and practices. Ending or concluding old routines may include various physical activities such as final ceremonies or moving to a new location to signal separation from the previous practices. The second phase is the neutral phase in which the organizational members are separated from their old way of doing things but not yet fully engaged in the new. This pause or "time out" between the old and new allows people to adjust to the upcoming change emotionally. The third phase involves practicing new approaches and making those new ways of doing things routine so that organizational members do not fall back into old habits. Success after the changes reinforces members' commitment to the new and encourages them not to regress backward. If the changes are unsuccessful, it is easy for people to want return to the way things used to be.

It may be challenging for you to think of examples of transformational leaders unless you know something about the history of an organization, but history is full of great examples of transformational leaders. For example, every one of us benefits from the transformational leadership of William Anderson who became CEO of National Cash Register in the early 1970s. His story was explained in a keynote conference presentation (Meyer, 1987; See also http://www.ncr.com/company/company-overview/history-timeline). At the time Anderson became CEO, National Cash Register was on the brink of failing because the computer revolution was taking off; and although it was producing computers as well, it was still producing the old mechanical cash registers like you see in movies. The former CEO said "our customers have no interest in new-fangled gadgets" (Meyer, 1987, p. 10). When Anderson took over from the short-sighted CEO, he took drastic steps to enact his new vision for the organization by announcing that they would only produce computerized registers from then on, a clear indication the old way of doing things was changing. During the transition, he reinforced the transformational change symbolically by changing the company name to NCR; and he reinforced the change physically by actually bulldozing the old single-story, campus-like company headquarters and replacing it with a steel and glass multistory building that stood out in the Dayton, Ohio, skyline. He also first wrote off $135 million in mechanical cash registers and the replacement parts as losses. Then they apparently were still able to sell those parts to customers who wanted to maintain their old cash registers as a shortage of replacement parts developed. In this way, he created a profit for the organization in the following years. But the growth and success of NCR was largely the result of it creating the first commercialized bar code scanners that are standard in all retail stores today. Chances are you can probably see or find a bar code right where you are (like on the back of this book!). The transformation of the organization was so complete and successful that AT&T purchased the company in 1991—although it later spun it off, and it again became NCR. As you shop in the future, look for NCR at the checkout. This clear example of transformation leadership may assist you in recognizing other transformational leaders in businesses, sports teams, educational settings, and nonprofit organizations.

Institutional Leadership

Each of the previous types of organizational leadership has focused on creating or changing an organizational culture. The final type of organizational leader is different than the previous three. Institutional leadership focuses largely on *maintaining* the culture. With this focus, institutional leadership may seem like managerial leadership because it seems to enact the decisions and vision of someone else. Institutional leadership is different from managing in that the leader is in the position to decide to sustain the current culture actively and encourages others to maintain it actively as well. A manager does not have the authority to make that decision. As discussed in Chapter 6, organizational culture is the result of a structuration process in which the culture is created and recreated through the actions of the organizational members. By deciding to maintain the culture actively, the institutional leader recreates and sustains the culture. Harrison Trice and Janice Beyer (1991, 1993) identify four important characteristics of an institutional leader.

First, an institutional leader *sustains* the mission, distinctiveness, and basic organizational culture. The leader does not perceive that there is a crisis or problem that needs to be addressed because the organization is successful in achieving its goals. If there is a problem, the leader believes it can easily be addressed without changing the culture. Due to this assessment, the institutional leader focuses on maintaining the organization instead of changing it.

Next, the institutional leader *embodies* those values, beliefs, and practices. By example, the leader demonstrates a strong commitment to the organization's current culture. If thriftiness is an organizational value, then the institutional leader exhibits financial restraint in the furnishings of the CEO office and may fly coach instead of first class on business trips.

Third, the institutional leader *defends* the organizational culture and makes its values seem stable and secure. Through communication, the leader points to the organization's success, based on its values, and presents an optimistic view of the future based on maintaining those values. These messages and the institutional leader's behaviors create a sense of security about the organizational culture.

Finally, although generally maintaining the culture, the institutional leader also *refines* the organizational culture. The leader does make an effort to improve the organization and makes adjustments as a result of a changing environment. These changes are minor changes in the culture during its recreation, but the overall culture will seem largely unchanged.

It is probably easy to think of leaders who are institutional leaders, individuals who maintained the culture of the organization when they assumed the role as the head of an organization. This practice might be particularly common when children take over a family business. To illustrate institutional leadership, we present an historical example of a son succeeding his father as CEO of a major corporation (Levinson & Rosenthal, 1986; see Rodgers, 1969; Trice & Beyer, 1991, 1993).

Thomas Watson Sr. was instrumental in founding IBM and served as its CEO for 40 years. His son, Thomas Watson Jr., followed him as CEO. The son generally acted as an institutional leader even though he and his father disagreed with each other frequently. For example, to uphold the value of "high standards of performance, attention to detail, and high moral and ethical standards," he called the head of the IRS personally to report a minor accounting mistake discovered two years after the fact and paid the additional taxes. He continued the concern for employees by making speeches at many IBM locations to be able to meet them personally, sent flowers to the wife of a manager he kept late to apologize to her, and maintained the open door policy established by his father so that employees could skip levels of management to discuss matters with him directly, if needed. He also maintained the practice of making sure that suppliers and communities were not overly dependent on IBM for their livelihoods. This meant making sure that a supplier did not have more than 30% of its business directly related to IBM and that the number of employees in a community did not exceed a certain percentage of their population or more than 6,000 employees. However, he did make changes in practices over time. The community policy was later amended because plants were located in larger metropolitan areas. He also demonstrated creativity by directing the company toward new products and later restructured the organization while maintaining the value of producing leading products. These changes influenced the success of the organization while maintaining much of its culture.

Framing Theory

The different types of organizational leadership we present have been descriptive without any underlying or unifying theory of leadership. Furthermore, across these well-known models, communication is often listed as an aspect of leadership but is often not described as central to its essence and expression. Professor Gail Fairhurst, however, puts forth a theoretical perspective that provides a way of synthesizing these different types of organizational leadership from a communication perspective. That perspective is summarized by the phrase "leadership framing." The central idea of framing is that leadership involves managing meaning by presenting a particular frame or description of a situation that encourages followers to take up a particular way of understanding and responding to the situation. "To hold the frame of a subject is to choose one particular meaning (or set of meanings) over another. When we share our frames with others (the process of framing), we manage meaning because we assert our interpretations should be taken as real over other possible interpretations" (Fairhurst & Sarr, 1996, p. 3). Both the meanings that are included and emphasized as well as those meanings that are excluded or discredited provide understanding of the situation (Fairhurst, 2011b).

Framing theory directs our attention to the idea that communication is not merely an "instrument" of leadership or reflective of leader's thoughts but is the substance of how leadership influence actually works. To understand that idea, it is important to know that a *frame* refers to beliefs about how the world works (or is supposed to work). *Framing* involves attempting to shape others' frames. Framing devices such as stories, metaphors, contrasts, jargon, and spin are a few common communication-based ways that leaders shape our beliefs about the world. Take, for example, an organizational leader who engages in framing the meaning of long work hours and comparatively low wages. Long work hours and comparatively low wages can lead some organizational members to frame those ambiguous facts as indicating that they are overworked and underpaid. Obviously, if those meanings were accepted, employees would probably experience low satisfaction and consider leaving the organization. Conversely, imagine a communicatively savvy leader who might engage in framing the meaning of long work hours as indicative of organizational members' "hard working character" through the use of a different frame. The leader might engage in framing the meaning of comparatively low wages as indicating "organizational members' commitment" and "real heart" in working toward the organization's goals to help customers and one another. Obviously, if those meanings were taken up by employees, it would probably result in much stronger organization–member relationships.

Fairhurst's (2011b) explanation of the principles of leadership through framing suggests a process. First, based on a reflection of themselves and their goals, leaders must have an understanding of a vision for the organization. Without a well-formulated understanding of the situation and a vision for action, leaders' attempts at framing will likely be unsuccessful. Next, leaders must also recognize the opportunities and constraints that exist in their environment, including those within their organizations and external to them. For example, events such as a key employee leaving provide an opportunity for framing, but the framing may be constrained if the loss of that employee is a particularly emotional event for others. The critical step involves the leaders

Framing and Managerial Leadership

Framing theory not only applies to organizational leadership but also to managerial leadership. Consider how framing theory can be important for managers whether they are viewed from a trait, style, situational, or contingency approach. In particular, consider how framing may be important in managing dialectical tensions.

communicating effectively to enable others to have a shared understanding of the situation and of the vision of what the organization can be.

Communication discourse can include a range of framing devices. For example, metaphors show similarities, contrasts show differences, and stories attract attention and are easily remembered. Successful framing by leaders using these and other framing devices results in organizational members accepting the leaders' frame and responding in kind. Framing tends to be rather conscious when writing or delivering prepared messages; however, significant forethought and practice at the skill can help leaders use framing even in spontaneous communication (Fairhurst, 2005, 2011b).

Framing is clearly a part of each of the four types of organizational leadership presented. For example, the charismatic leader has to frame the current situation as a problem that needs to be addressed, whereas institutional leaders frame the current situation as not problematic. Visionary and transformational leaders have to be able to frame a clear vision of change that will be perceived as better than the current situation. Institutional leaders have to be able to frame the organization as not in need of significant change. Each of the examples demonstrates how the leaders frame situations to influence the understanding of the other organizational members including using symbolic behavior such as rituals and routines to reinforce the meanings that they desire.

Organizational Leadership of Volunteers

Nonprofit organizations that rely on volunteers for the majority of the effort needed to achieve their goals need charismatic, visionary, transformational, and institutional leaders as well. Well-known founders of organizations like Clara Barton, founder of the

American Red Cross, or Millard and Linda Fuller, founders of Habitat for Humanity, appear to have been either charismatic or visionary leaders. Jan Levy, although far less widely known, is a graduate of the Seattle-based Leadership Tomorrow program who is considered a transformational leader because she built and expanded the program after becoming its executive director (Riggio, Bass, & Orr, 2004). Research indicates that transformational leadership is associated with positive energy, enthusiasm, and effort among employees of nonprofit organizations (Freeborough & Patterson, 2015). However, once these organizations began reaching their goals, institutional leaders usually followed. Organizational leadership is clearly important for nonprofit organizations at the local level as well as at national and international levels.

The Dark Side of Managerial and Organizational Leadership

So far our discussion has viewed managers and leaders in a positive light as men and women who help organizational members accomplish routine tasks and positive goals. Unfortunately, many leaders use their influence to achieve goals that harm others. Without ethical standards, the same communication can be used to accomplish prosocial or antisocial goals (Fairhurst, 2011b).

A summary of the components of ethical behavior suggest that ethical leadership behavior included four important factors (Hackman & Johnson, 2000). *Moral sensitivity* considers how different courses of actions will affect others. *Moral judgment* involves choosing the most appropriate actions from those options. *Motivation* for the choice needs come from moral values and concern for others rather than gaining personal wealth or power. *Moral action* involves implementing the choice. If organizational leaders follow these principles, then historical examples like Kenneth Lay at Enron or Bernadine Healy of the American Red Cross being disgraced for financial improprieties would not have occurred.

Comparing Managerial and Organizational Leadership

We began the chapter by pointing out that the distinction between managerial and organizational leadership is not as distinct as we have made it here because the lines between the two are often blurred. Managers may have a vision for their department. Organizational leaders have to use managerial leadership skills to work with their immediate contacts in the organization. So what makes managing and leading different?

Warren Bennis (2009), among others, makes clear distinctions between managerial leadership and organizational leadership. Table 8.2 highlights some of the major differences. Looking at the list should help you see why we have divided the chapter into two sections. Managerial leadership has a different focus than organizational leadership, but looking at the list should also make it easy to see why the distinction is not always so clear. Good managers may focus on maintaining the organizational operations, but to do so may require some vision beyond the day-to-day operations. Organizational leaders may be focused on the future and innovations but have to pay some attention to maintaining operations or the organization will fail. Good managers may accomplish a lot through positional power that allows them to control and direct members of their department or group, but being able to inspire those people will result in more success. Organizational leaders may inspire trust so that organizational members accept or buy into a vision for the organization, but at times the members likely just do "what the boss wants." So although it is easy to make two lists and consider them as

TABLE 8.2 Difference Between Managerial Leadership and Organizational Leadership

Characteristics of Managerial Leadership	Characteristics of Organizational Leadership
Good at administration	Good at innovation
Asks how and when	Ask what and why
Is a copy of others who imitates them	Is the original who initiates new ideas
Accepts and maintains the status quo	Challenges the status quo and changes it
Eyes on the bottom line and efficiency	Eyes on the horizon and vision
Relies on control to influence others	Inspires trust to influence others
Short-range perspective	Long-range perspective
Is the classic good soldier	Is his or her own person
Makes decisions affecting specific tasks	Makes decisions affecting the organization
Communicates primarily one-on-one	Communicates frequently one-to-many
Does things right	Does the right thing

separate and nonoverlapping, it is probably better to think of them as continuums instead of dichotomies such that people in leadership positions in organizations emphasize one end of continuum more than the other; however, much like dialectical tensions discussed earlier, they need some of both. During your career, you are more likely to be in positions of managerial leadership than organizational leadership, but you will have opportunities to demonstrate characteristics of both in your various roles as organizational members.

Summary

In this chapter, we addressed one of the most important topics in organizational communication. Throughout your life you will be managed or led by someone and you will manage and lead others either in your career or in your other life experiences as a parent, volunteer, or community member. The distinction between managerial leadership and organizational leadership helps clarify some of the important differences between working closely with a group of people and leading an entire organization of people. Managerial leadership may be based in part on personal traits, although the evidence is weak that some people are natural leaders. Managers have different styles—they sometimes respond to the situation, and other times they adapt their styles based on contingencies in the situation or in the group members. Managers balance dialectical tensions between choices to focus on task or relations and internal or external audiences. Organizational leadership involves framing situations in ways that creates meaning so that followers understand the situation and know how to respond. Charismatic and visionary leaders create organizational culture, whereas transformational leaders change existing cultures and institutional leaders maintain them while making some changes or adjustments. Your future leadership experiences will likely include both managerial and organizational leadership.

Communication
and Decision-Making

When the meeting of the department heads at the local department store occurred that Wednesday, the store manager specifically charged them with developing a new policy to address the employee tardiness problem. During that initial meeting, tempers sometimes flared as managers had different ideas on what to do. There was no agreement on a policy by the end of the meeting. At the end of the second meeting there was less conflict and eventually the committee recommended a policy to upper management for implementation. The policy included incentives for employees who are on time and mild consequences for employees who are late.

· · · · ·

Decision-making is a mainstay of organizational activity that is accomplished through communication. Each day individuals and groups of people in organizations make dozens of decisions. These decisions range from small decisions such as what color paper to use for a project to major decisions about which services a business should provide that could affect the viability of the organization. These decisions may be effective or ineffective; they may have a major impact on an individual or the organization; or they may make little short-term or long-term difference.

As an organizational member, you will be involved in many individual decisions, including the decision to join or leave an organization. Our focus in this chapter is not on how individuals make decisions but on how groups of people make decisions that affect the group or the larger organization. The longer you are in an organization, the more likely you are to be involved in making decisions that directly impact others. In this chapter, we focus on understanding how decision makers work together in organizations with the goal of improving decision-making. To accomplish this, we begin by examining some prescriptive models that attempt to prescribe how decisions should be made. Then we explore a number of descriptive models that try to describe how groups of people actually make decisions based on observing groups in action. These descriptive models are followed by some alternative approaches to understanding decision-making. Finally, we look at some explanations of why groups make ineffective decisions.

A Prescriptive Model of Decision-Making

The Model

A careful examination of most of the advice on how to make effective decisions will reveal that most of it is some variation on John Dewey's (1910) reflective thinking model. Dewey was primarily concerned with individual decision-making, but the ideas in his model have been applied to group and organizational decision-making as well. The basic model involves five steps.

1. The first step is to *define and limit the problem*. The idea here is that decision makers need to make sure that they have narrowed down the problem to something specific and that they understand the causes and effects of the problem. Without a clear understanding of the problem to be addressed, it will be difficult to solve it effectively. So in this step, the tardiness policy committee mentioned previously might try to discover the scope of the tardiness problem, such as its causes, while making sure that they do not address issues of absenteeism or understaffing, which are different problems.

2. The second step is to *establish criteria for evaluating a solution*. Here the decision makers focus on the important characteristics or requirements for the solution. This does not involve considering specific solutions yet but just what any solution must do. So, for example, based on the tardiness problem defined in the first step, the tardiness policy committee may decide that a solution must

Improving Decision-Making Through Brainstorming

Most groups that use brainstorming rarely follow the actual guidelines for it. The formal rules for brainstorming are (a) state as many ideas as possible, (b) encourage wild and creative ideas, (c) improve or combine ideas (piggy-backing), (d) accept without criticism all ideas, and (e) record all ideas for future consideration (Osborn, 1957). Accepting ideas without criticism is the key to achieving a wide range of ideas. Groups that follow these rules generate more ideas than those that do not; but research has consistently shown that if group members use the nominal group technique (NGT) in which members brainstorm on their own without interacting and then share their ideas, they will produce more nonredundant ideas than an interacting brainstorming group (Diehl & Stroebe, 1987). So one way to improve decision-making and have more ideas to consider is to think outside the box for solutions by following the rules of brainstorming or NGT. What could you do if a group is "brainstorming" but not following the rules and begins criticizing immediately?

reduce tardiness by at least 20%, be inexpensive to implement, and treat hourly employees differently than salaried employees.

3. The third step is to *suggest and consider alternative solutions.* During this step, the decision makers should suggest and consider as many alternatives as possible. Most groups and individuals could probably improve their consideration of alternatives by using some sort of formal process to generate possible solutions such as brainstorming or nominal group technique (NGT; see Communication Challenge above). However, most groups simply start suggesting ideas and begin evaluating (criticizing) them almost immediately. This pattern leads to group members considering fewer ideas than they could, as members are reluctant to suggest something for fear of criticism. So the tardiness policy committee might start with a few suggestions such as docking people's pay, giving them warnings before firing them, or offering incentives for those who consistently arrive on time. Because they begin discussing the merits of these suggestions as they come up, they likely do not consider very many other possible options. Following the

formal rules of brainstorming or NGT likely would have increased the number of ideas considered.

4. The fourth step is to consider *the advantages and disadvantages of the solutions* that have been mentioned. If the group followed the brainstorming or NGT, they begin comparing the solutions at this point. They should also consider which solutions best meet the criteria that they developed in the second step. Here the tardiness policy committee might see that dismissing employees for tardiness might be very expensive for the organization because of the cost of hiring and training replacements, and that the cost of incentives could add up over time. So they may decide on a policy that gives hourly employees one warning for tardiness per month, but then docks their pay for subsequent tardiness. The policy allows salaried employees to use flextime and either stay late or shorten their lunch hours to make up for when they are tardy.

5. The final step is to *implement the best solution*. Having selected the best solution to the problem, the individuals then go about executing the plan. If the process was rational and logical as Dewey (1910) suggested it should be, then the plan should work. The plan the tardiness policy committee recommended to management would be put in place and presumably reduce the tardiness problem by at least 20% and cost the organization very little to implement.

Descriptive Models of Decision-Making

Prescriptive decision-making models like Dewey's (1910) probably seem rather idealistic. We can all recognize that we individually, or in decision-making groups, frequently do not follow this sort of carefully plotted out process of decision-making. As an alternative to prescribing how groups should make decisions, a number of researchers have focused on descriptive models of decision-making. These researchers observed groups making decisions in laboratories or natural settings and then systematically analyzed their communication processes to be able to describe how groups make decisions accurately. There are a variety of these descriptive models.

Phase Models

Some of the earliest descriptive models of decision-making focused on the phases that groups go through in making decisions. There are a variety of these models proposed by a range of scholars over the years (e.g., Bales & Strodtbeck, 1951; Bennis & Shepard, 1956; Tuckman & Jensen, 1977). These models all have some sort of introductory phase, followed by a phase or two of disagreement and evaluation, followed by a phase or two where the group gradually comes together to reach a decision. Rather than review and compare all of these, we provide a detailed presentation of one such model developed by Fisher (1970) as representative of the others. Based on a very complex analysis of the decision-making of a wide range of groups that reached consensus on a decision, Fisher described four phases of decision-making: (a) orientation, (b) conflict, (c) emergence, and (d) reinforcement. Each phase includes both a task dimension of communication related to making an effective decision and factors that affect the social relationships among the group members. These two dimensions are consistent with the research on managerial leadership we discussed in Chapter 8, which suggests task and social forces often demand a balanced approach.

Fisher (1970) labeled the first phase he observed in groups making decisions the *orientation phase*. During this time, individuals might begin by introducing themselves to each other if they did not already know one another to begin creating social relationships. They also likely clarified the goal of the group so that everyone was working on the same issue or problem. During this time, they also voiced some of their attitudes toward the issue. However, they voiced them in very tentative or ambiguous ways to maintain relationships early at this point in the process (see strategic ambiguity in Chapter 1). This ambiguity allowed them to determine if their opinions were compatible with that of others in the group and maintain positive social relationships. Their tentative discussion of the problem perhaps included topics like how big the problem was in their department or some of the ways that they have tried to address the problem in the past. Focusing on the problem and how it was addressed in the past allowed them to be ambiguous about their preferences for addressing the problem now because they did not commit to any particular solution to the problem.

After the polite and ambiguous orientation phase, Fisher found that decision-making groups typically entered a *conflict phase*. As they continued discussing the issues, they addressed the task using less ambiguity and more forcefully voiced their opinions. They voiced agreement or disagreement more clearly over different potential choices that were being discussed. Individuals in the group began to form alliances with others who agreed with them. The conflict often intensified as these subgroups or cliques became clearly defined based on similar attitudes. These subgroups affected the social relationships within the larger groups. Disagreement became the dominant form of communication during the conflict phase between subgroups with different opinions, although agreement within groups was also common. There was a significant reduction in ambiguity as group members clearly stated their opinions. During this phase of the tardiness policy committee deliberations, the committee members started clearly voicing their opinions on which solutions to the problem they favor. There was agreement between some individuals on using sanctions to correct problem employees. Others joined together to push for incentives as positive rewards instead of sanctions. A third group simply wanted to fire employees who were problematic. According to the scenario, there were heated discussions between the groups about these differences of opinions and the first meeting apparently ended with the group still in the conflict stage. Because this committee involved more than one meeting to reach a decision, it is likely that some of these different subgroups may have informally discussed their views outside of the meeting and then sat together at the beginning of the second meeting. An observer of the conflict stage might think the group would never reach consensus.

The conflict phase of a group could be brief or quite long, even carrying over several meetings if the group used a series of meetings to make a decision. Eventually, Fisher (1970) found that groups entered an *emergence phase*. During this time, the group started finding areas of agreement and began reducing the discussion to fewer options or even just one option that more and more people could support. The use of ambiguity during this phase increases for two reasons. Moving from strongly worded opinions to more ambiguous ones allows individuals to change their opinions without clearly contradicting their previous statements. Also, ambiguous statements allow more agreement to emerge. During the emergence phase, there are fewer disagreements; and the subgroups that formed during the conflict phase start to dissipate, and the group becomes more unified socially again. During this phase of the tardiness policy committee, members of some of the subgroups will soften their stance, perhaps by taking positions that are somewhat ambiguous, such as "you make a good point about incentivizing good behavior, but I think we still need some sort of consequence for being late." Statements like this allow various members to come together and reach tentative agreement and eventually reach consensus. As this occurs, the group gradually becomes more unified and the subgroups no longer seem to exist.

The final phase according to Fisher (1970) was the *reinforcement phase*. During this phase, the group reached consensus on a decision. After they have worked out the details of how they will implement the decision, usually with a minimal amount of disagreement, they often congratulate themselves for the work they have done. If consensus

TABLE 9.1 Phases of Decision-Making Leading to Consensus

Phase	Task Dimension	Social Dimension
Orientation	Narrowing of topic Providing context Voicing opinions tentatively	Initiating and introducing Maintaining positive relations
Conflict	Disagreeing on solutions Advocating opinions clearly	Developing cliques and subgroups based on opinions
Emergence	Finding areas of agreement Moving toward consensus	Diminishing presence of subgroups
Reinforcement	Reaching consensus Clarifying the decision	Merging of the subgroups Celebrating accomplishments

was truly achieved, as opposed to some members simply giving in to the majority opinion, there was likely a sense of unity and accomplishment in the group. The group was now ready to implement the decision they reached. For the tardiness policy committee, the group members worked on specific details of the policy including some incentives for being on time (extra employee discounts) and consequences for those who are late (minutes deducted for hourly employees) and when the policy will go into effect and who will enforce it. They seemed quite pleased with their decision and expected it will help reduce the problem.

Fisher (1970) emphasized that the phases are not necessarily of equal length. For example, a group may have a very short orientation phase if they already know each other or may have an extended conflict phase that lasts for several meetings. The transition between phases is determined by the change in communication patterns, not the amount of time.

Alternative Descriptive Models

There are some significant limitations to phase models of decision-making. This description of a group going smoothly through the phases of decision-making may seem familiar, or we may be able to make one of our group decision-making experiences fit into the phase model, but we can likely think of other experiences that do not fit this pattern. Research by other scholars suggests some alternative descriptive models to the typical phase model.

The Spiral Model

Scheidel and Crowell (1964) proposed that groups often do not move smoothly through the phases like Fisher's (1970) model might suggest. Instead, they found that groups often move back and forth between phases. A group may move from orientation to conflict, onto emergence, back to conflict, and repeatedly visit previous phases until it gradually reaches a decision. According to them, there is a gradual spiral toward reinforcement/conclusion rather than a linear progression.

The spiral model is particularly likely to occur if the decision-making process actually involves a series of small decisions rather than only one large decision. For the tardiness policy committee, it might be possible to describe the process as fluctuating back and forth between conflict and emergence as a committee makes a series of decisions. For example, they may first decide that they need a company-wide policy; then decide that they need to provide incentives for promptness and consequences for tardiness; then determine what the incentives should be; then what the consequences should be; and then finally, who will implement the policy. Each of these smaller decisions may involve periods of orientation, conflict, and emergence, but eventually an overall policy is adopted. This spiraling toward a final comprehensive decision likely describes our own experiences with groups as well. It is not quite a step-by-step process like the phase models, but it still suggests a sequential but flexible approach to decision-making.

Multiple Sequence Model

Through a series of studies using alternative groups and an alternative method of analysis, Poole (1981, 1983a, 1983b) provided compelling evidence that decision-making groups often do not follow anything resembling the traditional phases of decision-making. As an alternative to phase models, Poole proposed that decision-making groups instead have three activity tracks that occur simultaneously: (a) task process activities related to managing its task, (b) relational activities related to managing relationships among group members, and (c) topical focus activities related to specific issues or arguments at a particular point in time. These three activity tracks overlapped and interacted in no particular order; but through a series of breakpoints, the group gradually moved toward a decision. A common type of breakpoint was a topic shift that moved the group to a new activity or focus or reintroduced a previously discussed topic. A second type of breakpoint included delays in which the group was in a sort of holding pattern where they addressed a particularly difficult topic for an

Leading Group Decisions

As the leader of a decision-making group (a committee), you recognize that conflict is a normal part of the process. However, the group you are leading seems to be stuck in conflict after two meetings with little movement toward any decision. Should you allow your committee to move at its own natural pace or use communication strategies to help urge it along toward a decision? If you choose to move it along toward a decision, what communication strategies can you use to help the group?

extended period of time as they increased their comprehension of a particular issue or had a period of high creativity. The third type of breakpoint was disruptions or even failures. These are points at which conflict is quite intense or the group recognizes that it is failing to address the decision sufficiently and must readjust either to manage the conflict or reconsider the issues. These three types of breakpoints caused shifts in the three activity tracks, but the group still eventually reached a decision. The multiple sequence model might describe the tardiness policy committee deliberations similarly to the spiral model by examining how breakpoints caused the committee to move forward and backward in a gradual movement toward a final decision. However, the multiple sequence model would focus more attention on examining the three tracks: (a) periods of time when the group focused on facilitating a decision, such as asking if there was agreement on a particular part of the policy proposal; (b) time spent addressing relational issues that were affecting the group, such as disagreement between two individuals; and (c) time spent discussing particular issues, such as incentives or consequences.

Vigilant Interaction Theory

An alternative to the previous models describes decision-making in terms of specific communication behaviors needed for effective decision-making. Vigilant interaction theory (VIT) by Hirokawa and Rost (1992) suggests that effective decision-making groups address four important communication activities:

1. What problem or issue in the current state of affairs needs to be addressed?
2. What do we want to achieve or accomplish in addressing the problem?

3. What are the choices available to us?

4. What are the positive and negative aspects of these choices?

The two researchers used historical case studies, studies of groups in laboratories, and naturally occurring groups in organizations to verify the theory. They reviewed several studies and found general support for the usefulness of these four principles for enhancing the quality of groups' decisions. However, they also found that most of the improvement was related to encouraging groups to explore the possible negative consequences of their choices. Conversely, encouraging groups to explore the potential positive consequences of their choices was not found to be related to solution quality because most groups are optimistic about their choices without much prompting (Orlitzky & Hirokawa, 2001).

A comparison of VIT to Dewey's (1910) reflective thinking model finds some consistency between them. Both focus on defining the problem carefully and considering the positive and negative aspects of various choices. What seems to distinguish VIT from Dewey's model is the sequential flexibility that VIT suggests for decision-making. Whereas Dewey's model suggests going through a step-by-step, linear process to make a decision, in VIT, it is not important what order the consideration of these factor occurs in, just that they are completed at some point. So according to VIT, the tardiness policy committee could be effective even if it started with considering the negative aspects of imposing consequences for tardiness, then worked on what the real problem was, then considered other solutions, then later redefined the problem differently, but eventually came to a consensus in the end. The decision would be effective because they completed all four communication activities as part of their decision-making process even though they did them in a somewhat random order.

TABLE 9.2 Comparison of Rationale Decision-Making Models

Dewey (1910) Rational Decision	Fisher (1970) Phase Model	Scheidel/Crowell (1964) Spiral Model	Poole (1981, 1983a, 1983b) Multiple Sequence Model	Hirokawa/Rost (1992) Vigilant Interaction Theory
Define problem	Orientation	No set order for phases	Task activities	What problem?
Establish criteria	Conflict	Back and forth between phases	Relational activities	What to achieve?
Consider alternatives	Emergence		Topic focus	What choices?
Advantages and disadvantages	Reinforcement			What positive and negative aspects?
Implement plan				

Alternative Decision-Making Processes

A comparison of Dewey's (1910) model to the others (see Table 9.2) suggests that our understanding of decision-making has not progressed as much as we might expect over the years. The spiral, multiple sequence, and VIT models still have some of the same assumptions as Dewey's model that people make decisions through a largely rational process. Zey's (1992) critique of decision-making models finds that they include a number of assumptions related to rational decision-making that frequently are not true. Some of these assumptions concern decision makers processing information effectively, which frequently may not happen. For example, a group may not consider a wide range of options that limits their ability to make effective decisions. A group may not consider the appropriate criteria for achieving the objectives they want to accomplish because they are unaware of some of the factors that could influence the outcome. They may not correctly understand the information they have available about the problem. They may inadequately consider the positive outcomes or negative consequences of the costs and benefits of their decision in part because it may be impossible to know or accurately predict them. As a result, what seems like a good idea may have a negative outcome that could not be known ahead of time. For example, the tardiness policy committee seemed to have only considered incentives and consequences when other possibilities may exist. There may be scheduling issues within the organization that are creating the tardiness problems rather than the personnel involved, but information concerning improving scheduling was apparently never examined. In addition, although offering incentives seems like a good idea, they may not realize that offering incentives will actually create additional conflict between supervisors and their subordinates as they squabble over how early is early. In this way, the new policy may have a negative influence of employee morale that they were unable to anticipate.

The rational models also make some assumptions about the people involved in making the decision (Zey, 1992). The models assume that group members are committed to finding the best solution, but we have all worked in groups where at least one member was a social loafer who lacked such a commitment and was content to let others do the work (Latane, Williams, & Harkins, 1979). The rational models assume people have the time or resources to gather the information they need to make an effective decision while still meeting some decision deadline. They assume that people will not grow tired of the decision-making process and will continue to think critically about the issues rather than simply agreeing to what seems like a majority opinion.

In the case of the tardiness policy committee, the group may have been rushed for time and may not have considered the problem serious enough and so failed to gather important information that would have guided their decision-making in a different direction. After the conflict in the first meeting, they may have quickly endorsed a plan that was mentioned without thinking it through completely so that they could avoid conflict and get back to their other duties, which they consider more pressing. Given these problems with viewing decision-making as a very rational process, a number of scholars have described decision-making with alternative processes.

Satisficing

The satisficing decision-making process describes how participants actually tend to reach decisions in real situations when faced with an overwhelming amount of information or resource limitations (Connolly, 1980; Simon, 1972). A satisficing decision-making process describes how decision makers tend to be profoundly disadvantaged by bounded rationality or an inability to consider large amounts of information in making a decision. Limits to rationality included the complexity of the situation leading to an incomplete consideration of alternatives, incomplete information about the known alternatives, and uncertainty about the consequences of each known alternative (Simon, 1972). Faced with this bounded rationality, decision makers tend to search for options and then settle on a sufficient (not necessarily the best) choice discovered quickly, or one that will satisfice (apparently a combination of satisfy and suffice). This process might be described as discovering "a good enough" solution to the problem rather than trying to discover the optimal, rational solution through additional searching of an unending amount of information. Satisficing also implies that the outcome of the decision is monitored and then adjustments are made in response to the positive and negative consequences of the outcome. Much like players in a chess match or other strategy game, the individual or group decision maker arrives at a satisficed decision but then monitors the opponent's move to determine if an adjustment in strategy is needed.

In addition to occurring when faced with overwhelming amounts of information, satisficing also likely occurs when other characteristics of rational decision-making models are absent. In particular, satisficing often occurs when the decision makers are not particularly motivated to make an optimal decision either due to lack of personal involvement or because they consider the issue of limited importance. So despite the fact that we can analyze the tardiness policy committee's communication patterns according to each of the descriptive models in the previous section, it is quite possible that what actually occurred was satisficing. It is likely that only some of the committee members considered the problem important. As a result, when a "pretty good" or "adequate" sounding solution was proposed based on a reasonable amount of information gathered by those with a strong vested interest in solving what they consider an important problem, the entire group quickly reached consensus. Then they will monitor the new policy once it is established and make any adjustments if they are needed.

Garbage Can Model

Although satisficing does not fit the purely rational processes described in models like Dewey's (1910), it is possible to argue that satisficing is a very rational response to many real-life situations. As has been noted by a number of people, "A good decision taken in a timely manner is always better than an excellent one taken too late" (Pomerol, 2013, p. 241).[1] Because the cost and amount of effort to seek additional information does not result in an appreciable improvement in the final decisions (Connolly, 1980), it is actually fairly rational to select a good solution that emerges in a timely manner rather than getting caught in an unending cycle of seeking more information rather than making a decision or missing a deadline. By contrast, the final model, known as the garbage can model, does not attempt to portray decision-making as always resembling a rational approach; however, the garbage can model attempts to be honest about the ways some organizational decisions are actually made.

The garbage can model of decision-making essentially disregards all of the premises of rational decision-making and the systematic processes of the descriptive models, however flexible or inflexible they may be. The model describes decision-making as occurring in an almost random or chaotic manner in organizations at times. According to the garbage can model, decisions sometimes occur when streams of choices, attention, problems, solutions, and participants accidentally come together (Cohen, March, & Olsen, 1972). Accordingly, it takes participants paying attention to the situation and making choices that connect solutions and problems for these types of decisions to occur. However, these streams can begin at different times and in any order rather than in the orderly manner of the descriptive models introduced earlier. The following example of the tortilla warmers illustrates the garbage can model quite effectively.

Tortilla Warmers

Tortilla Warmer

. . . . .

A retail store had a large supply of tortilla warmers (Styrofoam-like containers with lids to keep tortillas warm on the table) on its shelf in the housewares department. Despite reducing the price on them by 50 percent, there were few sales and the store manager was considering writing them off as a loss and removing them from the shelves. About this time, a customer came in and asked the manager, "Where do you keep your bait boxes?" When the manager asked what he meant by bait boxes, the customer replied, "you know, those Styrofoam boxes you keep your worms in for fishing?" Realizing that the customer was describing the tortilla warmers, the manager took him to housewares, and the customer was happy to find the "bait boxes" at such a discounted price. Then the manager moved the tortilla warmers, now labeled as "bait boxes," to the sporting goods department. He marked them up to full price and they sold quickly.[2]

. . . . .

Notice how the solution to the customer's problem existed prior to knowledge of the problem. In fact, to the store manager, the tortilla warmers were actually perceived to be a problem in search of a solution and not *a solution in search of a problem*. Somewhat accidentally, the manager, who had been stewing over the failed attempts at solving the problem of the tortilla warmers, and the customer, who needed bait boxes, happened to meet. If the customer had arrived when the manager was on break or not working, the problem may never have been solved. Then only because the manager was paying attention and matched the customer's problem to a potential solution and made the correct choice by moving the tortilla warmers to the sporting goods department were both problems solved. Although you can certainly argue that the manager made a rational choice by being flexible enough to see tortilla warmers as bait boxes, there certainly was no step-by-step decision-making process; the decision was largely fortuitous.

Retrospective Rationality

There are probably numerous examples of satisficing and garbage can decision-making in organizations that go unreported. There are actually quite a few examples of products that were invented accidentally, suggestive of a garbage can model. For example, the well-known lubricant product WD-40 was invented for quite different purposes than it is now used by most consumers. Few consumers know of its original purpose: water displacement (WD). WD-40 was the 40th attempt at producing a product designed at preventing rust on aerospace missiles, but gradually the employees and customers found numerous other uses for it (http://www.wd40company.com/about/history/). Similarly, most people would be surprised to know that chocolate chip cookies, probably one of your favorite cookies, were accidently invented by Ruth Graves Wakefield when she ran out of baker's chocolate and substituted a Nestlé's chocolate bar for it. She was surprised when it did not melt and mix into the batter like she thought it would and remained in chunks. She decided that the chocolate chunks in the cookies would make a good consumer product (http://iml.jou.ufl.edu/projects/fall09/saval_j/history.html). Undoubtedly, we are largely unaware of countless of examples of satisficing and garbage can decision-making because organizations are reluctant to share just how haphazard so many of their decisions and discoveries are.

Another reason we rarely hear of satisficing and garbage can decision-making processes can probably be explained as the result of what is called *retrospective rationality*. The process of retrospective rationality involves decision makers going backward after

ETHICAL ISSUE

Retrospective Rationality

A small business owner accidently creates a new computer application that has potential to make millions in sales if it can be mass produced. To achieve this, the entrepreneur must attract venture capitalists to fund its production. During a presentation on what the product will do, one of the potential investors asks how she invented the product. Is it ethical for her to present a rational explanation of product development to solidify the investor's interest or should she simply admit that it was a rather serendipitous accident?

they perceive a decision to have been effective and then creating a rational description of the decision-making process (Connolly, 1980). So even though the decision was arrived at haphazardly and with less than maximum effort, the decision maker presents the decision-making as if it were a rational process. The reason for doing this is fairly easy to understand. Because communication involves impression management, presenting a rational explanation for a less than rational process helps improve the image of the decision makers and the organization. Imagine if a business went around explaining that they were not particularly thorough in seeking information before making decisions and often they just fell into most of their decisions accidentally. It would be difficult to recruit employees and investors, as well as customers and clients. Because our society values rational decision-making versus "flying by the seat of our pants," decision makers and organizational spokespersons usually present rational explanations for their decisions while masking examples of satisficing and garbage can decision-making.

Faulty Decision-Making

So far we have described decision-making in terms of characteristics of effective decision-making. We realize that decision makers in organizations frequently make poor decisions as well. The headlines throughout the last decades are frequently filled with examples of poor decision-making. Famous examples of ineffective decision-making include the failed Bay of Pigs Invasion (1961), the Watergate break-in (1972), the Bhopal disaster (1984), the Hubble telescope fiasco (1990), the Enron collapse (2001), and the financial crisis that led to the 2008 recession. More recently (2015), the executives of Volkswagen seem to have made poor decisions concerning the emissions on their clean diesel engines. In all of these examples, and many more, decision makers made ineffective decisions that led to significant problems, whereas alternative choices would have been more effective. The goal of this next section is not to second guess decision makers but to point out some of the problems that lead to ineffective

In September 2015, the Environmental Protection Agency found that many VW (Volkswagen) cars being sold in America had a "defeat device"—or software—in diesel engines that could detect when they were being tested, changing the performance accordingly to improve results. The German car giant has since admitted cheating emissions tests in the United States, and its reputation has subsequently been tarnished.

decisions to encourage decision makers to avoid making these same mistakes. We begin by looking at the most famous explanation of ineffective decision-making known as groupthink, developed by Irving Janis (1972). Then we explore other reasons groups make ineffective decisions.

Groupthink

Groupthink describes a decision-making process in which highly cohesive groups make poor decisions due to a number of errors in their decision-making processes. In the early conceptualization, Janis (1982) looked at examples of poor decision-making by policy makers, such as the Bay of Pigs Invasion, and used seven major decision-making defects that lead to poor decisions in selecting examples of groupthink:

1. Decision-making groups limited their discussion to only a few alternatives rather than considering many options
2. Decision makers did not consider the implicit values in the choices they were making or the objectives they were attempting to achieve
3. The decision makers failed to reexamine initially favored actions for risks and drawbacks, especially non-obvious ones, and so failed to consider potential problems with their planned actions
4. Decision makers failed to consider possible benefits of alternatives rejected by the group and so never seriously considered other alternatives
5. Groups made little or no attempt to consult experts outside the group and so instead trusted themselves and their collective knowledge
6. Decision makers demonstrated selection bias by only collecting information that supported their initial view and disregarding information that did not
7. Decision makers spent limited time deliberating about their decision and had no contingency or back-up plan for any problems or obstacles that got in their way

These were the starting points for explaining the concept of groupthink that guided other researchers.

Street (1997) provided a comprehensive model of groupthink based on the work of Janis (1982) and other scholars who followed. According to Street, there are three antecedent conditions, or preexisting conditions, that lead to the possibility of groupthink: (a) *high cohesion* among group members, which is a necessary but not sufficient condition; (b) *structural faults*, such as group isolation from others; and (c) a proactive situational context that requires timely action, such as an *external threat* to the group causing it stress. These antecedent conditions lead to concurrence seeking, or the biased information seeking that Janis identified.

Next, Street (1997) identified three symptoms of groupthink or conditions that develop as a result of the antecedent conditions and the biased information seeking: (a) an overestimated or inflated view of the group such that they have an *illusion of invulnerability* and a sense of group morality in that they think they cannot fail because they are doing what is right or correct; (b) *close-mindedness* to other ideas including collective rationalization and stereotyping of outgroup members such that they demonize those who oppose them; and (c) high levels of pressure to conform, such as an *illusion of unanimity* and *self-censorship*, such that no alternative perspectives are even voiced. It seems likely that given the other characteristics of groupthink, no other opinions may be voiced because there actually are no dissenting opinions.

These symptoms of groupthink are the essence of the decision-making defects Janis (1982) defined. There is an incomplete examination of alternatives and information, a failure to examine preferred or rejected choices for positive and negative consequences, continued selection bias, and a lack of a contingency plan. These decision-making defects lead to various negative and often disastrous outcomes.

Groupthink has primarily been used to analyze situations retrospectively in which groups made poor and disastrous decisions. There seem to be two primary problems in the way groupthink has been applied. First, most of the examples of groupthink are of decisions made that have large, political, or national consequences. It seems likely that decisions made by many groups and organizations that are less political also involve groupthink. It is fairly easy to present an analysis of the actions of various cults or extremist groups as examples of groupthink. Rarely does a year go by without some university campus group making headlines based on some poor decision-making that leads to some embarrassing incident or death. One example of this would be the Florida A&M death of the drum major during a hazing ritual in 2012 that led to charges against 13 band members (http://www.nytimes.com/2012/05/03/us/13-charged-in-hazing-death-at-florida-am.html?_r=0). The fact that the band continued hazing even after the state law in Florida made hazing a felony suggests that the band members exhibited many of the characteristics of groupthink, including antecedent conditions such as high cohesion and group isolation and symptoms of groupthink such as believing they were invulnerable and so would never be caught. They clearly did not carefully consider the possible negative consequences of their actions, consider alternative options, or have a contingency plan if something went wrong like it did. There are likely multiple other examples of groupthink that fail to make the national headlines in small and large organizations.

Second, the term *groupthink* has become such a common term that it seems to be routinely misused to describe any poor decision-making by a group. For example, it is hard to imagine that most student groups in college classes or committees in most businesses who make poor decisions are actually victims of groupthink, and yet the term is often applied to such groups. Other than a negative outcome, at best, these decision-making groups exhibit one or two of the characteristics of groupthink but rarely display very many of them. They likely fail to exhibit the characteristics of effective decision-making such as those identified as reflective thinking (Dewey, 1910) or VIT (Hirokawa & Rost, 1992), but that does not mean they fell into groupthink. It is due to this overuse of the term groupthink that we present another examination of ineffective decision-making next.

Other Characteristics of Ineffective Decision-Making

On January 28, 1986, the Space Shuttle Challenger exploded during takeoff. A number of scholars have argued that the decision to launch was an example of groupthink (e.g., Esser & Lindoerfer, 1989). Other scholars have argued that the decision to launch was an example of faulty decision-making without claiming it is an example of groupthink. In their analysis, Gouran, Hirokawa, and Martz (1986) identify a number of ways that groups make ineffective decisions due to various errors in their decision-making process. They divide these mistakes into three areas: cognitive influences, psychological influences, and social influences.

Cognitive influences include questionable beliefs and questionable reasoning (Gouran et al., 1986). Questionable beliefs amount to having and/or believing incorrect information. In the case of the Challenger decision, some of the decision makers believed there were backup systems for the O-rings when there were none and that the equipment would operate correctly in low temperatures even though they had never been tested for that. Questionable reasoning amounts to drawing unjustified conclusions. In the Challenger decision, the decision makers also seemed to have concluded that because past risky decisions had not led to any catastrophic outcomes, they would not in this case. As with the stock market, past performance is no guarantee of future performance, and yet that seems to have been the (il)logical reasoning used by the

Avoiding Groupthink and Ineffective Decision-Making Practices

It is clearly in the best interest of groups to avoid groupthink and other ineffective decision-making practices. A variety of suggestions have been made for avoiding these problems. Among them are assigning a critical advisor (aka, a devil's advocate) to question ideas and assumptions of the group, using a standard agenda so the group goes through a decision-making process rather than jumping to conclusions, inviting dissenting opinions, allowing for anonymous voting so that dissenting opinions are noted, having each person in the group list potential risks they see in the decision, and delaying the final decision until the next meeting to allow for reflection. Which of these seems most likely to be effective? What other actions could a leader do to make sure a group is avoiding decision-making errors and groupthink?

decision makers. Similarly, cognitive influences can affect other decision makers. For example, the owners of a temporary employee agency that provides employees to other businesses may have incorrect information about their capacity to open a second location in another community and may also draw incorrect inferences about their competitors' market growth in that town based on patterns from the last two years.

Psychological influences include perceived pressure and presumptive shift (Gouran et al., 1986). Perceived pressure means that some of the individuals involved felt pressured to agree with someone, probably higher in the hierarchy. In the case of the Challenger, the Thiokol managers felt pressured to reverse their recommendation against launching by the higher level NASA managers to whom they reported. Presumptive shift has to do with changing the decision-making criteria in an unexpected way. In the case of the Challenger, previously the decision-making criteria was to cancel the launch if there was *any doubt* of its safety; but suddenly the criteria changed on this particular day to proceed *unless there was conclusive evidence* that it was unsafe to launch. It is much easier to present a possible problem than it is to prove an inevitable one. The engineers were unprepared to prove it was unsafe to launch; they could only demonstrate that it might be a problem. Similar psychological influences could influence decision-making in a business. The owners of the temporary employee agency may feel pressured to open a second location because they feel that is what their investment partners expect or the investment partners may ask them to prove that opening a new location will be a financial disaster when they were only prepared to demonstrate that there are potential problems with expanding.

Social influences include ineffective persuasion and ambiguous language (Gouran et al., 1986). *Ineffective persuasion* means that individuals who had reason to oppose a decision did not make effective and forceful arguments to support their position. Using ambiguous language rather than precise language allows the receiver freedom to interpret the message somewhat differently than it was perhaps intended. In the Challenger disaster, the engineers admitted that they were unable to convince the managers at NASA not to launch in part because they said "Rockwell cannot assure that it is safe to fly," which can be interpreted as it might be safe to launch. "We recommend that you do not launch this morning" would have been less ambiguous and perhaps more persuasive. Of course, the managers at NASA may not have been convinced to change their minds by any message from the engineers. For the owners of the temporary employee agency, the business manager who correctly understands why the owners should not open a new location may lack public-speaking skills to address them and convince them to wait for another year or two before expanding. The manager may soften a critical comment so that it is ambiguous rather than stating it forcefully in an effort to avoid offending a senior owner who makes hiring and firing decisions.

This list of cognitive, psychological, and social influences is by no means a complete list of factors that can lead to ineffective decision-making. Zey's (1992) critique of rational decision-making models offered other reasons—such as insufficient information, inability to predict outcomes accurately, and lack of commitment of decision makers, among others. Additional explanations for poor decision-making can be easily added. The important point to take away from this list is that there are many reasons that decision makers in groups make poor decisions. Rather than jumping to an inappropriate conclusion that a poor decision is always the result of groupthink, it is important to explore other potential explanations for negative outcomes.

Decision-Making in Volunteer Organizations

Most of the discussion of decision-making so far can easily be applied to volunteers and nonprofit organizations by simply changing the examples. Volunteers face decisions just like members of for-profit and government organizations as groups of volunteers routinely make decisions about actions to take. They likely try to follow rational decision-making processes and to be vigilant in making good decisions. Because volunteers often lack a long-term commitment to the organization, as it is often less important to them than their work and family, volunteer groups may be more prone to satisficing than other organizations. They likely stumble across good decisions from time to time in a pattern that is consistent with the garbage can model. No doubt, they make ineffective decisions at times for various reasons. When voluntary associations are based on strong ideological commitments, it would not be surprising if members practice groupthink due to like-mindedness, high cohesion, and a belief in the superiority and unassailability of the morality of their goal and decision-making. The Jonestown massacre in 1978, where cult members committed mass suicide by drinking cyanide-laced Kool-Aid, likely represents groupthink. Various radical groups appear to exhibit groupthink tendencies as well.

A study of individuals who serve as members of boards of directors for nonprofit organizations suggested that the volunteer context has similarities to for-profit business settings but also had some differences (Castor & Jiter, 2013). In general, the volunteer board members thought that there were many similarities between their experiences in businesses and nonprofits. In both contexts, it was important to understand the culture of the organization to make appropriate decisions. In both contexts, decision makers were expected to use their personal knowledge and expertise to make decisions that benefitted the organization. An important difference was that the general expectations for them as board members were ambiguous, making it unclear what their decision-making responsibilities were or if they were simply supposed to be fundraisers and cheerleaders for the organization. They reported that decision-making and implementation simply moved slower in nonprofit organizations, in part because of the reliance on volunteers and in part due to infrequent meetings. Finally, they felt that there was more ambiguity about leadership in the nonprofit setting. As board members, they were in some ways the leaders who should make decisions for the organization and its volunteers, but they also felt like they were there to serve the organization's director and volunteers. They also often lacked a clear leader or mentor to help them make decisions on behalf of the organization. So although the nonprofit setting with volunteers was generally quite similar to other business settings, there were differences that impacted the decision-making processes.

Summary

Decision-making is a critical part of participation in organizations. Although newcomers have to make many individual decisions that affect their own jobs when they join an organization, they typically are not involved in many decisions that affect their work-group or department initially. Later, as they become more involved in the organization and assume positions involving more responsibility, they likely play a larger role in decision-making for others and not just themselves.

In this chapter, we have provided insight into how decision-making might work in an organizational setting. There will probably be an expectation that individual and group decisions will be made using a rational process as suggested by Dewey (1910). Groups making decisions may follow linear phases (Fisher, 1970), but they may be just as likely to spiral toward a decision by circling back and forth between phases (Scheidel & Crowell, 1964) or arrive at a decision via multiple sequences (Poole, 1983b) that occur in no particular order. The group may include many of the characteristics of rational decision-making, but the decision-making process may occur in somewhat random order as suggested by VIT (Hirokawa & Rost, 1992). At other times, groups may make decisions by satisficing due to various factors such as too much information or lack of commitment to reaching an optimal decision (Connolly, 1980). Sometimes groups will almost randomly make good decisions as described by the garbage can model (Cohen et al., 1972). Of course, at other times they will make poor decisions due to various cognitive, psychological, and social influences (Gouran et al., 1986). In some instances, when the group is highly cohesive and feels invincible, they may demonstrate characteristics of groupthink (Street, 1997). It is likely that some retrospective rationality goes into all of these types of decisions as decision makers attempt to make their decision-making process seem rational (Connolly, 1980). For the organizational member, it is challenging to work with all of these different types of decision-making processes in organizations.

CHAPTER 10

Communication and Conflict

The retreat planning committee was charged with planning the annual retreat for all of the department heads in the company. This included selecting a location for the annual retreat, designing the program, arranging for any guest speakers, and communicating the whole plan to everyone so that they would enthusiastically participate. The committee had met four times and work was moving along toward completion of the task, but there were certain predictable patterns in the group.

Terry, the chair of the committee, focused on facilitating the group process rather than dictating the outcome so everyone had a chance to influence the decisions in important ways. Of course, this meant there were certain disagreements and occasionally there arose outright conflict.

When it came to selecting the location, one member, Jesse, suggested the new Red Rock Retreat Center located about an hour away. A few people mentioned they liked where they went last year, so they did not make a decision at the first meeting. After Jesse distributed full-color brochures at the second meeting, everyone seemed to agree they should try Red Rock.

Deciding what the topic should be was a lot more challenging. Kendall was an outspoken proponent for training on leadership, and Hayden was quite insistent that the topic be on creating a positive organizational climate and culture. As they discussed potential topics, two members, Lane and Kai, began arguing with each other, vehemently disagreeing with the other's points. Near the end of the second meeting, this conflict developed into personal attacks, with Lane accusing Kai of being uninformed and Kai saying that Lane's views were rigid and old-fashioned. No one seemed to know how to respond to the situation, and Terry failed to provide any guidance. After some awkward moments, the group decided to wait until the next meeting to finalize the topic.

Fortunately for everyone, between meetings Reese learned about a consultant who had done a workshop for another company on transformational leadership that emphasized the process of changing organizational culture. After a rather brief discussion and a quick visit to the consultant's website, Kendall, Hayden, and everyone else agreed that was a great topic idea—that is, everyone except for Lane and Kai. They still found reasons to disagree with each other on every little detail. The committee decided to go with the consultant anyway and asked Terry to come to the next meeting with recommendations on the remaining details.

At today's meeting, everyone hoped that they could make some final decisions based on Terry's recommendations. Secretly they hoped that Kai and Lane would miss the meeting.

. . . . .

We tend to think of conflict as negative and something to be avoided. We might particularly consider conflict negative in organizational settings. Some people perceive the word so negatively that they insist that although they have "disagreements" with other people, they do not have any "real conflicts." This relabeling practice implies that the two terms are not overlapping phenomena, as a discussion of the meaning of conflict suggests. However, as we discuss more thoroughly later, conflict *can be* positive as well. For example, athletic achievements are the result of contestants competing with one another for the same prize or record—a form of conflict.

Conflict will be part of your organizational experience throughout your lifespan. If you are fortunate, you may not experience intense conflict on a routine basis. You may insist that you only have disagreements at work, no conflicts. More than likely, there will be periods of time when conflict in your workplace is prominent enough to cause you to consider whether to remain in a group, department, or organization or go somewhere else.

In this chapter, we examine the issue of conflict in organizational settings. We begin by defining conflict, and then we looks at some of the many types of conflict that influence our organizational experiences and some possible positive outcomes that can result from conflict. We explore some of the common styles of managing conflict that individuals use before looking at some ways that others intervene in the process. Finally, we explore in more depth two particularly detrimental forms of conflict that can occur in organizational settings involving abusive coworkers: bullying and sexual harassment.

Defining Conflict

A common definition of conflict is "the interaction of interdependent people who perceive opposition of goals, aims, and values, and who see the other party as potentially interfering with the realization of those goals" (Putnam & Poole, 1987, p. 552). This general definition emphasizes some important components of conflict. First, for conflict to occur, the two people or parties (groups) must be interacting or communicating with each other. Second, the two people or parties must have an interdependent relationship to be in conflict. Only if what the one party does affects the other party is there the potential for conflict. Third, they must perceive that the other party is interfering with their ability to achieve their goals, aims, or values, whether that perception is accurate or not. If both parties can achieve their goals, by definition there is no conflict. So if two employees can both get the same raise, there is no conflict. But if one employee perceives that they cannot both get the same raise, then conflict is possible. Likewise, if there is only one promotion available for the two people, then there is a conflict because they cannot both achieve their goals. It does not mean that they will fight with each other or be angry with the other person for getting the promotion. It does mean that conflict is present.

In addition to defining when conflict occurs or exists, it is important to define when it is resolved. Conflict does not end when it is no longer visible because a decision has been made, one side has won, or the parties have moved on to other issues. Instead, conflict is resolved when the issues have been addressed to the satisfaction of everyone; if the conflict has merely been suppressed or delayed, it is not actually resolved (Pondy, 1967). If it is only suppressed, it may become hidden or dormant, but then it has a strong potential to erupt again in the future.

The definition of conflict should seem quite similar to the causes of emotion discussed in Chapter 7. Emotion occurs when there is a discrepancy between expectations and actual experience. So when we expect to achieve some goal, aim, or value, and someone else is trying to or succeeding in preventing us from achieving it, then not only is there conflict, but some emotion is necessarily involved as well (Guerrero & La Valley, 2006). The more important the goal is, the more intense the emotion experienced. Perhaps the reason people do not consider "little disagreements" conflict is that the goal in question is of low importance, such that the emotion is not very intense. From that perspective, conflicts are only those situations where there is intense emotion. Based on the definition we are using, it is the *incompatible goals and not the intensity of the emotion* that defines conflict as discussed in this chapter. So in the planning committee, the decision on where to have the retreat was a conflict because different parties wanted different locations initially, but the conflict was not intense and it was easily resolved. The conflict over the topic for the retreat was much more intense and more challenging to resolve.

Typologies of Conflict

Next it is important to think about the types of conflict that occur in organizations. There have been at least three different ways of considering conflict based on the level of conflicts, the content of the conflicts, or the stages of conflict.

Level of Conflicts

Conflict occurs at multiple levels in organizations. Scholars have generally divided these into four levels: the intrapersonal level, the interpersonal level, the group level, and the organizational level (e.g., Putnam & Poole, 1987).

Intrapersonal Conflict. Some of the conflicts we experience in organizational settings are really internal or intrapersonal conflicts between different expectations we have for ourselves. Sometimes those conflicts are *intrarole conflict*, or, conflicts within a role. For example, an employee may experience conflict within the role of sales associate between providing personal customer service and being efficient so as to serve more customers. Many of us experience *interrole* conflict between various roles that we expect ourselves to fill. Many employees experience conflict between their work roles and their family roles. We will address this more fully in Chapter 12. A common intrapersonal conflict is *role overload*. Sometimes we simply do not have enough time in the day or week to fulfill all our expected roles. Role overload can include the conflict that arises from our attempts to fulfill too many demands created by the various roles at work (e.g., supervisor, peer, mentor, subordinate, completing paperwork, etc.) and nonwork roles (e.g., family member, health club member, volunteer). These various types of intrapersonal conflicts create stress for us and can inhibit our ability to fulfill our job duties as an organizational member. They may or may not be visible to others.

Interpersonal Conflicts. Conflicts between people, interpersonal conflicts, probably receive the most attention because these are often very visible. These often can be considered intragroup conflicts because they tend to involve conflict between two individuals within the same group, department, or division. A common type of conflict is *interpersonal role conflict* in which two or more people are vying for the same role. This may be conflict over some formal role, such as two people trying for the same leadership role. It can also be over informal roles, such as if two members of a group each want to influence group members to their opinion or viewpoint. Some interpersonal conflicts result from receiving different role expectations. Sometimes two different supervisors provide competing expectations and create what is sometimes called *intersender role conflict*. A student working retail told how two different supervisors gave her different directions on cleaning the glass cases in the jewelry department. These differing directives put her in conflict with one or the other because it was impossible to do it both ways. Finally, interpersonal conflict can be the result of *role ambiguity*. When it is unclear who has what responsibilities, conflict often results because some individuals are not meeting unstated expectations or two people try to assume the same responsibilities.

Intergroup Conflicts. Due to issues like scarce resources within an organization, it is common to have intergroup conflict or conflicts between departments or groups. These are intraorganizational conflicts because both groups are within the same large organization. In addition to conflicts over budget and personnel allotments, a common intergroup conflict relates to space allocation. When a new building opened at one university where Michael Kramer taught, a small department tried to claim classrooms exclusively for their department. Fortunately, an administrator eventually gave the small department priority scheduling in the rooms but also scheduled other departments in the rooms to resolve the conflict.

Interorganizational Conflicts. Organizations are hindered in their goal achievement by other organizations, which results in conflict between organizations. Organizations compete for the same resources, such as supplies, personnel, and customers. Even when organizations agree to cooperate with each other in interorganizational collaborations, there are still often conflicts between them as the two organizations have different cultures, different past experiences, and different motivations for being involved. These *external* conflicts create potential conflicts *within* the organization, and organizational members will have different opinions about how to address these conflicts, which can trigger further conflicts.

Content of Conflicts

A second typology of conflict focuses more on the content or nature of the conflict, particularly as it applies to groups in organizations. From this approach, it is extremely common to distinguish between task and relational conflict—but it may be important to consider a third type, process conflict (Behfar, Mannix, Peterson, & Trochim, 2011). *Task conflict* involves differences of opinion and ideas on how to address a particular problem, decision, or goal. Conflict occurs because people perceive different ways of achieving group goals. *Relational conflict* involves factors that affect the ability to maintain positive personal relationships. Personality differences and communication incompetence can cause conflict. Some people have trouble working with others regardless of the task. Relational conflicts are usually personal, with the focus on stopping or hurting the other person rather than on achieving some task-related group goal (Putnam, 2006). *Process conflict* concerns issues of time management, scheduling, and contribution to the group effort. This includes having trouble finding times to meet and conflicts over whether everyone is contributing their share to the group effort. The combination of task, relational, and process conflict creates high potential for conflict in group settings.

Visibility of Conflicts

Research by a number of scholars suggest that conflict develops through five stages (Pondy, 1967). However, viewing these five stages in terms of the visibility of the conflict divides them into two categories: latent and manifest conflicts (Lipsky & Seeber, 2006).

Latent conflict is really the potential for conflict. If, for example, there are limited resources or different goals for different parties in the organization, this creates the potential for conflict; however, until people become aware of these issues, it is only latent or the potential for conflict. Latent conflict may be perceived and felt when one or more individuals recognize the conflict exists. This awareness likely leads to stress or anxiety concerning the conflict. The other parties involved may be unaware of this latent conflict.

Latent conflict becomes *manifest conflict* when the conflict becomes public and visible. Public expression of the conflict may only involve the two parties in conflict. Public communication of the manifest conflict may include anything from relatively calm statements of disagreement to heated arguments. In most instances, manifest conflict is noticed by other observers as well. They may choose to enter the conflict by choosing one side over the other, trying to reduce or resolve the conflict, or they may choose to continue to be observers.

Application

These different typologies are applicable to the retreat planning committee. It is possible that some of the group members are experiencing intrapersonal conflict as they are wondering how they can balance being on this committee with their other work roles or wish they could avoid the retreat all together. The committee may have to compete with other committees for funding to hire the consultant or compete with other organizations who want to hire the consultant for the same dates. Most of the conflict for the committee seems to be at the interpersonal or intragroup level.

The committee experiences task conflicts regarding where to have the retreat and what topic to address at it. These conflicts are manifest quickly as the members discussed the merits of the choices, but these task conflicts do not seem particularly intense. The task conflicts were resolved with the hiring of the consultant doing the transformational leadership workshop.

By contrast, the relational conflict between Lane and Thai was latent during the first meeting to most committee members, but was probably perceived or felt by the two of them. Near the end of the second meeting, the conflict became manifest to everyone as the two began to disagree vehemently and attack each other personally. The rest of the committee hoped it would return to its latent form during the fourth meeting.

Any process conflict in the committee meetings seems relatively subtle. Some of the members probably wish Terry was more active in guiding the decision-making process, whereas others were happy with the rather hands-off approach to leading the group process. Yet, most of the group wished Terry would help them work through the relational conflict in a positive manner, although no one ever voiced this concern.

Conflict as Dysfunctional and Functional

Scholars often state that conflict can have positive effects, such as reducing groupthink; however, the focus of most scholarship is on eliminating the negative psychological and physiological effects of conflict on organizational members (Pondy, 1967; Putnam, 2006).

The negative effects of conflict are many. They include effects at the personal level, such as tension, emotional strain, and harmed emotional well-being. Conflict can have negative effects at the group and organizational levels by leading to productivity losses because the time spent addressing conflict, especially relational conflicts, distracts from getting work done and can even lead to the breakdown and malfunction of the system.

Conflict also has potentially positive effects. At the individual level, learning to manage conflict is essential for the development of mature and competent human beings. Group and organizational conflict can lead to innovation, progress, and even productivity.

Conflict can prevent stagnation and can foster internal cohesiveness as group or organization members join together to compete with other groups or organizations.

These effects of conflict are somewhat general; however, research also reveals specific types of conflict can have specific kinds of effects. Studies of groups find that moderate levels of task conflict can be beneficial. For example, when work teams performed routine tasks—such as processing orders—task conflict was detrimental to the team productivity and satisfaction. But when the work teams dealt with unusual or nonroutine tasks—such as developing a new product—task conflict was actually beneficial in many cases, as it led to better performance and satisfaction (Jehn, 1995). By contrast, relational conflicts tended to have a detrimental effect on groups, particularly on outcomes such as group satisfaction and commitment (Behfar et al., 2011; Jehn, 1995). In addition, process conflicts over logistics or contribution are also negatively related to group outcomes.

Overall, conflict is *functional* or *dysfunctional* based on whether it "facilitates or inhibits the organization's productivity, stability, or adaptability" (Pondy, 1967, p. 308). In the case of the retreat planning committee, it appears that the task conflict over the topic for the retreat had a positive effect, as the group developed a creative solution that addressed the differences of opinion of group members. The relational conflict may not have had a detrimental effect on the final group decisions, but it was having a negative effect on members' satisfaction and interest in continuing to work on planning the retreat.

Conflict Styles

Perhaps the most widely researched topic on conflict concerns how people manage or respond to conflict. The majority of this research explores different styles individuals use to respond to conflict. Shockley-Zalabak (1988, p. 304) created a summary graph (see Figure 10.1) of three of the most popular conflict style models at the time. The model is a synthesis of theorizing done by Blake and Mouton (1964), Hall (1973), and Thomas (1974). All three of these models of conflict are based on two dimensions, similar to the managerial grid presented in Chapter 8. One dimension focuses on concern for getting the task done and achieving goals. The second dimension focuses on concerns for people and relationships. This pattern leads to five general styles that people or groups use to manage conflict:

Avoiding: An avoiding style or withdrawal style involves little regard for how the task is completed or personal preferences and little regard for the relationships (1,1).

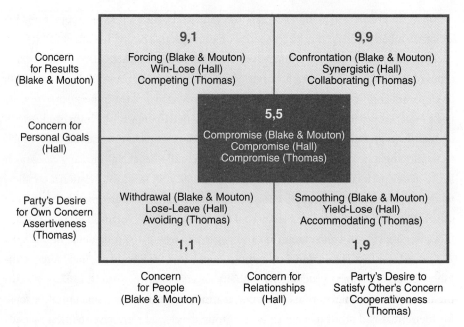

Figure 10.1. Composite of Blake and Mouton (1964), Hall (1973), and Thomas (1974) Two-Dimensional Conflict Grid

Individuals using this style avoid communicating about the conflict usually either by delaying addressing the conflict or withdrawing so that they do not have to discuss it. They usually appear disinterested in the conflict.

Accommodating: An accommodating or smoothing style shows little regard for how the task is completed or personal preferences, but is very concerned with maintaining relationships and so accepts the other parties' approaches (1,9). Individuals using this style communicate an acceptance of the opinions of others and may appear to be people pleasers who overlook or downplay differences.

Competing: A competing or forcing style is concerned with completing the task in a way that meets personal goals and has little concern for how achieving those goals might affect personal relationships (9,1). Individuals using this style generally communicate in an aggressive, competitive manner and are willing to confront those who disagree with them.

Compromise: A compromising style is equally concerned about accomplishing the task and meeting personal goals and maintaining relationships (5,5). Individuals using this style communicate a willingness to split differences in a give-and-take manner that allows everyone, including themselves, to get something they wanted; but no one likely gets everything they wanted.

Collaborating: A collaborating style has high concern for accomplishing the task and meeting personal goals and for maintaining positive relationships (9,9). Individuals using this style communicate a need to look for creative solutions that meet everyone's needs and interests. This can involve challenging and time-consuming efforts.

There are a number of points to make about identifying people's conflict styles. First, it is important to note that a comparison of the different ways that conflict styles are measured indicates that they are only moderately associated with each other; additionally, the measures are known to produce similar, but sometimes widely varied, results when the same individual completes the test even a few weeks apart (Thomas & Kilmann, 1978). In other words, do not assume results are stable or permanent. Our preference and self-perceptions about conflict management can change rapidly.

Second, the way different styles appear on the graph suggests that collaborating is the preferred style of managing conflict, but this seems quite unrealistic in many situations. For example, conflict is often the result of scarce resources; yet, in actual practice, situations often require additional resources to collaborate effectively. Minimally, it takes more time and energy for the parties involved to reach agreement. So there may be times when each strategy is appropriate. Consider a situation in which a conflict arises because a powerful team member directs others to behave unethically for the sake of the team or task. Such circumstances may call for courageous members to engage in a "competing" conflict management style with the one who requests unethical behavior (Redding, 1985). Likewise, other issues or decisions can arise that are quite trivial, and maintaining positive relationships is too important for collaboration to be needed or realistic. In such cases, an "accommodating" style might be most appropriate. Table 10.1 gives some guidelines for thinking through which conflict management style is appropriate.

Next, although research suggests that people do have differences in their preferred way to manage conflict, it also suggests that people adapt depending on how the conflict continues to develop and if it is not resolved. For example, although male and female supervisors did not differ in their initial approaches to dealing with a conflict involving a subordinate, if the subordinate did not respond in the desired manner, male

Conflict Management Style	Collaborating	Accommodating	Competing	Avoiding	Compromising
The task or issue is	Complex and important	More important to the other party	Extremely important personally	Trivial	Equally valued by both parties
Can decisions be made slowly?	Yes	Yes or No	No	Yes	Yes
Other considerations:	One party cannot solve the problem alone	Preserving the relationship is important	Wrong decision by other parties can hurt you or others	Cooling-off period helps preserve the relationship	Collaborating cannot be reached

Note: Adapted from Rahim (2015).

supervisors moved more quickly toward competing, aggressive behaviors than female supervisors (Conrad, 1991). Other individual differences and contextual factors such as the size of the conflict and the urgency of the situation influence choices as well.

Finally, although the two-dimensional models of conflict styles are certainly common to conceptualizations of conflict, limiting the discussion to only these two dimensions likely limits our ability to consider alternative factors beyond tasks and relationships. Professor Anne Nicotera (1993) presents an interesting third dimension for conflict style based on whether it is disruptive to the relationship in the short term or the long term. For example, an avoidance style suggests a short-term indifference to the other person and the task, but an estranged style suggests that ignoring the issue is the result of a long-term negative relationship. However, both styles involve withdrawing from the situation. A collaborative style suggests positive agreement on the task and relationship, but a begrudging style suggests that the agreement satisfied both task and relational concerns in the short term, but that it was not a friendly agreement and may inhibit future work relations, although both styles result in a positive resolution to the conflict. There are likely other factors beyond task and relationships and intensity/ length that should be considered.

A number of different conflict styles are apparent in the retreat planning scenario. After a brief conflict over where to hold the retreat, the group accommodates Jesse's suggestion and agrees to hold it at the new facility. The group uses a collaborative style by coming up with the transformational leadership workshop that combines a focus on leadership with a focus on culture, satisfying both Kendall and Hayden. Lane and Kai seem to use an aggressive or competing style in an effort to have their own way at the expense of the other one and the group. Finally, the leader, Terry, and the rest of the group seem to be using a withdrawal or avoidance style to respond to the relational conflict of Lane and Kai.

Bargaining and Negotiation in Conflict

Conflicts are resolved through communication. The process involves bargaining or negotiation as different parties attempt to resolve the conflict in ways that satisfy them. Scholars have generally classified bargaining strategies into two main categories (Putnam & Poole, 1987). *Integrative strategies* are cooperative strategies that work to bring the parties together and reach mutually satisfying resolutions to the conflict. These strategies are associated with compromising and collaborating conflict resolution styles. *Distributive strategies* are competitive strategies that focus on gaining an advantage and achieving personal goals at the expense of the other parties. These strategies are especially associated with competing conflict resolution styles.

It would be nearly impossible to catalogue all of the strategies for bargaining and negotiating that have been identified. What follows is just a partial list of strategies identified in various reviews of strategies (e.g., Forgas, 1998; Putnam & Jones, 1982). The bargaining process involves offering proposals and counterproposals in an effort to reach agreement. Integrative strategies include inviting proposals, focusing on problem solving, requesting and sharing information, making concessions, and exhibiting positive emotion to build relationships. Integrative strategies involve offering persuasive arguments based on statistical support, examples, analogies, and causal relationships and even presenting information that supports the other party's position.

ETHICAL ISSUE

Ethical Bargaining

Examine the five types of unethical bargaining identified by scholars listed in the text. Now consider the distributive bargaining strategies listed in the text. Do any of these distributive strategies seem unethical because the objective of the strategies is to achieve personal goals at the expense of the other party?

Distributive strategies include rejecting proposals, withholding information, delaying, dominating, making threats or demands, and maintaining emotional distance or acting irritated and tense. Distributive strategies often include presenting persuasive messages that directly attack the opponents' positions.

An assumption in the previous paragraph is that those involved in bargaining are operating in what would generally be considered an ethical manner. Scholars identified five strategies that are generally considered unethical (e.g., Robinson, Lewicki, & Donahue, 2000):

1. *Competitive bargaining* in which proposals or demands are significantly higher or lower than any expected outcome in an attempt to gain additional benefits.
2. *Attack the opponent's network* by threatening to influence their position in their organization negatively by harming their reputations.
3. *Making false promises* while knowing that they will not likely be kept.
4. *Misrepresenting* your own or your opponent's information to gain advantage.
5. *Inappropriate information gathering* by secretly finding out information about your opponent's position.

These strategies are clearly distributive as well in that they are designed to gain personal advantage in the conflict negotiations.

In the retreat planning scenario, most of the committee used integrative communication strategies, presenting their arguments and reasons for their positions with a focus on problem solving. By contrast, Lane and Kai used distributive strategies that focused on attacking each other.

Managing Conflict through Third Parties

Focusing on different styles used to resolve conflicts suggests individuals primarily manage conflicts on their own. In many situations, the incompatible goals and differences of opinion cannot be resolved by the parties involved. Group members struggle because the conflict consumes so much of their time that they are unable to proceed. In situations like these, it is common to use a third-party intervention to address the concerns. When third parties enter a conflict situation, they generally assume one of two similar but different roles: mediator or arbitrator (Putnam & Poole, 1987). Both mediators and arbitrators are expected to assume a neutral position, not siding with either party. In addition, they are both expected to investigate the conflict by listening to all the sides of the conflict.

The difference between a mediator and an arbitrator has to do with their role in determining how the conflict will be resolved. A *mediator* facilitates discussion of the issues so that the parties involved come to an amicable decision. The mediator does not have any stake in the final decision and only tries to help those involved find a mutually satisfying outcome. An *arbitrator* has decision-making power. After gathering the information, the arbitrator makes a ruling or decision, and the parties have to abide by it. In some large organizations, there is an official mediator to handle internal conflicts, sometimes called an *ombudsperson*. Ombudspersons are mediators who tend to be free from hierarchical oversight to reduce the influence of power differentials on their work in resolving conflicts. In organizations with grievance procedures, a designated grievance committee may serve as an arbitrator.

These definitions work well for formal mediation and arbitration. Of course, when two coworkers or two departments are in conflict with each other, and they ask someone to intervene, it is often not clearly stated what type of intervention is expected. If they ask a supervisor to intervene, the supervisor's own conflict style may determine the nature of the intervention. More competitive and controlling supervisors are likely to become arbitrators. More collaborative and facilitative supervisors are likely to become mediators. When asking for a third-party intervention, it is important to clarify which role is expected at the beginning.

If the planning committee needed to work together over the long term, they might ask an outside mediator to come in to help them manage the conflict between Kai and Lane. It may take a neutral party to get to the bottom of the relational conflict between them. An arbitrator would be an ineffective choice in this case because the relational conflict cannot be merely "ordered" to stop by an outside authority or ruling.

Communication and Conflict with Abusive Coworkers

In Chapter 7, we discussed common communication relationships in organizations, including those with supervisors, peers, mentors, and friends. Unfortunately, not all interpersonal relationships and interactions in organizations are positive, ethical, or healthy. Customers can be verbally abusive; peers can displace their anger toward one another. We expect to be treated with civility at work; we expect communication behaviors that suggest mutual respect, rather than behaviors that humiliate, discourage, and harm us (Kassing & Waldron, 2014). When these expectations are not met, we experience intense emotions and conflict. The focus here is not on isolated, short-term incidents involving unpleasant communication and conflicts that quickly pass or involve low levels of incivility (even though such incidents do create some emotion and conflict). Instead, the focus here is on repetitious abuse in the workplace—forms of incivility that create ongoing interpersonal conflict. In the following section, we describe organizational communication research on two forms of workplace conflict: bullying and sexual harassment.

Workplace Bullying

Defining Workplace Bullying. When we think of bullying behavior, we might think of scuffles on the playground or in the hallways of a junior high school and not interactions occurring among working professionals. Unfortunately, workplace bullying occurs all too frequently.

Bullying is defined "as repeated and persistent negative acts towards one or more individual(s), which involve a perceived power imbalance and create a hostile work environment. . . . Bullying is thus a form of interpersonal aggression or hostile, anti-social behaviour [sic] in the workplace" (Salin, 2003, pp. 1214–1215). Workplace bullying can be described across four specific features: intensity, repetition, duration, and power disparity (Lutgen-Sandvik, Tracy, & Alberts, 2007). *Intensity* refers to the severity of the bullying acts the target reports experiencing. *Repetition* concerns how frequently the bullying actions recur. *Duration* considers how long of time over which the bullying occurs. Persistence longer than six months is a common criteria for differentiating bullying from other negative behaviors. Finally, bullying involves a *power disparity* such that the target of bullying feels unable to stop or prevent the continuation of the behavior. This power disparity likely changes over time as the target feels increasingly helpless. Defining bullying this way emphasizes that the behavior is repetitive, rather than a one-time incident or infrequent experience, and that the persistent behavior creates a hostile work environment for the target of the bullying and possibly others. This definition also emphasizes that the target of bullying feels a power imbalance that makes it difficult to confront the behavior effectively.

Workplace bullying can include at least five distinct types of tactics or behaviors (Kassing & Waldron, 2014). *General physical aggression* involves overt behaviors such as invading someone's personal space, physical intimidation, verbal abuse or shouting, and even pushing or shoving. In contrast to these physically aggressive behaviors, *self-confidence attacks* are more psychological and include communication tactics such as constant criticism, belittling remarks, ridicule, or spreading rumors. *Manipulation of the workplace* is perhaps more subtle but achieves similar psychological damage by various strategies that discourages the persons from accomplishment of their work—whether it be by setting unrealistically high goals and assigning excessive workloads or assigning meaningless tasks and removing responsibilities. *Ostracizing or isolating* involves excluding or ignoring the person or making the person feel like an outsider, perhaps through practical or insider jokes or ridicule. Finally, *threats* emphasize a power differential by indicating that the bully can hurt the person physically, professionally, or personally.

Based on this general understanding of bullying, a study of over 400 employees in the United States from a range of occupations and locations found that around 9% self-identified as being the targets of bullying. Interestingly, as many as 28% of the sample of adults reported being the target of chronic negative behaviors lasting longer than six months (Lutgen-Sandvik et al., 2007). Thus, many of the working adults were the targets of bullying by definition but did not necessarily label or frame themselves as such. Another study of over 6,000 employees found that over 12% reported being bullied in the past year, and 24% reported being bullied at some point in their career

ETHICAL ISSUE

Wanting to Belong and Participation in Social Bullying

Imagine that you are new to your organization and a colleague called you a couple hours prior to a big departmental meeting. Your colleague invited you to join with several others who are gathered to discuss some upcoming decisions in private, prior to the meeting. You were glad to be included and sought out for your input so you decide to join the group. Once at the gathering, your colleague begins to explain how awful "everyone" there thinks another member of the department is; then, others voice similar stories. Consider how situations like these could lead to social bullying. How might you overcome the appeal of being included as a new member in a group that talks constantly about others negatively?

(Namie & Lutgen-Sandvik, 2010). Clearly, workplace bullying is a common communication experience in the modern workplace.

Causes. There are no simple explanations for why bullying occurs. Bullying is the result of a complex interaction of characteristics of the perpetrators, victims, and the environment (Harvey, Heames, Richey, & Leonard, 2006).

Characteristics of Perpetrators. According to Harvey et al. (2006), research supports the idea that there are certain biological factors related to brain activity and genes that seem related to bullying behavior. In addition, many adult bullies were victims of bullies when they were children. Bullies tend to be politically aware; and because they are socially aware, they take advantage of situations in which it is possible to bully someone while avoiding organizational sanctions. Some research suggests bullies are psychopathic, but others see them as more opportunistic (Harvey et al., 2006; Kassing & Waldron, 2014). Bullies also tend to be in supervisory positions.

Although most conceptualizations of bullying focus on a single perpetrator and victim, bullying is often a social phenomenon involving others. Social bullying can include others' active participation in the bullying behaviors as accomplices, such as adding additional verbal abuse or supporting the threat, or passive participating, such as watching passively or not taking action to prevent additional bullying (Namie & Lutgen-Sandvik, 2010). In their study, Namie and Lutgen-Sandvik (2010) found that 20% to 30% of bullying situations included multiple harassers.

Characteristics of Targets. According to Harvey et al. (2006), targets of bullying behavior often share certain characteristics. In comparison to their peers, victims often have low self-esteem in areas like their cognitive abilities, their emotional stability and maturity, their character, their professional accomplishments, or even their physical characteristics. Victims tend to be passive and isolated from their peers and are often out-group members who have been victims of bullying in the past. Individuals who do not fit these characteristics may become targets for bullying if perpetrators view them as rivals. Women are more often victims of bullying than men, but women make up 40% of the perpetrators, and they primarily target other women (http://www.workplacebullying.org/tag/women-bullies/).

Environmental Factors. The culture of the organization, including its values and practices, plays an important role in shaping the intensity of bullying that occurs

(Harvey et al., 2006). Perhaps the most critical factor is a cultural norm that tolerates a low standard of treatment and high incivility that makes bullying behavior seem acceptable. For example, accepting abusive behavior as normal treatment for initiating new organizational members can make bullying behavior seem appropriate, at least in certain situations. Other factors include ineffective training of managers and supervisors so that they are unable to identify or correct bullying behavior. The arrangement of the workplace can contribute to bullying by physically isolating employees so that bullies can act without being detected. Kassing and Waldron (2014) cite research that suggests organizations that promote internal competition for rewards and promotions create a situation in which individuals may exhibit bullying behaviors more often to gain an advantage.

Effects of Bullying. Research has suggested a wide range of negative effects from bullying. The effects on the individual targets of bullying include psychological or emotional, physical, and work-related effects (Meglich-Sespico, Faley, & Knapp, 2007). *Psychological or emotional effects* include depression, anxiety, irritability, low self-confidence, hostility, nervousness, social withdrawal, and even suicidal thoughts. *Physical effects* included insomnia, chronic fatigue, weight gain, and more susceptibility to illness and disease. *Work-related effects* include an inability to concentrate; lower productivity; as well as increased sick leaves, reassignments, and terminations.

In addition to individual effects, there are a number of potential negative organizational effects (Kassing & Waldron, 2014). Organizations that fail to address bullying and respond appropriately when it is reported risk employees (other than the victims) being negatively affected in similar ways. Observers of bullying may begin to fear that they will be the next victims, which can lead to a general loss in productivity in the unit or organization. In addition to the economic costs of reduced productivity of the victim and others concerned about bullying, there can be health costs, absenteeism costs, and the additional costs of recruiting and replacing employees who leave when bullying is not addressed. If a bully is in a supervisory position, as is typically the case, the positions below the bully can become revolving doors in which new hires are set up for failure before they even begin (Lutgen-Sandvik et al., 2007).

Coping with Bullying. Lutgen-Sandvik (2008) found that individuals who deal with bullying cope through a three-phase communication process. During the *pre-bullying phase*, bullied individuals are often uncertain whether they are actually being bullied, although they know that they are uncomfortable with what is occurring. By talking to others they can confirm or dismiss their perceptions and, in the process, validate their self-worth. If their suspicions are confirmed about being bullied, during the *bullying phase,* individuals make their concerns public to gain support from others and, at the same time, tarnish the reputation of the bully. If the organization takes supportive action, they regain some of their self-image but also lose the sense of security that they may have felt as an organizational member prior to the bullying. During the *post-bully phase* when either the target or the bully has moved to a new location or organization or ceases their bullying behavior, the victim often grieves the loss of security and then tries to recreate a positive self-image. Given the amount of effort that coping with bullying takes, it is not surprising that there are many psychological, physical, and work-related effects.

Addressing Bullying. Given the frequency of bullying behavior and the negative impact that it has on the individual and the organization, it is important that organizations develop policies that communicate intolerance for such behavior. The critical first step in any effort to address bullying is a willingness to believe victims when they report a problem. A survey of victims found that as many as 71% were never believed, and only 9% felt that they were believed and never doubted (Namie, 2014). Victims of bullying can feel victimized a second time when they are not believed by other organizational members.

Harvey et al. (2006) recommend three broad areas of response that organizational leaders should pursue:

1. Leaders should conduct a self-analysis to determine what in its environment is allowing bullying to occur—whether it be the climate or the physical layout—and then develop training programs and policies to correct problems.

2. Leaders need to support the individual during and after bullying events, including providing a safe reporting process that prevents retaliation. And they need to provide programs to assist the victim in coping or provide the opportunity to relocate within the organization.

3. Leaders need to restructure jobs to reduce the bully's interaction with victims and potential victims, provide training and coaching to change behaviors, and be willing to terminate chronic bullies.

The policy the organizational leaders adopt needs to be comprehensive (Meglich-Sespico et al., 2007). It should include an informal, confidential complaint procedure and timely investigation of complaints that protect the target(s) and perpetrator(s). It also needs to protect victims against retaliation and implement corrective action for the bully, including dismissal if warranted. It should include awareness training for all employees, and management should monitor the policy over time.

Sexual Harassment

A second type of negative interpersonal interaction that harms workplace relationships is sexual harassment. Sexual harassment is a particular type of social-sexual behavior. Social-sexual communication and behavior in the workplace involves "any non-work-related behavior having a sexual component; it includes sexual harassment, initiating dating, flirting, and the like" (Gutek, Cohen, & Konrad, 1990, p. 560).

Defining Sexual Harassment. Defining sexual harassment is more challenging than it might first appear because it is a form of social-sexual behavior. Generally, sexual harassment is defined as negative personal communication that is sexual in nature, unwelcomed by the target, severe, repetitive, and contributes to a hostile work environment (Robinson, Franklin, Tinney, Crow, & Hartman, 2005). The definition of sexual harassment is problematic because non-harassing social-sexual behavior is defined similarly. Non-harassing social-sexual behavior includes behavior "such as making sexual comments intended to be taken as complimentary, attempts to initiate dating, flirting, presenting sexually-oriented jokes or cartoons, wolf whistling, and making sexual comments that are mildly annoying but not offensive enough to be labeled harassment" (Gutek et al., 1990).

ETHICAL ISSUE

Sender or Receiver Priority

Determining whether a particular behavior is or is not sexual harassment often comes down to determining whether the sender's intent or the receiver's reaction should be given more weight. Suppose the sender says, "I was just joking" or "I was just flirting"; and the receiver says, "Your words made me feel harassed and unsafe in the work place." Whose perspective should be given priority in this conflict?

Certain behaviors are easily defined as sexual harassment. In particular, "quid pro quo" (Latin for "this for that") requests in which a sexual favor is demanded in exchange for a raise, promotion, or some similar benefit clearly meet definitions of sexual harassment, even if the behavior is not repeated. Similarly, use of graphic, crude language or displaying pornographic pictures or videos are defined as sexually harassing behaviors because they contribute to a hostile work environment.

Problems with defining harassing versus non-harassing social-sexual behaviors tend to occur when behaviors are more ambiguous. Research has consistently shown that men and women make significantly different interpretations of the same behaviors (Garlick, 1994; Solomon & Williams, 1997). For example, men were less likely than women to consider behaviors such as putting their hand on a shoulder or asking about someone's dating life as inappropriate, and men were less uncomfortable than women with those behaviors (Garlick, 1994). In addition, characteristics of the initiator and amount of harm to the target shape what is considered sexual harassment. For example, expressing sexual interest is rated as more harassing when the initiators were unattractive and the targets attractive, and men were less likely to perceive behavior as harassing when the initiators were women (Solomon & Williams, 1997).

Another complication is that even when men and women discuss sexual harassment, they may use similar language but intend different meanings for that similar language. In other words, there can be an illusion of shared interpretation in mixed-gender discussions of sexual harassment. For example, in research involving interviews of men and women concerning perceptions of sexual harassment, both men and women talked about not "crossing the line" between flirting and sexual harassment; yet, on closer inspection, the two groups held very different understandings of what "crossing the line" meant (Dougherty, Kramer, Klatzke, & Rogers, 2009). This meaning-based dynamic makes it difficult to determine what behaviors cross the metaphorical line between initiating romance and sexual harassment.

The research is clear: Sexual harassment is very common. Reports on sexual harassment include statistics suggesting that 42% of women working for the federal government, 70% of women in military service, 50% of female students and 30% of faculty at universities, and up to 92% of clerical and professional women report experiencing some form of sexual harassment in the workplace (Wood, 1992). Although sexual harassment by supervisors receives the most attention, and women are more often victims than men, peers are also perpetrators. Furthermore, men are frequently victims, too, and same-sex harassment is also a problem. Research conducted in the restaurant industry indicated that sexual harassment is extremely common from managers (66% for women, 50% for men), coworkers (80% for women, 70% for men), and customers (78% for women, 55% for men)—with inappropriate touching (30% for women and 22% for men) being a common occurrence (http://time.com/3478041/restaurant-sexual-harassment-survey/).

Causes of Sexual Harassment. Given the prevalence of sexual harassment, it is important to understand its cause. The cause of non-harassing social-sexual behavior is generally accepted as resulting from personal attraction toward another person and a desire to pursue an interpersonal friendship and, potentially, a sexual relationship (Gutek et al., 1990). The resulting relationships are usually mutually beneficial. However, personal attraction does not explain sexually harassing behavior. The most common explanation for sexually harassing behavior is that it results from the blatant exercise and abuse of power and authority (e.g., Gutek et al., 1990; Wood, 1992). The exercise of power is clear in quid pro quo harassment when someone in a supervisory position can influence various economic outcomes; however, the exercise of power also explains other types of sexually harassing behaviors, including harassment from peers. The harasser is generally trying to gain control or dominance over the other person for personal benefit, although some perpetrators likely convince themselves that their motives are positive and romantic.

Effects of Sexual Harassment. Sexual harassment victims suffer essentially the same negative effects as bullying victims. The individuals who experience sexual harassment experience negative psychological and work-related outcomes (Schneider, Swan, & Fitzgerald, 1997). Victims have lower psychological well-being and life satisfaction and experience more life stress in general. At work, they experience greater job stress and are less satisfied with their work, their coworkers, and their supervision. They have lower organizational commitment and have higher levels of absenteeism and tardiness and are more likely to quit. These negative effects begin to occur even with very low levels of harassment and increase as the harassment levels escalate.

Effects are not only limited to victims: Others who observe harassment that goes unaddressed or stopped can see themselves as potential victims, which can lead to them to begin experiencing the same negative effects. When victims of sexual harassment make their accusations public, it can have reputational and economic effects for the organization at large (Dougherty, 2009).

Coping with Sexual Harassment. Victims of sexual harassment often try to cope on their own by avoiding the harasser. One of the largest hurdles victims face in coping with sexual harassment is getting others to believe them. Ironically, although the greatest fear for women after experiencing sexual harassment is that they will not be believed if they report the problem, they also tend to agree that most women who claim they have been sexually harassed have fabricated the harassment (Dougherty, 2000). Men likely experience similar disbelief if they report being harassed with unwanted sexual advances.

Support from peers provides some of the most important assistance for coping with sexual harassment. Not only does support involve accepting the accuracy of the victim's story of harassment, but it includes other women and men who help create a sense of supportive community in opposition to the harasser. At times, support can include the use of humor in which the perpetrator is made comical in the retelling of the event—further enhancing the sense of community that includes the victim but excludes the harasser (Dougherty & Smythe, 2004). Unfortunately, when victims feel unsupported by colleagues, victims may seek to cope by removing themselves from the situation or organization altogether.

Addressing Sexual Harassment. The Equal Employment Opportunity Commission Policy Guidance on Current Issues of Sexual Harassment makes it clear that organizations must address sexual harassment (U.S. Equal Employment Opportunity Commission, 1990). The Commission sets guidelines for evaluating evidence of harassment, for determining whether the behavior is unwelcome, and for determining what constitutes a "hostile work environment." Organizations should have clear policies against sexual harassment, develop a system for filing complaints that protects the victim and other witnesses from retaliation, respond to complaints with immediate and appropriate action, and provide appropriate sanctions for harassers. Any organization receiving federal funding, such as universities, must also provide sexual harassment prevention training to employees.

Developing policies like these and communicating those policies and programs to organizational members is considered the best way to prevent sexual harassment. But victims of harassment are often concerned about being victimized by the system a second time if they are not believed. Support from management, by responding immediately and appropriately to incidents that are reported, can help communicate intolerance of sexual harassment and encourage individuals to come forward and report sexual harassment.

Conflict in Nonprofit/Volunteer Settings

Conflict is equally prevalent in nonprofit organizations and in interactions involving volunteers. Conflict occurs at intrapersonal, interpersonal, group, and organizational levels. Conflict can be task, relational, or process related. Conflict can be functional, leading to creativity, or dysfunctional, leading to volunteers becoming discouraged and quitting. Individuals manage conflict using the various conflict styles and use various communication strategies as they bargain and negotiate to resolve the conflicts. Despite the similarities, some aspects of conflict are different in these settings.

Due to the fact that volunteering is often a role taken on in addition to work and family roles, volunteers often temporarily or permanently quit their volunteer roles when they experience role overload (Kramer, 2011a). Due to the voluntary nature of their participation, they also may be more prone to quitting over conflicts, particularly intense ones, rather than putting in the effort it takes to use integrative communication strategies to create collaborative resolutions to conflicts. Of course, volunteers who are deeply committed to organizations will not be so quick to leave.

Volunteers are also probably unlikely to continue if they experience bullying or sexual harassment. However, given the social motivation of many volunteers, acceptable behavior may be defined differently. In particular, behaviors that might be considered sexual harassment in a work setting and as creating a hostile work environment were considered playful social behavior that was acceptable in a setting like a community theater group (Kramer, 2002). So the volunteer context may change what is interpreted as conflict and harassing behavior for the parties involved. Like work settings, when behavior is considered inappropriate, the organizational leaders need to address it in ways that support victims.

Summary

Conflict is an inevitable part of organizational participation. We experience it at least periodically, if not constantly, from the time we join an organization until we leave; it may even be part of our motivation for leaving. Conflict may be experienced internally, such as when we experience conflict over which role to prioritize. Interpersonal conflict occurs due to differences in opinions or methods of accomplishing some goal or can be due to personality clashes. Conflict may be between groups within an organization as those groups compete for resources. We tend to respond to conflict using some conflict management style ranging from avoiding to collaborating. When we address a conflict, we use various communication strategies in an effort either to find an integrative solution that satisfies all the parties involved or distributive one that serve self-interests.

Two forms of interpersonal conflict, bullying and sexual harassment, are particularly toxic to organizations. They create damaging emotions and conflicts, not only for the victims of these behaviors, but also for others who observe these behaviors. Organizations need to develop policies and practices that support victims of such misconduct and that either correct or remove the perpetrators of these offenses.

CHAPTER 11

Communication, Power, and Resistance

Power is an important concept to consider in organizational communication. A number of scholars, especially critical scholars, argue that power is the central or defining characteristic of organizations because the exercise of power pervades every aspect of organizational life (Russell, 1938). Although people use the term *power* quite frequently to describe a wide range of situations, it is important to begin by recognizing the complexity of the concept of power. Power is not simply something that one person *has* that others do not have.

If you are a fan of HBO's television series *Game of Thrones*, you might recognize this discussion of power between two of the main characters:

LORD VARYS:	*Power is a curious thing, my lord. Are you fond of riddles?*
TYRION:	*Why? Am I about to hear one?*
LORD VARYS:	*Three great men sit in a room: a king, a priest, and a rich man. Between them stands a sellsword [a soldier]. Each great man bids the sellsword kill the other two. Who lives? Who dies?*
TYRION:	*It depends on the sellsword.*
LORD VARYS:	*Does it? He had neither crown, nor gold, nor favor with the gods.*
TYRION:	*He has a sword, the power over life and death.*
LORD VARYS:	*But if it's swordsmen who rule, why do we pretend kings hold all the power? When Ned Stark lost his head, who truly was responsible? Geoffrey, the executioner, or something else?*
TYRION:	*I've decided I don't like riddles.*
LORD VARYS:	*Power resides where men believe it resides. It's a trick, a shadow on the wall, and a very small man can cast a very large shadow.*[1]

· · · · ·

Consider how this conversation eliminates any simple understanding of power. If we think of power as something someone has and can use to make things go a certain way, it is rather difficult to determine who has power in this situation. We usually think of high-ranking people as having the power. In this riddle, the king has political and military power, the priest has religious power, and the rich man has financial power. Yet, in the end, the soldier has the sword and so he has "power over life and death." Only to the degree that one of the three can influence the soldier does he possess the power that matters most in this situation. And of course, the soldier could decide to kill all three. As this riddle suggests, power is a much more complex issue than identifying who holds a special title or status as having power.

The statement, "Power resides where men [sic] believe it resides" makes the issue of power even more complex. The saying suggests that power is not something that a person *has* but something that *is attributed to them* by others willing to follow. In other words, because we think that an individual has power over us, they do.

In this chapter, we consider issues of power and resistance. We begin by looking at some definitions of terms related to power. We then consider some of the ways power has been understood as an observable, surface-level phenomenon. Then we consider how power often resides as a deep structure that is not easily observed. Finally, we look at how individuals in organizations can resist power.

Definitions

It seems valuable to make distinctions between words that are often included in discussions of power, including the word *power* itself. This distinction among related terminology may help eliminate some confusion throughout the rest of the chapter.

Power and Influence

Power is often defined as "A has power over B to the extent that he [or she] can get B to do something that B would not otherwise do" (Dahl, 1957, pp. 202–203). According to this definition, if a manager is able to get a group of subordinates to work late when they would rather leave, the manager has power over them. This definition provides a rather narrow focus because power is also exercised when A devotes his [or her] energies to creating or reinforcing social and political values of self-interest so that B is prevented from bringing up issues that might be different than what A prefers or that might be harmful to A's interests (Bachrach & Baratz, 1962). If the manager is able to reinforce the values of honesty and hard work to the point that none of the employees shirk their jobs or steal from the company, the manager also has power over them.

Although both these definitions have intuitive appeal, they both focus attention "on the manifest *exercise* of power and not on power as a potential or dispositional quality of actors" (Mumby, 2001, p. 588). In the first definition, the exercise of power causes something to *happen* that A prefers, whereas in the second definition the exercise of power causes something to *not happen* in line with A's preferences. In this way, both definitions define the exercise of power, which might more accurately be considered as definitions of influence. *Influence* is generally defined as action or communication that causes someone else to act or think in a certain way that they would not have otherwise done. When people discuss power in organizations, they are often actually pointing to the exercise of power or influence. That distinction makes it important to consider what power is apart from behaviors that influence others.

Although some scholars do not make a distinction between power and influence (e.g., Frost, 1987), others do. During his graduate program, the Michael Kramer's professor, Robert Hopper, began a class discussion by announcing that he did not believe in the existence of power, only influence. The graduate students in the class struggled with providing examples or evidence of power that could not be more easily described as influence. Certainly power is associated with influence; allocating resources and controlling situations leads to certain interpretations of events and the achievement of goals (Stohl & Cheney, 2001). We concluded that power is more an attribute or meaning that we assign to people or institutions when we accept them as capable of influencing our actions, attitudes, or beliefs. From a communication perspective, there is a subjective component to the relationship of power and influence. Thus, power exists to the degree that organizational members assign meaning to actions and others accept those meanings; however, they may resist or choose alternative meanings instead (Frost, 1987).

Power, then, is exercised in "the production and reproduction of, resistance to, or transformation of relatively fixed (sedimented) structures of communication and meaning that support the interests (symbolic, political, and economic) of some organizational members or groups over others" (Mumby, 2001, p. 587). Furthermore, "***power is exercised through a dynamic process in which relationships of interdependence exist between actors in organizational settings***" (Mumby, 2013, pp. 159–160). These conceptualizations of power are consistent with the idea that power is not something that someone possesses over others. Because power must be produced and reproduced by the system (through a structuration process), it takes the interaction of interdependent parties to exercise power. Although some organizational members clearly have more resources to bring to the process than others, everyone has some resources and individual agency that can be leveraged. Even someone with very limited resources can potentially resist or change the system as it is produced and reproduced (however slightly).

Two concepts flow out of this sort of understanding of power and influence. *Dominance* occurs when resources are perceived as so unevenly distributed that one individual accepts the influence of another all or nearly all of the time. So for employees who believe that they have few if any resources and that the manager has large quantities of resources, the exercise of power or influence may flow almost exclusively from the manager and the existing system toward employees. *Empowerment* involves making individuals aware of their own ability to exercise power or influence by recognizing their own resources and role in producing and reproducing the system.

Apply these concepts to the example of a manager trying to get a group of employees to work late: The manager is trying to influence the employees to reproduce a system that will likely benefit the manager or owners more than the group of employees. If they agree to stay late routinely because they assign the power to influence them to the manager, they recreate an organization in which managers seem to hold the power, and a system of dominance exists. Alternatively, if they become aware that they have an important resource—labor—which the manager needs, they may exercise their own influence through interaction with the manager to resist the request or at least to request changes to the system. They become empowered when they request compensated time off the following day, and the manager agrees out of necessity. In other words, it would not be accurate to construe the supervisor–subordinate situation as one in which the manager has power and the employees have none. Rather, power was enacted through communication as the manager and the employees produced and reproduced the organizational system.

Ideology (or Ideologies)

Closely related to the topic of power is the concept of ideology. Because the exercise of power generally supports the interests of some organizational members or groups (usually those in high-ranking or high-status positions over others), it is usually their values and ideas that are favored or made to seem incontestably good. However, ideology is more than just a set of practices that benefit one group more than another. For example, stock options for executives benefit one group more than another but are not an ideology. However, stock options may be the result of a broader or higher level ideology. An *ideology* is a framework for understanding reality and social systems (such as organizations) that provides individuals in the social system with an identity and set of criteria for evaluating what is right or wrong, good or bad (Mumby, 2001). An ideology focuses individuals' attention on certain assumptions about the social system while constraining their ability to consider other possibilities. As such, ideology is a way of seeing reality that at the same time is a way of not seeing (Poggi, 1965). For example, in our country with its individualistic ideology, it is often difficult to consider the value and benefits of a collectivistic ideology.

Organizational systems tend to embrace a set of ideologies, not just one. The original ideological critique by Karl Marx focused on economic ideologies (Deetz, 2001). Different sets of values and assumptions distinguish economic ideologies such as capitalism, socialism, and communism from each other. As a country, the United States generally embraces an ideology of individualism over collectivism (Mumby, 2013). Individualism complements a capitalistic economic ideology by rewarding individual accomplishments economically. This combination of ideologies is reinforced communicatively by the notion of achieving success by picking yourself up by your "bootstraps." Another set of assumptions creates an ideology concerning reasoning. The focus on technical rationality with an emphasis on controlling scientific measurement and means–ends or cause–effect relationships makes other forms of reasoning based on instinct or belief systems seem irrational (Deetz, 2001). Political ideologies include, among others, democracy in which everyone has the opportunity to participate in decisions; theocracy in which religious leaders make decisions; oligarchy in which a small number of (usually wealthy) people make decisions; and monarchy in which members of the ruling family make decisions. At the risk of generalizing too much, in the United States, most organizations embrace a capitalistic ideology based on economic growth, reinforced with an individualistic ideology of personal gain, based on technical rationality, and function as an oligarchy in which a small group of people, usually upper management and owners, make the decisions. Obviously, there are exceptions to this pattern. Power and influence in organizations serve to create and reinforce these values usually in ways that benefit some organizational members more than others. Critical scholars focus their attention on this inequity and on the struggle for power and influence that surrounds it in organizations.

Surface and Deep Structure Power

In further considering definitions of power, it is important to consider that power exists both as a surface level activity in organizations and deeply embedded in the organizational structure (Frost, 1987). *Surface level power* is usually quite easy to observe or detect. If a manger says to an employee, "Stay late to finish this report and I'll owe you a favor," the supervisor is using a form of surface level power to influence the employee to act. *Deep structure power*, by contrast, may be virtually undetectable. For example, the organizational structure in most organizations is set up based on an assumption that managers can give orders and distribute rewards (a favor) or punishments (or you'll be fired) and that employees should generally go along with those assumptions. Deep structure power is like organizational culture in that it involves assumptions that may never be questioned. Ideology generally is part of the deep structure power because it includes assumptions that are rarely questioned. Given the distinction between the two, we consider surface and deep structure power separately.

Surface Level Power

A number of scholars, especially during the post-World War II era, focused on understanding power at the surface level. Research on power at the surface level includes identifying the types of power and the reasons for those types of power relationships that exist in organizations.

Types of Power

Based on the more traditional definition of power as the ability of A to get B to act or think in a particular way, French and Raven (1959) identified five bases or types of power. These are all examples of surface level power because they can easily be observed and identified in routine communication interactions in organizations.

1. *Reward power* involves the ability to provide various incentives or rewards for behaving or thinking in a desired manner. Supervisors and managers can provide pay raises, promotions, increased responsibility, or flexibility as potential rewards.

2. *Coercive power* is essentially the opposite of reward power. It involves threatening to impose negative consequences or punishments unless certain behaviors or attitudes occur or imposing those consequences if they do not. These consequences include a range of possibilities from assignment to less desirable work, to reduced hours or pay, or dismissal.

3. *Legitimate power* is essentially power related to a particular role or position. In organizations, the authority to make and impose certain decisions is often

associated with a position. For example, a department head is expected to have more influence on decisions and even has the authority to make certain decisions without consulting others. A vice president has even more positional power to make decisions and expects others to accept them because most organizations are oligarchies in which those at the top make the important decisions.

4. *Expert power* is based on knowledge rather than position. Different organizational members have different levels of knowledge about organizational functions and activities. Those with more knowledge are usually granted more influence on decisions as a result of their perceived expertise. Information technology personnel whose position in the organizational hierarchy would suggest that they have little legitimate power often have a great deal of expert power that influences decisions and even organizational budgets.

5. *Referent power* is based on one individual identifying strongly with or liking another person or group. Because of this strong identification and desire to be similar to that person or group, the individual imitates the behaviors and attitudes of the person or group. This phenomenon can easily be observed on many college campuses during rush week for sororities and fraternities, but it occurs in many other places. A manager who admires the accomplishments of an organizational vice president may begin to adopt the same behaviors as the vice president in an effort to achieve the same career trajectory.

This typology of power has sometimes been reduced or expanded by various people. For example, French and Raven admit that reward and coercive power can be combined as *sanctions* but emphasize that they often do not have the same effects. Rewards tend to improve the relationship between two people, whereas punishments tend to decrease the attractiveness of the relationship. Legitimate power is sometimes discussed in terms of *status*. When individuals reach certain positions or statuses, there are expectations about the authority associated with that status. Expert power is sometimes characterized as information power. Those with the most information often are considered the experts.

Two of these types of power are particularly consistent with the idea that power is not something a person possesses but rather something attributed to the person—and that power resides there because people think it does. Expert power may be granted to an individual who does not actually have more knowledge or information than others but is *perceived* to have more information than others. An extreme case of this was

In the film, *Catch Me if You Can*, Leonardo DiCaprio's character, Frank Abagnale, was able to convince those around him that he was an expert in a variety of professions due to his ability to imitate the knowledge of actual experts through communication.

chronicled in the 2002 movie *Catch Me If You Can* about the life of Frank Abagnale who was able to convince people that he was an airline pilot, a doctor, and a prosecutor. People attributed expertise to him due to his ability to imitate the knowledge of actual experts in his communication performances. Referent power is also granted to a person in some cases without personal knowledge of the power. If an employee is trying to imitate the behaviors of an admired manager by dressing the same, attending the same seminars, and practicing the same work ethic, the manager may be unaware of possessing referent power.

Reward, coercive, and legitimate power bases are known as *positional power* because they tend to be connected with organizational authority and status. Expert and referent power are known as *personal power* because these power bases are attributed to the individual, whether they have obtained high organizational authority and status or not.

Increasing Personal Power

The study of communication helps us learn how to grow our personal power base. Being seen as knowledgeable (expert) and likeable (referent) by others will be much more likely when communicators are perceived as competent, professional, and relational—the very skills that communication majors learn. Given what you already know about communication, can you think of three ways of enhancing your personal power through good communication practices?

Rahim, Antonioni, and Psenicka (2001) demonstrated that when individuals have positional power, others in the organization are much more likely to attribute expert and referent power to them as well. In other words, these power bases are not necessarily isolated but tend to form clusters of associations and attributions in actual practice. Similarly, Pfeffer (2009) noted how individuals in organizations tend to assume those with organizational authority are especially intelligent and ethical, whether that is actually the case. That common attribution speaks to how surface level power can emerge from deep level power we describe later in the chapter.

Reasons for Power Relationships

Power as Resource Dependency. One of the most common explanations for surface power relationships is resource dependency. Resource dependency basically argues that to the degree that Person A has a resource that Person B wants or needs, Person B is dependent on Person A; this dependency gives Person A certain power or influence over Person B (Emerson, 1962). In such a situation, the greater Person B's desire for what Person A has and the less likely it is that Person B can obtain the same resource elsewhere, the more likely Person B will do what Person A requests. For example, if a manager has control over a subordinate's promotion, the subordinate may stay at work late and accept the least desirable jobs to impress the boss. That supervisor may knowingly or unknowingly be taking advantage of the subordinate.

Organizational newcomers tend to be resource dependent on established employees because they need information to learn their jobs, want to create relationships with others, and need to understand the culture and power relationships of the organization (Kramer, 2010). Fortunately, resource dependency varies over time. As newcomers gain knowledge and competence, they gain resources that make them less dependent. Once they are familiar with "how things are done around here," they are no longer as dependent on others and may even become resources for individuals who join the organization after them.

Resource dependency is not only descriptive of power relationships between individuals. It can also describe power relationships between an individual and a group or power relationships between organizations. For example, a new employee who has strong social needs may take on the worst jobs and work the longest hours to gain acceptance from a peer group. A small manufacturing plant facing potential layoffs due to lack of business may accept a low bid for its product from a national retail chain because it needs the orders to stay in business. Resource dependency puts the person or organization in need of the resource at a power disadvantage.

Power as Social Exchange. Although resource dependency is a popular explanation of power and is easy to understand, it fails to represent the concept of power adequately. Resource dependency implies that power resides in the person who has the desired resource, whereas the dependent person has no power at all. To be consistent with a dynamic definition of power, it is more appropriate to think of the basis of power as a social exchange process. Unlike a resource dependency explanation, a social exchange explanation of power recognizes that both parties have resources, albeit not necessarily distributed evenly (Mumby, 2013).

A social exchange perspective on power indicates that in social interactions between individuals, both parties are involved in an exchange of costs and benefits even though the exact exchange rate and the time frame for completing the exchange may be unspecified (Roloff, 1981). These exchanges are also not limited to economic or financial concerns. In social relationships, the exchanges may involve money, goods, services, information, status, and affect or friendship (Foa & Foa, 1980). It is worth noting that some of these are closely related to French and Raven's (1959) types of power or Maslow's (1954) hierarchy of needs.

A social exchange perspective on power recognizes that even when one party has more resources, it must still give up something to fill its needs. This perspective is actually implicit in the examples used so far in this chapter. The manager who persuades employees to stay late must exchange resources to gain their labor. That may be providing flexible work hours the next day if the exchange remains in the economic category, but it could also mean that the manager may need to give additional status to those employees and consider their opinions more in future decisions. Alternatively, it could mean that the manager loses resources by compelling them to work. The employees may reduce the number of extra-job duties that they complete in the future (loss of services). The employees may no longer respect the manager (loss of status and/or friendship) and so other aspects of the work environment may suffer, including productivity. In the case of the small manufacturer, if the large retail company demands too low a price, in the future, the small company may find a competitor to sell to instead; or when it is doing better, the manufacturer may not renew its agreement with the large company.

Power and Personal Characteristics. Viewing power as personal characteristics is somewhat inconsistent with a perspective of power as a dynamic exchange because it seems to imply that power is something that someone has or possesses. Although that may have been the perspective of some of the researchers who studied power as personal characteristics, it is more appropriate to think of personal characteristics as *resources*— not power per se—that individuals possess. Because these resources are not evenly distributed, some people have an advantage in the exchange of resources that can lead to opportunities to exercise power.

One personal characteristic associated with power is a *predisposition for power* (Frost, 1987). Some people have a high need to be influential and exercise power in social settings. Most of us know individuals who are ambitious, highly verbal, and seem to like to take charge in situations to influence the process and outcomes as they see fit. Individuals who desire power are more likely to gain positions where they can exercise power in organizations (Frost, 1987; Russell, 1938).

A number of *personal abilities* are also associated with power. For example, people with higher levels of self-confidence and higher levels of cognitive differentiation (i.e., the ability to perceive nuanced differences in a phenomenon) are more likely to gain positions where they can exercise power. For example, higher levels of cognitive differentiation were associated with job level and upward mobility for employees in a large insurance company headquarters over four years (Sypher & Zorn, 1986).

Previous experience in power is also associated with future exercise of power (Frost, 1987). Individuals who were in positions where they influenced others, were successful at it, and were rewarded for it are also more likely to seek positions of power in the future. In this sense, those who have had been able to exercise power in the past are more likely to seek positions where they can exercise power in the future.

One negative personal characteristic associated with power is *Machiavellianism*, named after the 16th-century author of a short book, *The Prince*, by Niccolo Machiavelli. In the book, Machiavelli encouraged his prince to be unemotional and detached from conventional moral views as well as to use deception and manipulation to achieve goals. People who score high on measures of Machiavellianism tend to be successful manipulators, resistant to attitude change, task oriented, and have a tendency to give more orders and directives to others than they receive, particularly in competitive situations (e.g., Drory & Gluskinos, 1980).

There are likely other personal characteristics associated with people who exercise power. Because of differences in these personal resources, some individuals more readily gain access to positions that enable them to exercise power. These different personal resources could be considered various types of expert power.

Deep Structure Power

As mentioned previously, deep structure power is more difficult to observe because it is embedded in the organizational structure as *assumptions* about the way organizations in general or a particular organization "should" work. Critical scholars are particularly interested in deep structure power because it is often the basis for creating disadvantages for some organizational members while providing advantages to others. For example, few of us question who benefits or is harmed by the traditional five days a week, 40-hour work week or question why employees with college degrees should be paid more than those without one for doing the same work. Unquestioned rules or norms like these are part of the structure of organization and are part of its deep structure of power.

Dennis Mumby (1987) provided a summary of the characteristics of communication that are associated with deep structure power. He used a story told about an incident at IBM to illustrate these characteristics. The story, told in a biography of the former CEO of IBM, Tom Watson, includes the following details about a confrontation between Lucille Burger, a security guard at one of the IBM plants, and Watson, the CEO at the time. According to the story, Lucille Berger was

> [A] twenty-two-year-old bride weighing ninety pounds, whose husband had been sent overseas, and who, in consequence, had been given a job until his

return. . . . The young woman, Lucille Burger, was obliged to make certain that people entering security areas wore the correct clearance identification. Surrounded by his usual entourage of white-shirted men, Watson approached the doorway to an area where she was on guard, wearing an orange badge acceptable elsewhere in the plant, but not the green badge, which alone permitted entrance at her door. "I was trembling in my uniform, which was far too big," she recalled. "It hid my shakes, but not my voice. 'I'm sorry,' I said to him. I knew who he was all right. 'You cannot enter. Your admittance is not recognized.' That's what we were supposed to say." The men accompanying Watson were stricken; the moment held unpredictable possibilities. "Don't you know who he is?" someone hissed. Watson raised his hand for silence, while one of the party strode off and returned with the appropriate badge. (Rodgers, 1969, pp. 153–154)

An analysis of this story as representative of the organization's culture concluded that it expresses the important values of IBM. It particular, the story suggests that the organization values employees who follow the rules (assume custodial roles) and that everyone, even the CEO, is obligated to follow the rules (Martin, Feldman, Hatch, & Sitkin, 1983). A script analysis would suggest that both Berger and Watson are heroes for upholding the company values. The members of the entourage might be considered villains for suggesting that it was appropriate for the CEO to break the rules.

This cultural interpretation fails to recognize the political nature of the story and the way it communicates and reinforces the deep structure power of the organization. Mumby (1987) and other scholars have identified some of the key characteristics of communication and deep structure power. One characteristic of deep structure power is that communication *represents sectional interests as universal*. This involves making it appear that something that actually benefits a particular group of individuals is equally good for everyone. In this story, it appears that having everyone follow the rules benefits everyone equally. In fact, Watson, as CEO and stock owner, benefits significantly more (financially, socially, and otherwise) from all of the employees following the rules and procedures than the employees themselves benefit. This characteristic might be summarized as "it will be good for everyone."

A second characteristic of deep structure is that the communication *denies or transmutes contradictions*. When there is a contradiction in a situation, communication can refute the contradiction exists or, more often, deny it exists by failing to address it. This allows the contradiction to go unnoticed. For example, in this story there is a fundamental contradiction that is being ignored or overlooked: Watson did not have to follow the security rules if he choose not to do so. Because as CEO he makes the rules, he can change them to fit his needs. By contrast, Lucille must follow the rules or risk losing her job. However, by not addressing the power difference between the two and focusing on following the rules, the narrative denies that such a contradiction exists or is worth considering.

A third characteristic of deep structure is that communication *naturalizes and reifies the present.* Repeated communication within a group can establish or reinforce a practice in ways that make it seem like the only plausible or rational behavior in a situation. Few people question what seems perfectly natural. In this case, the story reinforces that having security check points for employees is perfectly natural. The story also makes it seem apparent and obvious that it is appropriate to distrust employees. You must monitor them so they will follow rules. The story also makes it seem natural that even a CEO must go through security checkpoints and have the correct badge. The story also suggests that it is perfectly natural to trust a small, young, unskilled worker with this important job even though she would probably be unable to prevent untrustworthy people from entering by restraining them physically.

A fourth characteristic of deep structure power is the *systematic distortion of communication,* typically in the form of self-deception. This concept involves individuals failing to recognize that they are deceiving themselves through their communication. Burger is deceiving herself if she thinks that she could actually prevent Watson from entering the section of the plant, even though it is her job. Watson is deceiving himself by suggesting that he must comply with her request when he knows he could have fired her if he had chosen to do so. He deceives himself and the entourage into thinking that he is very egalitarian, just another employee, who must follow the rules as well.

The term *hegemony* is frequently used as a general term for oppression or control or dominance by those in power. To distinguish that general meaning of hegemony from the more narrowly defined use here, the final characteristic of deep structure power to discuss is that it involves *hegemonic participation.* Hegemonic participation describes the process by which the ideas of those in charge are so readily accepted by others that they willingly participate in their own oppression and consent to their role without recognizing the oppression involved (Gramsci, 1973). Burger is involved in hegemonic participation. Because she is grateful for her job at IBM while her husband is at war, she accepts her role as guard without questioning why she (or any woman) is not part of

Muting Voices of the Mistreated

Communication researchers interviewed 69 employees of a large organization, known for having problems associated with mistreating employees (Meares, Oetzel, Torres, Derkacs, & Ginossar, 2004). The researchers analyzed how participants from diverse racial and cultural backgrounds responded to employee mistreatment. Management's repeated silencing of resisters and their ambiguous and lukewarm responses to employees' feelings of being mistreated muted the employees' voices over time. The scholars used ideas about hegemony from scholars such as Gramsci (1973) and Mumby (2001) to explain how resisters of the employee mistreatment became numbed to the mistreatment over time. Some even resigned themselves to its normalcy. What changes in communication would be necessary to break this cycle of mistreatment and silence?

Watson's entourage. Similarly, although they are at a much higher status in the organization, the members of the entourage submit to Watson's authority willingly to maintain their positions. Notice how readily one scurries to get Watson's badge rather than having him retrieve the badge himself.

The acceptance of the ideas of those in charge is really an acceptance of the dominant ideology. Although the dominant ideology may shift over time, there are a number of aspects of the dominant ideology in the U.S. workforce that are also evident in the IBM story. For example, we tend to accept the principles of capitalism as defining the "appropriate" way for a business to function. We tend to accept the principle of oligarchy in which a small group, usually those in high status positions like Watson, make the decisions. These assumptions mean there "should" be a chain of command in which managers make the rules and employees follow them. It is easy to see that these and other characteristics of the dominant ideology are present in the story.

When focusing on the deep structure power within an organization, it is also valuable to reconsider how surface power is also involved simultaneously. Certainly, Watson did not have to comply with Burger's request and could have fired her. The deep structure would have supported his actions, and the structure would have been reinforced or recreated in the process. At the surface level, there would have been a cost to Watson. Once employees knew that the rules did not apply to everyone, there would have been a loss of respect for Watson and most likely a loss of willingness to comply with organizational rules. Over time, the deep structure that would be recreated would have changed because widely held assumptions would have changed. The new structure would still likely benefit a few people like Watson more that than security guards, but there would have been some cost, albeit possibly quite small, to Watson and the others due to the changes.

Of course, not everyone responds to someone in a position associated with power the same way because power is something attributed to someone rather than something a person has. At the end of the Lucille Burger story, Al Good, who was the director of security, commended Lucille in an unusual manner because he "understood the nervousness of the men in Watson's party. 'I guess it was the sort of thing they couldn't mention to him if they were close to him. With me, it was just a job, and it didn't bother [me]'" (Rodgers, 1969, p. 154). This fascinating quote suggests that the upper management personnel in Watson's entourage were actually more intimidated by Watson's power than he was despite their high status in the hierarchy. Because they worked more closely with Watson than people lower in the hierarchy, such as people in security, they felt less able to challenge him. This reinforces the idea that power is attributed. The entourage apparently attributed more power to Watson than people in security like Al Good.

Resistance to Power

The ability to exercise power is never absolute. Because of the dynamic interplay necessary to exercise power to influence another person or group, the exercise of power can always be resisted. Even a threat to fire an employee unless a report is finished by the end of the day may not influence the employee's behavior. Firing does not influence or change the employee's behavior; it removes the employee from the situation but does not get the report completed. *Threats* of termination may influence behavior, or not. Perhaps the most effective exercise of power occurs when those who use it are able to make their interpretation of the organization and the actions needed seem so natural or obvious that other organizational members embrace those interpretations as part of their own identity—and as a result, do not resist and instead accept those interpretations as their own (Zoller, 2014). Such is often the case with deep structure power; it seems natural to comply with those who exercise power.

There is plenty of evidence to suggest that attempts to exercise power in organizations regularly fail to achieve at least some or all of the goals. Employees fail to comply with organizational rules frequently or even when they comply with the desired behaviors, they may not exhibit the desired attitudes and commitment to organizational goals. Sometimes noncompliance is simply a mistake. An employee may have been improperly trained and so fails to comply with organizational directives. Sometimes noncompliance is the result of something unrelated to organizational membership. An employee may arrive late due to a sick child. At other times even when an employee is well-informed and able to comply, the noncompliance can be an act of resistance. Knowledge of the constraints that the exercise of power institutes to gain or maintain control can lead to either compliance or resistance (Conrad & Haynes, 2001; Fairhurst, 2011a). An employee may deliberately not follow the new procedure management recently implemented to resist the change. Employees may deliberately take extra-long lunch breaks to resist the expectations from management that they stay late. There is a constant tension or struggle between control by those exercising power and resistance to that influence from those who are being controlled (Zoller, 2014). Conversely, employees can resist bureaucracy through "malicious compliance" with its rules. In such cases, employees resist the rules by attempting to follow all the rules obsessively to the point that collective action virtually ceases. Malicious compliance creates a work slowdown or stoppage by following the rules too closely.

Clearly, resistance can come in many forms. Some forms of resistance are overt and clearly visible to those in positions of authority, such as a labor strike by employees. Many are more covert or secretive in which individuals resist the exercise of power while expecting that those attempting to exercise power will not be aware of their actions. For example, a study of faculty members' interactions with institutional review boards (IRBs), which have the power to decide whether professors can conduct research involving human subjects, found a number of covert forms of resistance. Covert resistance included avoiding IRBs completely, using strategic ambiguity to mask their real actions, and appearing to cooperate while actually circumventing the system (Dougherty & Kramer, 2005). These covert methods of resistance allowed the researchers to continue doing their research without complying with the organizational rules and without being detected by the IRBs.

Resistance can also be what is described as "decaf resistance" or "real resistance" (Contu, 2008). In the same way that decaf coffee does not contain caffeine, decaf resistance does not actually resist the exercise of power in a way that attempts to create

Ethics and Decaf Resistance

Decaf resistance does not seek to change work issues substantively, but some individuals believe it helps them relieve stress created by the job. Some "real" resistance efforts can be attempted on principled grounds to create ethical change in the workplace, such as trying to resist managers' directives to fool customers into buying more services than they need. Yet, because decaf resistance does not attempt to create change, is it ever principled or ethical? What would principled or ethical decaf resistance sound like?

change. For example, staff on cruise ships are required to manage their emotions and put on a positive face all the time, even when not working; "bitching" about customers behind the scenes when managers are not around creates comradery among crew members and relieves some of the stress in complying with those difficult work expectations (Tracy, 2000). Disney ride operators face similar expectations to be positive to even the rudest guests but find ways to slap particularly offensive guests "accidently" with the seatbelt while strapping them in to rides as ways of getting even (Van Maanen & Kunda, 1989). These acts of resistance may help the employees cope with their situation, but they are decaf resistance because they do not affect change by confronting the system of power arrangements directly.

Zoller and Fairhurst (2007) list a wide range of actions that are forms of resistance. These include symbolic and material forms of resistance that vary in terms of how covert or overt they are and in terms of whether they are decaf or real resistance. One form includes complying with requested *behaviors* but not complying with the requested *attitudes* by showing resignation or tolerance instead of enthusiasm. Others involve overt resistance, including noncooperation, personal confrontation, formal complaints within the organization, collective or legal action by going outside of the organization, and even violence. Covert strategies include theft and sabotage.

Some of the most common forms of resistance in organizations—such as cynicism to management; parody and humor, which make fun of those in charge; or gripe sessions among employees to talk about how it would be "if we were in charge"—involve little or no cost for the employees. However, because these are forms of decaf resistance, they have little if any chance of actually producing change in the power relationships. According to Contu (2008), these ineffective forms of decaf resistance need to be replaced with real resistance in which the individual takes responsibility for the action; however, real resistance may also involve significant costs. Some of the overt forms of resistance listed previously, such as formal complaints or legal action, have the potential for real change but at a cost.

Voice and Resistance

One common way for organizational employees to communicate their resistance overtly regarding some organizational policy or practice is by voicing dissent. *Voicing dissent* involves taking verbal responsibility for resistant actions. Voicing dissent holds the potential for incurring significant cost, but it also holds the potential for making meaningful changes in an organization by confronting issues publicly. Employee voice, a broad term, describes a variety of communication that can be constructive, such as suggesting new ideas or participating in decision-making, or destructive, such as complaining or badmouthing; and it can include expressions of job dissatisfaction or principled disagreement with organizational practices (Gorden, 1988). It is this last form of voice, expressing disagreement with organizational policies or practices, that exemplifies the concept of voicing dissent as a form of resistance to the exercise of power in organizations (Kassing, 2009).

Voicing dissent is a form of resistance because it expresses disagreement or contrary opinions about workplace policies and practices in an effort to change how power is exercised in the organization. Kassing (2009) summarizes many of the findings concerning employees' dissent. Employees may articulate dissent to supervisors and management, a form of real dissent, or they may displace their dissent to family and peers, a form of decaf dissent. They are more likely to engage in upward dissent when they have higher levels of self-esteem, better communication skills, and more positive relationships with their supervisors. They are also more likely to resist by expressing dissent after some specific triggering event occurs that violates their expectations for how power should be exercised, such as unfair or harmful treatment to themselves or others, poor decision-making, or implementation of an organizational change. So, for example, if an employee observes that an incident of sexual harassment reported by a co-worker was never investigated by management, that employee may voice dissent with company policy in an attempt to change an attitude of "boys will be boys" that has been practiced by those in authority. This articulated, voiced dissent is more likely if the employee has high self-esteem and a good relationship with a supervisor. Voice then becomes a form of resistance to power that can cause change.

Voicing dissent is more likely to be an effective form of resistance that will produce change if the individual uses communication strategies that are perceived to be competent. Five strategies seem to be particularly common for communicating upward dissent (Kassing, 2005). A *solution presentation* focuses on communicating about some triggering event and ways to solve the problem or prevent additional occurrences. In a *direct-factual appeal*, the dissenter presents information, facts, or physical evidence that support the need for change in policies and practices. In *repetition*, the employee reminds the supervisor repeatedly and regularly of the issue and perhaps even has other employees participate in voicing their dissent as well.

The previous strategies for voicing dissent with organizational policies or practices typically involve communicating to a direct supervisor, the person with legitimate authority, directly above an employee in the hierarchy. However, because these forms of resistance do not always lead to the desired changes, in some instances, employees *circumvent* their immediate supervisor to voice their dissent to someone higher in the chain of command, skipping at least one level in the hierarchy. Circumvention is most likely to occur for one of these three reasons (Kassing, 2009):

1. *Supervisor inaction:* Employees expect the supervisor will act on their complaint and take action but find that no changes occur.
2. *Supervisor performance:* Employees become aware that the supervisor lacks the skills to handle issues competently or has treated employees unfairly in the past.
3. *Supervisor indiscretion:* The supervisor behaved inappropriately or unethically in the past or is part of the problem that needs to be addressed.

As these three reasons suggest, individuals will circumvent their immediate supervisor to resist organizational policies or practices primarily when the supervisor is part of the problem. If the supervisor seems unlikely or incapable of assisting the employee in creating change in the way power is currently being exercised in the organization, circumvention is a possible, albeit risky, strategy.

Although obviously risky, the employee may voice dissent by *threatening resignation*. This strategy can backfire if the person is not willing to resign if no action is taken, but it may be effective in resisting an unsafe, unethical, or illegal practice.

In comparing these strategies (see Table 11.1), a solution presentation was perceived as the most competent approach, followed by direct-factual appeal. These two strategies

TABLE 11.1 A Comparison of Five Upward Dissent Strategies

Upward Dissent Strategies	Definition	Perceived Competence: Rank Ordered from Most to Least Competent
Solution Presentation	Providing solutions to address dissent-triggering issues.	1
Direct-Factual Appeal	Supporting one's dissent claim with factual information.	2
Repetition	Reminding others about one's dissent claim.	3
Circumvention	Dissenting to someone higher in hierarchical authority.	4
Threatening Resignation	Giving an ultimatum that the dissent-triggering issue should be corrected or the dissenter will exit the organization.	5

were perceived as similar in effectiveness. They were also seen as significantly more effective than repetition and circumvention. Finally, threatening resignation was perceived as the least effective strategy (Kassing, 2005). Regardless of their perceived competence, all of these are forms of dissent that qualify as employee resistance.

Whistleblowing is final form of voicing dissent and resistance that involves voicing the dissent publicly outside of the organization. In general, after becoming aware of some unethical, immoral, or illegal practice within an organization, the individual begins resisting by voicing dissent to their immediate supervisor and then moves on to higher level administrators. Voicing dissent and resistance *within* the organization about unethical, immoral, or illegal practices is termed *boat rocking*, to differentiate it from whistleblowing. Only when the issue is not addressed or resolved properly are boat rockers more likely to become whistleblowers as they finally go outside the organization if the issue is still not addressed in an effort to change the practice

ETHICAL ISSUE

Boat Rocking and Whistleblowing

When should a dissenter stop boat rocking and start whistleblowing? Does the issue matter? Does management's receptiveness matter? Does timeliness of addressing concerns matter? Does the way concerns are addressed matter? What other aspects of the decision to move from boat rocking to whistleblowing should be considered?

(Stewart, 1980). By going public outside the organization, the whistleblower takes responsibility publicly and often incurs significant costs. Although whistleblowers are legally protected from retaliation and firing, this does not prevent or control the emotional, social, and financial costs that whistleblowers often incur (Gorden, 1988).

Voice is a common way to communicate to resist the exercises of power in organizations. Voice is generally done internally and typically only results in whistleblowing when the issue is not addressed and is severe. It seems likely that voicing dissent most frequently addresses surface level expressions of power because these are more likely to be visible triggering events that violate expectations. The more subtle, deep structure exercise of power is such an assumed part of the organization that employees are less likely to notice it and be able to resist it.

Power and Resistance in Nonprofits and Volunteers

Power and resistance differ in an important way with volunteers. Because volunteers have prosocial motivations rather than economic ones, they do not have the same resource dependency on organizations as employees who rely on paychecks for their livelihoods. As a result, it would be easy to make the mistake of characterizing power in nonprofit organizations as being almost the reverse from the way it works in businesses and government agencies. For example, the resource dependency often appears to be in the reverse direction with NPOs dependent on the generosity of volunteers. NPOs, from religious organizations to disaster response agencies, such as the Red Cross, are dependent on volunteers to achieve their goals.

Such a characterization of power in relationship to volunteers is overly simplistic. Volunteers are also dependent on NPOs to achieve their goals, and NPOs provide forms of nonfinancial rewards to volunteers. For example, community theater volunteers are motivated by a desire to perform and create relationships, but they can only achieve their goals if the director casts them (Kramer, 2005). Generally, volunteers can only achieve their goals of service to the community by cooperating with the NPO's training requirements and by following the guidelines and rules of the NPO. As with other organizational settings, because power is a dynamic of interaction, there is an exchange process as power is exercised with volunteers in relationships with others.

Power operates at both a surface level and deep level simultaneously in relationship to volunteers. For example, at the surface, community theater volunteers give long hours of service based on their expertise as performers in exchange for the opportunity to be rewarded by the applause at the end of the performance, the development of friendships, and other potential benefits. At a deeper level, however, selection into a community theater is often perceived as a political process that favors some insiders over newcomers or outsiders (Kramer, 2004b). As another example of the deep structure power, new volunteers for a search and rescue team were only allowed to do the grunt work, such as inventory supplies—not the exciting work like riding in helicopters—until they conformed to the expectations of the established volunteers, including demonstrating appropriate humility (Lois, 1999). This ability of established volunteers to determine the roles of the new volunteers seems natural and in the best interests of the long-term stability of the program. Thus, the practice naturalizes the present and represents the sectional interests of the established volunteers as universal.

Resistance to power is also common among volunteers. A study of volunteers in three organizations found that volunteers often resisted the rules communicated down to them through formal channels. When social services volunteers were told to avoid touching and hugging clients, they often violated the rule because they felt it was more important to be compassionate when interacting with their clients than to comply with professional rules (Onyx, 2013). Other studies demonstrate that volunteers respond to directives from the organizations' upper management with a variety of forms of resistance (McAllum, 2013). For example, some volunteers used forms of decaf resistance—including gossiping, humor or irony, and resentment—to relieve tension and create comradery without attempting to effect change. Other volunteers avoided certain directives or provided reluctant compliance in which they waited until the last minute to produce required reports. In other cases, volunteers exhibited real resistance by simply refusing to comply with directives. Volunteers can also choose to leave, as an expression of resistance, but many are reluctant to do so because of their identification with the volunteer activity (McAllum, 2013). Furthermore, leaving often does not necessarily create change anyway. Many of the search-and-rescue volunteers quit when they were not accepted and given more interesting duties quickly, but that did not change the way newcomers were treated (Lois, 1999).

At the organizational level, nonprofit organizations are often resource dependent and must link to those with more economic resources (Shumate & Contactor, 2014). As a result, large and more established nonprofit organizations are more likely to have formal collaborative relations with other nonprofits because they are more appealing partners than newer, smaller ones due to their access to more resources (Guo & Acar, 2005). This dynamic often gives the larger more established NPOs more ability to exercise power in relationship to small ones when working together.

The relationship of NPOs to volunteers has not been extensively studied from a power perspective. Perhaps this is due in part to the lack of economic motivations that are so integral to the constitution of power arrangements in business settings. Yet the limited research now available on volunteers does suggest that power works quite similarly, with surface level exchanges and deep structure power controlling expectations and behaviors in important ways.

Summary

In this chapter, we explored many of the issues related to power and resistance in organizations. We emphasized the importance of viewing the exercise of power or influence as a dynamic process that develops between two parties rather than seeing power as something that one party has over another. At the surface or easily observable level of power, individuals exchange resources such as money, service, or status. These resources are not evenly divided, as some individuals have legitimate power based on their position, can control rewards more easily, or have more knowledge and expertise. Their own personal characteristics may also contribute to how they exercise power in relationship to others at the surface level.

At the deep structure level, power is built into the structure of the organization and the meanings that people assign to the way the organization operates. These factors serve as assumptions that naturalize the current way of doing things and frequently represent the interests of one group, usually upper management and owners, as mutually and equally beneficial. When these structures and meanings are particularly powerful, individuals willingly participate in their own oppression through hegemonic participation.

Because power emerges through interaction and is not absolute, individuals can comply or resist attempts to exercise power, although surface power is easier to identify than deep structure power. Resistance may come in the form of decaf resistance such as griping or joking, which does not cause any changes and often results in compliance, or resistance may be real when it challenges the surface or deep level power in an effort to facilitate change.

CHAPTER 12

Communication and Work-Nonwork Issues

Robin had an unusual group of friends at Underwriters Insurance Conglomerate (UIC). For one, they had all joined the company about the same time just after graduating from college. More unusual, they all stayed with the company for their entire careers—an unusual feat these days.

Their perspectives on the company's family-friendly policies changed over the years. When they were starting, they really preferred to keep their work and personal lives separate but found it especially difficult to prevent work from interfering with their personal lives. They wanted to show they were truly committed employees and so they often ended up "volunteering" to put in more hours than they wanted. This overcommitment happened in part because they were unmarried without children. As a result, their managers seemed to expect them to be able to work late and on weekends. Meanwhile, their colleagues with children were excused from such extra work because they had parenting duties, soccer games to attend, and parent–teacher organization meetings to run. The managers did not seem to think their Thursday evening volleyball league was an adequate reason for them not being able to stay late. It was also clear that the managers would only call the employees without families on weekends if an urgent job needed to be done. Robin remembered thinking at the time that the family-friendly policies seemed more like a burden on those who did not have families.

Of course, as they married and had children, their perspective on the policies changed. They were happy to be able to have some of the benefits of the policies, although it was not always so easy to take advantage of them as they thought. Taking maternity leave involved negotiating time off and a return time. That was tricky because you were committed to your career and you wanted to be sure to appear that way while asking for leave time. It was even more challenging to take paternity leave. Colleagues resented the extra work they had to do for what was perceived as an unnecessary perk. It did seem like more men were willing to risk taking paternity leave as time went on than when the policy was first adopted.

Some of Robin's friends seemed to find ways to integrate their work and family lives. It was not unusual for them to interrupt work to take personal phone calls and respond to personal emails. Others kept strict boundaries between work and other life activities. As a result, there was sometimes friction between the two groups. The first group thought nothing of occasionally having a child at work for a short period of time, and the managers allowed it if it did not interfere with work. The second group thought having children in the workplace created an unprofessional atmosphere.

The group of friends was growing in their appreciation of the policies now that many of them were caring for elderly parents. The ability to use flextime hours to take their parents to doctors' appointments was proving to be particularly valuable. Robin was amazed at how many appointments two elderly people could have.

· · · · ·

Organizational communication is often studied with some unstated assumptions. One common assumption is that people's organizational or work roles are their primary concern and that their organizational or work roles operate somewhat independently from any other roles the individuals may have. Of course, that is not the case. As we discussed briefly in Chapter 10 on conflict, individuals often experience conflict between multiple work roles, but they also frequently experience conflict between work roles and other nonwork or life roles, such as being a family member or volunteer. In this chapter, we examine some of the communication issues related to the intersection of work and other life roles.

The Changing Workplace

Issues of work-nonwork or work-life balance have become increasingly prominent over the last few decades for a number of reasons. One reason is the increase in the number of women in the U.S. workforce. In 2010, approximately 72 million women worked outside the home, with 72% of them employed in full-time jobs and 28% in part-time work; they comprised 47% of the U.S. labor force in 2010 and are projected to account for over 51% of the labor force by 2018 (U.S. Bureau of Labor Statistics, 2010). A second reason is that the same studies show the percentage of married women, mothers, and dual-career families has also risen significantly over the last four decades. Although there were work-life issues prior to these changes, the changing makeup of the workforce has focused scholars' attention on the issues that were previously ignored.

General Causes of Work-Life Conflict

As Robin's scenario indicates, conflict between work and nonwork roles can take many forms. A key article by Greenhaus and Beutell (1985) identified three primary reasons for conflict and stress between work and other life roles: time-based conflict, strain-based conflict, and behavior-based conflict.

Time-Based Conflict. Time-based conflicts are the easiest to understand. Conflict occurs because time spent on one activity cannot also be spent on another activity. Although we have expectations that individuals spend time at work and away from work, time-based conflict occurs when expectations for the amount of time spent on each role are not met. The discrepancy may involve the individuals' own expectations or the expectations of others at work or away from work. Time-based conflicts occur primarily in two forms: (a) They occur when time pressures of one role make it physically impossible to comply with the time pressures of another role, and (b) they occur when pressures in one role leads to a preoccupation with that role while attempting to fulfill another role halfheartedly (Greenhaus & Beutell, 1985). These conflicts can flow from work to nonwork roles or from nonwork roles to work roles. For example, if a parent works overtime one evening, it makes it impossible to spend that evening with family. Alternatively, an employee who is taking care of an elderly parent may be preoccupied with medical care issues and as a result be unable to concentrate at work.

Research on time-based conflicts indicates a number of interesting trends related to working women. A somewhat dated study found that women working part-time jobs actually tend to experience more conflict than women working full-time (Hall & Gordon, 1973). This dynamic appears to occur for a couple of reasons: Working part-time may not satisfy an internal conflict women have about holding a career because the part-time work is often not particularly challenging. In addition, some women are also mothers, and some mothers are also wives. A recent report by the U.S. Census Bureau (2014) reports that only a little more than half of U.S. adults live with a spouse, and significantly fewer of those U.S. households include one or more children. For some of these women, working part-time may mean struggling with role overload, as they may still be expected to perform all the domestic duties while also trying to juggle the additional role of working part-time, whether or not they are the only adult in the household. Statistics from the U.S. Department of Labor Women's Bureau (2015) revealed that more than 65% of first-time mothers worked full- or part-time during their pregnancies in 2008 as compared with 44% during the early 1960s.

Research reveals husbands of wives in managerial/professional roles experience more work-life conflict than husbands of wives in nonmanagerial/nonprofessional roles (Greenhaus & Kopelman, 1981). It is likely that wives in managerial/professional roles need to dedicate more time to their work and that this results in their husbands experiencing more stress from taking on additional domestic duties, including in some cases child care responsibilities. In addition, because it is more common now for wives to earn more than their spouses, it would be interesting to see how the relative income of the spouses affects these issues. Clearly, household dynamics are shifting nationwide. In 2012, 40% of mothers were the sole or primary income earner of their household as compared to just 11% in 1960. Yet, in spite of this trend, mothers with children under 18 in the United States earn only three-fourths the income of fathers with children (U.S. Department of Labor Women's Bureau, 2015). Little is known currently about how issues regarding role sharing and role overload plays out in same-sex couples.

Strain-Based Conflict. Strain-based conflict occurs when the challenges of completing one role makes it difficult or challenging to fulfill the other roles. For example, if the effort and stress of a particularly challenging or negative work role creates negative emotions, those negative emotions can spill over to family roles. The negative emotions create fatigue, tension, and worry that are displaced into personal life such that the individual does poorly as a friend, parent, or spouse. By contrast, if an individual experiences a lack of support from a partner or spouse away from work, the lack of career support can make it more difficult to do well on the job.

Behavior-Based Conflict. Behavior-based conflict occurs when the behaviors in one role are not appropriate (or less than optimal) in the other role, but the individual fails to adapt behaviors appropriate to the other situation. For example, in the workplace, a manager may be expected to be self-reliant, aggressive, and directive; yet those same behaviors can be problematic in a family setting. A number of movies over the years have illustrated behavior-based conflict when a member of the military treats family members as if they were part of a platoon instead of acting toward them in a loving and caring manner. These movies include classics such as *The Sound of Music* in which Captain von Trapp treats his children like a platoon until Maria enters his life. More recently, the comedy *The Pacifier* has Lt. Shane Wolfe assigned to babysit a family of five children instead of his usual military operations. Movies like these illustrate that behaviors that are successful at work are inappropriate in the home. Conversely, if parents practice nurturing and caring behaviors toward their children, those same behaviors may be ineffective in a managerial role in the workplace.

In the opening scenario, time-based conflicts were the most obvious. Employees with children could not work overtime and coach their children's soccer team at the same time. Taking time to drive elderly parents to doctor's appointments meant revising work schedules to manage time-based conflicts. It is likely that strain-based conflicts occurred frequently, for example, when employees' anxiety about their children affected work or when a stressful situation at work made it difficult to focus on showing concern for a parent. Because working in an insurance organization does not involve particularly extreme directing or caring behaviors, it is unlikely that there were many behavior-based conflicts for the group of friends as they progressed through their careers.

Specific Causes of Work-Life Conflict

The time-based, strain-based, and behavior-based conflicts that employees experience are influenced by a number of specific work, life, and personal characteristics (Kirby, Wieland, & McBride, 2006). *Work factors* that affect work-life conflicts include the type of work (e.g., physical demands, amount of challenge), work schedules (regular day shifts vs. irregular shifts), level of work autonomy, and work group relationships (e.g., level of conflict or support). *Life factors* include family characteristics such as the nature of the household (single- vs. two-parent families), sources of household income (single provider vs. dual income), and status of children (number and age). *Personal factors* include how central the work or family role is to an individual's identity, and personality characteristics such as emotional stability, agreeableness, and conscientiousness. These three factors affect the nature of the work-life conflict. For example, in the scenario, Robin as a single person with no children likely experienced less time-based and strain-based work-life conflict than a friend working evening shifts who was a single parent with young children. However, if they both identified strongly with their work roles, the level of work-life conflict would be greater than for some other employees.

Social Norms that Increase Work-Life Conflict

Work-life role conflict seems to have increased due to a number of additional reasons. At least for individuals in what are traditionally called "white collar" jobs like in the scenario, society seems to have communicated expectations that lead to increases in work-life conflict. These expectations, described in what follows, are communicated as the motherhood norm, ideal worker norm, individualism norm, and consumerism norm (Drago, 2007; Kramer, 2010). We also add an additional norm, the technology norm.

According to Drago (2007), the *motherhood norm* communicates that women are expected to be interested in and willing to do unpaid caregiving, such as raising children and caring for the elderly. This expectation has the potential to create a number of conflicts for them. It suggests that women should be willing to be full-time moms or caregivers even when they are working part-time or full-time; men are generally not held to this same expectation. This uneven distribution of work contributes to additional work-life conflict for women but can also create additional conflict within the family if partners have different expectations concerning this norm. The motherhood norm may also create role conflict in the workplace as women are expected to be more nurturing than men or are expected to volunteer for various roles, such as planning social events or assuming duties such as coffee maker at the office. Differences in these expectations create conflicts in the workplace. It is idealistic to think that the changes in role expectations for women and men over the last few decades have eliminated these issues.

The *ideal worker norm* communicates that dedicated professionals should be willing to prioritize work over family and friends. The norm often means putting in long hours of unpaid labor because most professionals receive a salary rather than hourly pay. The ideal worker norm makes working at home in the evening or on weekends seem like a normal expectation. Those who are unwilling to do this kind of work may run the risk of communicating that they are uncommitted or unwilling to carry their workload by not meeting the ideal worker norm expectations. Because of the fear that *other* employees will work the long hours, an employee who may not want to work such long hours often feels pressured to live up to the ideal worker norm. As is discussed in more detail later, technology also plays a role in the increased pressure to be an ideal worker by making it easier for employers to contact employees 24 hours a day, 7 days a week. On an airline flight, Michael Kramer overheard two young women who were apparently account executives for a public relations firm complaining that they had not agreed to be 24-hour "slaves" of the organization. However, they also seemed unable or unwilling to determine an appropriate way to put boundaries on requests from their supervisors. By contrast, some people resist this norm by not checking work email or using caller ID to screen work calls outside of normal working hours.

To Work or Not to Work, That Is the Question

When we think of dual-career households, we likely imagine two professionals and assume that they can afford child care or after-school care if they have children. In many cases, second spouses take jobs that are closer to minimum wage. Sometimes when that is the case, the couple experiences almost no economic gain because most of the secondary income pays for day care. Of course, the economics of the situation are not the only consideration. The second spouse may value working as a career activity. Does it make more sense to not work if there is so little financial gain for the couple? Does it make more sense to work so the spouse feels a sense of accomplishment and contribution? What other contextual factors might influence the decision to work or not work?

The *individualism norm* suggests that as Americans, we are "rugged individuals" who should be able to manage challenges on our own. It communicates that we should not need the help of others, or at least not beyond the help of our family members. This norm tends to makes U.S. employees hesitant to expect organizations to provide affordable, on-site day care for children or to provide leave time to care for a family member. Other political and economic systems communicate alternative values that make it the responsibility of the government or community to provide these types of services. In the United States, we tend to expect people to take care of their nonwork life individually so that it does not interfere with being a productive and ideal worker. This focus on individuality actually increases work-life conflict by increasing stressors on the employee.

The *consumerism norm* is perhaps a foundational problem for work-life balance. In our consumer culture, we are constantly encouraged through personal and mediated communication to purchase more and better material goods and to do more elaborate and lavish activities. To pick an obvious example, a couple can get married for the cost of a marriage license (usually under $50). Although most couples spend less than $10,000 on their weddings, the average cost of a wedding in the United States is now $26,000, not counting the cost of the honeymoon (The Wedding Report Incorporated, 2015). The recent trend toward destination weddings will likely drive these costs higher, particularly when the cost to those attending the wedding is included. There are many other examples of consumerism prompting our need to earn more money according to advertisers: the size of home we should own, the cars we should drive, the vacations we should take, the jewelry we should own, the restaurants we should frequent, and the expensive entertainment or sporting events we should attend. This consumerism norm pressures people to earn more and more money, which results in a need for them to work longer hours to obtain the necessary resources. It often makes dual-career couples seem like a necessity. Less consumerism would reduce work-life conflicts and likely reduce stress at work and at home.

We add the *technology norm* to the list of norms that increase work-life conflict. Many people simply expect everyone to have constant access to communication technology through computers or a smartphone. The expectation leads to assumptions about individuals being available 24/7 for work or nonwork communication. Some supervisors expect to be able to contact employees at any time and place, including during employee vacations, reinforcing the ideal worker norm. These expectations can create a sort of white-collar sweatshop in which individuals are working longer and longer hours at work and at home due to their availability through technology without additional compensation (Fraser, 2001). Similarly, some friends and family members expect access throughout the workday and become upset when they do not receive a timely response to an email or text message. Although behaviors supporting the technology norm are far from universal, that does not prevent individuals from feeling pressured to comply with it.

Taken together, the motherhood, ideal worker, individualism, consumerism, and technology norms create significant work-life tensions. Each of the norms pressures individuals to focus additional time and energy on one role over the other, creating additional time-based or strain-based tensions. These norms, in combination with the changing demographics of the workplace, make work-life issues more prominent. In the scenario, the ideal worker norm seems to have been particularly influential. The young, single professionals work extra hours to demonstrate they were committed employees. As individuals negotiated maternity and paternity leaves, they were concerned about maintaining an ideal worker image so that their careers would not be hurt by taking advantage of the policy.

Outcomes of Work-Life Conflict

Research has consistently found negative outcomes associated with work-life conflict. High levels of work-life conflict are consistently associated with lower levels of *job satisfaction* (Kossek & Ozeki, 1998). In addition to reduced job satisfaction, increases in work-life conflict are associated with work alienation, lower morale, job stress, and burnout (Kirby et al., 2006). These negative relationships are generally worse when work interferes with family than when family interferes with work (Kossek & Ozeki, 1998). These results suggests employees' attitudes about their work is affected more negatively when, for example, work causes them to miss a family activity than they are when a family emergency interferes with their ability to do their work. Of course, some research suggests the opposite pattern where family interfering with work creates more job stress (Frone, Russell, & Cooper, 1992). That study found that family-to-work conflict (when family issues interfere with work) was more disruptive than work-to-family conflicts (work interferes with family), leading to job stress and depression. This pattern is perhaps due to perceptions of failure to meet the standards of ideal worker norm expectations.

Similarly, high levels of work-life conflict are consistently associated with low levels of *life satisfaction* across many different studies (Kossek & Ozeki, 1998). The negative response affects a variety of other outcomes, including increased health risks and likelihood of sleeping disorders and mental health issues, along with reduced effectiveness in parenting roles, and it reduces marital satisfaction and family well-being (Kirby et al., 2006). In general, these negative relationships are greater for women than for men, although they do not seem to differ for single versus dual career couples (Kossek & Ozeki, 1998). These results suggest that working women are more likely to become dissatisfied with their family situation than men due to work-life conflicts. This difference is possibly due to failure to satisfy the motherhood norm.

Managing Work-Life Boundaries

Individuals develop coping strategies to manage work-life conflicts that occur due to their many different roles as employees, family members, and volunteers, to name a few. Scholars suggest these coping strategies range along a continuum from high segmentation to high integration (Ashforth, Kreiner, & Fugate, 2000). Many individuals are not at the extreme ends of the continuum and instead use a combination of strategies based on situational factors. Each approach has its own advantages and disadvantages.

Individuals who use a high segmentation strategy attempt to make very clear and distinct boundaries between their work and nonwork lives. They believe that it is important to separate work from other nonwork activities such as family, volunteering, or leisure activities. They attempt to minimize any overlap between work and nonwork activities and to maintain clear and impermeable boundaries between their work and personal lives or roles. This separation is accomplished communicatively: *High segmenters* might manage others' expectations about their communication patterns in ways that compartmentalize activities. For example, high segmenters could proactively tell others at work about their personal policy to "keep work at work" or add a note to the end of emails explaining that "I observe email-free evenings and weekends on this account." Furthermore, high segmenters likely have separate email accounts for work and personal activities. To keep boundaries clear, they may avoid checking their work email account in the evenings or on weekends or checking their personal email during the workday.

By contrast, individuals who use a high integration strategy observe few, if any, boundaries between work and the rest of their lives. They believe it is important to address work or personal issues as they arise. They have very flexible and permeable boundaries between their work and personal lives. They also accomplish this flexibility communicatively. For example, *high integrators* may have separate work and personal email accounts, but they have both accounts forwarded to their smartphone where they

COMMUNICATION CHALLENGE

Choosing Communication Media for Boundary Management in Global Virtual Organizing

A study of a globally distributed virtual team revealed that telecommuting managers chose communication technologies that allowed them to segment or compartmentalize their work from their home life. Even in the media rich work environment required of virtual teamwork, members choose their media, in part, according to how well the media allowed them to maintain work/life boundaries. The researchers found that managers tended to prefer lean and asynchronous communication media, such as email, in contrast to video conferencing because it allowed them to "segment work from their personal lives" better (Ruppel, Gong, & Tworoger, 2013, p. 18). What kinds of communication media choices do you make when communicating work-related messages? Do those media choices help you manage work-life boundaries as either a segmenter or integrator?

access both whether at work or not. Because they integrate work and personal life, they think nothing about responding to a work email on the weekend or interrupting work to respond to a personal email or text message.

A number of factors influence how easily individuals maintain their preferred work-life boundaries, regardless of whether they are segmenters or integrators (Kreiner, Hollensbe, & Sheep, 2009). Similarities or congruence between an individual's preferences and the behaviors of others makes it easier or harder to manage boundaries. Certain occupations make it difficult to use a particular boundary management style. For example, it is nearly impossible for an individual to be a successful real estate agent and a segmenter; the job requires being available for clients nearly 24/7. By contrast, we do not expect that small restaurant owner to be available to customers after hours. In addition, family members can either support or disregard an individual's preferred approach to managing boundaries. If a spouse calls a segmenter at work for minor issues regularly or if an aging parent refuses to call an integrator at work even for major problems, their behaviors do not support the individual's preferred approach to managing boundaries. A family member or coworker may also screen calls to support a segmenter's efforts to maintain boundaries so that only urgent calls get responses. Similarly, work supervisors, colleagues, subordinates, and clients can support or ignore an individual's preferred approach. Calling a segmenter on the weekend with a work-related question violates that employee's preferences. Failing to update an integrator about the progress of a project that occurs after hours ignores that employee's preference. Congruence between an individual's preferences for managing boundaries and the occupation and communication behaviors of family members and work-related people can make it easier or harder to manage boundaries.

Segmenters and integrators both often have rituals or patterns of behavior that help maintain their approach to multiple roles (Ashforth et al., 2000; Kreiner et al., 2009). These behaviors serve as tactics for maintaining preferred work-nonwork boundaries. High segmenters often have rituals to help them maintain the boundaries between roles. They may enjoy a long commute because it gives them time to switch roles. They may change clothes immediately when they get home to communicate to others that they are no longer in their work roles. They may maintain separate work and nonwork calendars. High integrators have different rituals to help them integrate their roles. They may live nearby work to make both easily accessible. They may regularly check their messages and discuss work and personal issues openly in both settings. These behaviors communicate to others that they are willing to integrate their roles.

The advantages and disadvantages of these two strategies are quite opposite. High segmenters are more able to focus on one role at a time without many distractions, although they are not immune to strain-based conflict when they think about one role while performing another one. Because they are used to focusing on one role at a time, they become unsettled when another role interferes or overlaps with the current role. For example, segmenters are much more likely to be upset and flustered when they receive a phone call at work that says their child is sick and needs to be retrieved. Because of the boundaries they attempt to keep, they lack practice in dealing with interruptions of their normal role separation. By contrast, such a phone call would likely not fluster or upset high integrators because they are used to switching roles quickly throughout the day on a regular basis. However, they may have trouble focusing on completing the activities of one role, whether it is a work or nonwork role, because of the routine interruptions that occur and redirect their attention to another role. People who are not at the extremes of the continuum likely have an ability to adapt a segmenting or integrating strategy depending on situational factors. For example, when something is urgent, such as a sick child, they may quickly switch roles. When they perceive the situation as less critical, perhaps a partner letting them know that their child did poorly on a report card, they likely choose to deal with it later and may even chastise the partner for interrupting their work.

Communication is the key process for managing boundaries in a preferred manner. Segmenters and integrators, and all those between the extremes, need to communicate explicitly their expectations to others. Then when violations of their expectations occur, they need to confront the violators and communicate their expectations again. In the scenario, the group of friends seemed to have trouble maintaining their preferred work-life boundaries when they were young. They wanted to segment work and life, but the lack of support for that practice by managers, who encroached on their nonwork time, made it difficult for them to maintain their work-life boundaries. Later in their careers, there was some conflict between the integrators who appreciated being able to be flexible in their work hours and bring their children to work as necessary and the segmenters who thought the presence of children was unprofessional.

Family-Friendly Work Policies

The increased awareness of work-life conflict has led the management of many organizations to adopt various family-friendly policies and practices to assist segmenters and integrators with managing work-life issues. It is impossible to mention all of the possibilities. Table 12.1 presents some broad categories of policies with a brief explanation

TABLE 12.1 Common Work-Life Policies or Practices

General Issue	Policy or Practice	Goal/Accomplishment
Work Policies	Flexible work schedule (e.g., other than 9–5)	Schedule work around home life issues (e.g., child care)
	Compressed workweek (e.g., work 4, 10-hour days)	Reduces days at work/increases time with family
	Telework/remote work	Working at home reduces travel time, creating more family time
	Job sharing (one job filled by two or more employees)	Allows employees flexibility for work and life roles; may reduce overtime concerns
	Paid time off/emergency time off (e.g., bank hours)	Using hours instead of days reduces use of vacation days for emergency/sick children
	Part-time options	Maintains career with reduced current effort
	Maternity/paternity leave policy	Allows continuation of career goals after interruption
Facilities	Adequate health care	Reduces financial concerns
	Lactation rooms for breast feeding/pumping	Allows mothers to continue breastfeeding after returning to work
	On-site/in-house day care	Reduced travel, support of breastfeeding
	Health wellness facility or health club	Makes healthy options more accessible before, during or after work
	Nearby day care/schools	Reduces travel, increases sense of security
Location Options	Nearby health clubs	Makes healthy options more accessible

of what they accomplish. Some policies, such as providing 12 weeks of unpaid maternity leave with job protection, are mandated by the Federal Family and Medical Leave Act for certain types of employees, most often full-time employees. Providing the same benefits for other types of employees, such as part-time employees, or providing *paid* maternity leave are optional.

Policies and practices like these communicate to employees that they are valued and that the management supports their efforts to balance work-life issues. The absence of such policies indicates that employees are expected to abide by the individualism norm and take care of work-life issues on their own.

In the scenario, UIC adopted a number of family-friendly work policies. These policies included flexible work schedules and maternity/paternity leave. These policies supported parents and employees caring for elderly parents. The employees were able to manage work-life issues more effectively because of the policies.

Positive Effects of Family-Friendly Policies

It is easy to find evidence suggesting that family-friendly policies are advantageous for employees and the organization providing them. For example, adopting flexible work arrangements has been shown to lead to positive effects for the organization such as reductions in absenteeism and improved customer service; employees feel that they have more control in managing work-life issues and as a result experience less stress and pressure while having more time for family and community issues (Bailyn, Fletcher, & Kolb, 1997). Others studies find that family-friendly policies reduce work-family conflict, which is related to job and family satisfaction; in addition, supervisor support reduces both work to family and family to work conflicts, which increases job satisfaction (Frye & Breaugh, 2004). Taken together, these and other studies indicate that having family-friendly policies and direct supervisors who support use of those same policies are generally associated with positive outcomes for work and family life. In the scenario, if supervisors supported the use of a company policy of flextime to manage life issues, Robin and other employees likely experienced fewer work-life conflicts and had more positive attitudes about work as a result. However, some large organizations that provide ample on-site services to employees (e.g., child care, shopping, dry cleaning, and vehicle maintenance) may actually exacerbate role conflict because these services often come with the implicit expectation that employees will work long, unusual, and inflexible hours.

Unintended Consequences of Family-Life Policies

Professors Mary Hoffman and Renee Cowan (2008) analyzed the websites of Fortune 500 magazine's "100 Best Companies to Work for." The websites tended to tout the organizations' excellent track record of policies and practices that encouraged work-life balance—a competitive advantage in hiring and retaining highly qualified employees. The researchers demonstrate how even apparently positive corporate rhetoric about work-life policies reinforces and normalizes notions such as work (not family) as the most important aspect of life and organizations as having a right to control work/life programs (not employees). How do the ways we talk about work and life (including those very terms) highlight and hide assumptions about what is important and valuable?

Problematic Issues of Family-Friendly Policies

Even though organizations may adopt family-friendly policies, employees often do not take advantage of the policies (Bailyn et al., 1997). A number of factors seem to contribute to the employees not using family-friendly policies.

Career Repercussions. One of the primary explanations employees give for not taking advantage of family-friendly policies is fear that their careers will suffer if they do. Especially career-oriented mothers, single employees without spouses, and fathers are concerned that they will receive smaller raises and be overlooked for promotions if they take family leaves because colleagues will interpret their leave as demonstrating weak commitment to the organization and their careers (Bailyn et al., 1997). These fears show the influence of the ideal worker norm that suggests employees should be willing to sacrifice their personal lives to demonstrate their commitment to their careers and organizations (Drago, 2007). As a result of these fears, employees often take shorter leaves for childbirth than they are entitled to take or continue to "work" while on paid family leave. The same fears about lack of commitment likely help explain the large accumulation of unused vacation days by many employees and why two thirds of certain types of employees take work with them on vacations (e.g., Mohn, 2013).

Similar concerns over career repercussion reduce employees' willingness to tele-commute. Even though studies suggest that individuals who work from home actually work longer hours than those who work in the office, employees tend to believe that they need to be seen by their supervisor or they will have fewer opportunities for promotion to management positions (Hylmö & Buzzanell, 2002). This observation suggests that even though the telecommuter may fit the ideal worker norm better than the in-house employee, the perception of who better fits the ideal worker norm can reduce employees' willingness to use family-friendly policies.

Difficulty Negotiating Leave Policies. Even when an organization has a family-friendly policy like family leave for the birth or adoption of a child, it does not necessarily mean that taking such a leave is a simple matter. A group of scholars found that the negotiation of family leave is quite complex (Miller, Jablin, Casey, Lamphear-Van Horn, & Ethington, 1996). For example, mothers-to-be must convince others that they will return to work and that their contributions to the workplace will not decline before and after the leave. They may be concerned about being pressured to finish projects prior to the beginning of their leave rather than being allowed to pass them on to someone else. They may be concerned about being assigned to menial work before and after the leave instead of important projects. During their leave, they face problems of determining how to stay up to date on long-term projects so that they can be up to speed on returning. Negotiating these issues can lead to solutions that may be less supportive of employees than expected. Most mothers-to-be work into their ninth month. Many work during their family leave in amounts that range from keeping in touch to conducting significant amounts of work from home. We know of professors who graded papers and read lengthy dissertation proposals while in the hospital on maternity leave, despite the fact that many universities have generous paid leave policies. If negotiating a family leave for a mother-to-be is challenging, then it is likely that it is even more challenging for negotiating leave for fathers-to-be given society's general expectations for men. The independence norm suggests that fathers-to-be should not really need to be absent from work for substantial periods of time for the birth of a child.

Peer Pressure Against Using the Policy. With family-friendly policies, most of the focus is on the how the policy influences the lives of the benefactors of the policies. Some policies affect employees fairly equally—for example, flextime. Other policies, such as family leave, benefit employees who are parents without providing similar benefits to other employees. Furthermore, when one employee is given leave time, this can have repercussions for the rest of the work unit. Unless the unit is allowed to hire a temporary replacement, which is often not the case, the remaining employees must assume additional responsibilities.

A study of one organization found that there was such intense pressure from peers against taking all of their eligible leave time under the federal Family Medical Care Act that they titled the article, "The policy exists, but you can't really use it" (Kirby & Krone, 2002). The title emphasizes the bind employees felt regarding taking family leave, *according to* federal and organizational policies. For example, when they returned after maternity leave, new mothers often felt resentment from other employees who had to work harder while they were gone. When one male employee asked for two weeks of paternity leave, only a portion of what he could have requested, his supervisor discouraged him from applying at all. Many employees discussed how the family policies created inequities among employees, as those with children and spouses received preferential treatment that single individuals did not receive. As a result, they either intentionally or unintentionally pressured employees not to take advantage of leave policies.

Resistance to Work-Life Integration. Although individuals who are integrators welcome the opportunity to integrate their work and nonwork lives, segmenters prefer the opposite. This means that when organizations have policies that allow children to be present in the workplace, there is often conflict between the two types of individuals. For example, professors at universities often enjoy the freedom to bring their children to work for periods of time that range from a few minutes to several hours. This allows those professors to integrate work and family life in a small way. However, colleagues are often less than enthusiastic about such practices. Professor Bonnie Dow (2008) writes bluntly, "we all want our colleagues to bring their new baby to the office–once– so that we may share their joy in their new family member. What we don't want is pack-n-play set up in their office three days a week so that they don't have to arrange for child care during their office hours" (p. 161). She goes on to point out how the presence of a child, even a quiet one, disrupts work for people in adjoining offices, for example, when well-meaning coworkers stand in a doorway and chat about the child.

In the scenario, some of the issues created by family-friendly policies are evident. Some of the men in particular seemed reluctant to take paternity leaves for fear of career repercussions. As a young employee, Robin resented taking on extra work in the evenings and weekends so that colleagues with children could attend events and

"ALL IN FAVOR OF BANNING ROGER'S KIDS FROM FUTURE BOARD MEETINGS..."

What happens when work and life overlap?

volunteer at their children's schools. At the same time, when Robin had children, the policies were a valuable resource for managing work-life issues, but the policies continued to create conflict between segmenters and integrators.

Work-Family Third-Place (Life Enrichment) Balance

Most of the research on work-life balance focuses on issues related to work and family. In fact, most of the early research used the terms such as work-*family* conflict instead of work-*life* conflict. The old label represented two implicit biases. First, the label communicates a general assumption that only married couples (and mostly married couples with children) experienced work-life balance issues and that single individuals do not. Of course, single people have families and friends and other nonwork activities that are important to them. For example, in the scenario, Robin's group of friends resented being asked to work on Thursday evenings because that was their volleyball night. The change of label to work-life balance attempts to correct for the assumption about only married couples with families experiencing work-life balance issues, although most companies still have "family-friendly" policies.

A second assumption implicit in the work-family label is that people need to balance only two important roles—employee and family member. Some scholars recognized that people have "third-place" roles. These are roles that are different from or in addition to work and home life roles (Ashcraft & Kedrowicz, 2002). Most of the attention on third-place roles has been on volunteering in various community and religious organizations, but third-place roles could broadly include regular participation or memberships in other social domains such as recreational sports leagues, health clubs, or routine hanging out at the neighborhood bar (Ashforth et al., 2000). In the scenario, the "family conflicts" that some parents experienced were actually third-place conflicts, as they had responsibilities in the parent–teacher association at their children's schools—a voluntary role, not a family role. Robin's friends playing volleyball every Thursday evening was a third-place social role rather than a volunteer role.

Calling these roles "third place" communicates a bias as well. It implies that work and family are the primary roles (without specifying an order for the two). However, you may know people for whom these third-place roles actually are their most important or primary roles. Some individuals' whole lives center around so-called third-place roles. This focus may be due to their religious beliefs or a commitment to some community service such as addressing poverty or protecting the environment. For these individuals, work may simply be a means of supporting themselves so they can focus on their "primary" role.

Because most of the research focuses on volunteering and voluntary membership in organizations rather than the more informal social roles, we focus on issues related to work-life balance and participation in life enrichment groups or organizations (Kramer, 2002). People join these formal organizations to meet a variety of needs or interests and then must maintain work-family-life enrichment balance.

Volunteer Roles

Individuals who become volunteers clearly have a different organizational role than employees. The general definition of a volunteer is someone who (a) performs tasks or works of their own free will (b) without receiving any payment or financial benefit (c) for the benefit of others (Lewis, 2013). Although this definition fits most situations, there are exceptions to all three criteria. For example, students are sometimes required to complete service learning hours or judges may assign people to complete community service hours. Peace Corps volunteers receive pay, although it is quite limited compared to what they might make elsewhere. Some volunteers receive mutual benefits from their actions, such as a parent coaching their child's soccer team. The broad definition does communicate our general expectations for volunteers.

Because they are not paid, volunteers have different motivations than employees for completing their "work." As discussed in Chapter 4, the internal motivations for people to volunteer typically include some of these reasons: (a) to express values that are consistent with the organization; (b) to gain understanding or grow personally through new experiences; (c) to enhance their self-image by helping others; (d) to gain social acceptance or belongingness by developing friendships; (e) to gain career-related benefits through new skills or making new contacts; and (f) to protect their self-image to relieve guilt over their own good fortune or to escape from personal problems by becoming busy (Clary et al., 1998).

Although this list seems comprehensive, it fails to recognize that people often volunteer as an extension of their other work or family roles. For example, some people volunteer in connection with their work roles. If they work in an organization that values corporate social responsibility, they may feel some sense of duty or responsibility to volunteer in their community; the organization may even give them some paid-time off to volunteer (Pompper, 2013). According to one study, one in three large companies have employee volunteer programs and nine of ten large companies in America encourage voluntarism (Tuffrey, 1997). It would not be surprising if your university has a "volunteer office" to encourage students, faculty, and staff to volunteer. Others volunteer in connection with their family roles. Obvious examples of this are parent–teacher organizations and youth sports programs. Nearly all volunteers in these organizations join the organizations initially because of their role as a parent of a child who benefits from the program.

Motivations to continue volunteering are often different than motivations to begin. For example, a study of zoo volunteers found that many volunteers were internally motivated as a means of expressing their values and gaining new knowledge, but continued to volunteer due to the friendships they developed with other volunteers (Kramer & Danielson, 2016). Other individuals may become volunteers to aid their children's activities as part of the family role but continue to volunteer because of the friendships they develop with other parents. The parents who had voluntary roles in the scenario seem largely motivated to assist their children, although they likely felt that the organization expressed their values as well. The organization did not give them time off to volunteer but did support them by relieving them of overtime duties so they could volunteer.

Types of Volunteering

There are a multitude of types of organizations in which individuals can volunteer as part of their life enrichment roles. A concise list suggests six types of organizations that rely heavily on volunteers: (a) social services, such as family assistance including food-banks or counseling; (b) community development, such as environmental protection or community redevelopment groups; (c) education, including after-school programs like 4-H or scouts; (d) health care, including substance abuse services or mental health programs; (e) foreign assistance, such as disaster relief or refugee resettlement; and (f) cultural activities including community theaters or arts festivals (Salamon & Abramson, 1982). Another way to classify organizations that need volunteers is to focus instead on who is served: (a) the general public, such as Meals on Wheels or a community orchestra; (b) the members of the organization, such as professional groups and religious organizations; or (c) a voluntary association, such as an informal grass roots organization (Frumkin, 2002).

Lewis (2013) identifies a number of different types of commitment volunteers hold. Some volunteers make long-term commitments, often more than a year, such as joining the Peace Corps or becoming a full-time missionary. These full-life volunteers often resign from other work roles to commit full time to their volunteer role. Episodic volunteers are the most common. Some episodic volunteers make large commitments for a short period of time and then may repeat that commitment multiple times. For example, community theater volunteers typically commit to one or two months for the duration of the production but then take time off until they decide to participate in another production. Other episodic volunteers are habitual or routine volunteers who offer their time and efforts for one activity on either a weekly, monthly, or annual basis. This description of a volunteer is perhaps our stereotype, someone who volunteers at the hospital or zoo the same day, every week, for months or years at a time. Others may help organize a community arts festival each year. Other episodic volunteers are more sporadic and volunteer as they have time. They may help sort food at the food bank a few times a year.

You can likely think of types of volunteers and organizations not covered in the last two paragraphs, but the purpose is not so much to be comprehensive as to give a sense of the diversity of opportunities for volunteering in life enrichment activities. It is also important to note that the type of volunteering and organization involved affect the types of work-family-life enrichment balance conflicts individuals experience. The parent volunteers in the scenario seemed to be episodic volunteers who likely attended regularly scheduled (monthly or quarterly) meetings and participated in other events sponsored by the organization. It seems unlikely that they will continue in the organization after their children leave the school, but the friendships they may have developed may lead them to volunteer in the parent association jointly at the next school the children attend.

Work-Family-Life Enrichment Balance

Although it was mentioned earlier that for some people their voluntary role is actually their primary role, the reality for many people is that any voluntary membership or role is a lower or a "third-place" priority compared to work or family. The level of priority has certain implications for work to life to life-enrichment balance.

In some instances, individuals manage the work-family-life enrichment balance of voluntary roles by making temporary commitments that prioritize the voluntary role for a short period of time. They communicate their priorities to others to create expectations about their temporary commitment. Then, they revert back to prioritizing work and/or family ahead of their voluntary role when that short-term commitment is over. For example, volunteers may clear their schedule of all work and family activities for the week of summer camp sponsored by their nonprofit organization so that they can devote all of their energies to that event. Once the event is over, their volunteer role goes back to its normal level of involvement, such as a few hours a week or month. Similarly, individuals who go on short-term mission trips make this type of short-term commitment. They typically use vacation days from work and make a full-time commitment to

---

ETHICAL ISSUE

Disingenuous Volunteering?

Many organizations offer employees paid leave to volunteer at local nonprofit organizations. The idea is that serving in these roles can often expand employees' social networks, which can then be leveraged to increase perceptions of the organization's credibility and legitimacy. Connections gained while volunteering can also be leveraged to generate sales leads for identifying potential customers. What are the ethical implications of such a practice? Does volunteering with these motives matter or reduce the importance of volunteering?

that volunteer role for a week or two; they often travel at their own expense to some international location to assist others and share their beliefs (e.g., Frederick & Mize-Smith, 2013). Community theater members often make decisions about whether to try out for productions based on whether they will be able to commit enough time to the production. Once involved, they communicate to family and friends that they will be largely unavailable during the duration of the production; they may neglect aspects of their family roles (e.g., housecleaning or mowing lawns), and some even skip work during production week to be rested and healthy for performances (Kramer, 2002). Once the short-term volunteer commitment is over, the volunteers return to their normal way of balancing work to life to life-enrichment activities.

For individuals who make longer term commitments to episodic volunteering, such as weekly volunteering at the zoo, managing work-family-life enrichment roles can result in role overload. It can become unmanageable for individuals to maintain all three roles at the same time. Quitting one role is a common solution. In most instances, this means quitting the voluntary-life enrichment roles. They are the easiest to quit, unlike work and family roles, and there are relatively few negative consequences for doing so, perhaps only losing social contacts with friends. As an alternative to quitting, volunteers often manage role overload by taking temporary leaves from their volunteer roles. They become transitory members of their volunteer organization who fluctuate from full volunteers to non-participants at different times. For example, transitory voluntary members of a community choir might participate for a semester, then take off a semester or year due to work-family role priorities, but then return to the choir the following year (Kramer, 2011b). This sort of transitory membership creates communication problems for organizational leaders who rely on volunteers, particularly when the individuals fail to communicate their status to the organization. The lack of communication from the transitory volunteers makes it difficult for organizational leaders to separate transitory volunteers, who are likely to return, from former volunteers who will never return. This challenge probably explains why many nonprofit and voluntary organizations continue to communicate through mail or electronic messages to individuals long after they no longer consider themselves volunteer members.

In the scenario, it appears that the employees of this company are not having much trouble balancing their work-family-life enrichment roles. They receive some support from the organization in this regard. Perhaps they also managed to avoid role overload, or at least it was not mentioned.

Summary

In this chapter, we explored the intersection of work and nonwork life. It is common for people to experience stress between work and life roles due to time-based, strain-based, or behavior-based conflict between their roles. These conflicts are intensified due to a number of social norms that encourage overcommitment to work roles. These include the motherhood, ideal worker, individualism, consumerism, and technology norms. These conflicts have a negative influence on work satisfaction and life satisfaction. People manage these conflicts through strategies that range from trying to separate work and life roles completely to trying to integrate them completely; most people likely fall somewhere in between these extremes. Many individuals also have third-place or life enrichment roles when they volunteer or participate regularly in social activities. These roles create additional needs to balance various life roles. Although some individuals prioritize these life enrichment roles, when most people experience role overload, the life enrichment role is the one that receives reduced priority.

CHAPTER 13

Communication and the Changing Work Environment: Technology, Diversity, and Globalization

Peyton thought managing an athletic shoe store would be easy, never imagining how many factors influenced sales. For example, running shoes were constantly changing. The latest trend was "wavespring" technology. It was important to stock the latest shoes for competitive runners who wanted them as soon as they came out. Then there were "plodders" who defiantly announced, "I want the same shoes I've been running in for years." Unfortunately, it was challenging to find some of those old shoes. Now there were "mud-runners" who wanted high-top running shoes so they wouldn't lose them in mud holes. In addition to running shoes, it was important to keep up with the most popular brands of walking shoes and cross-training shoes as well.

Employees and customers were changing, too. Customers were increasingly a more diverse mixture of ethnicities and nationalities reflecting the changing community surrounding the store. Peyton found it was important to understand that customers from different backgrounds often had different expectations for an athletic shoe store. It was important to understand those different expectations to adapt to the changing environment. Adapting also meant hiring a more diverse sales staff to match the community demographics.

More and more customers at the store were asking about technology for improving their workouts. Some simply want reliable watches to time themselves. Others want a device that can track their workouts, monitor their heart rate, and record their food intake. Some just want to know a good app for their phone that will help them. Peyton was considering adding a new section to the store stocking a range of such products.

Peyton never imagined that events around the world would directly affect local shoe sales. Recently, when the news reported that a major shoe manufacturer was using sweat shops in China for production of its shoes, sales of that brand dropped dramatically. Now Peyton was overstocked in that name brand and understocked in others. The challenges never seemed to end.

· · · · ·

f you have attended your university for even two years, you probably have experienced some changes, perhaps in how you register for classes and buy textbooks, in what food options are available on campus, or in the number and types of students on campus. You probably welcomed some of the changes but responded negatively to others. In this chapter, we consider communication and organizational change. We begin by discussing systems theory to explore how change enters organizations. Then we examine how people respond to change, including the diffusion of innovation, emotional responses, and resistance. Finally, we look at three specific areas of change: technology, diversity, and globalization.

Systems Theory

Generally we have treated organizations as if each one is an independent entity. We have focused on organization's internal operations, such as internal communication, management theory, and decision-making. In reality, organizations are not independent but interact with their environment to gain resources and disperse products and services. While interacting with their environment, they must adapt to environmental changes and challenges to survive and thrive. Systems theory explores the interaction between organizations and their environment and helps explain how changes or innovations enter organizations.

Developed by biologist Ludwig von Bertalanffy (1968), systems theory explored the interrelationships of the physical environment but was quickly applied to organizations. Systems theory emphasizes that organizations are open systems that interact with their environment to survive, just like plants and animals must do. As a result, organizations import energy and resources from the environment (input), transform those resources (throughput), export the transformed resources into the environment (output), and then the cycle repeats as new resources enter the organization (Katz & Kahn, 1978). For example, beginning with its financial resources, the owners of a local athletic shoe store like the one in the opening scenario purchase shoes wholesale from manufacturers, along with furnishing and utilities, among other things, from the environment and hire employees who may be unskilled and must be trained. The employees transform these resources into information, retail products, and customer services. The organization then exports those products and services into the environment when customers purchase them. Other outputs include waste and perhaps skilled employees. From customer purchases, the organization gains new financial resources to purchase and import additional resources as the cycle continues.

Kast and Rosenzweig (1972) identified important characteristics of organizations from a systems theory perspective related to change. From a communication perspective, positive and negative feedback from the environment are critical. Negative feedback suggests the need for change or innovation. Organizational survival involves its ability to adapt to a changing environment. Failure to adapt to negative feedback possibly results in its decline and death. For an athletic shoe store, if people begin to purchase less of their products because they want less expensive shoes or more trendy brands, or they want better customer service, the organization needs to adapt by offering a wider selection of expensive and inexpensive shoes and needs to improve its customer service or face declining sales and eventual closure.

Another characteristic of open systems is that organizations are part of a *hierarchy of systems*. This concept is different than organizational hierarchy or status. In systems theory, hierarchy is the idea that an organization is made up of subsystems (systems embedded within it) and is part of suprasystems (systems larger than it). An athletic shoe store has subsystems such as the men's, women's, and children's sections or floor, maintenance, and office staff. Some employees possibly work in multiple subsystems. The organization is also part of suprasystems. Even if the store is not part of a national chain like Footlocker (a possible suprasystem), it is still part of larger systems such as the other athletic shoe stores in town, all local stores selling shoes, the retail shoe industry nationally, and so forth. What happens in these subsystems and suprasystems affects its ability to maintain fitness with its environment. A dysfunctional subsystem, for example, poor customer service, can lead to negative customer feedback and reduced sales. A new competitor opening in town may influence it negatively. The organization must adapt to maintain equilibrium with its environment. The open systems concept of *equifinality* indicates that there are multiple ways of adapting to the environment.

There are additional systems theory concepts, but these key concepts illustrate how systems theory contributes to understanding how organizations respond to change. As new technologies become available or community demographics change, organizations must adapt to maintain fitness with their environment. The ability to adapt affects their ability to grow, maintain, or survive. For example, technology for an athletic shoe store has changed. The shoes have new technologies, and there are new fitness assistance devices like Fitbit. There are also new technologies for helping to understand the particular type of shoes a particular runner should purchase to maximize performance. New cash registers (computer systems) provide speedier and more accurate service. Some can manage inventory by alerting managers to low inventory on specific items or even automatically placing orders. The workforce is more diverse by age, race, and nationality. Organizations, including locally owned shoe stores, must adapt to many such changes in their environment to survive.

Defining Change

You've probably heard the cliché "the only constant is change." Because we explained culture as an ongoing structuration process creating and recreating culture (see Chapter 6), change is constant; but if everything is change, then the term becomes meaningless. For this chapter, we consider that organizations, or their subsystems (department or teams), have periods of relative stability with minor, undecipherable changes and periods when the system is significantly modified. Those kinds of changes are the focus of this chapter.

In classifying organizational change, Laurie Lewis (2011) classifies changes along three dimensions. First, changes may be *small or large*. Creating a new procedure for internal reports is a small change; merging with another organization is a large change. Second, changes may be *material or discursive*. Material changes include updating technology or changing the office configuration from cubicles to individual offices. Discursive changes include changing the language by referring to employees as "associates" or revising the organization's mission statement. Third, changes may be *planned or unplanned*. Planned changes might include moving to a new location or creating a new department. Unplanned changes might be new government regulations or the ripple effects of planned changes. Changing product lines at the athletic shoe store is probably a small, material, planned change. The changing demographics of the community likely creates larger, unplanned, discursive changes for the store.

Unfortunately, these distinctions are not always clear. One organization ended funding a morning coffee break for employees to cut costs. This small, planned, material change had a much greater influence than expected. It resulted in large, unplanned, discursive changes. The change hindered informal communication; most employees no longer interacted informally with upper management. The employees eventually distrusted management because they felt uniformed and thought management was deliberately withholding information. Classifying changes may also be challenging because some changes may be so gradual that they can only be detected from a long-term perspective. For example, employee demographics may change slowly and go unnoticed, but over time, these small, incremental changes eventually result in major changes. Despite problems classifying some changes, the framework provides a useful way to consider organizational changes.

Reactions to Change

Individuals and organizations collectively adapt to the changes in their workplaces and the environment. However, they do not all respond the same. We examine three perspectives on responses to change using the lens of diffusion of innovation, emotion, and resistance.

Diffusion of Innovation

Everett Rogers (1995) developed an extensive line of research about how people adopt innovations. His diffusion of innovation theory involves four main principles:

1. *Innovation:* An innovation is an idea, practice, or object perceived to be new or different. Innovations include new technologies, processes, or ways of understanding that change current ways of understanding or doing things. An innovation must be perceived as new, whether or not it actually is.

2. *Communication Channels:* An innovation must be communicated through various channels so that others learn of the innovation and its potential for change. These communication channels may include anything from face-to-face interactions to mass media messages.

3. *Time:* The diffusion of innovation begins when the first person passes information about the innovation to one or more other people and continues until the innovation has saturated the system.

4. *Social System:* The diffusion of innovation occurs within a system. Consistent with systems theory, innovations may occur within a subsystem (a department), a system (an organization), or a larger suprasystem (an industry). The process is facilitated by *opinion leaders* or *change agents* who influence others to adopt the change through any available communication channels.

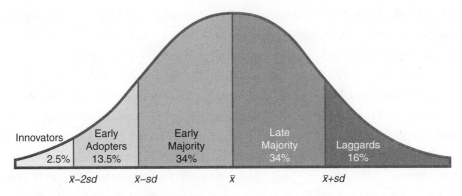

Figure 13.1. Adopter Category for Innovations

This conceptualization provides a useful way of examining change whether it is small, large, material, discursive, planned, or unplanned. Someone conceives of a change, communicates it to others, and over time it is implemented throughout the system.

In addition to these characteristics of innovation, studies involving a wide range of technologies, practices, and ideas indicate that there is a consistent pattern in how individuals adopt changes. This pattern is illustrated in Figure 13.1 (Rogers, 1995):

1. *Innovators* are adventurous individuals who look for new ideas and ways of doing things. Innovators often have strong network ties with other innovators. They are particularly connected to innovators outside their primary organization.

2. *Early Adopters* are situated in their organization and are respected by their colleagues for carefully considering innovations before adopting them. They serve as role models for others.

3. *Early Majority* adopters represent about one third of the system, frequently interact with early adopters, and are influenced by them to adopt a change.

4. *Late Majority* adopters also represent about one third of the organization. They adopt changes already adopted by the majority because of increasing pressure, including economic necessity.

5. *Laggards* probably has a negative connotation, but it really just means that they lag behind the vast majority in adopting an innovation. They maintain the old way of doing things longer than others before adopting the change.

It is important to realize that people may differ in their classification depending on the specific change. For example, a customer at the athletic shoe store may be an early adopter when it comes to purchasing a new product like a Fitbit, but a laggard when it comes to adopting new shoes. You may purchase the latest communication technology immediately, but resist adopting changes in organizational traditions.

Roger's (1995) understanding of the diffusion of innovation is more complex than this brief discussion, but this basic understanding provides a general sense of how individuals and organizations respond to change. For better or worse, some individuals and organizations lead the way when it comes to embracing innovations and change; others respond slowly, often adjusting only out of necessity. For example, when Microsoft announced that it would no longer provide service support to Office 2007 after October 2012 and would discontinue support completely in October 2017, the announcements had no impact on most users who had already adopted newer technologies. However, these policies will force laggards to adopt newer technologies or risk problems, such as new viruses. From a systems theory perspective, the environment is providing negative feedback to systems relying on the old technology. Failure to adapt could be detrimental to organizational survival.

Change and Emotion

It should not be surprising that change is often associated with emotion. Organizational change alters the organizational culture in small or large ways. As Terrance Deal and Allan Kennedy (1982) stated

> Change always threatens a culture. People form strong attachments to heroes, legends, the rituals of their daily lives, the hoopla of extravaganzas and ceremonies—all the symbols and settings of the work place. Change strips down these relationships and leaves employees confused, insecure, and often angry. (p. 157)

Although it is easy to see how a change in leadership or a new building changes an organization's culture, it may not seem like small change also potentially changes the culture. Small changes in the rituals of daily life, like coffee breaks mentioned earlier, can change the culture. For example, enrollment procedures changes at one university meant that students no longer stood in line for consent cards to enroll in classes. This change was welcomed for sure, but it changed the student culture. Students no longer shared stories of arriving early (i.e., 4 a.m.) to get near the front of the line or commiserated while they waited. This change in the ritual changed students' relationships to each other by eliminating this bonding ritual.

Deal (1985) suggests that individuals may experience the equivalent of a grieving process during organizational change because they miss the way things used to be. The grieving process can involve (a) denial and isolation, (b) anger, (c) bargaining, (d) depression, and (e) acceptance (e.g., Kübler-Ross & Kessler, 2008). It is easy to imagine employees going through these stages during a major change. Recall the story of the transformational leader, William Anderson of NCR, who dramatically changed NCR's culture by renaming the company and bulldozing its headquarters to build a skyscraper. It easy to imagine that some employees went through the stages of grief. They may first have denied that the changes would occur, expecting the board of directors to stop Anderson's plan. Then, they may have become angry at Anderson for the proposed changes. They may have tried to bargain with him to maintain the old name or keep some of the original buildings. As bulldozers demolished the buildings and they worked in temporary offices, they may have become depressed before finally accepting the changes and perhaps embracing them when the changes resulted in success and their new offices outshined their old ones.

We do not want to give the impression that we think organizational change is comparable to the loss of a loved one; we simply agree with Deal that strong emotions can be associated with change for some employees. Additionally, not everyone experiences strong emotion related to change. Innovators and early adopters are comfortable with change and may rarely experience negative emotions related to change. Late adopters and laggards more likely have stronger emotional ties to the way things were before the change. And finally, individuals do not necessarily go through the stages of grief in linear steps. Individuals skip steps, fall back on previous steps, and so forth in various patterns. It seems unlikely that changes at the athletic shoe store will result in strong emotional reactions, although some customers will likely become upset when their favorite shoes are no longer available; and the community may feel a sense of loss if the store closes because it fails to adapt to its environment.

Resistance

Due in part to an emotional attachment to the current practices, change is often met with resistance. Resistance attempts to stall or hinder implementation of changes. It involves a struggle over change. The term conjures up romantic images of some domineering, powerful (and probably bad) organizational leader imposing new ideas on lower level (and probably good) employees who rise up and assert their independence and power through resistance (Deetz, 2008). Lewis (2011) provides a convenient continuum or range of resistance behaviors. At the subtle or weak end of the continuum is *ambivalence* toward change. Ambivalence is generally experienced internally and individually. It involves a reluctance to embrace change due to uncertainty and fear concerning its effects. *Peer-focused dissent* involves complaining to others inside or outside the organization. Although more active than ambivalence, it has little influence on implementation of the change. Peer-focused dissent amounts to "venting" emotional reactions to change. *Upward dissent* is a positive form of resistance that involves discussing and negotiating with management. It is a more proactive method of resistance because there is the potential that leaders will make adjustments in implementing the change based on the concerns voiced. *Sabotage* involves actively working to make the change efforts fail, with the goal of returning to the pre-change situation. Sabotage can range from passive actions, such as not putting adequate effort into a task so that it fails, to active forms, such as deliberately breaking new equipment or omitting steps in the new procedure to guarantee its failure. The most overt forms of resistance include *activism, refusal,* or *exit*. Activism involves organizing resistance with others. Refusal involves not complying either by continuing to do things the old way or simply not completing the duty at all, perhaps as collective action. Exit involves leaving the organization. This does not have an impact unless enough people leave so that organizational leaders are forced to reconsider the change. At an athletic shoe store, we would not expect a lot of evidence of resistance. However, runners and sales staff may complain to each other about the new shoes as a form of peer-focused dissent. Other customers may simply refuse to adopt to the new fitness technology. Some sales staff may actively discourage customers from purchasing such items.

There is evidence that some resistance to change is an individual predisposition or characteristic. Individuals who value routine in their lives, feel stress when change occurs, have a short-term focus, and are cognitively rigid (unlikely to change their minds) are more resistant to change than others (Oreg, 2003). In addition, people who resist change tend to avoid risks and sensation seeking; they tend to be dogmatic and have low tolerance for ambiguity.

Resistance to change is so common that nearly every popular book on organizational change has a section or chapter on managing resistance to change (Lewis, 2011). It takes effective communication to address resistance.

Resisting Changes or Change Communication

Ryan Bisel and Kevin Barge (2011) studied a home health care organization that underwent large changes to its executive leadership. The board of directors (BOD) removed the organization's leadership and then threatened employees with termination if they discussed the issue with one another or the media. Interviews revealed that many employees supported the leadership change but felt threatened and mistreated by the change communication from the BOD. The employees resisted the change because the change communication implied they were untrustworthy. This led to distrust between employees and the BOD. In sum, employees can resist changes, but they can also resist change communication. How should the change have been communicated differently to employees?

Communication and Change

Informative and persuasive communication strategies can help organizational members discontinue previous ways of working and increase the likelihood of adopting new approaches. Effective leadership communication during change can reduce resistance to change and soften the strong emotions employees can experience during changes. Lewis (2011) suggests five communication strategies for increasing employees' acceptance of change.

First, it is important to *disseminate information and solicit feedback* early in the process of adopting organizational changes. Keeping individuals informed reduces their uncertainty and stress during changes. Genuine solicitation of feedback in which employees' opinions potentially create adjustments in the change adoption provides a sense of involvement and control that can increase acceptance and reduce anxiety.

Two-sided persuasive messages help reduce resistance. One-sided messages only present the change agent's perspective. Two-sided messages acknowledge and address the concerns of opposing views. Communicating two-sided messages demonstrates thoughtful and thorough consideration of various issues related to changing and concern for others.

To maximize the persuasiveness of change messages and provide employees with a sense of urgency, it is important to use a mixture of gain and loss frames. *Gain frames*

Design a Ceremony

Consider yourself a consultant to William Anderson at NCR. Design a ceremony to celebrate the past while also building excitement about the future as part of the process of changing the name and replacing the old headquarters with a new glass and steel skyscraper.

emphasize the advantages of the change. *Loss frames* emphasize the disadvantages of the current approach. Both frames provide reasons for adopting the change.

Lewis (2011) suggests using a mixture of blanketed and targeted messages. *Blanketed messages* go to everyone affected by the change. *Targeted messages* address the concerns of particular subsets of individuals. Changes often affect various subgroups differently. Blanket messages inform everyone of the broad influence of the changes. Targeted messages explain how particular groups and individuals will be affected.

Finally, Lewis (2011) also suggests a mixture of *discrepancy* and *efficacy* messages. Discrepancy messages emphasize the urgency of change; they explain that failure to change will have detrimental effects. Efficacy messages stress the goals that will be accomplished by changing. Similar to frames, discrepancy messages create a need to discontinue the current practices, whereas efficacy messages stress the advantages of adopting the change.

In addition to these recommendations, Deal (1985) suggests providing symbolic recognition of the old practices through a ceremony to assist individuals in moving forward. Ceremonies help provide individuals with closure. For example, retirement parties help employees deal with the changes that occur from personnel changes. Deal suggests similar ceremonies may help employees accept changes in technology in particular.

For the athletic shoe store in the opening scenario, it is probably important that the managers keep the sales staff informed of which products are being added and discontinued so that they can inform customers. Emphasizing the gains that will occur and the ease with which those changes can be accomplished (efficacy) are probably sufficient communication strategies given the magnitude of the changes involved.

Changing Communication Technology

In addition to these general issues related to change, we now focus on one particular change affecting organizational communication in the 21st century. Technology in general and communication technologies specifically are changing rapidly. If you were born after 1990, you may have difficulty imagining life without email and smartphones. In 1990, there were about 5 million mobile phone users in the United States; by 2000, there were over 100 million mobile phone users, about a third of the population. By 2014, over 90% of U.S. adults owned mobile phones, but only 64% had smartphones (http://www.pewinternet.org/data-trend/mobile/device-ownership/). In 1991, after finishing his PhD, Michael Kramer only checked email once a day because he rarely received messages. As a Samsung Galaxy S6 commercial said, "today we are a nation of checkers" who often miss the current moment and time because we are checking on other places and things.

By the time you read this, the "latest technologies" likely will have changed again. Email seems to be a permanent part of organizational life, although how we receive emails continues to evolve, from receiving them on stationary desktop computers to mobile devices. Text messages, Twitter, and various social media formats are common today; however, it is hard to predict which ones will remain important and what new technologies will replace them. Given the pace of technology changes, we focus on broad issues related to technology and the expectations for its use. You should apply these issues to whatever technology is current as you read this.

Media Richness Theory

Given the variety of communication choices, it is important to compare how the characteristics of various communication channels affect organizational communication. Media richness theory explains the differences between communication channels. According to the theory, different media vary in how *rich* or *lean* they are along four dimensions: (a) the ability to convey multiple cues such as verbal, nonverbal, visual, and audio; (b) the capacity for timely feedback, ranging from immediate to slow; (c) the level of personalization, ranging from very individualized to very impersonal; and (d) the variety of the possible language used, ranging from complex informal language to simple numeric-based language (Daft & Lengel, 1984, 1986).

Each dimension describes the degree to which a communication channel has rich or lean *information-carrying capacity.* The greater the channel's ability to convey multiple information forms, provide immediate feedback, be personalized, and be informal, the richer the media. Face-to-face communication is the richest media. It allows for multiple verbal and nonverbal cues, immediate feedback, and personal, informal messages. A paper newsletter sent to all employees is a lean communication channel. It conveys primarily words, limits feedback, and is written in an impersonal, formal style.

In addition to different information-carrying capacities, media differ in their *symbol carrying capacity* (Sitkin, Sutcliffe, & Barrios-Choplin, 1992). *Symbol carrying capacity* is the idea that our cultures attribute socioemotional value to particular media. A face-to-face talk can convey social warmth and friendliness that an impersonal email cannot. Depending on local culture, the symbolic meaning of the media is sometimes more important than whether the media can convey information. We know of a highly technical workplace in which emailing an officemate (even one five feet away) is perfectly acceptable. The workplace norm is to use emails to document ongoing project conversations. Email use likely has different symbolic meaning elsewhere.

If you Google "fired by email," you get over 1,800 hits. Links include stories of individuals being fired via email or groups of employees being fired via mass emails. Some stories discuss the frequency, appropriateness, ethicality, and legality of doing so. Many people take offense with these media choices because of the symbolic meaning of the impersonal media chosen and not the information conveyed. Certainly a mass email conveys the information, but its symbolic meaning suggests an impersonal relationship in which recipients are not valued. Interestingly, although we may take offense at firing employees via impersonal emails, it is really not so different than the notorious "pink slips" that have been used for decades. So, in addition to considering the ability of communication technologies to convey information, it is important to consider the symbolic meaning of choices.

Various studies demonstrate the importance of media choices. In a representative example, Waldeck, Seibold, and Flanagin (2004) studied the influence of three types of communication channels based on media richness. They distinguished between face-to-face (FtF) communication; advanced communication and information technologies (CITs) including email, instant messaging, intranet, cell phones, and teleconferencing; and traditional communication forms such as landline telephones, company newsletters, memos, and company handbooks. FtF communication was perceived as the most important in helping new employees adjust to their new organizations, followed by advanced CITs, and finally traditional communication forms. The study emphasized that although communication technologies were important, the richness and social presence of FtF communication is still extremely important in many organizational settings.

Changes in Communication Expectations

Communication technologies change organizational communication patterns. These patterns include changing how meaning is established, changing decision-making expectations, and changing interpersonal interactions (e.g., O'Connell, 1988). Each of these potentially changes the habitual way of performing work, and thus change organizational culture.

Changing How Meaning Is Established. Technology influences how meaning is established by providing access to information otherwise unavailable. For example, social media, including external sources such as Facebook and Twitter, and internal organizationally owned social media systems, provide additional means of sending and receiving information. According to Leonardi and Treem (2012), social media changes access to organizational information in at least four important ways:

1. It enables individuals to increase their visibility by communicating with additional organizational members; at the same time, it provides other members access to the information without having personal relationships with the individual.

2. It provides more persistent or permanent records that can be reviewed repeatedly; other communication forms, such as FtF communication and phone calls, generally leave no interaction record.

3. It allows individuals to carefully craft their image editing of their posts; synchronous, real-time communication limits communicators' ability to carefully edit their images.

4. It creates and reminds organizational members of social connections and associations frequently through practices such as tagging, friending, and grouping; this relational information must be explicitly shared in other communication channels.

These principles are clearly seen in the way some organizations use social media to check on potential or current employees. It is not difficult to find stories of individuals who were not hired due to their social media posts.

Communication technologies also change the way meaning is created. In FtF communication, we are able to find meaning from people who speak in a wide range of patterns from those who present it in a very strict order to those who speak in unpredictable, almost random order with frequent tangents and diversions. As communication becomes more technologically driven, we may change our expectations for conciseness, accuracy, speed, and access. The norms for receiving and responding to emails and text messages are not established. Heavy users of emails and text messages may expect fast, short, responses and may assign meaning to individuals who take days to respond or who write what are viewed as excessively long messages. In these ways, technology influences how we assign meaning to messages or lack of messages.

Changing Decision-Making Expectations. As we saw in Chapter 9, individuals and groups make decisions through a wide range of patterns from very rational and linear processes to fairly random processes. Computers, however, process information in a linear manner. A variety of meeting systems have been developed and new ones will continue to be created as virtual meetings of people geographically dispersed become increasingly common. These systems vary in media richness and their influence of the decision-making process. The use of group decision support systems (GDSS) can influence the way groups make decisions compared to groups who meet in one location and without the aid of a mediated platform (e.g., Poole, DeSanctis, Kirsh, & Jackson, 1995). Groups that actively adopted the GDSS tended to follow the agenda in a rather linear process. However, the GDSS was not deterministic. Some groups ignored the system and worked on their own, and others tended to blame the system for problems they encountered.

Other studies also indicate that technology influences the decision-making processes for geographically dispersed groups—but again, not in a deterministic manner. For example, the group size, number of locations, and number of time zones involved influences the way technology was used. Furthermore, characteristics of the communication, such as how argumentative, thorough, and responsive it was, also influenced group outcomes such as their satisfaction and identification with the group; however, the technology only influenced the outcomes for certain types of communication (Timmerman & Scott, 2006). For example, groups that were thorough and responsive had better outcomes when they increased their use of FtF communication but experienced worse outcomes when they increased electronic communication. These and other studies of technology and decision-making show that the use of technology influences decision-making, but they do not support the idea that technology determines the quality of group outcomes per se. Individuals are quite imaginative in their ability to use the technology in a variety of ways—for better or worse.

COMMUNICATION CHALLENGE

Creating a Collaborative Organizational Policy of Internet Usage

Because employee Internet use can cause damage, such as with bullying or sexual harassment, organizational leaders look for advice on creating Internet usage policies. The planned change communication research offers great advice such as engaging in two-way communication in which employees co-create such policies. Work by Arnesen and Weis (2007) recommends a number of potentially helpful aspects of a reasonable employee Internet use policy, including the following:

1. Employees shall post no junk mail or spam.
2. Employees may use the Internet and email for reasonable limited personal use providing such use does not interfere with job performance or productivity.
3. The employer shall disclose to all employees the extent of monitoring, the level of detail, and who receives reports about employee use.

These include rights and responsibilities for both employees and employers. What other issues should be considered in crafting this kind of policy?

Changing Interpersonal Communication Interactions. Perhaps the most apparent influence of technology is in the way that it changes interpersonal interactions in organizations. Some changes are unsettling, such as the rise of bullying or harassment perpetuated online. Other communication technology uses provide a platform for the perpetuation and deepening of interpersonal and professional relationships among geographically dispersed individuals. In general, increases in electronic communication mean less FtF communication and the potential for fewer and less personal relationships.

Technology also influences communication at FtF meetings. With smartphones, computer tablets, and mini-laptops, technology may encourage us to become less mentally present at organizational meetings. At times, communication technologies can be quite advantageous for workgroups as they have access to information to assist group decision making. At other times, it can be detrimental when group members are distracted and inattentive while checking their electronic devices. Research suggests that individuals with greater experience with electronic communication are more likely to multitask with their electronic devices during meeting (Stephens & Davis, 2009). In addition, group members who observed other members using devices were more likely to use devices during meetings. Interestingly, whether the individuals thought they were overloaded with communication in their job did not affect their use of technologies in meetings.

Multitasking at meetings influences communication patterns by inhibiting listening and participation, but it is not clear whether electronic device usage is more distracting than doodling or daydreaming. In any case, some leaders discourage the use of communication technologies explicitly because they believe it is detrimental to group interactions. Of course, one wonders how much multitasking is personal and not work related. An Internal Revenue Service study of its own employees estimated that as much as 51% of employees' online usage was personal. Likewise, a study by the Cranfield School of Management found that 30% of small to medium businesses were "losing a day of work each week due to employee Internet and email use" (Arnesen & Weis, 2007, p. 54).

The use of social media includes both public (e.g., LinkedIn, Facebook) and company-owned social media sites. Scholars have identified three important ways social media influences communication and relationships in organizations (Leonardi, Huysman, & Steinfield, 2013). First, social media serve as a *leaky pipe*. A leaky pipe spills water in places it was not intended to go. Social media often broadcasts messages to unintended individuals, resulting in changes in relationships, much like gossip does when shared indiscriminately. Second, social media can serve as an *echo chamber*. People with similar attitudes tend to connect through social media while also

Using Social Media to Convey and Express Private Opinions

A Facebook user recently reported that at a previous company, the individual had to fight to get equal pay for equally qualified male and female applicants. Because many of the people who read the post knew the individual's employment history, they could rather easily identify the company involved. Sharing such information in a face-to-face conversation does not share the information so broadly or permanently. Do you think it is appropriate to post such information on social media? Given how easy it is for employees to share experiences with large groups online, what additional, ethical considerations should employers make?

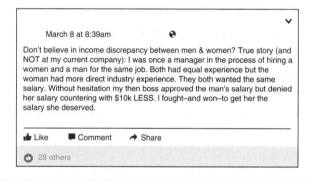

insulating themselves and avoiding information and opinions that differ from their own. This dynamic can result in cliques or subgroups of like-minded people. These subgroups may have positive effects by helping people accomplish positive goals (e.g., a running group) or create conflict, isolation, and perpetuate extreme views. Third, social media may serve as a *social lubricant*. Social media makes it easier for individuals to know more about each other and link to new people.

Another significant workplace change due to technology is the ability for employees to work from home instead at the office. This change influences relational dynamics and work attitudes for both telecommuters and those who remain in the office (e.g., Hylmö & Buzzanell, 2002). Telecommuters perceive themselves as less likely to be promoted due to the lack of FtF interaction with supervisors and coworkers. They also experience more stress because they feel they must be available 24 hours a day. In fact, they do work outside normal business hours more frequently than in-house employees. In-house employees often develop negative attitudes toward telecommuters as less productive workers despite evidence to the contrary. These different experiences create relational issues for both electronic and FtF interactions.

Finally, new technology also has increased surveillance within organizations. This monitoring has increased safety, but it also has increased monitoring of employee activity. Foucault (2000) and others warn of a time of "panopticon" (or all-seeing) control in which organizations monitor employees much like prisoners are monitored by guards. Research on call centers suggests very high levels of surveillance in which supervisors monitor call takers' behaviors—such as time at the desk, length and number of calls, and even keystrokes per call—and then use the information to evaluate employees (Bain & Taylor, 2000). Fortunately, the amount of effort necessary to monitor employees carefully in many settings makes this kind of near-total surveillance impossible. That said, it is easy to find news stories of employees being fired over their use of computers for visiting inappropriate websites, for distributing inappropriate content, or simply for wasting company time. Sales associates at one electronics chain are monitored to see if they sell sufficient numbers of extended warranties. Likewise, Arnesen and Weis (2007) remind us that emails sent on organizational servers (such as those ending in ".edu") are not private, can never be completely deleted, and are lawfully subject to monitoring and inspection in the United States at any time by the organization without prior warning. In the end, the increased surveillance resulting from new technologies changes the relationships between managers and employees if for no other reason than changing the level of trust in the relationship.

Summary of Changing Communication Technology

Technology is an important input for organizations from the environment that leads to change and innovation. Some new technologies, like changes in the way shoes are designed in the shoe store scenario, have limited effect on communication. Changes in communication technology significantly influence organizational communication patterns by changing how meaning is created, how decisions are made, and how interpersonal relationships develop. Because communication channels vary in their media richness, it becomes increasingly important to determine the appropriate use of communication channels in organizational settings.

Cultural Diversity: The Changing Workforce

There are many different ways to consider diversity in organizations. Some of the more frequently discussed ways include diversity based on sex, (dis)abilities, generations (baby boomers, millennials), sexual orientation, race, ethnicity, and nationality. It would certainly be possible to write extensively on each of these.

In the following, we focus on just one form of diversity. Cultural diversity brought on by the changing workforce has produced important issues for organizational communication (see Chapter 12 for a discussion of women in the U.S. workforce). The workforce in the United States is changing, in part, because its population is changing. Historical data included in Table 13.1 from the U.S. Census Bureau updated in 2013 indicates the following demographic trends (http://quickfacts.census.gov/qfd/states/00000.html).

From 1910 to 1960, the racial and ethnic demographic characteristics of the U.S. population were relatively stable. Since 1960, there have been significant changes in those demographics that have been accelerating. The labor force mirrors these changes. Most projections suggest non-Hispanic white individuals will be less than 50% of the work force sometime in the next 30 years. These changing demographics tend to change the culture of organizations gradually.

Cultural Diversity and Communication

The increase in workplace diversity results in increased opportunities for intercultural or interethnic communication, as more people from different backgrounds interact. These interactions can, at times, create high levels of uncertainty for people, in part because individuals from different backgrounds communicate differently.

Part of the uncertainty in these interactions comes from differences in expectations about the communication process that are characteristics of cultures of different racial,

TABLE 13.1 Racial and Ethnic Demographics of the U.S. Population

Race/Ethnic Group	1910	1960	1970	1980	1990	2000	2010	2013
African American	10.7%	10.5%	11.1%	11.7%	12.1%	12.3%	12.6%	13.2%
American Indian, Eskimo	0.3%	0.3%	0.4%	0.6%	0.8%	0.9%	0.9%	1.2%
Asian and Pacific Islander	0.2%	0.5%	0.8%	1.5%	2.9%	3.8%	4.9%	5.3%
Hispanic (of any race)	0.9%	3.2%	4.4%	6.4%	9.0%	12.5%	16.3%	17.1%
Non-Hispanic White	88.1%	85.4%	83.5%	79.6%	75.6%	69.1%	63.7%	62.6%

ethnic, or national groups. In the foundational work on these differences, Geert Hofstede (1997) identified four general dimensions of culture. Hofstede's study of thousands of employees of the multinational IBM organization revealed some patterns in the way different national groups valued aspects of communication. These include whether the culture focuses on *collectivism versus individualism, masculinity versus femininity, hierarchical versus flexible power distance,* and *uncertainty avoidance versus acceptance.* When people of diverse backgrounds communicate, these cultural differences can result in confused, hurtful, or unproductive interactions. For example, a supervisor with a flexible understanding of power distance, as is typical of U.S. employees, may expect subordinates to initiate interactions to identify problems or provide upward feedback. A subordinate from a culture with a hierarchical view of power distance, as is typical of employees from many Asian cultures, may wait for the supervisor to initiate the interaction out of respect and deference to the position. In such a situation, both the supervisor and the subordinate may evaluate the other as an ineffective communicator for failing to meet their own cultural communication expectations.

In addition to these general differences in expectations based on cultural backgrounds, a review of studies on intercultural communication indicates that people from different cultural backgrounds often vary in specific communication behaviors. For example, they may differ on how prone they are to self-disclosure in initial interactions, how they express nonverbal cues, how much they rely on nonverbal cues to understand interactions, how many questions they ask to reduce their uncertainty, and how frequently they communicate overall; in addition, the prejudices and stereotypes they have for people who are different than they are influence their interactions with them (Baldwin & Hunt, 2002). The combination of different cultural backgrounds and different communication behaviors create the potential for frequent misunderstanding and ineffective communication.

Cultural Diversity in the Workplace

Although the U.S. workforce is increasingly diverse, that diversity is not equally distributed across organizations, occupations, or regions. Research suggests that organizations fall into one of three categories (Larkey, 1996). *Monolithic organizations'* members are largely homogenous from similar cultural backgrounds. *Plural organizations'* members have a mixture of cultural backgrounds, but diversity is compartmentalized in certain segments of the organization. Often diversity appears in the entry

Creating Teams

You are given the job of creating five project teams in your department. Out of 25 members, there are only 7 individuals from non-white backgrounds, including three who were born outside the United States. Should you consider diversity in assigning groups? If you do, how do you balance the need for increased intercultural interaction for everyone with the issues associated with being the only minority member of a group?

level or lower management positions, whereas upper management is still largely homogenous. *Multicultural organizations'* members are heterogeneous with a diverse workforce distributed equally throughout the organization, from bottom to top.

To become multicultural, many organizations have to progress from a monolithic organization to plural to multicultural gradually. Even if an organization has a goal of becoming multicultural, the surrounding community affects an organization's ability to become multicultural. It may be easier for an organization in California to become multicultural than an organization in Wyoming due to the demographics of its community.

The diversity of the organization in general affects the diversity and communication at the group level in at least two important ways. First, when a group has only one non-majority member, group members tend to use categorization rather than specification to interact with that person (Larkey, 1996). *Categorization* is essentially stereotyping or tokenism. Majority members tend to view a single non-majority member as representative of the underrepresented group. Because many stereotypes are negative, this creates potential for negative communication relationships. Another common mistake is for group members to expect the non-majority individual to speak for or represent the viewpoints of an entire group. Perhaps you have been in situations where you were the only man, woman, or other minority member, and the rest of the group expected you to be the spokesperson of "your group." Conversely, when there are multiple non-majority members, majority members are more likely to use *specification* in their communication, which involves viewing each person individually and responding more based on the individual's characteristics rather than a stereotype.

Next, the organization's diversity influences the number of non-majority members in typical workgroups or departments and their communication behaviors. A study of mixed-race groups found that Asian minority members communicated differently when they were the only minority member in the group as compared to when there was at least one other member of their ethnic group present (Li, Karakowsky, & Siegel, 1999). When they were the only minority in the group, they rarely participated; when there were at least two members of their ethnic group, they participated at levels consistent with the majority group members. Think back to your own experiences again. If you were the only man, woman, or other minority member in a group, your participation was probably somewhat guarded, but if there was at least one other person you perceived as "like you," you likely participated in your usual manner.

Influence of Diversity on Group and Organizational Effectiveness

Given the potential for unproductive communication in intercultural interactions, it might seem likely that diverse groups would be less effective than more homogenous ones. In general, research does not support such a conclusion. A variety of studies compared the performance of homogenous groups to heterogeneous groups. A wide range of personal characteristics were used in these studies as indicators of diverse background including cognitive ability, sex, race, and personality. In most cases, heterogeneous groups performed the same or better than the homogeneous groups on a variety of group tasks (Shaw, 1981). The general explanation for these results is that the more heterogeneous the group, the more likely it is to have the diversity of information and skills needed to be effective; whereas homogenous groups have more limited variety and so may be less effective.

Despite these general findings, individual studies of the effect of cultural diversity on team performance often have produced contradictory findings. For example, one study found that culturally homogenous groups of students perform better on conducting case study analyses than heterogeneous groups (Thomas, 1999). Another study found that culturally diverse groups of students produced higher quality ideas that were rated more effective and feasible than those produced by homogenous groups (McLeod, Lobel, & Cox, 1996). Another study found that although in the short term, homogenous student groups performed better on a case study analysis, over time with feedback, the performance of the heterogeneous group was no different (Watson,

Kumar, & Michaelsen, 1993). This pattern suggested that the uncertainty of communicating and working together initially created some problems for culturally diverse groups, but that over time, the groups overcame those difficulties through their communication. This pattern suggests that intercultural communication in groups may indeed need to be managed carefully to obtain the unique and special benefits heterogeneous groups can generate, such as creativity.

In an effort to determine if we can make any general conclusions about the influence of cultural diversity on group outcomes, a group of scholars conducted a "meta-analysis" of the research of diversity in groups. A meta-analysis is a statistical procedure for combining the results of multiple different studies. The authors offer the following general conclusions across studies (Stahl, Maznevski, Voigt, & Jonsen, 2010): (a) There was no significant difference between culturally diverse and homogeneous groups on performance in general or in their overall communication effectiveness; (b) culturally diverse groups demonstrated greater creativity and experienced greater satisfaction than homogenous groups; (c) culturally diverse groups experienced more task conflict, particularly on complex tasks, but not more relational conflict; and (d) culturally diverse groups felt less of a sense of social integration or unity than homogenous groups. When taken together, it seems that culturally diverse groups generally do the same or better than homogenous groups but that a number of factors, such as the task, the makeup of the groups, or length of time together may have more of an influence than the group's diversity. In addition to support from these outcome-based studies, some organizations may decide there is a social and cultural value all unto itself to build a multicultural organization that esteems diversity for its own intrinsic importance.

Summary of Cultural Diversity

A culturally diverse workforce is another important input from the environment that is changing organizations. Diversity can be a source of innovation and change as it brings in new ideas, challenges old assumptions, and creates new practices for the organization. Although the uncertainty of the initial interactions between individuals from different backgrounds can create communication problems and issues, these are most likely short-term problems; and in the long term, groups and organizations are more effective and better able to adapt to their changing environment when they capitalize on the unique perspectives offered by a diverse workforce. Even a small local shoe store, like the one in the opening scenario, is influenced by the changing demographics of the community. Interactions among employees and with customers will change as a result. Small and large organizations need to recognize and adapt to those changes.

Globalization

A third important issue influencing organizations is globalization. *Globalization* is the gradual integration of ideas, practices, products, and other aspects of culture across national boundaries. Globalization has increased in intensity and is the result of increased ease of global travel and advances in worldwide communication. Globalization is most apparent in multinational corporations such as Coca-Cola, McDonalds, and Sony, which have facilities and sell their products throughout the world. Their products and practices have been exported worldwide including in both developed and emerging economies. Although the United States is clearly not the only participant in the process of globalization, it is a dominant one at this time as it exports its product, business practices, and capitalistic ideology to other countries. That trade occurs as U.S. organizations search for new markets to sustain the economic growth that drives its economy and culture (Steingard & Fitzgibbons, 1995). Put in other words

> In many respects the corporate sector has become the primary institution in modern society, overshadowing the state in controlling and directing of individual lives and influencing collective social development. Workplace values and practices extend into nonwork life through time structuring, educational content, economic distributions, product development, and creation of needs. Modern corporations affect society by both their products and their income distribution but also by the practices internal to them. (Deetz, 1992, p. 17)

The increased interdependence resulting from this globalization creates many economic, political, and social issues. Taken to its logical conclusion, globalization should create a singular, homogenous world culture as a result of corporations colonizing or spreading their worldview across the globe. Yet globalization makes economic disparities between economically developed and emerging economies more visible. Differences in labor laws and work conditions become more apparent. Resentment of and resistance to globalization are common.

Rather than discussing the social and economic issues of globalization further, we focus here on a three specific ways that globalization affects organizational communication.

Globalization creates a need for *communication convergence* in the form of compatible communication technologies and similar communication practices and language (Stohl, 2001). This does not mean that everyone must speak the same language, although English does seem to dominate world commerce. Convergence involves creating compatible methods of communication and a common understanding. To accomplish convergence, multinational organizational members have to adapt their organization's culture to that of the location of the facility and vice versa, although the adaptations are not always distributed equally. For example, when a multinational organization opens a facility in another country, it must create compatible and interdependent communication technologies and practices to function effectively. To do so likely means that the technology of the multinational company will be adopted, but it may have to adapt some of the ways that the technology is used to meet the needs and practices of the local culture. For example, this may mean avoiding the use of the technology or conducting business on certain days or times of the day out of respect for the local religious and national holidays.

At the same time, organizations must allow for *communication divergence* as cultural differences must be recognized and appreciated (Stohl, 2001). The daily practices and rituals of countries that influence the local organizational culture must be acknowledged. For example, the use of time varies significantly across national boundaries. Some cultures are monochronic, such as the United States and many northern European nations. *Monochronic* national cultures view time as linear and precise and expect that only one activity is scheduled or conducted at a time. Other cultures are polychronic, especially Mediterranean and Arab countries; *polychronic* national cultures view time as diffused or approximate and schedule multiple activities simultaneously; and relationship development is prioritized over punctuality. To conduct business successfully in a culture with a different time perspective requires acceptance of divergence.

Some social and economic issues resulting from globalization also influence the need for *external communication*, as organizations must respond to the social and economic issues created by globalization. Issues like fair trade and fair wages make headlines, and organizations have to respond to these issues. Every couple of years, some organization, like Nike, is accused of producing its product in factories operated in developing countries that produce unsafe products, pay inadequate salaries to employees, or have unsafe factory conditions. These issues may seem unrelated to a local store; but when toys imported from China reportedly contain lead-based paint, for example, the issues affect many organizations that need to respond to consumers' concerns.

Due to globalization, there is an increasing interdependence between organizations across national boundaries. As this occurs, individuals and organizations must attempt to balance managing environmental, social, and technological pressures and practices in ways that are similar to others located internationally while maintaining their local cultural identity and differences (Stohl, 2001). Not only must they balance these needs, but they can be called on to defend their practices when they fail to meet the expectations of local communities. We might think of globalization as a trend only multinational organizations deal with, but even a small local athletic shoe store like the one in the opening scenario needs to adapt to the implications of globalization—for example, when negative stories about one of its popular brands makes international news. Globalization calls on organizations to be more knowledgeable, innovative, flexible, and responsive as part of a rapidly changing global system (Stohl, 2001).

Change and Nonprofit Organizations and Volunteers

It should be apparent that change affects nonprofit organizations and volunteers in many of the same ways as discussed so far. As part of many different systems, including local communities, national organizations, and government regulations, nonprofits and their volunteers must adapt to changes. Some adopt innovations in technology or processes quickly, whereas others are slow to respond. Volunteers sometimes respond emotionally to changes in their context and resist those changes or quit in protest. As the population changes, the demographics of volunteers change, creating issues associated with cultural diversity. We highlight some of the unique changes that nonprofit organizations and volunteers face.

Changes in Funding and Collaboration

One of the more apparent changes for nonprofit organizations is that they are being encouraged or required to collaborate to receive the funding they need to provide their services. Collaboration is seen as an important way for nonprofit organizations to pool resources, share new ideas and expertise, and maximize the services they provide (Sowa, 2008). Collaboration has pitfalls and benefits. Collaboration can be time consuming, and not every collaborative effort will receive funding or accomplish its goals.

These failures can be due to a variety of reasons. For example, there may be insufficient coordination between organizations due to lack of communication, one organization may be perceived as more important or powerful, or ineffective leadership may discourage real collaboration (Keyton & Stallworth, 2003). Benefits include enhanced image in the community, competitive advantages in gaining funding and additional volunteers, and improved chances of survival (Sowa, 2008). These changes mean that leaders of nonprofits need to be more proactive in communicating with other organizations to develop a network of interorganizational contacts to develop collaborations and secure funding. Failure to do so will likely inhibit their ability to survive.

Changing Volunteers

Volunteers, one of the most important resources for nonprofit organizations, seem to be changing as well. For some time, observers have decried a general decline in people's willingness to be involved in civic life including volunteering, as they prefer to "bowl alone" rather than be involved in their communities (Putnam, 1995). Others have argued that people volunteer at similar rates; it is just that now they often volunteer online through listservs and social network sites rather than FtF; participating electronically still allows them to assist with decision-making, fundraising, communication, marketing, and consulting (Lewis, 2013).

In addition, volunteers seem more interested in short-term, one-time, or episodic volunteering and are more reluctant to make long-term commitments to regular volunteering (Lewis, 2013). They may also be reluctant to work directly with organizations. Some volunteers organize themselves through social media rather than deal with the slow process of working with nonprofit organizations and government agencies that coordinate volunteers in crisis situations like flooding (McDonald, Creber, Sun, & Sonn, 2015). Organizations with long FtF training programs that prevent volunteers from serving immediately will likely need to adjust to the changing attitudes and behaviors of volunteers.

Culturally Diverse Understandings of Volunteers

In the United States, we have a broad but consistent understanding of volunteering and the same general expectations for volunteers. As our population becomes more diverse, different cultural groups have different understandings of volunteers. For example, the

American Red Cross has significantly more unpaid volunteers than paid employees (17 to 1) compared to its Turkish equivalent (1 to 1); the reason for this is that the general public in Turkey does not trust volunteers to provide adequate service (Gossett, 2015). In another situation, Bhutanese refugees in Atlanta expected U.S. volunteers to continue to serve them, much like the government workers in refugee camps, whereas the volunteers expected the refugees to develop independence over time (Kumar & Dutta, 2015). Recognizing these divergent understandings of volunteering can reduce the tensions and improve communication between diverse groups of volunteers and the people they serve.

Globalization and Volunteers

Volunteers and nonprofit organizations who provide services internationally are part of globalization. They export values and practices from their home country to other nations. They may even assume that their own social and economic system is superior. For example, the Peace Corps assumes that "American exceptionalism," the supposed superiority of our system, should be exported to less fortunate nations (Hanchey, 2015). By viewing people in the country in which they volunteer as the "serviceable other," international volunteers position people in other nations as in need of adjusting their ways to coincide with our expectations; volunteers are often disappointed when this does not happen (Craig & Russo, 2015).

Globalization, as a result of volunteers, can also have unexpected effects on a community. After interacting with short-term volunteers, many young people in a Filipino community developed upward and geographic mobility aspirations that led them to leave their communities; this changed the community demographics dramatically, as the community consisted primarily of older adults and families with children after many of the young adults left (McAllum & Zahra, 2015). Whether those changes were positive or negative depends on whose perspective is considered.

Summary

It is impossible to deny that change affects organizational life and communication regularly. From a systems theory perspective, changes exists in the environment, and organizations must adapt to it or risk decline. The process of the diffusion of innovation provides an understanding of how changes are dispersed throughout one organization or a group of organizations. Individuals often respond emotionally to change and resist it through a variety of strategies. Technology is a particularly significant part of change because it affects how we create meaning, make decisions, and create relationships with others. The increasingly diverse workforce creates change as organizations move from being monolithic places dominated by people of similar background to pluralistic ones with people from many diverse backgrounds. Effective communication strategies, including ceremonial separation from the past, can facilitate the implementation and maintenance of change. Globalization, the gradual interdependence of economies, people, and practices from around the world is both the result of change and the cause of change. Change requires both communication convergence, so that similar meanings develop, and communication divergence, the acceptance of differences.

CHAPTER 14

Communication During Career and Organizational Transitions

It had been a year of transitions. Amari began the year working for a small production company, Irata, in Chicago. The company specialized in developing computer graphics, banners, lighting, and staging that other companies use to promote themselves at technology exhibitions around the country. The year was going well when the owners decided to promote Amari to a supervisory position in February. The job involved new responsibilities and new challenges. For example, Amari had to manage former peers like TJ, Corey, and others. Amari did not have any issues with TJ, who accepted that a former coworker was now the boss, but Corey seemed to think that "former coworker" status meant getting special privileges and insider information. However, Amari knew better than to create jealousy among subordinates.

Then, in June, the owners called a company-wide meeting for a big announcement that caught employees by surprise. The announcement was that a larger company was diversifying their product base and so was "merging" with Irata. Irata's owners were going to serve on the board of the new company but would no longer be involved in the day-to-day operations of their former company. They assured the employees that this merger was not going to affect their jobs because the new company was committed to maintaining Irata and its services; their jobs were secure.

It did not take long for that promise to be broken. In September, Amari was called into the office and told that there were going to be layoffs because business was slumping. It was not a surprise because rumors had been going around for a few weeks that layoffs were inevitable. Amari's job was secure according to the Vice President of Human Resources (VP of HR), but TJ and Corey were mentioned as being among those being let go in four weeks. The announcement was being made in a couple of hours.

After Amari's meeting, Corey tried to get some inside information by asking about the purpose of the meeting. Amari simply replied, "Just some management issues." When the announcements were made that there would be layoffs at the end of the month, Amari avoided eye contact with TJ and Corey for obvious reasons. The VP of HR offered all terminated employees one week's severance pay for every year they worked for the company and provided the services of an employment agency at no cost to the former employees. After people like TJ and Corey found out they were losing their jobs, most of them cleared out before the end of the month; and some of those who were not terminated elected to find jobs elsewhere. Apparently, those employees decided they were not going to wait around for the other shoe to drop.

The other shoe dropped last week. This time there were no layoffs. Instead, Amari learned that the company was transferring all of Irata's former services to California so that they would be closer to the main headquarters. The company offered a generous relocation package to anyone willing to move. Amari had one week to decide whether to transfer to California or find a new job in Chicago. How would Amari's family respond to this potential transfer? What a way to spend the holiday.

· · · · ·

Transitions are the constant of modern organization life. Individuals tend to experience significant changes throughout the course of their careers. Individual transitions between jobs, organizations, and organizational levels are common across one's career. Organizations also experience significant changes across time. Organizational transitions such as relocations, downsizing, layoffs, mergers and acquisitions, and growth are also common throughout the lifespan of an organization. In short, individuals and organizations go through a variety of transitions over the years.

Whereas in the previous chapter, we focused on organizational change in general, in this chapter, we focus on how individuals make sense of the career transitions they experience while working within one organization. We begin by exploring the process of "sensemaking" in general. Next we examine a few of the individual career transitions you may experience, followed by some of the organizational transitions that you might experience that may affect your career.

Sensemaking Theory

The basic premise of sensemaking theory is that when we experience a discrepancy in our routine way of doing things, it triggers an interpretive process as we attempt to understand or make sense of it in our social world (Weick, 1995). In other words, once we have learned our job, work becomes fairly routine so that we are able to function without much mental effort—almost as if we are on autopilot. We already understand our situation, what our own and others' expectations are for the situation, and how to act in it. When a disruption or discrepancy occurs in our routines, we are faced with equivocality or the possibility of many different meanings. We find it difficult to act until we have located the meaning of a situation, and so the disruptions to our routines trigger an attempt to assign meaning to unusual events (i.e., sensemaking). When facing equivocality and the disruption of routines, we ask two questions: "What's the story?" and "Now what should I do?" (Weick, Sutcliffe, & Obstfeld, 2005). Answering these two questions is the sensemaking process, and how we answer these questions serve as springboards for action.

According to Weick (1995), there are seven general principles to sensemaking:

1. Sensemaking is *retrospective*. We make sense of what has already happened, some discrepancy or difference that we experienced.

2. Sensemaking is *enactive* of sensible environments, which means that the environment constrains possible meanings and actions in a given situation.

3. Sensemaking is a *social* activity. We must interact with others to develop an agreement on the meaning of our experiences; generally, we cannot do this individually.

4. Sensemaking is *ongoing*. Because we experience minor to major discrepancies on a regular basis, we frequently must understand the story that is occurring to determine our actions. Sensemaking is always happening but only becomes visible when a disruption of our routine slows it down and makes it more effortful.

5. Sensemaking is based on *extracted cues* or a subset of all possible inputs for interpretation. Because there are simply too many possible cues in the environment and too much equivocality in the cues to consider all of them carefully, we focus on a few of the cues and generalize from those.

6. Sensemaking is *driven by plausibility* rather than accuracy. In other words, when we make sense of a situation, it must seem reasonable, but it does not have to be correct. The interpretation only needs to be a reasonable way to guide our course of action in a given situation.

7. Sensemaking always involves *identity*. When we select a particular interpretation or meaning for a situation, we are selecting an identity for ourselves and rejecting other possible identities. Of course, these principles often occur simultaneously.

To make these principles seem a bit more real, consider the situation of Amari's co-workers at Irata as they face a series of changes. Sensemaking is retrospective and ongoing as they experience first Amari's promotion, then the acquisition of the company, and then some of them are laid off. In each case, they must determine what they believe the story is, how it relates to them (their identity), and what their next actions should therefore be. In the first change, their friend was promoted. This disruption of the routine probably made sensemaking more visible as it involved them determining retrospectively what the story was behind Amari's promotion and why they were not promoted instead. They likely talked to each other, and possibly Amari or the owners, to gather possible explanations. As they talked, they focused on certain cues in the environment while ignoring others. They may have discussed that Amari has good work habits but also goes to lunch with the owners more often than they do. They may forget to consider Amari's training. They were constrained from making certain interpretations. Because Amari was not the longest serving employee at their level, the promotion cannot be explained on the basis of seniority. Eventually, they may need to decide between two plausible explanations: Amari's promotion was likely due either to merit (hard work) or favoritism created by brown-nosing or some other personal connection. The choice they make affects their identities and how they act next. If they make sense of the promotion as merit based, that means their identity as organizational members is consistent with the American dream that employees can get ahead through hard work in this company. If they make sense of the promotion as based on favoritism, then their identity is more likely consistent with those who feel that organizational life is often too political. Such an interpretation might encourage them to identify as organizational outsiders rather than insiders. The identities they choose by making sense of the promotion will influence how they make sense of the other changes they experience during the subsequent acquisition and layoffs.

This preceding analysis of sensemaking draws attention to two more principles of the communication process of sensemaking. In situations where people do not feel there is any discrepancy, it may be necessary to first communicate "sensebreaking" messages. *Sensebreaking* is communication that challenges current understandings of a situation as incorrect. Sensebreaking undermines or destabilizes current routine understandings to create a situation in which others reengage in effortful sensemaking (Pratt, 2000). In other words, sensebreaking creates a discrepancy or void for the receiver by making the routine understanding of the situation seem inappropriate. When sensebreaking is successful, it opens the opportunity for "sensegiving" messages. *Sensegiving* is communication that tries to influence others to accept a certain interpretation or understanding of the situation (Gioia & Chittipeddi, 1991; Sharma & Good,

COMMUNICATION DURING CAREER AND ORGANIZATIONAL TRANSITIONS

2013). Sensegiving provides information in support of a particular plausible explanation of the story. When successful, sensegiving results in sensemaking that is consistent with the desired interpretation. However, because sensemaking is a social activity, multiple parties are involved in sensebreaking and sensegiving as the interpretation of the situation emerges from the communication.

To continue with the example, if the coworkers have made sense of the promotion as an example of favoritism and politics in the organization, the owners may create sensebreaking messages that point out that they actually take everyone to lunch about the same number of times. They may follow up with sensegiving messages that point out the Amari has the highest productivity of anyone in the department and is the only person in the department with an organizational communication degree. Amari's former coworkers may accept that the promotion was the result of merit, or after talking among themselves conclude that the owners value college degrees over work experience.

We have presented the basic concepts of sensemaking theory. The theory provides a valuable perspective for examining how individuals respond to various personal and organizational changes throughout their careers. We now turn first to individual career transitions and then organizational transitions, although sometimes the two overlap.

Individual Career Transitions

Communication and Promotions

Most of the readers of this text will receive a number of promotions during their careers. Promotions tend to be viewed positively because they often involve increases in rank (hierarchy), responsibility, or pay. They suggest upward mobility, part of the American Dream. To gain an understanding of communication during job promotions, we examine some important factors that influence the selection process, how individuals are selected for promotions, and finally examine the process of promotion.

Promotion Selection Context

Although we might like to think that everyone has an equal opportunity for a promotion, a number of contextual factors may systematically disadvantage some individuals from receiving promotional opportunities. There are at least three different scenarios that influence the selection process for promotions (Shen & Cannella, 2002).

Promotion Types and Bias

Research demonstrates that hiring managers tend to look to promote others who are demographically similar to themselves, and many managers are quite unaware of that bias (Roth, 2004). What are the ethical advantages and disadvantages of each type of succession strategy in reducing the potential for systemic bias in an organization's promotion practices? Should organizations always use one kind of succession or a mix? Explain the ethical issues involved. Consider the implications for the culture of the organization.

In *heir apparent successions* there is an expectation that a particular individual will take over a supervisory or management position after someone leaves. One individual is considered to have the inside track on the position either because he/she is the most skilled, has the longest tenure, or had inside connections with upper management. In *contender successions*, multiple parties contend to replace an outgoing supervisor or leader. Contenders may make a case that they will maintain the status quo like the predecessor, or they may instead indicate that they will be different than their predecessor. In *outsider successions*, those higher in the organization have determined that there is no one within the department or division who has the skills needed to be promoted and so choose to hire an outsider, often with the hope that the new person will make changes. Employees make sense of the different messages management communicates to them according to which of these patterns it adopts for promotions.

The Selection Process for Promotions

The context of the promotion influences who is ultimately selected for promotion. When there is an open selection process (no heir apparent), the selection process generally considers three important characteristics of candidates being considered for promotion (Katz, 1974). First, the candidate needs to have the *technical skills* needed to perform and supervise the job. The person must have knowledge and analytical or physical skills required by the new position. Second, the person must have the *human skills* needed to manage others in communicatively competent ways. Promotions can involve supervising or overseeing other employees or volunteers. The ability to communicate in ways that helps achieve productivity goals while maintaining positive working relationships is important and highly desirable to many employers. Third, the person should possess the *conceptual skills* for the position. Conceptual skills involve being able to see the larger picture, such as how the groups or departments in the organization are interrelated and how management relates to the work done by entry-level employees. These conceptual skills are related to the external communication skills of managerial leaders discussed in Chapter 7, such as ambassador, task coordinator, scout, and guard (Ancona & Caldwell, 1992).

Promotion Process

The promotion process involves three phases. Researchers investigated these phases from both the perspective of the person being promoted (Kramer & Noland, 1999) and the perspective of those in the department or group in which the promotion occurs (Ballinger & Schoorman, 2007). During the *pre-promotion phase*, individuals discover a promotion opportunity exists through either formal or informal communication channels. This phase may begin with a formal announcement or a rumor that someone is leaving or being promoted, thereby creating a promotion opportunity. If there is an heir apparent, little active sensemaking is necessary because there is agreement on who will be promoted whether or not it is deserved; in other words, in these cases sensemaking has already occurred. In the case of outside succession, applicants are solicited from outside the workgroup. In the contender succession, those who are interested in being promoted "apply" for the promotion. This application may be as simple as letting someone in management know of their interest in the position or as complex as submitting documentation to the human resources department to be considered. In other cases, a higher level manager may actually approach individuals about the promotion opportunity. The actual selection process for the position may include formal interviews, especially in the case of outsider succession, or can be as simple as a higher level manager offering the promotion. The longer the decision-making process takes, the more likely productivity in the workgroup could decline as workgroup members attempt to make sense of the situation by discussing who should be promoted or who should not. The current supervisor or manager may leave prior to the selection of the person for the promotion or after it is announced.

During the *shifting phase*, the newly promoted person assumes the position officially. Sometimes the person has already been serving in the role informally. A variety of communication and relationship issues can occur at this point as people make sense of the changes created by the promotion (Kramer & Noland, 1999). For example, former peers can sometimes become subordinates. This relational change can create communication problems, as former peers may expect special privileges or insider information from their new supervisor. In addition, the person promoted has new peers who used to be of a higher rank but now are equal in the hierarchy, such as other managers. Those peers may have trouble viewing the newly promoted manager as an equal and continue to treat the person as a subordinate.

The individuals who are promoted gain access to new information that was previously unavailable to them. For example, they may have access to personnel files of others in their department. They likely attend meetings and receive communication that provides information that they previously only knew about if their supervisor shared it with them or through rumors. Learning how to manage that new information is one of the challenges newly promoted individuals face. As they make sense of their new roles, they must decide what information to share and what to keep to private.

In addition, during this phase, newly promoted individuals may face testing or hazing from former peers or other organizational members. In a study of newly promoted employees in the restaurant business, testing involved appropriate challenges to see if the people were competent in their new jobs, whereas hazing involved excessive or aggressive behaviors designed to annoy or irritate (Kramer & Noland, 1999). In that study, testing might include quizzing a new manager over the menu items or procedures for handling a particular situation. Hazing might involve yelling at the new kitchen supervisor in front of others to work faster when the particular job requires a fixed amount of time to be completed. Newly promoted employees needed to prove that they deserved their promotions by working hard and handling the testing and hazing professionally.

The *adjustment or stabilization phase* indicates that the newly promoted individual and the workgroup have made sense of a new routine. The emergence of a new routine is probably not marked by some event but more likely develops gradually over time. At this point, the newly promoted individuals have made sense of three important issues. First, they have reconciled their expectations for the new positions with their experiences. Much like newcomers who experience unmet expectations (see Chapter 3), the reality of their new positions is often different than they expected. They likely have experienced a mixture of positive outcomes, such as increased authority, new challenges, and additional freedom; however, they also likely have some negative experiences, such as increased stress, unexpected responsibilities, and more difficulty maintaining work-life balance (Nicholson & West, 1988). Second, they have learned to manage conflicts with their former peers. The testing and hazing has ended, and former peers have learned to interact with them as their manager instead of their peer. Third, they have made sense of their new relationships with subordinates (former peers), peers (former supervisors), and their new supervisors (former second-level removed managers). The workgroup has made sense of the new situation as well.

How the workgroup makes sense of their new situation often depends on the situation they faced prior to the promotion. If the workgroup perceived itself as largely successful, they will respond positively to the promotion of someone who maintains the status quo; if they perceived themselves as struggling or unsuccessful, they will likely welcome someone who will make changes (Moreland & Levine, 1982).

In addition, the type of relationship individuals had with the outgoing supervisor influence how they make sense of the change (Ballinger & Schoorman, 2007). Individuals who had a partnership or insider relationship (high LMX; see Chapter 7) with the outgoing supervisor may appreciate an heir apparent succession in which the new supervisor will maintain the current approaches. Individuals who had an overseer or outsider relationship (low LMX) will likely appreciate someone with new ideas and approaches because it could result in positive changes in their supervisor–subordinate relationship.

In the scenario, Amari's promotion exhibits one way that a promotion may develop. The owners approached Amari and offered the promotion. There was no contender succession where others had an opportunity to apply for the position. After the promotion, Amari faced some of the usual challenges involved. One former peer, Corey, expected special favors and insider information, whereas TJ adjusted quickly to the new difference in status. Amari had to learn to manage those relationships to former peers. There did not seem to be any overt testing or hazing, but Amari had to manage confidential information shared by the owners and decide whether to share the information or not after learning about the layoffs. TJ and Corey likely made sense of Amari's decision not to share the information by considering their new supervisor "one of them," the management team that treated them unfairly.

Communication and Job Transfers

For people who work in large organizations with multiple business locations, a second type of individual transition is also common. A job transfer or job relocation involves moving from one physical organization site to another. Although it is not common for

students working part-time jobs to be transferred, it can happen. Some organizations allow students to transfer their jobs from their hometown to their college town. For full-time employees, transferring is common. On average, over 240,000 transfers per year occur in just Fortune 500 companies alone (Worldwide ERC, 2014). One corporation was jokingly referred to by employees as "I've Been Moved" (i.e., International Business Machines, IBM) some years ago. Many government agencies and smaller corporations also transfer employees; and of course, military personnel are transferred routinely. Job transfers include domestic transfers within the home country and international transfers to other countries.

Communication and Domestic Job Transfers

Purposes of Domestic Job Transfers. Domestic job transfers serve both the organization and individuals involved. Vacant positions occur after retirements, resignations, promotions, or other transfers. Particularly for higher level positions, it is often less expensive for an organization to move a qualified internal employee to a different location than to hire and train a new employee. Some transfers are lateral moves from one position to a similar position, but many transfers include promotions. As a result, transferred employees develop new skills, gain a broader understanding of the organization, and often develop a stronger commitment to their careers and the organization (Stroh, 1999). Employees perceive career benefits from transfers because they believe transfers provide opportunities for career development as they learn new skills and increase their chances for future career advancements, especially when moved into upper management positions (Brett, Stroh, & Reilly, 1993). Employees may also seek out job transfers for less career-oriented benefits, such as moving to a more desirable location, living closer to family, or enjoying a preferable climate

(Kramer, 2010). Domestic job transfers can benefit both the organization and the transferees.

The Process for Job Transfers. Research suggests that there are three phases to the job transfer process (Kramer, 1989, 1995). These include a pre-move or loosening phase, a transition phase, and a tightening or adjustment phase.

Pre-Move or Loosening Phase. The first part of the pre-move phase involves communication regarding the opportunity for a job transfer. In this time period, messaging moves from discussions about the possibilities of a transfer through to the formal departure.

The possibility of a job transfer can occur in a variety of ways. About 80% of the time, management approaches individuals after determining that they have the necessary technical or supervisory skills to recommend a transfer opportunity (Pinder, 1977). When management initiates the discussion of a transfer, employees may feel that they must accept the transfer because rejecting it will result in negative career consequences (Brett & Werbel, 1980). They may accept a transfer to an undesirable location because they fear that they will not be considered for future promotions or transfers if they do not. In many of the remaining 20% of the cases, a human resources department posts transfer opportunities and individual employees initiate the transfer by applying for the opening. In these cases, there may be competition for desirable positions, which could mean that there may be an interview and selection process. Employees who initiate their own transfers and view them as promotions tend to be more satisfied in their new positions (Pinder, 1977).

Communication and work relationships change once an employee decides to accept a job transfer. The transferring employee works at finalizing current projects and does not accept any new ones that will last beyond the transfer date. Transferring employees may need to convey certain critical or confidential information to others so that there is continuity in the workplace after their departures. Colleagues often begin to treat transferees differently because they consider them "short-timers" who no longer have a long-term perspective on their workplace. Usually there will be some sort of ceremony or ritual to mark the departure of the employee. These ceremonies help individuals make sense of the changes they are experiencing.

Transition Phase. The transition phase begins when the transferee leaves the old location to move to the new one, but it often begins earlier. It is not unusual for there to be communication with future supervisors, particularly with today's technology. When this occurs, it helps the transferee have a more accurate understanding of what to expect at the new location. Sometimes transferees are even consulted on certain issues prior to arriving at the new location, particularly if they are moving into a position with a lot of organizational authority, because they may have to handle the situation once they arrive. Lower level transferees rarely are involved in this type of communication. It is also not uncommon for the transferee to continue to communicate with coworkers from the old location while past tasks are finalized.

Once they arrive, transferees must "get up to speed" by making sense of their new work. Although they may be familiar with the overall culture of the organization, they still need to learn the subculture of the particular location and its norms, practices, and politics. Some of the differences may be due to the way the geographical location influences the local work norms. For example, there are likely different norms in a Los Angeles location versus one in Indianapolis, even within the same company. If the transfer involved a promotion, then the transferee must learn the new work and communication skills associated with the job. Transferees who receive social support and feedback from their supervisors and peers during the first weeks and months on the job are more satisfied and experience less role ambiguity (Kramer, 1995, 1996).

Work-life issues also affect the transition phase. One study found that transferees average an eight-week separation from spouses and family members when they move to their new location (Brett, 1982). Although communication technology changes have made this less of an issue than in the past, it still often means that transferees are living in temporary quarters waiting for their family and belongings to arrive. Transferees and their families must make sense of many changes once the move is complete. They must find new places to shop, new schools to attend, and new places for life enrichment activities such as gyms and places of worship. Transferees who experience fewer unmet expectations for family and community adjustment are more satisfied and confident in their work roles as well (Jablin & Kramer, 1998).

The Tightening Phase. Over time as transferees make sense of work in the new location, they no longer feel like newcomers. They develop routine communication relationships with supervisors, peers, and subordinates, along with a network of contacts at the new location. Their communication with former colleagues and friends decreases gradually, despite new communication technologies, as new responsibilities and new work relationships and friendships become more pressing. Work-life issues also matter. Some transferees do not feel like the transition is over until they have celebrated one or more major holidays in their new location. They are more satisfied in the jobs when their spouses and families have settled into new schools, found new jobs, and become focused on their new situation rather than thinking about the transition (Stroh, 1999). Of course, in organizations where transfers are common, such as the military, there may never be a sense of reaching stability, as preparations for the next transfer begin soon after arrival.

Effects on the Workgroup. Although the research on job transfers focuses on the person who is relocating, coworkers being left by the transferee need to make sense of the move as well. For example, when it is announced that someone is transferring, other employees at the old location may contact the person to understand why they are leaving and to discuss their own career concerns (Kramer, 1989). Sometimes this motivates the other employees to seek out job transfer opportunities. Those employees must also make adjustments to their work environment as they divide work responsibilities or adjust social relationships to compensate for the loss of a coworker. At the new location, the transferees create uncertainty for the workgroup as newcomers (Gallagher & Sias, 2009). Workgroup members assist in teaching the transferees the local norms of the organization. As they do, they must make sense of how the work habits of the transferee will influence their own work. They need to accommodate and integrate the transferee into the communication networks. Like the employees in the old location, they may be motivated to seek career opportunities through job transfers based on their experiences with the transferee.

Communication and International Job Transfers

Multinational organizations have the opportunity to transfer employees to various international locations in addition to within their home country. International transfers are used to attempt to create continuity or consistency across different branches of the company (Kostova & Roth, 2003; Stroh, 1999). Management expects that placing key personnel from their home country in international locations will help create a unified culture across national boundaries. There are strong parallels and important differences between domestic and these international transfers, also known as expatriate assignments. We highlight some of the important differences briefly here.

When job transfers are international, the process is similar, but with more intense implications for the individual. An important difference is that international transfers are usually for a fixed period of time, which can range from six months to a number of years. *Before* international transfers, employees need cross-cultural training, including in many cases language training, for both the work and nonwork environments.

Providing training to the expatriates and their family members who are involved helps the expatriates to develop skills and perform more effectively in their jobs (Black & Mendenhall, 1990) and helps them make sense of the culture outside of the workplace as well (Mendenhall, Dunbar, & Oddou, 1987). *During* expatriate assignments, mentoring from host country nationals assists expatriates in adjusting to their new locations and understanding international business issues while increasing chances of successful completion of the overseas assignments and higher satisfaction with the experience (Carraher, Sullivan, & Crocitto, 2008; Feldman & Bolino, 1999).

Despite such efforts, international transfers are frequently *unsuccessful*, with as high as 40% of expatriates returning home prior to completing their assignments (Black, Mendenhall, & Oddou, 1991). These failures are often due to either the hardships experienced by the families of the expatriate or the expatriates themselves failing to adjust to the culture of the new location (Bolino, 2007).

After an incomplete international appointment, creating opportunities for success and career development can communicate to the employees that any concerns they have about crippling their careers are inaccurate. But even when the overseas appointment is successful, expatriates need to receive the promotions and career advancement opportunities they expected, or they often seek employment in other organizations (Kraimer, Shaffer, & Bolino, 2009).

In the scenario, Amari has an opportunity to be transferred to California. This transfer was initiated by management, which may mean that Amari feels that there is little choice in accepting it or not. Amari will likely take work-life issues into account while weighing the decision. The attitudes of family members toward moving to California will likely influence the decision. If the company continues to grow and purchase companies in locations around the world, Amari may have opportunities for an international assignment.

Communication and Career Plateaus

The American Dream is that through hard work individuals can continue to climb the ladder of success to higher and higher positions. The reality is somewhat different. In small organizations, there are often fewer opportunities for advancement. Diagrams of hierarchies of large organizations are shaped like pyramids because there are fewer and fewer individuals at the top of the hierarchy. Not everyone has the skill to succeed at the next higher level of an organization. In other situations, systemic discrimination accounts for a lack of individuals' upper mobility. In still other cases, the only opportunity for advancement is the retirement of someone in a higher position. These, and other forces, mean that most people reach one or more points in their careers where they face a career plateau, a temporary or permanent stopping place. Although this might not seem like a transition, a career plateau is a transition, at least psychologically, as the individual must make sense of a situation in which additional advancements are unlikely. In some cases, the adjustment may be easy because the individuals have achieved their goals or even exceeded them. In other cases, the adjustment may involve disappointment or anger from being passed over for a promotion by a newer or younger employee, which can lead to reduced work effort. Research demonstrates that objective measures of a career plateau such as number of years at a rank was not associated with job dissatisfaction or intentions to quit; however, subjective perceptions of reaching a career plateau was associated with a dissatisfaction with work, supervisors, and the organization, along with perceptions that an organization's promotion and reward system was inequitable (Tremblay, Roger, & Toulouse, 1995).

Management can communicate in ways that eliminate some of the negative consequences of perceptions of career stagnation. Management can provide opportunities for employees to be mentors or to serve on special or high-profile projects that create visibility or can provide development opportunities such as training to become experts in a new area. Employees can make sense of themselves as valuable and developing employees by taking on these opportunities, despite reaching a plateau. Employees who cope with their career plateau by seeking new job assignments (lateral moves), accepting special projects, or taking on mentoring roles experience more positive satisfaction, along with increased effort and commitment; those who cope by blaming their supervisors or the organization, reducing their effort, and even engaging in substance abuse, became increasingly dissatisfied and reduce their effort and commitment to the organization (Rotondo & Perrewé, 2000). Others may leave the organization looking for career opportunities elsewhere. Given that large numbers of employees reach career plateaus, managers interested in retaining skilled employees should be aware of when employees are perceiving that their careers have become stagnant and communicate opportunities such as mentoring, special training, and special projects to those employees.

In the scenario, Amari does not appear to have reached a career plateau yet. There seem to be opportunities for advancement in California or in another organization in Chicago. Of course, it is likely only a matter of time before those upward mobility opportunities will become increasingly rare. If Amari finds more satisfaction in the technical work than in managerial work, a lack of advancement opportunities may never become a concern.

Organizational Transitions

So far in this chapter, we have focused on career transitions that individuals experience, whether it is being promoted, transferred, or reaching a career plateau. There are many different organizational transitions that could be examined that also affect individuals during their careers. We focus on two common ones: mergers and acquisitions (M&As) and reductions-in-force (RIFs) or layoffs.

Mergers and Acquisitions

An M&A involves two organizations becoming one. There are technical differences between the two. A *merger* occurs when two roughly equal partners or organizations join their material assets, operations, technology, personnel, and culture into one; by contrast, an *acquisition* involves one organization, usually the larger of the two, buying the other organization and absorbing it into its operations and culture (Buono & Bowditch, 1989). We treat them as the same, as mergers often imitate acquisitions because usually the communication practices and culture of one of the organizations is more dominant after the two join together.

The motives for M&As are generally to increase size, gain new technologies or profits, broaden markets, increase profitability and market share, or encourage innovation. These goals are usually accomplished in one of three ways (Goldberg, 1983). In a *vertical integration*, the primary organization tries to gain control over suppliers, production, and distribution of the secondary organization. For example, a meat packing company may acquire commercial farms or a grocery chain to gain control over the entire process from farming to consumer. In a *horizontal integration*, the primary organization tries to eliminate competition by absorbing a rival organization or by creating capacities that smaller organizations cannot match. For example, a furniture rental company may acquire competitors in the nearby communities to have control of the market for an entire region. In a *conglomerate strategy*, the primary company acquires various companies to diversify into new areas. For example, in 1991, AT&T purchased

NCR, the company discussed under transformational leadership in Chapter 8, to diversify into other computer technologies besides telecommunications. It maintained NCR as a subsidiary before returning it to an independent company in 1996 when AT&T determined that NCR no longer fit its conglomerate strategy.

This last example illustrates another important point about M&As. Despite positive plans and intentions, research generally finds that about 75% of M&As fail to accomplish their intended goals (Marks & Mirvis, 2001); as a result, the larger company often divests itself of the smaller one after some time. There are a variety of explanations for this pattern. Poor communication is a primary explanation for the failure of M&As. For example, inadequate communication prior to an M&A often results in poor choices for M&A partnerships. Poor communication after an M&A often results in a failure to integrate the two companies into one.

The M&A Process

The M&A process is described as occurring in four time periods or phases marked by critical differences in events and communication (Napier, Simmons, & Stratton, 1989): a pre-merger phase, an in-play phase, a transition phase, and a stabilization phase. Throughout these phases, organizational members must make sense of the changing situation.

The Pre-Merger Phase. The *pre-merger phase* is characterized by secretive talks exploring the possibility of merging between the high-ranking officials of the two organizations, such as the owners, CEOs, or boards of directors. The goal of secrecy seems to be to avoid embarrassment in the case that the two companies decide not to complete the merger and to keep employees from worrying. However, rumors tend to develop despite the efforts of secrecy; and employees and other stakeholders attempt to make sense of the possible merger without any official information. Some researchers suggest that it is better to have open communication instead of being secretive because it is easier to manage information and attempt to frame the sensemaking process through official sensegiving communication rather than trying to control rumors.

The In-Play Phase. The *in-play phase* refers to the time from when the official announcement of the M&A occurs until the actual combining of the organizations begins. During this time, individuals in both organizations experience high levels of uncertainty and must make sense of what is going to happen (Napier et al., 1989).

Rumors and Sensemaking

Sensemaking conversations are likely wherever routines are disrupted and anxiety is created. Many organizational members turn to one another to discuss (i.e., make sense) about what is going on. This can be especially true for large organizational changes, such as M&As. One study collected nearly 800 rumors from employees of a large health care organization that was undergoing large changes (Bordia, Jones, Gallois, Callan, & DiFonzo, 2006). Not surprisingly, most rumors were negative and predicted trouble. The most common kind of rumor was about whether and which employees would lose their jobs. The study also revealed that when participants reported negative rumors and making sense of the change as fearful, they also, in turn, experienced significantly more change-related stress than those who reported positive and optimistic rumors. What communication practices should management use to control rumors?

In any M&As, employees experience uncertainty concerning how organizational practices, procedures, information systems, and cultures must be combined. In what is officially a "merger," it may be unclear if one organization will dominate after the combination is complete. Mixed messages often contribute to confusion during this time. Management in both organizations may tell the employees that their jobs are secure while at the same time telling investors that the M&A is going to be beneficial because they will become more profitable by cutting costs; unions may reassure their members that their jobs are secure, but insist that they need the union to maintain job security (Greenhalgh & Jick, 1989). During this uncertain time, employees must make sense of how their individual work will be affected by the M&A.

Transition Phase. The *transition phase* begins after all of the legal aspects of the M&A have been completed and the two previously separate organizations begin to integrate into one combined organization. The combined organization may take the name of the larger partner, but sometimes a new name is created. For example, the name Bank of America was created after a series of M&As over a period of many years. Integrating two companies triggers a need for changes such as replacing old signage, letterhead, and a host of other organizational symbols. For example, when two airlines merge, the planes need to be repainted, the signage at the airport check-ins needs to be changed, and personnel need to wear the uniform of the surviving or new organization. More challenging than standardizing the symbols to create a unified image is integrating two different sets of procedures, computer systems, and sets of cultural norms and values. Integrating personnel is particularly challenging, as departments and management personnel may be merged and facilities may be closed. For example, two separate human resource departments and managers must begin to work under one leader.

Communication during the in-play and transition phases is critical as demonstrated in a field experiment of two comparable plants involved in the same merger (Schweiger & Denisi, 1991). The one plant received only the official announcements. The other plant implemented a strategic organizational communication plan. All employees received a realistic merger preview (like a realistic job preview in Chapter 2), went to weekly department meetings to discuss progress, received newsletters with a question-and-answer section, and could call a rumor hotline. Personnel in both plants experienced increases in uncertainty, stress, and absenteeism as well as declines in commitment and satisfaction. However, the plant with the strategic organizational communication plan had higher levels of trust, commitment, and satisfaction and lower levels of uncertainty than the other plant. The differences were so significant that the comparison or control organization ended the experiment early and began its own strategic organizational communication program. This study reinforces the idea that it is important to communicate during changes so that employees can make sense of their situation.

The communication needs of different personnel are usually not the same in M&As. Employees in an acquired organization are primarily concerned with their own job security and job duties, whereas those in the acquiring organization are more concerned about how the combining of the organizations will change their work routines, duties, and coworkers (Zhu, May, & Rosenfeld, 2004). Management can provide sensegiving messages to assist both types of employees in making sense of their situation. For example, symbolic gestures like appointing some of the management from the acquired organization to important positions in the combined organization provides some sense of job security. Also, providing high-quality or accurate information quickly can help employees make sense of their situation (Cornett-DeVito & Friedman, 1995).

Communication involved in merging two different cultures can be quite challenging. A study of the acquisition of a small equipment leasing company by a larger local bank identified some of those challenges (Bastien, 1992). The leasing company had a fairly informal culture. Decisions were made quickly and sealed with handshakes. Employees wore casual clothes that matched their customers. By contrast, the bank, which acquired the leasing company to diversify its services, had a very formal culture. Decisions were expected to follow the chain of command, and agreements had to be carefully written and signed. Employees wore business suits that fit the bank's refined architectural facility. To make sense of their situation after the M&A, the employees of the leasing company used one of three coping strategies. Some of them decided that it made sense to switch to the bank's culture. They began wearing suits and followed formal rules and the chain of command carefully. These employees tended to move to the bank headquarters as they received career advancement opportunities. The second group of employees

ETHICAL ISSUE

Leading the Combining of Two Cultures

Imagine you are on a management team that is leading your organization through an acquisition. Your company purchased another. To what degree do you feel responsible to honor the acquired organization's culture? Should members of the acquired organization be expected to adopt your organization's culture and drop their own? Now consider that you are on a management team that is leading your organization being acquired by another organization. To what degree would you like the acquiring organization's leadership to honor your organization's established culture and norms? What does this perspective-taking teach us about how to manage and communicate M&As successfully?

made sense of the situation by practicing "code switching" to try to balance the two cultures. When they were interacting with personnel from the bank, they practiced more formal communication and dressed formally. When they were working with lease customers, they maintained their previous casual culture. These employees tended to leave the organization after a while, perhaps to look for employment where they could maintain more consistency in their communication and self-presentation. The third group rejected the bank's culture. For them it made sense to continue to maintain the leasing organization culture to be able to work with their customers. They tended to remain at the leasing location and were not offered opportunities for advancement.

The Stabilization Phase. The *stabilization phase* is conceptualized as the time when the combined organization reaches a sense of "business-as-usual." This is primarily a psychological state and it may be more of an illusion than a reality that the two cultures have combined. In some cases, members of an acquired organization maintain a secret organization within the combined organization. In one such case, years after an airline was acquired by another one, the employees of the no longer existing business continued to have "company picnics" and participated in other symbolic activities such as secret tattoos (Pierce & Dougherty, 2002).

In the scenario, Amari and the other employees were involved in an acquisition. A larger company purchased Irata to diversify their products and services. Irata's owners apparently managed to maintain secrecy concerning the negotiations during the pre-merger phase because the announcement caught the rest of the employees by surprise. Irata's owners tried to address job security concerns of their employees in their announcement, and the owners of the new company made a symbolic statement that Irata's employees had a place in the combined company by appointing Irata's owners to the board of directors of the combined company. Before the M&A transition seemed complete, Amari and the other employees faced another organizational transition.

Reductions-in-Force or Layoffs

Because almost 75% of M&As fail to meet their goals, it is not uncommon for the M&A transition to be followed by another type of transition—RIFs or layoffs. Of course, RIFs occur for many other reasons as well. Although it is fairly easy for leaders to frame M&As positively—despite the uncertainty that many employees feel—it is nearly impossible to frame RIFs in a positive light. Clearly, for the people who lose their jobs, the consequences are negative; but evidence suggests that communication to the survivors of the RIF (those not laid off) is also very important in helping them make sense of their situation.

Given the negative connotation of layoffs, it is not surprising that companies created a number of euphemisms for them—including human resource reallocations, streamlining, and rightsizing. RIFs are often the result of the general economic climate. In 2008 and 2009, many companies, small and large, laid off employees; and the unemployment rate rose dramatically due to a nationwide recession. In other cases, RIFs are due to problems in the local economy, mismanagement of resources, overexpansion, M&As, and a host of other possibilities.

When organizations need only a small reduction in their workforce, they can often accomplish this without announcing a RIF or laying off any employees. If it has the time and resources to do so, the organization may simply enact a hiring freeze where no new employees are hired and natural attrition occurs due to voluntary exits such as retirement or career and life changes. If it works, this strategy can allow management to state that they have never laid off an employee. In other cases, this strategy is inadequate and layoffs occur. Like M&As, it is advantageous to think of a RIF as occurring in three phases: a pre-announcement phase, the announcement phase, and the post-layoff phase (Kramer, 2010).

Pre-Announcement Phase

During the *pre-announcement phase*, it is unusual for a RIF to come as a complete surprise for employees because of the changes that occur in the workplace prior to a RIF. Employees likely observe that there is less work to do and employees are often idle or that they have fewer customers and clients. They may see upper management and/or owners holding secret or closed-door meetings. As they make sense of what is happening, they talk to each other frequently and rumors begin to develop. Some employees begin considering looking for work elsewhere. The uncertainty that they experience and the time spent discussing rumors can create a downward spiral of decreased productivity, which leads to additional organizational problems.

Announcement Phase

The *announcement phase* often involves two steps. First, there is a general announcement that there are going to be layoffs followed by individual announcements where employees find out their own fate. A 2009 movie, *Up in The Air*, illustrates what most people would consider an inappropriate way of laying off employees; the main character travels around the country laying off employees in a very impersonal way through a video link to avoid personally interacting with them. Michael Kramer heard of a large company that used voicemail messages to announce layoffs, also a seemingly inappropriate approach. More effective individual announcements may include offering severance packages based on tenure, or the organization may provide job placement services to help individuals find new positions.

Reducing the time between the general announcement and the individual announcements seems important, as employees will be trying to make sense of their own situation; and productivity is likely to slump, as sensemaking and adjustments become more effortful. Reducing the time between the announcements and the last day of work also seems valuable, as employees who are laid off are unlikely to be highly productive. In some instances, if there is a long period of time between the general announcement and the actual layoffs, management may use that time to evaluate who will be retained. The employees continue to work side by side even after they know their futures. Under those circumstances, survivors have higher levels of trust in their managers and colleagues, but both types of employees experience high levels of uncertainty (Tourish, Paulsen, Hobman, & Bordia, 2004).

Post-Layoff Phase

In the *post-layoff phase*, the individuals who keep their jobs after a RIF, often experience "survivor guilt" as they try to make sense of why they kept their jobs while others did not. This survivor guilt can lead to one of two very different behaviors. If the survivors make sense of keeping their jobs as due to their work ethic, they may work harder, especially as they take on work previously done by employees who were laid off; if they make sense of it as random chance, they will experience lower self-esteem, fear additional layoffs, and decrease their productivity (Brockner, Grover, O'Malley, Reed, & Glynn, 1993). Sensegiving communication from management can assist survivors in making positive adjustments.

Survivors tend to experience high levels of information deprivation as they try to make sense of their situation. Despite this problem, likely due to impression management concerns, they are reluctant to ask questions of management directly and instead increase their use of observation and third-party information seeking (Casey, Miller, & Johnson, 1997). Of course, talking to other peers may not provide accurate or current information. Due to their lack of information, survivors are uncertain about their careers in the organization and consider leaving. In fact, employees in work areas unaffected by a first round of layoffs experience higher levels of uncertainty about their careers than those in work areas that experienced layoffs (Casey et al., 1997). Because a second round of layoffs is not uncommon, it likely makes sense to them that their workgroup will be the next to experience layoffs.

Communication and social support from supervisors and other workgroup members can improve their work satisfaction and reduce the desire to leave (Johnson, Bernhagen, Miller, & Allen, 1996). Unfortunately, although management usually could provide information, it is often reluctant to do so. Often management decides that because they cannot provide complete information, they should not communicate any information. As a result, employees make sense of their situation on their own. However, providing even partial information, while admitting to being unable to provide more, assists survivors in making sense of the situation and improves morale compared to being secretive and waiting until complete information is available (DiFonzo & Bordia, 1998).

In the scenario, Amari found out about the layoffs shortly before most of the employees but was told to keep the information secret. This created problematic relationships with coworkers. The company did try to support the individuals they laid off with a small severance package and job placement services. Not surprising, some of the survivors of the layoff also chose to look for jobs and found them. They felt too much job insecurity to remain in the company and likely had other options to pursue.

Individual and Organizational Transitions for Volunteers

Volunteers can experience many of the same transitions we discussed in this chapter, but because their volunteer role is often less central to their identity than their paid work, the changes are often not as important or as common. The most likely transition is when a volunteer is promoted to supervising other volunteers. Transfers are uncommon because many organizations relying on volunteers have only one location. Some large organizations, such as the American Red Cross and many religious organizations, allow or encourage volunteers to transfer their memberships when they move. Of course, employees in large nonprofit organizations may transfer just like employees in other organizations. Occasionally, two nonprofit social agencies or two congregations in the same religious denomination or two social movement organizations will merge, usually for the same reasons as for-profit companies: to increase size, efficiency, and impact. When this occurs, volunteers must make sense of their role in the new combined organization. Organizations that rely on volunteers never lay off volunteers, but if they are experiencing a decline as an organization, there may be fewer opportunities for volunteers to serve.

Summary

You are likely to experience a variety of transitions while participating in a single organization. We have discussed a few of these in this chapter. At the individual level, these included promotions to positions higher in the organization, either domestic or international job transfers, or career plateaus where further advancement is unlikely. At the organizational level, we explored M&As and RIFs or layoffs. In all of these situations, we examined how communication assists individuals in understanding their changing situations based on sensemaking theory. The principles of sensemaking we used in this chapter can be applied to the other transitions you may experience.

CHAPTER 15

Communication During Organizational Exit

Kelly was not enjoying this week as the owner of a Sweep Away franchise. Sweep Away's business model was fairly simple. It contracted with various local businesses to clean their office space overnight. It was actually a fairly lucrative business due to the increasing demand for its services. Most businesses found it cheaper to hire an outside company like Sweep Away to do the work than to hire their own staff. Kelly was pleased to have the business growing so quickly, but with that growth came personnel problems. This week several problems came to a head.

Kelly always knew that Justice was going to quit sometime in May after graduation. Working for Sweep Away had just been a way to pay for college and have some extra cash for fun. Kelly once tried to convince Justice to join the business, but it simply was not going to happen. Justice was pursuing a dream career in pharmaceutical sales.

Harley's resignation was not really a surprise either. Kelly noticed that the quality of Harley's work was no longer good—or even average—during recent inspections of the offices after they were cleaned. Whatever had motivated Harley to do a good job at first was no longer there. Kelly was not surprised by Harley's resignation but was very annoyed by the lack of two weeks notice before quitting. Good employees usually gave two weeks notice, but what can you do if someone stops showing up? Unfortunately, this probably meant Kelly would have to step in for a few nights until a replacement could be found.

And then there was Jayden, who never had been a very good employee. Kelly trained and retrained Jayden three times, but nothing seemed to change. After the last training session, Jayden was given specific goals to meet or be let go. After Kelly documented that the goals were not met on three different occasions in the last month, it was time to let Jayden go.

So the rest of the day was going to be taken up primarily with a meeting to terminate Jayden's employment, followed by taking Justice out to eat one last time, followed by filling in for Harley. Sometimes being a franchise owner was not a lot of fun.

· · · · ·

ost certainly, you will leave a number of organizations during your career.
Chances are you have already left a number of organizations as a student, employee, or volunteer. Although a great deal of research focuses on the process of organizational entry and being an employee or voluntary member of an organization, the process of exiting or leaving is relatively understudied. In this chapter, we address communication during organizational exit. To understand the issues involved, we first present social exchange theory to help provide an explanation of the exit process. Then, we investigate communication surrounding the two primary forms of exit: voluntary and involuntary. Then, we explore another form of exit that does not fit neatly into those two categories in which employees are encouraged or induced to leave through subtle or not-so-subtle efforts. We end the chapter by noting some important differences in the way that volunteers exit organizations compared to employees.

Social Exchange Theory

Social exchange theory (SET) is a general name for a theoretical perspective that focuses attention on how individuals weigh the costs and benefits of beginning, continuing, or ending their social relationships. SET has been applied to various social relationships such as interpersonal relationships (e.g., supervisor–subordinate relationships in Chapter 7) or employee to organization relationships.

According to SET, individuals participate in two types of exchanges: economic and social (Roloff, 1981). In economic exchanges, people know the exact rate of exchange, such as the salary or hourly compensation they will receive in exchange for work. In social exchanges, the costs and benefits are more ambiguous. For example, if a co-worker does a favor for you, it is often unclear whether you owe a favor in return, exactly how much of a favor you owe, or how soon you are obligated to return the favor.

Organizational membership for employees or volunteers include a combination of social and economic changes. Employees and volunteers alike exchange money, goods, services, information, status, affect, and friendship (Foa & Foa, 1980). For example, a high-performing employee may be given a raise and, in turn, become more committed (affect) to his/her manager and the organization as a result. A manager may give an employee some valuable information and receive status from the employee who admires the manger as a mentor.

According to SET, decisions to begin, continue, or end relationships, such as organizational membership, are based on two calculations: the comparison level and the comparison level of alternatives (Thibaut & Kelley, 1959). The *comparison level* is an examination of the ratio of costs to benefits. For an employee, this could be as simple as a comparison of the amount of work (time, effort, challenge, etc.) compared to the salary. The better matched the cost–benefit ratio is, the more likely an individual is to pursue or continue the relationship. It likely is more complex than just salary, however, because the benefits could include other factors besides pay such as the pleasantness of the work environment and the ability to maintain work-life balance through a flextime policy. For a volunteer, this might be a comparison of the amount of time and effort involved in volunteering compared to the sense of accomplishment or quality of friendships that develop as a result.

The *comparison level of alternatives* looks at the comparison level of the current relationship but also considers the comparison level of possible alternative relationships. So for employees, the comparison level of alternatives would compare the cost–benefit ratio of a current workplace to the cost–benefit ratio of other possible workplaces. So even if employees feel that the current pay is lower than it should be, if there are no other job openings or those that have openings have poor work-life policies, the employees may stay because the cost–benefit ratio in the current organization is better than the alternatives. Similarly, volunteers, who may be unhappy with the inefficiencies of the agency they serve currently, may continue to serve it because other agencies are more poorly funded and it would take a lot of effort to create new friendships there.

SET, however, is often criticized for being too rational to adequately reflect actual human behavior. Certainly most people probably do not spend a lot of time consciously calculating the costs and benefits of their organizational memberships on a routine basis. However, circumstances often lead us to considering the advantages and disadvantages of staying in an organization or moving to a new one. When that happens, we may begin thinking in terms of costs and benefits. Employees and volunteers likely use some calculations when they make their membership decisions, particularly when deciding to leave one organization or join another.

SET is useful in examining the two main categories of organizational exit: voluntary and involuntary. It provides a framework for examining why people make voluntary decisions to leave an organization. It also provides a framework for understanding why managers decide to dismiss employees during an involuntary exit.

Voluntary Exit

Research suggests that there are three main reasons why people leave organizations voluntarily: (a) planned exits, (b) shocks, and (c) gradual dissolution (Lee, Mitchell, Wise, & Fireman, 1996). For each of these, individuals may complete a search for their next place of employment prior to quitting, or they may quit without having a definite plan for their futures.

Planned Exits

Planned exits refer to expected membership dissolutions. Planned exits tend to be predictable and are not usually surprising to other organizational members. Instead, planned exists occur because of an event, usually apart from the organizational setting, that causes a person to leave an organization. Typical events that might trigger a planned exit could include graduating, getting married, moving, a spouse or partner's promotion or transfer, or a variety of similar events. Most of these events are known in advance, although not always. Conscientious employees typically discuss many of these possible or expected events with their supervisors ahead of time. Sometimes these events occur somewhat unexpectedly. For example, if a spouse receives an offer to transfer to another city, the partner might resign without much warning because the couple has a plan for that situation. In planned exits, individuals have determined that the costs of continuing in the organization are greater than the benefits of pursuing other new options; as a result leaving is often simply the best choice for them. They also are usually very open about communicating their intentions and gratitude to their supervisors and peers. In the opening scenario, Justice exited the cleaning company due to a planned exit, graduation from college, and the resulting opportunity to pursue another career.

Shocks

Shocks are significant disruptions or discrepancies in the workplace. These can range from very personal events, such as being passed over for a promotion (see career plateau in Chapter 14), or being bullied or sexually harassed (see Chapter 10). In other cases, the shock might be the result of an organizational event, such as the announcement of merger (see Chapter 14) or discovering that management has been conducting business in an unethical manner. These shocks cause the person to reevaluate the costs and benefits of staying in the organization. If the person determines that the costs are too great compared to the benefits, they will likely leave, especially if there are acceptable alternatives.

This definition of shocks is similar to the description of the causes of emotional reactions discussed in Chapter 7. Shocks often cause strong emotional reactions. When the shock and reaction are severe enough, an individual may resign almost immediately without a plan. In less severe cases, the person may develop an alternative plan, such as finding a position in another organization before resigning. The choice between these two actions may be related to both the comparison level and the comparison level of alternatives. When the shock is a severe violation—such as a quid pro quo sexual harassment proposal from a supervisor—the victim may leave immediately because the situation is intolerable. When there are few alternatives to the person's current position or the shock is not so severe, an employee may be more reluctant to quit without first securing a new position elsewhere. In a study by Lee et al. (1996), many nurses were able to quit without first finding another job after they experienced a shock—in part because they were confident they could find comparable employment elsewhere.

A person seeking opportunities elsewhere before leaving will likely be secretive about their job search. They may only discuss their plans with family and close friends. A person who quits immediately after a severe shock will likely announce it quickly and then exit. By contrast, supervisors prefer that an employee discuss the concern with them so that they can address the concern or at least make plans to keep operations moving forward smoothly in the absence of the employee. For example, if an employee explained her concern about being harassed by coworkers, the supervisor could take steps to eliminate the harassment, and perhaps retain the employee. In the opening scenario, it is possible that Harley experienced some shock a few months ago and so began looking for work elsewhere without ever talking to Kelly. This could explain the decline in Harley's work performance. Once employment was secured elsewhere, Harley resigned. A more likely explanation of Harley's departure is that it involved gradual disenchantment, the third explanation for voluntary exit.

Gradual Disenchantment

The most studied type of voluntary exit is based on gradual disenchantment. As the name suggests, *gradual disenchantment* occurs when an employee who once was a committed organizational member gradually becomes less committed and finally leaves the organization voluntarily. Hundreds of studies have tried to identify the best predictors of preventing voluntary turnover. These studies can be grouped into a number of areas.

Many studies have explored how various attitudinal factors like job satisfaction, job commitment, and other similar concepts are associated with intent to turnover or actual turnover (Griffeth, Hom, & Gaertner, 2000). For example, one study demonstrated that person-organization fit (P-O; see Chapter 2) was a significant predictor of job satisfaction and employee retention (McCulloch & Turban, 2007). Another study revealed that small business owners who develop inclusive and empowering relationships with their employees (comparable to partnership relationships in Chapter 7) had employees who were more satisfied with their jobs and were less likely to turnover (Marcketti & Kozar, 2007).

Consistent with SET, studies like these illustrate that when employees' attitudes toward their organization decrease, the cost–benefit ratio of the current position becomes unacceptable. If there are not many alternatives to the current workplace due to the general state of the economy, the location, or the specialized work involved, a person might continue to work in an unsatisfying situation for a long time before securing employment elsewhere and actually exiting. When alternative options are plentiful, voluntary exit is a likely result.

Role stress and burnout are specific forms of gradual disillusionment that often lead to voluntary exit. Role stress and burnout are particularly common problems in the social services area of employment and volunteering, but they can affect any type of work or volunteering. *Role stress* is an emotional frustration that is created by job and task requirements that are too much or too difficult (see Chapter 10). Role stress can be the result of role conflict and role ambiguity. Perhaps not surprisingly, role stress often leads to burnout (Miller, Ellis, Zook, & Lyles, 1990). *Burnout* is defined as a psychological state of emotional exhaustion, low sense of personal accomplishment, and depersonalization of others (Maslach & Jackson, 1981). In other words, burnout is the result of continued role and workload stress that reaches the point that an individual no longer has the emotional energy to put forth quality effort. As performance declines, the person's sense of accomplishment decreases, leading to a withdrawal from interactions with others. Burnout is associated with many negative outcomes for the person, such as physical maladies like high blood pressure and fatigue, as well as lower job performance, higher absenteeism, and turnover (Sand & Miyazaki, 2000). Burnout is distinct from simple job dissatisfaction and is often associated with cynicism toward others (Maslach & Jackson, 1981).

Social support both from within the organization (peers and managers) and from outside the organization (family and friends) can help reduce the emotional exhaustion and stress associated with burnout (Sand & Miyazaki, 2000). *Social support* refers to the perceptions that one is cared for and cared about by others. In addition, social support along with participation in meaningful decision making in the workplace can help reduce stress and provide a sense of personal accomplishment, which helps increase job satisfaction, commitment, and reduces turnover (Miller et al., 1990). Of course, it may be too late for these remedies if other organizational members do not notice the signs of stress and burnout as they develop gradually. Employees who communicate their problems and concerns with stress and overload can give their peers and supervisors an opportunity to provide the support they need before the problem leads to exit.

Mixed Reasons for Voluntary Turnover

So far we have presented planned exits, shocks, and gradual disenchantment as if they are separate reasons for a voluntary exit decision. Although they can work separately, they can also work together, making it difficult to classify the reason for turnover. Several situations demonstrate this confound of explanations.

Network Location. The erosion model of employee turnover suggests that organizational turnover has much to do with a person's location in the communication network (see Chapter 5). In particular, two types of individuals are prone to turnover more frequently than others in an organization: (a) those at the edge of the communication network and (b) those who are closely associated with those near the edge (Feeley, Hwang, & Barnett, 2008; Feeley, Moon, Kozey, & Slowe, 2010). Those near the edge of the network are not well integrated into the organization's communication and find it more difficult to gain social support. As a result, they can easily become disillusioned with the organization. They tend to experience unmet expectations because the workplace does not meet their needs and so will often leave voluntarily. In addition, the people most closely associated with those who leave are also more prone to leave. This voluntary exit may be due to experiencing a kind of "contagious" disenchantment with the organization, or it could be that the exit of a close peer serves as either a shock or a planned exit event. Supervisors and coworkers who recognize that someone is on the periphery of the organizational network may be able to help reduce some turnover by making an effort to communicate regularly with those on the edge and getting them to connect with others socially.

Those on the edge of the network become more integrated into the organization and its communication network through these efforts.

Career Opportunities. In some instances, employees choose to leave an organization because of the presence of unexpected alternatives. The employees may be quite satisfied in their current positions and not looking for another position, but a new opportunity may find them. In the business world, there are companies that specialize in what is called "headhunting." These recruitment services are hired by organizations to find suitable candidates for job openings. Typically, these openings are in higher level positions in organizations where particular skills or experiences are needed to be a qualified candidate for the job. These head hunters then recruit suitable candidates for the opening. The limited research on this process suggests that headhunters consider two primary factors that are essentially the same as those for other new employees discussed in Chapter 2 (Coverdill & Finlay, 1998). They tend to look for candidates with a strong match or fit to the organizational culture (P-O) and to the individual who will hire them. They also look for a strong fit to the skills and experience needed for the job (person-job fit [P-J]). What makes this process unique for the candidates from a social exchange perspective is that the employees may not have intended to leave their current jobs because they were satisfied with the cost–benefit ratio; but faced with a new alternative, they leave for another position. Although this may seem like a fairly rare phenomenon, it is actually quite common for certain executive positions or in certain occupations.

Career Changes. A career change is not simply switching from a job in one company to a job in another one. Rather a career change is switching from one type of work to another. For example, a real-estate agent might get training to become a high school teacher. Career changes are part of the ongoing role socialization across the lifespan in which an individual chooses to pursue a new occupation based on experiences after entering the workforce full-time. It is difficult to determine how frequently people experience these career changes. We have heard estimates that current college students will likely make three career changes before they retire.

Research indicates that individuals make career changes for a variety of reasons. These include disenchantment with their current jobs, pursuing a lifelong dream, or in response to a sense of calling to serve a higher ideal or purpose (Tan & Kramer, 2012). For example, after working in a public relations firm for years, a person may pursue a dream of being a freelance photographer or decide to enter into social work to serve community members who are less fortunate. Sometimes the disenchantment occurs immediately on entering a career; but in other cases, disenchantment with a career can develop gradually. Career changes can also occur due to planned exits from organizations, such as on completing a degree that allows for mobility to a new career or by taking advantage of a spouse or partner's transfer to a new city to explore a new career opportunity.

In general, individuals involved in career changes spend a significant amount of time communicating with others as they consider making the change (Tan & Kramer, 2012). They usually gather information from people in the new career and seek advice from friends, colleagues, and family members. Potential career changers often talk with their network contacts whom they expect will be supportive of the change while perhaps being secretive about their plans with those they think will not be supportive. For example, career changers who wanted to move into less prestigious careers sometimes kept their intentions secret from their parents until after they made the change so their parents would not try to persuade them from making the change (Tan & Kramer, 2012). By seeking information from people that they think will support a career change and avoiding those they perceive as likely to be unsupportive, career changers are able to develop social support for their decisions to exit one job and career for another.

Retirement. Retirement is a relatively new workplace phenomenon in industrialized countries that is due, in part, to increases in life expectancies. When the average American only lived to their late 40s in 1900, retirement was not a realistic possibility; as the average life expectancy in the United States rose to living until their late 70s by 2010, retirement became possible (National Center For Disease Control and Prevention, 2011). With the increase in opportunities for retirement, our society has developed a master narrative of retirement as freedom from work and an opportunity to pursue other activities and interests (Smith & Dougherty, 2012). Despite general agreement on this master narrative across all adult demographics, the decision to retire is often quite complex. Although anticipating retirement as freedom, pre-retirees also worry about the lack of routine and have concerns over their ability to maintain their lifestyle financially and so many may delay retirement (Smith & Dougherty, 2012).

The actual decision to retire can be brought on by any of the three primary motivations for voluntary exit. Retirement can be a simple planned exit. It may occur when a spouse retires or after reaching a certain milestone, such as a certain chronological age, number of years in the organization, or years in a retirement plan. Because many individuals work past their target retirement date, they have the option to retire at any time. For these individuals, a shock, such as a change in leadership or a merger, may trigger a sudden retirement. Other potential shocks include being offered an early retirement compensation package. If the work becomes less fulfilling or meaningful, gradual disenchantment can lead to retirement as well. Any combination of these causes can lead to a reevaluation of the cost–benefit ratio of continuing to work. Retirement does not usually involve entering a new organization as an employee, although many retirees continue to work part-time for years. Supervisors appreciate employees who keep them informed of their potential retirement plans.

The Voluntary Exit Process

With the exception of exits due to sudden shocks, most voluntary exits involve a communication process of a preannouncement phase, an announcement phase, and an exit phase (Jablin, 2001). Communication during each of these phases is distinctly different.

The Preannouncement Phase. The preannouncement phase is the decision-making phase of the process. People considering voluntary exit gather information to inform their decision to stay or leave. Because they do not want to jeopardize their current position, individuals considering voluntary exit are selective about who they communicate with during this time (Klatzke, 2008). If a shock or gradual disenchantment is involved, they are more secretive about their potential plans. They likely only discuss their options with close friends and family members so that their managers are unaware of their potential plans. For a planned exit, they can be much more open in their communication and inclusive of their intentions to leave without fear of consequences. In addition, they likely differentiate themselves from those in the organization (Jablin, 2001). They might see themselves as more capable or less tolerant of unpleasant work conditions than their peers. Creating this type of dissonance makes it easier for them to leave their colleagues behind. During this time, they often consider the cost–benefit ratio of staying versus the alternatives available to them.

The Announcement Phase. During the announcement phase, the exiting individuals have made a decision to leave. They likely announce their decision beginning with family and close friends and then direct their messaging to larger, less personal members of their communication network over time. They often create different messages or explanations for their departure depending on the audience and their reason for leaving (Klatzke, 2008). For example, exiting individuals can probably be quite open about their reasons for leaving if it is a planned exit or retirement. Since there is little to hide, the audiences may all receive the same information. However, in other situations, exiting individuals may wish to mask their real reason for leaving as they frame their decision to their supervisors or the human resources department to maintain positive relationships and keep options open in the event that they later wish to return to the organization. As with job transfers, exiting individuals may be approached about their reasons for leaving from people who are not a part of the common contacts in the organization as word of the departure spreads. They may also attempt to gain support for their decision by bolstering the image and prestige of their new position in their communication (Tan & Kramer, 2012).

If exiting individuals are leaving on positive terms, they may also develop concern for their former colleagues and make an effort to make the transition for their colleagues smooth after their departure (Jablin, 2001). This process likely includes making the announcement as far in advance as possible, not just the minimum two weeks. It may involve recruiting people to substitute for either their formal or informal duties in the organization. It often involves passing along key insider information to others so that they are able to function without the help of the person leaving.

One final communication activity involves a farewell event or ritual to mark the end of person's formal membership in the organization (Kramer, 2010). Meals, happy hours, or formal parties may represent such departure rituals. These events provide closure and signal the transition for the people leaving and those who continue in the organization.

The Exit Phase. During the exit phase, the individuals have left their organization officially. During this time, communication changes quickly and dramatically. Despite promises to stay in touch and continue relationships, the lack of contact during the work week results in limited communication. Even when individuals get together after the voluntary exit, they find that they have less to talk about because they are no longer involved in the same work projects and may be less able to talk about confidential topics and situations (Klatzke, 2008). This lack of commonality can quickly lead to infrequent communication. It is unclear whether social media and electronic messaging has changed this pattern. The cost–benefit ratio of continuing those relationships with former colleagues, other than the closest friends, suggests that most communication would subside quickly.

Communication during the exit phase similarly changes dramatically for retirees. Retirees reduce their relationships to former coworkers and managers in most cases (Avery & Jablin, 1988). If they have spouses, they spend more time communicating with them than they did previously. Retirement programs can help them make these adjustments after their voluntary exit.

In the cleaning service scenario, the exit process for the two voluntary exits was quite different. Justice was open about a planned exit with Kelly throughout the preannouncement and announcement phase. The two of them are sharing a meal one last time to signal the beginning of the exit phase. It seems unlikely that the two will communicate often in the future because they have little in common and so little reason to maintain a relationship. Harley has been secretive about leaving, which is making it difficult to determine the true cause of the voluntary turnover.

Exit Interviews. Some organizations, particularly larger ones, have formal exit interviews as a part of voluntary exit. The purpose of an exit interview is to determine the reason an employee is leaving voluntarily with the goal of implementing changes in the organization to reduce voluntary turnover. The exit interview can be conducted under many different circumstances. They often occur during the last week of employment but can occur after

COMMUNICATION CHALLENGE

Exit Interviews with College Interns

Professor Kathy Barnett (2012) conducted 59 exit interviews with undergraduate students from various majors who were completing internships. The exiting interns had some similar reactions to their work experiences. First, they described how they realized how important communication is to work life. That realization was often the result of difficulties they experienced on the job, such as communicating with supervisors and potential clients. Second, the interns described how their work experiences revealed to them how different organizational and corporate culture is from their campus and college culture. On one hand, the interns were pleasantly surprised by the positive and warm interpersonal relationships at work. On the other hand, they were frustrated by how little direction and instruction they were given by supervisors, especially when compared with the instructions provided by professors. Besides internship programs, what can colleges do to better prepare students for the entry into full-time work?

leaving. They can be conducted by a supervisor or by someone in the human resources department. During exit interviews, departing employees are asked about their positive and negative experiences in the workplace.

A common criticism of exit interviews, regardless of how they are conducted, is that they provide little valuable information because employees want to save face and leave open opportunities for returning. There is some evidence to support this concern. A study that matched the reasons employees gave for leaving during an exit interview to answers they reported eight weeks later on a survey found significant differences (Lefkowitz & Katz, 1969). Whereas in the exit interviews, employees frequently reported they left for no particular reason or a need to be at home, on the survey, they reported specific reasons like dissatisfaction with the work conditions, peers, or supervisors.

Too often exit interviews are viewed as obligations, are poorly designed, and provide little valuable information. There are a variety of common suggestions for helping exit interviews achieve their stated purpose and goals (e.g., Harris, 2000). It is recommended that the exit interview occur in a comfortable *neutral site* away from the work flow to avoid interruptions and encourage thoughtful communication. It is important to provide *sufficient time* so the departing employee does not feel rushed and so the interviewer can listen carefully and ask appropriate follow-up questions to clarify points. The interviewer must communicate a *willingness to listen* to whatever the departing employee says. If the interviewer defends the organization or criticizes comments made, the departing employee will stop disclosing information that might be valuable for the organization's improvement. During the exit process, many conscientious employees will try to help improve the organization even though they are leaving. They will provide more useful information if they sense that their comments will make a difference. The interviewer should cover *specific events*. This may include probing vague answers and asking about whether certain events, such as a recent merger or change in management, were factors in the departure decision.

In the cleaning service scenario, exit interviews have the potential to provide insights into voluntary turnover at Sweep Away. An exit interview of Harley's could provide information about work conditions or workplace relationships that contribute to turnover. Making changes based on the information gleaned from the interviews could help reduce future turnover. An exit interview of Justice may not help reduce turnover because planned exits are usually unrelated to workplace characteristics. The exit interview still could potentially provide some insight into potential areas for improvement in the company because Justice probably is interested in improving the company despite leaving.

Involuntary Exit

In contrast to voluntary exit, involuntary exit involves the forced removal of a person from employment. Although layoffs are a form of involuntary exit for groups of employees, the focus here is on dismissing specific individuals for their personal actions as an employee. Because of the unpleasantness of dismissing employees, we have created a variety of euphemisms for the action such as terminated, fired, dismissed, let go, and released. Despite slight differences in connotation, the end result is the same. Because management has concluded that the cost–benefit ratio of retaining the person is too high, the person is no longer part of the organization.

Immediate or Summary Dismissal

If an employee is protected by an official contract, the actions that can result in immediate dismissal are clearly identified in the contract and may be limited to a very small number of behaviors such as being under the influence of drugs or alcohol on the job, stealing from the organization, or committing a criminal act. Many employees have no such formal contract and because they were "hired at will," they can be "fired at will" or subject to immediate or summary dismissal (Granholm, 1991). Of course, because of potential lawsuits for unfair dismissals, few managers feel free to fire at will. Thus, in actual practice, the list of possible reasons for immediate dismissal is still somewhat limited. In addition to those mentioned already, the list often includes behaviors like gross insubordination, perpetrating repeated or severe sexual harassment or bullying, or representing the organization in a negative manner—including in some cases posting negative information on social media (see Fired Over Facebook). The list of reasons for immediate dismissal is not always communicated explicitly to employees. In addition, because some of the reasons for dismissal are ambiguous, such as gross insubordination, it is often not clear-cut when an immediate dismissal is appropriate.

Progressive Discipline

Employees who do not meet the criteria for immediate dismissal likely go through a process known as progressive discipline. Progressive discipline focuses on managing employees who are ineffective in their jobs and need to either improve significantly or be dismissed. Progressive discipline generally involves three important communication

Fired Over Facebook

Professor Loril Gossett (2013) described a case in which a restaurant server in North Carolina was terminated for complaining on her Facebook page about a customer who left a small tip after occupying a table for several hours. The restaurant was monitoring social media sites as a means of managing its public image. Once the post was discovered by management, the server was terminated. Does it surprise you that approximately 10% of U.S. companies monitor social networking sites (American Management Association, 2008)? Is it ethical for organizations to monitor their employees' social media usage and fire them for a message because management does not like or approve of it?

activities or events: a problem-solving breakpoint, an elimination breakpoint, and a dismissal meeting (Cox & Kramer, 1995; Fairhurst, Green, & Snavely, 1984).

The *problem-solving breakpoint* refers to the decision made by a manager that a subordinate's poor performance requires remediation or improvement. This decision can be a challenging one for a manager to reach. The manager involved believed at the time of the hiring that a specific employee had the requisite P-J or P-O and was optimistic that the individual would be able to do the job effectively. However, at some point, despite a sufficient period of time for improvement, the manager becomes aware that the individual's performance continues to fail to meet the standards for employment in the organization. This decision could be due to a variety of factors from absenteeism, to unprofessional conduct and communication patterns, to a lack of skill to perform the job competently. The problem-solving breakpoint occurs when a manager admits that the employee has a problem that needs to be addressed (Fairhurst et al., 1984).

The supervisor–employee relationship changes after the problem-solving breakpoint. The manager communicates the need to improve and directs or monitors the employee more closely by providing specific goals that must be met in a certain time frame (Fairhurst et al., 1984). Additional training may be given to enable the employee to meet the goals. The manager is willing to make these efforts to retain the employee because of the high cost involved in hiring and training a new employee. If these efforts to improve the employee's work are successful, the manager saves the organization

The EAGR Approach to Giving Corrective Feedback

The EAGR approach is a common technique used by managers for communicating a downward remediation plan. The technique has many variants and can be easily documented to produce evidence that improvements are, or are not, happening. In the technique, a supervisor "Explains" the situation that needs to be remedied as factually as possible with reference to specific behaviors (e.g., "I noticed you were late returning from lunch 15 minutes Wednesday, 10 minutes Thursday, and 20 minutes today"). Then, the supervisor "Asks" the subordinate how he or she intends to correct the problem. Excuses (legitimate or otherwise) are common at this point. The supervisor then "Gets" commitment to a timeline for the behavior to improve (e.g., "So, next Friday, when we speak again, you will have been on time returning from lunch everyday next week?"). Finally, the supervisor will "Revisit" at the agreed on time (e.g., Last time we talked you said you were going to be punctual returning from lunch all week. I see that you did that. Thank you."). Can you think of a different performance problem and craft your own EAGR feedback?

money and time by retaining the employee. Typically, the manager not only communicates specific goals at this time but also begins documenting any failures of the employee to meet those goals in the employee's file. If the efforts are not successful, a second breakpoint occurs.

The *termination breakpoint* occurs when the supervisor decides the employee should no longer be retained. The cost of retaining the employee is too high, and alternatives seem more positive. Often, the termination breakpoint will be followed by gathering documentation that can be used to defend the termination decision to executives and peers. Again, the supervisor–subordinate relationship changes in the wake of this decision. Attribution theory provides a framework for understanding this change. According to attribution theory, when we evaluate a person's performance, we attribute the cause of the person's behaviors to either internal traits and personal disposition or to external and situational circumstances beyond the person's control

(Feldman, 1981). If a subordinate's performance is *similar* to the performance of others in the same situation, managers tend to attribute the performance to *external* factors; when a subordinate's performance is *different* than others, managers attribute the performance to *internal* characteristics of the individual. During the problem-solving breakpoint, the supervisor is still attributing the poor performance issue to situational factors that can be remedied. By controlling the situation carefully and perhaps providing additional training, the hope is that the individual's performance will improve. At the termination breakpoint, the supervisor no longer believes that the problem is situational. Rather, the conclusion is that the problem is within the individual and unfixable.

With the change in attribution for the poor performance, progressive discipline proceeds with careful documentation of every major and minor performance issue. The goal is to accumulate enough evidence of the employee's failure to meet goals to dismiss the employee with cause. The supervisor likely makes the employee aware that the records are being made so that the employee cannot claim to be surprised when they are called into a dismissal meeting.

The *dismissal meeting* is the formal meeting when the individual's employment is officially terminated. When progressive discipline has occurred for weeks or months, these dismissal meetings are often not actually needed. Progressive discipline tends to make employees quite aware that they are being scrutinized and that documentation of their poor performance is accumulating. That awareness often motivates employees experiencing progressive discipline to look for other work and resign. This resignation gives the appearance of being "voluntarily," but it is clear that the employee is saving face by avoiding being fired.

Popular books provide advice for conducting dismissal meetings (e.g., Granholm, 1991). They suggest holding the meeting in a private setting; having at least two people present in addition to the employee so that there is a witness to what occurs; being even-tempered and professional throughout; and of course, having all relevant documentation that has accumulated. Some managers even suggest certain days and times of the week to hold these meetings, although the advice is not always consistent. The dismissal meeting usually includes a number of steps (Cox & Kramer, 1995). The first part of the meeting usually involves asking the employee about his or her performance and then presenting documentation of poor performance if the employee fails to acknowledge performance problems. The employee may then attempt to defend his or her record, or, in other cases, resign, thereby making the rest of the meeting unnecessary. Again, resigning before being fired allows the employee to save face in the situation. The second half of the meeting involves communicating more specifically the exact reasons for the dismissal and when employment will be terminated. The remainder of the meeting involves topics like final paychecks and other logistics like returning keys or losing access to computers. Sometimes the supervisor offers advice for doing better in future jobs. Oddly enough, there may even be a discussion about whether the employee can use the workplace as a reference. If the progressive discipline and documentation has been ongoing, the employee should not be surprised. Still, emotions can run high at the dismissal meeting because the employee's goals have been interrupted and the employee's identity is likely threatened. The more important those goals and salient the work identity were, the more intense the emotion will be. It is not surprising that supervisors would prefer to avoid dismissing employees.

Although the focus of progressive discipline is on the employee being dismissed, it is important to recognize that other employees in the work setting are also affected by the situation. Other employees must make sense of the situation throughout the process of progressive discipline (Cox & Kramer, 1995). For example, if there seem to be no consequences for poor performance, that communicates to the other employees a message about management's expectations and the amount of effort they need to put into their jobs. Dismissing a low-performing employee may influence other low performers or friends of the fired employee. Similar to the erosion model described previously, other low performers associated with the terminated employee may choose to leave rather than face similar sanctions. Other high-performing employees may take the firing as validation of their own work ethic. Because of its influence on other workgroup members, employee dismissals are really part of the ongoing changes for the other employees. Because it will be apparent to other employees that the dismissed employee is no longer working, they will attempt to make sense of the situation. Managers may provide sensegiving messages to assist them in interpreting the dismissal in a particular way. Frequently they are restricted in what they can say due to confidentiality issues, and so other employees develop their own explanations or rumors as they make sense of the dismissal.

In the cleaning company scenario, Kelly has been using progressive discipline with Jayden. After deciding that Jayden was a consistently poor performer (problem-solving breakpoint), Kelly tried to retrain Jayden and provided specific goals. After the third retraining session (termination breakpoint), Kelly focused on documenting Jayden's problems to accumulate evidence of a dismissal. Kelly no longer considered the problem a mere situational issue; it was clear to Kelly that the problem was Jayden. All that remained was the dismissal meeting, unless of course Jayden resigned prior to being let go.

A Third Form of Exit

Although the distinction between voluntary and involuntary exit seems quite clear, there is a third form of exit that blurs the distinction. In some situations, supervisors and peers focus attention on an underperforming employee with the intention of making the employee want to quit or leave rather than be terminated. Cox (1999) did an extensive study of the strategies that coworkers use to influence employees to leave. These strategies include subtle communication, such as speaking highly of job opportunities in other organizations or making the target employee aware of other job or career opportunities, as well as criticizing the current workplace to make it seem undesirable. Supervisors can use more overt strategies such as criticizing the work of the target employee directly or giving warnings or threatening to fire them. Other strategies that supervisors or peers can use involve making the workplace more intolerable. Supervisors can assign the target employee to extremely difficult or very boring tasks. They may reduce their hours or assign them to undesirable shifts. In the study, some peers withdrew support and no longer cooperated or helped their peer. Some peers even committed malicious acts to sabotage the target employee's work, such as deliberately soiling an area that the employee had just cleaned so that it had to be done again. All of these strategies seem designed to demonstrate to the target employee that the cost–benefit ratio of staying is too high so that the employee should leave of his or her own accord.

Managers provided explanations for this practice of creating a negative work environment so the employee leaves (Cox & Kramer, 1995). Most of the explanations had to do with saving money and effort. If the employee leaves quickly, there is no need to put in the efforts that go into progressive discipline. It eliminates the dismissal meeting as well, which is a generally unpleasant experience. The problem with this approach is that the target employee could level charges of bullying or harassment and likely have some evidence to support such a lawsuit. In other cases, if they have no alternatives, they may continue in the job despite the hints and negative work environment. Like employees who quit during progressive discipline, these encouraged or induced kinds of employee exits blur the line between voluntary and involuntary exit. On any official statistics, it will appear to be a voluntary exit. In reality, it hardly seems voluntary.

Exit and Volunteers

Volunteers leave organizations routinely and at a much higher rate than employees. The average turnover rate for employees is 3% to 4% annually (Bureau of Labor Statistics, 2014a). Turnover rates for volunteers are about 10 times higher, with average rates between 20% and 40% in recent years (Corporation for National and Community Service, 2014). That means that volunteer coordinators are busy recruiting a quarter to a third of their volunteers each year.

It is rare that a volunteer is "asked to quit." Of course, if volunteers violate organizational policy or break the law, they will no longer be allowed to volunteer. But it is much rarer for volunteers who lack competence at carrying out their responsibilities to be asked to leave, although it can and does happen. Michael Kramer has been a volunteer member of a number of different community choirs. In one case, a poor singer was surrounded by stronger singers with the hope that this support would enable him to sing better or at least not be heard when he made mistakes rather than ask him to quit. In a smaller community choir, a singer who insisted on singing incorrectly and loudly was finally asked to leave because he was so disruptive to his section. Of course, asking a poor performing volunteer to quit is rare.

Volunteers are much more likely to leave voluntarily. They leave for many of the same reasons that employees leave. The most common reason for leaving is likely due to life events. Changes at work, with the family, or even changes with another voluntary activity can motivate volunteers to quit. However, when volunteers quit, it is not necessarily permanent. Whereas employees generally do not quit and later return (although this does happen with summer jobs and seasonal work), it is not uncommon for volunteers to take temporary leaves due to life circumstances (Kramer, 2011a). An individual may volunteer periodically for years with the same organization.

In other cases, volunteers exit because they experience a shock. For example, if the leader of the nonprofit organization commits some unethical or illegal action or violates the values of the organization, volunteers often move to other organizations. They also can become dissatisfied with the organization over time and quit or move to another volunteer organization. Similarly, other volunteers move from one organization to another when they become dissatisfied.

Regardless of whether they are leaving permanently or temporarily, volunteers may notify the organizational leaders of their intentions or they may simply quit arriving to work. This pattern often makes it difficult for the organization to have an accurate record of active volunteers (Kramer, 2011a). Of course, given the low cost of leaving someone on the volunteer email list, there is less incentive to keep an accurate list now than there was when it cost money to mail information to them. At no real cost, the organization can continue to communicate its activities to inactive volunteers and perhaps they will return as volunteers at some later date.

Summary

In this chapter, we explored two types of exit based on SET principles. Voluntary exit occurs for one of three reasons: *planned exits*, such as finishing a degree; *shocks*, which cause individuals to reevaluate the cost–benefit ratio of continuing in the organization; or *gradual disenchantment* where the costs of continuing are outweighed by the benefits of continuing over time. The availability of alternatives also influences these decisions. There is often a process of a preannouncement phase, announcement phase, and exit phase as the person makes the decision to leave, communicates it to others, and finally leaves. For volunteers, exit is almost always voluntary.

Involuntary exit occurs when the managers of the organization determine that the cost–benefit ratio of retaining an employee is too high. At the problem-solving breakpoint, managers have determined that the employee is problematic but may still be able to be retained and so may offer additional training. At the termination breakpoint, managers focus on keeping records to justify dismissal of the employee. When sufficient evidence is collected, the managers call a dismissal meeting. In many instances, the employee resigns before formally being dismissed.

In a third type of exit, the supervisors and peers of underperforming employees work to change the cost–benefit ratio for the employees so that they resign on their own. They can facilitate this kind of exit by a variety of strategies from seemingly supportive suggestions that they would be happier somewhere else to very negative activities such as sabotaging their work. In these cases, it is difficult to classify the exit as voluntary or involuntary.

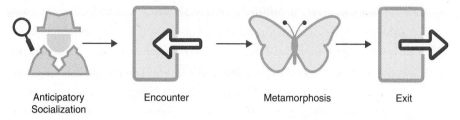

| Anticipatory Socialization | Encounter | Metamorphosis | Exit |

Figure 15.1. An Assimilation Model of Organizational Communication

Epilogue

In Chapter 1, we explained that this book takes a lifespan perspective on organizational communication because it explores how people participate in organizations from early in life until after retirement. We presented a preview of the textbook based on the assimilation model, which is repeated here (see Figure 15.1). Now we would like to review what we have presented and include some final thoughts.

In Chapter 2, we examined anticipatory socialization. This included anticipatory role socialization and anticipatory organizational socialization. We hope that at this point you can see that both of these processes continue throughout your life. Although you may select a career while finishing your formal education, you will continue to develop and change your work and volunteer roles throughout your life. Sometimes the changes will be dramatic, such as when you make a career change. Sometimes they will seem small, such as when you decide to volunteer for a new community group that becomes important to you.

In Chapter 3, we examined the newcomer experience of joining an organization. This encounter experience is going to be one you repeat numerous times throughout your life when you enter a new job, change careers, move to a new city, or begin volunteering in a new organization. Because of your previous organizational experiences, you will likely experience less uncertainty than you did in your first full-time job or first volunteer role, but you will still need to manage uncertainty when joining a new organization.

During your time in various organizations, the topics we covered in Chapters 4 through 14 will be part of your experience. You will experience some management theory from organizational leaders (Chapter 4). You will deal with the formal and informal communication channels and become part of the communication network as you manage your uncertainty and make sense of your experience (Chapter 5). You will learn the organizational culture, including its subcultures and ambiguities as revealed through artifacts, rituals, and stories (Chapter 6). You will develop communication relationships with supervisors, peers, and mentors (Chapter 7). In some organizations, you will take on managerial leadership roles, and either you will respond to organizational leaders or perhaps become one (Chapter 8). You will become involved in decision making and at times act very rationally and at other times perhaps accidentally discover a good solution (Chapter 9). You will manage task and relational conflicts and hopefully not be a victim of sexual harassment or bullying (Chapter 10). You will be aware of power issues in the organization (Chapter 11) and decide whether to participate with it (hegemonic participation) or resist it through your voice. Throughout your life, you will try to balance work, life, and volunteer roles, perhaps as a segmenter or an integrator (Chapter 12).

Your experience in the organization will be fluid and punctuated with transitions. The organization will face changes from the external system including a changing workforce, new technology, and the effects of globalization (Chapter 13). Some people will embrace the changes (early adopters), whereas others will resist it and mourn the loss of the old way of doing things. You will experience a variety of transitions (Chapter 14). These will likely include individual career changes, such as being promoted; or, if you are a member of a large organization, you may experience a national or international transfer. Your organization may merge with another or you may experience layoffs in troubled economic times.

You will exit numerous work and volunteer organizations over the years (Chapter 15). Hopefully, most of those exits will be voluntary as you change companies and careers or reassess your voluntary activities. If you become a supervisor, you may be involved in dismissing employees. If you reach the average life expectancy, you will most likely retire at some point, but you will likely continue to participate in organizations on a voluntary basis.

A Dark Side of Organizational Membership

When considering organizational membership, it is common to think of the positives associated with belonging to an organization. Through organizational membership we achieve personal and career goals and develop social relationships. However, when we say someone "drank the Kool-Aid," we recognize that being a part of an organization can have a dark side. The phrase refers to how the members of the People's Temple committed mass suicide by drinking arsenic laced Kool-Aid at the direction of their leader

Jim Jones in 1978. This, and other examples like it, demonstrate that people can become so identified with their organization that they commit violence to themselves and others that they would normally not consider. World War II demonstrated this same kind of problem at the societal level in Germany.

Cushman (1986) explored how organizations are able to socialize individuals to these extreme levels. For example, in extremist organizations, leadership prohibits recruits from communicating with outsiders who offer alternative perspectives. They create a mystical aura about their beliefs, and members often deify their leaders. They use the affiliation needs of recruits or members as a powerful resource by threatening to withhold membership unless they adopt the organization's entire belief system. Then, by having those members recruit new members, they reinforce the belief system.

Although it is unlikely that readers of this book will become so indoctrinated into some organization or group that they will "drink the Kool-Aid" to the point of suicide, many of the examples of groupthink (see Chapter 9) demonstrate how easily individuals can become swept into the values, beliefs, and practices of an organization so that they make poor decisions. Most of the issues affecting organizational members are far less life-threatening. For example, union members rarely question "Buy American" campaigns. Professors rarely consider the merits of tenure. Members of organizations with strong ideological commitments rarely question the assumptions behind their views. These examples suggest that the dark side of organizational membership is a matter of degree rather than an either/or situation.

Socialization and Individualization

As introduced in Chapter 1, organizational membership is a tension between socialization and individualization (Jablin, 2001). Socialization describes the efforts of organizational leaders to get members to adapt to its needs. Individualization describes the efforts of individuals to get organizations to adapt to their needs. A common criticism of organizational scholarship is that it demonstrates a managerial bias or a focus on socialization and the goals of the organizational leaders to the exclusion of individualization. At times, we probably are guilty of the same bias throughout the pages of this book.

That said, we want to emphasize some of the ways that the ideas presented in the book provide insight into how people can individualize organizations to meet their needs. During the selection process, we can select organizations that meet our needs (good person and organization fit) to minimize the need for individualization (Chapter 2). By being content and role innovators, we can make changes to the organizational system so that it better meets our needs (Chapter 3). By making small changes in the organizational culture as it is created and recreated through structuration processes (Chapter 6), we can gradually change the culture in small ways so that it better serves us. Small changes could include having the organization adopt anti-bullying and anti-sexual harassment policies (Chapter 10). When we are in leadership roles, we can hire and promote members of underrepresented groups to help create a more inclusive culture (Chapter 13), or we can promote better work-life balance (Chapter 12).

In addition to these small or subtle changes that may gradually individualize the organization, we can practice voice and resistance. In the fall of 2015, the graduate students and the football players of the University of Missouri united to voice their dissatisfaction with the policies and leadership of the university. The end result of their efforts was a variety of changes designed to create a more inclusive setting. Using their resource power, they even helped oust the university president and chancellor. Similar protests affected changes in diversity and inclusion at other universities, such as the University of Oklahoma. Although not all organizational members have the resources

The University of Oklahoma football team held a silent protest instead of practicing in response to a video showing members of Sigma Alpha Epsilon reciting a racist chant.

to influence such major changes, most have more resources than they realize to create changes that can make their workplace adapt to their needs.

Conclusion

Right now, you are a member of at least one organization, the university offering this course. Most likely, you are a member of many other organizations, perhaps a workplace, a volunteer organization, a student group, and many others. You will be part of many more in the future. We hope that applying the concepts discussed in this book will provide insight and understanding as you manage those experiences.

REFERENCES

Akhtar, S., Ding, D. Z., & Ge, G. (2008). Strategic HRM practices and their impact on company performances in Chinese enterprises. *Human Resource Management, 47,* 15–32.

Albrecht, T. L., & Hall, B. J. (1991). Facilitating talk about new ideas: The role of personal relationships in organizational innovation. *Communication Monographs, 58,* 273–288. doi:10.1080/03637759109376230

Albrecht, T. L., & Ropp, V. A. (1982). The study of network structuring in organizations through the use of method triangulation. *Western Journal of Speech Communication, 46,* 162–178. doi:10.1080/10570318209374075

Allen, N. J., & Hecht, T. D. (2004). The 'romance of teams': Toward an understanding of its psychological underpinnings and implications. *Journal of Occupational and Organizational Psychology, 77,* 439–461. doi:10.1348/0963179042596469

Allen, T. J. (1970). Communication networks in R & D laboratories. *R&D Management, 1,* 14–21. doi:10.1111/j.1467-9310.1970.tb01193.x

American Management Association. (2008). The latest on workplace monitoring and surveillance. Retrieved from http://www.amanet.org/training/articles/The-Latest-on-Workplace-Monitoring-and-Surveillance.aspx.

Ancona, D. G., & Caldwell, D. F. (1992). Bridging the boundary: External activity and performance in organizational teams. *Administrative Science Quarterly, 37,* 634–665. doi:10.2307/2393475

Arnesen, D. W., & Weis, W. L. (2007). Developing an effective company policy for employee Internet and email use. *Journal of Organizational Culture, Communication and Conflict, 11,* 53–65.

Ash, M. K. (2008). *The Mary Kay way: Timeless principles from America's greatest woman entrepreneur.* Hoboken, NJ: John Wiley & Sons.

Ashcraft, K. L. (2014). Feminist theory. In L. L. Putnam & D. K. Mumby (Eds.), *The Sage handbook of organizational communication* (pp. 127–150). Thousand Oaks, CA: Sage.

Ashcraft, K. L., & Kedrowicz, A. (2002). Self-direction or social support? Nonprofit empowerment and the tacit employment contract of organizational communication studies. *Communication Monographs, 69,* 88–110. doi:10.1080/03637750216538

Ashford, S. J., & Black, J. S. (1996). Proactivity during organizational entry: The role of desire for control. *Journal of Applied Psychology, 81,* 199–214.

Ashforth, B. E., Kreiner, G. E., & Fugate, M. (2000). All in a day's work: Boundaries and micro role transitions. *Academy of Management Review, 25,* 472–491. doi:10.5465/amr.2000.3363315

Ashforth, B. E., & Mael, F. (1989). Social identity theory and the organization. *Academy of Management Review, 14,* 20–39. doi:10.5465/amr.1989.4278999

Ashforth, B. E., & Saks, A. M. (1996). Socialization tactics: Longitudinal effects on newcomer adjustment. *Academy of Management Journal, 39,* 149–178. Retrieved from http://www.jstor.org/stable/256634

Avery, C. M., & Jablin, F. M. (1988). Retirement preparation programs and organizational communication. *Communication Education, 37,* 68–80. doi:10.1080/03634528809378704

Bachrach, P., & Baratz, M. S. (1962). Two faces of power. *American Political Science Review, 56,* 947–952.

Bailyn, L., Fletcher, J. K., & Kolb, D. (1997). Unexpected connections: Considering employees' personal lives can revitalize your business. *Sloan Management Review, 38,* 11–19.

Bain, P., & Taylor, P. (2000). Entrapped by the 'electronic panopticon'? Worker resistance in the call centre. *New Technology, Work and Employment, 15,* 2–18. doi:10.1111/1468-005X.00061

Baldwin, J. R., & Hunt, S. K. (2002). Information-seeking behavior in intercultural and intergroup communication. *Human Communication Research, 28,* 272–286. doi:10.1111/j.1468-2958.2002.tb00808.x

Bales, R. F., & Strodtbeck, F. L. (1951). Phases in group problem-solving. *The Journal of Abnormal and Social Psychology, 46,* 485–495. doi:10.1037/h0059886

Ballinger, G. A., & Schoorman, F. D. (2007). Individual reactions to leadership succession in workgroups. *Academy of Management Review, 32,* 118–136. doi:10.5465/amr.2007.23463887

Barker, J. R. (1993). Tightening the iron cage: Concertive control in self-managing teams. *Administrative Science Quarterly, 38,* 408–437.

Barnett, K. (2012). Student interns' socially constructed work realities: Narrowing the work expectation-reality gap. *Business Communication Quarterly.* doi:10.1177/1080569912441360

Bass, B. M. (1990). From transactional to transformational leadership: Learning to share the vision. *Organizational Dynamics, 18,* 19–31. Retrieved from http://dx.doi.org/10.1016/0090-2616(90)90061-S

Bastien, D. T. (1992). Change in organizational culture. *Management Communication Quarterly, 5,* 403–442. doi:10.1177/0893318992005004002

Baxter, L. A., & Montgomery, B. M. (1996). *Relating: Dialogues and dialectics.* New York, NY: Guilford Press.

Behfar, K. J., Mannix, E. A., Peterson, R. S., & Trochim, W. M. (2011). Conflict in small groups: The meaning and consequences of process conflict. *Small Group Research, 42,* 127–176. doi:10.1177/1046496410389194

Belschak, F. D., & Den Hartog, D. N. (2009). Consequences of positive and negative feedback: The impact on emotions and extra-role behaviors. *Applied Psychology, 58,* 274–303. doi:10.1111/j.1464-0597.2008.00336.x

Bennis, W. (2009). *On becoming a leaders: The leadership classic revised and updated.* New York, NY: Basic Books.

Bennis, W., & Nanus, B. (2007). *Leaders: Strategies for taking charge.* New York, NY: HarperCollins.

Bennis, W. G., & Shepard, H. A. (1956). A theory of group development. *Human Relations, 9,* 415–437. doi:10.1177/001872675600900403

Berger, C. R., & Calabrese, R. J. (1975). Some explorations in initial interaction and beyond: Toward a developmental theory of interpersonal communication. *Human Communication Research, 1,* 99–112. doi:10.1111/j.1468-2958.1975.tb00258.x

Bertalanffy, L. von (1968). *General system theory: Foundations, development, application.* New York, NY: George Braziller.

Bisel, R. S., & Arterburn, E. N. (2012). Making sense of organizational members' silence: A sensemaking-resource model. *Communication Research Reports, 29,* 217–226. doi:10.1080/08824096.2012.684985

Bisel, R. S., & Barge, J. K. (2011). Discursive positioning and planned change in organizations. *Human Relations, 64,* 257–283. doi:10.1177/0018726710375996

Bisel, R. S., Messersmith, A. S., & Kelley, K. M. (2012). Supervisor-subordinate communication: Hierarchical mum effect meets organizational learning. *Journal of Business Communication, 49,* 128–147. doi:10.1177/0021943612436972

Bisel, R. S., Messersmith, A. S., & Keyton, J. (2010). Understanding organizational culture and communication through a gyroscope metaphor. *Journal of Management Education, 34,* 342–366. doi:10.1177/1052562909340879

Black, J. S., & Mendenhall, M. (1990). Cross-cultural training effectiveness: A review and a theoretical framework for future research. *Academy of Management Review, 15,* 113–136. doi:10.5465/amr.1990.11591834

Black, J. S., Mendenhall, M. E., & Oddou, G. (1991). Toward a comprehensive model of international adjustment: An integration of multiple theoretical perspectives. *Academy of Management Review, 16,* 291–317. doi:10.5465/amr.1991.4278938

Blake, R. R., & Mouton, J. S. (1964). *The managerial grid.* Houston, TX: Gulf.

Bolino, M. C. (2007). Expatriate assignments and intra-organizational career success: Implications for individuals and organizations. *Journal of International Business Studies, 38,* 819–835.

Bordia, P., Jones, E., Gallois, C., Callan, V. J., & DiFonzo, N. (2006). Management are aliens! Rumors and stress during organizational change. *Group & Organization Management, 31,* 601–621.

Bormann, E. G., & Bormann, N. C. (1988). *Effective small group communication* (4th ed.). Minneapolis, MN: Gordon Press.

Botero, I. C., Fediuk, T. A., & Sies, K. M. (2013). When volunteering is no longer voluntary: Assessing the impact of student forced volunteerism on future intentions to volunteer. In M. W. Kramer, L. K. Lewis, & L. M. Gossett (Eds.), *Volunteering and communication: Studies from multiple contexts* (pp. 289–310). New York, NY: Peter Lang.

Boyd, N. G., & Taylor, R. R. (1998). A developmental approach to the examination of friendship in leader-follower relationships. *The Leadership Quarterly, 9,* 1–25. Retrieved from http://dx.doi.org/10.1016/S1048-9843(98)90040-6

Breaugh, J. A., & Starke, M. (2000). Research on employee recruitment: So many studies, so many remaining questions. *Journal of Management, 26,* 405–434. doi:10.1177/014920630002600303

Brett, J. M. (1982). Job transfer and well-being. *Journal of Applied Psychology, 67,* 450–463. doi:10.1037/0021-9010.67.4.450

Brett, J. M., Stroh, L. K., & Reilly, A. H. (1993). Pulling up roots in the 1990s: Who's willing to relocate? *Journal of Organizational Behavior, 14,* 49–60. doi:10.1002/job.4030140106

Brett, J. M., & Werbel, J. D. (1980). *The effect of job transfer on employees and their families.* Washington, DC: Employee Relocation Council.

Brockner, J., Grover, S., O'Malley, M. N., Reed, T. F., & Glynn, M. A. (1993). Threat of future layoffs, self-esteem, and survivors' reactions: Evidence from the laboratory and the field. *Strategic Management Journal, 14,* 153–166.

Brown, T. M., & Miller, C. E. (2000). Communication networks in task-performing groups: Effects of task complexity, time pressure, and interpersonal dominance. *Small Group Research, 31,* 131–157. doi:10.1177/104649640003100201

Brummer, J. J. (1991). *Corporate responsibility and legitimacy: An interdisciplinary analysis.* Westport, CT: Greenwood Press.

Buono, A. F., & Bowditch, J. L. (1989). The human side of mergers and acquisitions. Managing collisions between people, cultures, and organizations. San Francisco, CA: Jossey-Bass Publishers.

Bureau of Labor Statistics. (2011). *Current Population Survey, September 2010: Volunteer Supplement.* Inter-university Consortium for Political and Social Research (ICPSR) [distributor]. Retrieved from http://dx.doi.org/10.3886/ICPSR31861.v1

Bureau of Labor Statistics. (2014a). *Job openings and labor turnover survey.* Washington, DC: Government Printing Office. Retrieved from http://www.bls.gov/jlt/.

Bureau of Labor Statistics. (2014b). *Number of jobs held, labor market activity, and earnings growth among the youngest baby boomers: Results from a longitudinal survey.* Washington, DC: Government Printing Office. Retrieved from http://www.bls.gov/nls/79r25jobsbyedu.xlsx

Bureau of Labor Statistics. (2014c). *Volunteering in the United States, 2013.* Washington, DC: Government Printing Office. Retrieved from http://www.bls.gov/news.release/volun.nr0.htm

Caldwell, D. F., & O'Reilly, C. A. (1990). Measuring person-job fit with a profile-comparison process. *Journal of Applied Psychology, 75,* 648–657. doi:10.1037/0021-9010.75.6.648

Campbell, E. Q. (1969). Adolescent socialization. In D. A. Goslin (Ed.), *Handbook of socialization theory and research* (pp. 821–859). Chicago, IL: Rand McNally.

Carlone, D. (2001). Enablement, constraint, and the 7 habits of highly effective people. *Management Communication Quarterly, 14,* 491–497. doi:10.1177/0893318901143007

Carraher, S. M., Sullivan, S. E., & Crocitto, M. M. (2008). Mentoring across global boundaries: An empirical examination of home- and host-country mentors on expatriate career outcomes. *Journal of International Business Studies, 39,* 1310–1326.

Carver, C. S., & Scheier, M. F. (1990). Origins and functions of positive and negative affect: A control-process view. *Psychological Review, 97,* 19–35. doi:10.1037/0033-295X.97.1.19

Casey, M. K., Miller, V. D., & Johnson, J. R. (1997). Survivors' information seeking following a reduction in workforce. *Communication Research, 24,* 755–781. doi:10.1177/0093650297024006007

Castor, T. R., & Jiter, M. J. (2013). Learning by the "seat of your pants": The socialization of nonprofit board members. In M. W. Kramer, L. K. Lewis, & L. M. Gossett (Eds.), *Volunteering and communication: Studies from multiple contexts* (pp. 87–106). New York, NY: Peter Lang.

Chansler, P. A., Swamidass, P. M., & Cammann, C. (2003). Self-managing work teams: An empirical study of group cohesiveness in "natural work groups" at a Harley-Davidson Motor Company plant. *Small Group Research, 34,* 101–120. doi:10.1177/1046496402239579

Chao, G. T., O'Leary-Kelly, A. M., Wolf, S., Klein, H. J., & Gardner, P. D. (1994). Organizational socialization: Its content and consequences. *Journal of Applied Psychology, 79,* 730–743. doi:10.1037/0021-9010.79.5.730

Cheney, G. (1983). On the various and changing meanings of organizational membership: A field study of organizational identification. *Communication Monographs, 50,* 342–362. doi:10.1080/03637758309390174

Cheney, G. (2000). Interpreting interpretive research: Toward perspectivism without relativism. In S. R. Corman & M. S. Poole (Eds.), *Perspectives on organizational communication: Finding common ground* (pp. 17–45). New York, NY: Guilford Press.

Cheney, G., & Christensen, L. T. (2001). Organizational identity: Linkages between internal and external communication. In F. M. Jablin & L. L. Putnam (Eds.), *The new handbook of organizational communication: Advances in theory, research, and methods* (pp. 231–269). Thousand Oaks, CA: Sage.

Chinn, J. N., & Barbour, J. B. (2013). Negotiating aging and agedness in volunteer disaster response teams. In M. W. Kramer, L. K. Lewis, & L. M. Gossett (Eds.), *Volunteering and communication: Studies from multiple contexts* (pp. 223–244). New York, NY: Peter Lang.

Clair, R. P. (1996). The political nature of the colloquialism, "a real job": Implications for organizational socialization. *Communication Monographs, 63,* 249–267. doi:10.1080/03637759609376392

Clary, E. G., & Snyder, M. (1999). The motivations to volunteer: Theoretical and practical considerations. *Current Directions in Psychological Science, 8,* 156–159.

Clary, E. G., Snyder, M., Ridge, R. D., Copeland, J., Stukas, A. A., Haugen, J., & Miene, P. (1998). Understanding and assessing the motivations of volunteers: A functional approach. *Journal of Personality and Social Psychology, 74,* 1516–1530. doi:10.1037/0022-3514.74.6.1516

Cohen, M. D., March, J. G., & Olsen, J. P. (1972). A garbage can model of organizational choice. *Administrative Science Quarterly, 17,* 1–25. doi:10.2307/2392088

Comer, D. R. (1991). Organizational newcomers' acquisition of information from peers. *Management Communication Quarterly, 5,* 64–89. doi:10.1177/0893318991005001004

Connolly, T. (1980). Uncertainty, action, and competence: Some alternatives to omniscience in complex problem-solving. In S. Fiddle (Ed.), *Uncertainty: Behavioral and social dimensions* (pp. 69–91). New York, NY: Praeger.

Conrad, C. (1991). Communication in conflict: Style-strategy relationships. *Communication Monographs, 58,* 135–155. doi:10.1080/03637759109376219

Conrad, C. (2011). *Organizational rhetoric.* Malden, MA: Polity Press.

Conrad, C., & Haynes, J. (2001). Development of key constructs. In F. M. Jablin & L. L. Putnam (Eds.), *The new handbook of organizational communication: Advances in theory, research, and methods* (pp. 47–77). Thousand Oaks, CA: Sage.

Contu, A. (2008). Decaf resistance: On misbehavior, cynicism, and desire in liberal workplaces. *Management Communication Quarterly, 21,* 364–379. doi:10.1177/0893318907310941

Corman, S. R. (2000). The need for common ground. In S. R. Corman & M. S. Poole (Eds.), *Perspectives on organizational communication* (pp. 3–13). New York, NY: Guilford Press.

Cornett-DeVito, M. M., & Friedman, P. G. (1995). Communication processes and merger success an exploratory study of four financial institution mergers. *Management Communication Quarterly, 9,* 46–77.

Corporation for National and Community Service. (2014). *Volunteer retention rates—states.* Washington, DC: Author. Retrieved from https://www.volunteeringinamerica.gov/rankings/States/Volunteer-Retention-Rates/2014

Coverdill, J., & Finlay, W. (1998). Fit and skill in employee selection: Insights from a study of headhunters. *Qualitative Sociology, 21,* 105–127. doi:10.1023/A:1023464326912

Covey, S. R. (1989). *The 7 habits of highly effective people.* New York, NY: Simon & Schuster.

Cox, S. A. (1999). Group communication and employee turnover: How coworkers encourage peers to voluntarily exit. *Southern Communication Journal, 64,* 181–192. doi:10.1080/10417949909373133

Cox, S. A., & Kramer, M. W. (1995). Communication during employee dismissals. *Management Communication Quarterly, 9,* 156–190. doi:10.1177/0893318995009002002

Craig, B. J., & Russo, T. (2015). Implications for constructing the "servicable other": Desired and actual outcomes of Rotary's international service projects. In M. W. Kramer, L. K. Lewis, & L. M. Gossett (Eds.), *Volunteering and communication volume 2: Studies in international and intercultural contexts* (pp. 213–231). New York, NY: Peter Lang.

Crampton, S. M., Hodge, J. W., & Mishra, J. M. (1998). The informal communication network: Factors influencing grapevine activity. *Public Personnel Management, 27,* 569–584.

Creswell, J. W. (2007). *Qualitative inquiry & research design: Choosing among five approaches* (2nd ed.). Thousand Oaks, CA: Sage.

Cushman, P. (1986). The self-besieged: Recruitment-indoctrination processes in restrictive groups. *Journal for the Theory of Social Behaviour, 16,* 1–32.

Daft, R. L., & Lengel, R. H. (1984). Information richness: A new approach to managerial information processing and organizational design. *Research in Organizational Behavior, 6,* 199–233.

Daft, R. L., & Lengel, R. H. (1986). Organizational information requirements, media richness and structural design. *Management Science, 32,* 554–571. doi:10.1287/mnsc.32.5.554

Dahl, R. A. (1957). The concept of power. *Behavioral Science, 2,* 201–215.

Dansereau, F., Graen, G., & Haga, W. J. (1975). A vertical dyad linkage approach to leadership within formal organizations: A longitudinal investigation of the role making process. *Organizational Behavior and Human Performance, 13,* 46–78. Retrieved from http://dx.doi.org/10.1016/0030-5073(75)90005-7

Davis, K. (1968). Success of chain-of-command oral communication in a manufacturing management group. *Academy of Management Journal, 11,* 379–387. doi:10.2307/254887

Deal, T. E. (1985). Cultural change: Opportunities, silent killer, or metamorphosis? In R. Kilmann, M. Saxton, & R. Serpa (Eds.), *Gaining control of corporate culture* (pp. 292–331). San Francisco, CA: Jossey-Bass.

Deal, T. E., & Kennedy, A. A. (1982). *Corporate cultures: The rites and rituals of corporate life.* Reading, MA: Addison-Wesley.

Deetz, S. A. (1992). *Democracy in the age of corporate colonization: Developments in communication and the politics of everyday life.* Albany, NY: State University of New York Press.

Deetz, S. A. (2001). Conceptual foundations. In F. M. Jablin & L. L. Putnam (Eds.), *The new handbook of organizational communication: Advances in theory, research, and methods* (pp. 3–46). Thousand Oaks, CA: Sage.

Deetz, S. A. (2008). Resistance: Would struggle by any other name be as sweet? *Management Communication Quarterly, 21,* 387–392. doi:10.1177/0893318907310943

Delery, J. E., & Doty, D. H. (1996). Modes of theorizing in strategic human resource management: Tests of universalistic, contingency, and configurations performance predictors. *Academy of Management Journal, 39,* 802–835. doi:10.2307/256713

Detert, J. R., & Burris, E. R. (2007). Leadership behavior and employee voice: Is the door really open? *Academy of Management Journal, 50,* 869–884. doi:10.5465/amj.2007.26279183

Dewey, J. (1910). *How we think.* Boston, MA: D.C. Heath.

Diehl, M., & Stroebe, W. (1987). Productivity loss in brainstorming groups: Toward the solution of a riddle. *Journal of Personality and Social Psychology, 53,* 497–509. doi:10.1037/0022-3514.53.3.497

DiFonzo, N., & Bordia, P. (1998). A tale of two corporations: Managing uncertainty during organizational change. *Human Resource Management, 37,* 295–303. doi:10.1002/(sici)1099-050x (199823/24)37:3/4<295::aid-hrm10>3.0.co;2-3

Dougherty, D. S. (2000). Women's discursive construction of a sexual harassment paradox. *Qualitative Research Reports, 2,* 6–13.

Dougherty, D. S. (2009). Sexual harassment as destructive organizational process. In P. Lutgen-Sandvik & B. Davenport-Sypher (Eds.), *Destructive organizational communication: Processes, consequences, and constructive ways of organizing* (pp. 203–225). New York, NY: Routledge.

Dougherty, D. S., & Kramer, M. W. (2005). Organizational power and the Institutional Review Board. *Journal of Applied Communication Research, 33,* 277–284. doi:10.1080/00909880500149494

Dougherty, D. S., Kramer, M. W., Klatzke, S. R., & Rogers, T. K. (2009). Language convergence and meaning divergence: A meaning centered communication theory. *Communication Monographs, 76,* 20–46. doi:10.1080/03637750802378799

Dougherty, D. S., & Smythe, M. J. (2004). Sensemaking, organizational culture, and sexual harassment. *Journal of Applied Communication Research, 32,* 293–317. doi:10.1080/0090988042000275998

Dow, B. J. (2008). Does it take a department to raise a child? *Women's Studies in Communication, 31,* 158–165. doi:10.1080/07491409.2008.10162528

Downs, C. W., Johnson, K., & Barge, J. (1984). Communication feedback and task performance in organizations: A review of the literature. *Organizational Communication Abstracts, 9,* 13–47.

Drago, R. W. (2007). *Striking a balance: Work, family, life.* Boston, MA: Dollars & Sense.

Drory, A., & Gluskinos, U. M. (1980). Machiavellianism and leadership. *Journal of Applied Psychology, 65,* 81.

Drumheller, K. (2004). *Vehicles for entertainment or for legitimacy crisis? Revisiting legitimacy and image restoration efforts after film depictions of organizational crises.* University of Missouri, Columbia, MO.

Edmunds, A., & Morris, A. (2000). The problem of information overload in business organisations: A review of the literature. *International Journal of Information Management, 20,* 17–28. Retrieved from http://dx.doi.org/10.1016/S0268-4012(99)00051-1

Edwards, R. C. (1981). The social relations of product at the point of production. In M. Zey-Ferrell & M. Aiken (Eds.), *Complex organizations: Critical perspectives* (pp. 156–182). Glenview, IL: Scott, Foresman.

Eisenberg, E. M. (1984). Ambiguity as strategy in organizational communication. *Communication Monographs, 51,* 227–242. doi:10.1080/03637758409390197

Emerson, R. M. (1962). Power-dependence relations. *American Sociological Review,* 31–41.

Engler-Parish, P. G., & Millar, F. E. (1989). An exploratory relational control analysis of the employment screening interview. *Western Journal of Speech Communication, 53,* 30–51. doi:10.1080/10570318909374288

Esser, J. K., & Lindoerfer, J. S. (1989). Groupthink and the space shuttle Challenger accident: Toward a quantitative case analysis. *Journal of Behavioral Decision Making, 2,* 167–177. doi:10.1002/bdm.3960020304

Fairhurst, G. T. (2005). Reframing the art of framing: Problems and prospects for leadership. *Leadership, 1,* 165–185. doi:10.1177/1742715005051857

Fairhurst, G. T. (2011a). Discursive approaches to leadership. In A. Bryman, D. Collinson, K. Grint, B. Jackson, & M. Uhl-Bien (Eds.), *The Sage handbook of leadership* (pp. 495–507). Thousand Oaks, CA: Sage.

Fairhurst, G. T. (2011b). *The power of framing: Creating the language of leadership.* San Francisco, CA: Jossey-Bass.

Fairhurst, G. T., & Chandler, T. A. (1989). Social structure in leader-member interaction. *Communication Monographs, 56,* 215–239. doi:10.1080/03637758909390261

Fairhurst, G. T., Green, S. G., & Snavely, B. K. (1984). Managerial control and discipline: Whips and chains. In R. N. Bostrom & B. H. Westley (Eds.), *Communication yearbook 8* (pp. 558–593). Beverly Hills, CA: Sage.

Fairhurst, G. T., & Sarr, R. A. (1996). *The art of framing: Managing the language of leadership.* San Francisco, CA: Jossey-Bass.

Fayol, H. (1949). *General and industrial management.* London: Sir Isaac Pitman & Sons.

Feeley, T. H., Hwang, J., & Barnett, G. A. (2008). Predicting employee turnover from friendship networks. *Journal of Applied Communication Research, 36,* 56–73. doi:10.1080/00909880701799790

Feeley, T. H., Moon, S.-I., Kozey, R. S., & Slowe, A. S. (2010). An erosion model of employee turnover based on network centrality. *Journal of Applied Communication Research, 38,* 167–188. doi:10.1080/00909881003639544

Feldman, D. C., & Bolino, M. C. (1999). The impact of on-site mentoring on expatriate socialization: A structural equation modelling approach. *International Journal of Human Resource Management, 10,* 54–71.

Feldman, J. M. (1981). Beyond attribution theory: Cognitive processes in performance appraisal. *Journal of Applied Psychology, 66,* 127.

Fiedler, F. E. (1967). *A theory of leadership effectiveness.* New York, NY: McGraw-Hill.

Fisher, B. A. (1970). Decision emergence: Phases in group decision-making. *Speech Monographs, 37,* 53–66. doi:10.1080/03637757009375649

Foa, U. G., & Foa, E. B. (1980). Resource theory: Interpersonal behavior as exchange. In K. J. Gergen, M. S. Greenberg, & R. H. Willis (Eds.), *Social exchange: Advances in theory and research* (pp. 77–94). New York: Plenum.

Forgas, J. P. (1998). On feeling good and getting your way: Mood effects on negotiator cognition and bargaining strategies. *Journal of Personality and Social Psychology, 74,* 565–577. doi:10.1037/0022-3514.74.3.565

Foucault, M. (2000). Panopticism (Discipline and punish: The birth of the prison). In P. Rabinow (Ed.), *Foucault reader* (pp. 206–213). New York, NY: Pantheon Books.

Fraser, J. A. (2001). *White-collar sweatshop: The deterioration of work and its rewards in corporate America.* New York: Norton.

Frederick, K., & Mize-Smith, J. (2013). Making good: The identity and sensmaking of international mission volunteers. In M. W. Kramer, L. K. Lewis, & L. M. Gossett (Eds.),

Volunteering and communication volume 2: Studies in international and intercultural contexts (pp. 193–212). New York, NY: Peter Lang.

Freeborough, R., & Patterson, K. (2015). Exploring the effect of transformational leadership on nonprofit leader engagement. *Servant Leadership: Theory and Practice, 2,* 49–70.

French, J. R. P., & Raven, B. (1959). The bases of social power. In D. P. Carwright (Ed.), *Studies in social power* (pp. 150–167). Ann Arbor, MI: Institute for Social Research, University of Michigan.

Frone, M. R., Russell, M., & Cooper, M. L. (1992). Antecedents and outcomes of work-family conflict: Testing a model of the work-family interface. *Journal of Applied Psychology, 77,* 65–78. doi:10.1037/0021-9010.77.1.65

Frost, P. J. (1987). Power, politics, and influence. In F. M. Jablin, L. L. Putnam, K. H. Roberts, & L. W. Porter (Eds.), *Handbook of organizational communication* (pp. 503–548). Newbury Park, CA: Sage.

Frumkin, P. (2002). *On being nonprofit: A conceptual and policy primer.* Cambridge, MA: Harvard University Press.

Frye, N. K., & Breaugh, J. A. (2004). Family-friendly policies, supervisor support, work-family conflict, family-work conflict, and satisfaction: A test of a conceptual model. *Journal of Business and Psychology, 19,* 197–220.

Fulghum, R. (1986). *All I really need to know I learned in kindergarten.* New York, NY: Ballantine Books.

Gailliard, B. M., Myers, K. K., & Seibold, D. R. (2010). Organizational assimilation: A multidimensional reconceptualization and measure. *Management Communication Quarterly, 24,* 552–578. doi:10.1177/0893318910374933

Galanes, G. J. (2003). In their own words: An exploratory study of bona fide group leaders. *Small Group Research, 34,* 741–770. doi:10.1177/1046496403257649

Galanes, G. J. (2009). Dialectical tensions of small group leadership. *Communication Studies, 60,* 409–425. doi:10.1080/10510970903260228

Gallagher, E. B., & Sias, P. M. (2009). The new employee as a source of uncertainty: Veteran employee information seeking about new hires. *Western Journal of Communication, 73,* 23–46. doi:10.1080/10570310802636326

Garlick, R. (1994). Male and female responses to ambiguous instructor behaviors. *Sex Roles, 30,* 135–158. doi:10.1007/BF01420745

Geist, P., & Chandler, T. (1984). Account analysis of influence in group decision-making. *Communication Monographs, 51,* 67–78. doi:10.1080/03637758409390184

Gerbner, G. (1956). Toward a general model of communication. *Audiovisual Communication Review, 4,* 171–199. doi:10.1007/BF02717110

Gibson, M. K., & Papa, M. J. (2000). The mud, the blood, and the beer guys: Organizational osmosis in blue-collar work groups. *Journal of Applied Communication Research, 28,* 68–88. doi:10.1080/00909880009365554

Giddens, A. (1984). *The constitution of society*. Berkeley, CA: University of California Press.

Gilstrap, C. M., & White, Z. M. (2013). "Like nothing else I've ever experienced": Examining the metaphors of residential hospice volunteers. In M. W. Kramer, L. K. Lewis, & L. M. Gossett (Eds.), *Volunteering and communication: Studies in multiple contexts* (pp. 149–168). New York, NY: Peter Lang.

Gioia, D. A., & Chittipeddi, K. (1991). Sensemaking and sensegiving in strategic change initiation. *Strategic Management Journal, 12*, 433–448. doi:10.1002/smj.4250120604

Glaser, S. R. (1994). Teamwork and communication: A 3-year case study of change. *Management Communication Quarterly, 7*, 282–296. doi:10.1177/0893318994007003003

Goldberg, W. (1983). *Mergers: Motives, modes, methods*. New York, NY: Nichols.

Goodnow, J. J. (1988). Children's household work: Its nature and functions. *Psychological Bulletin, 103*, 5–26. doi:10.1037/0033-2909.103.1.5

Gorden, W. I. (1988). Range of employee voice. *Employee Responsibilities and Rights Journal, 1*, 283–299.

Gossett, L. M. (2013). Fired over Facebook: Issues of employee monitoring and personal privacy on social media websites. In S. K. May (Ed.), *Case studies in organizational communication: Ethical perspectives and practices* (2nd ed., pp. 207–217). Los Angeles, CA: Sage.

Gossett, L. M. (2015). An introduction to international and intercultural volunteering. In M. W. Kramer, L. K. Lewis, & L. M. Gossett (Eds.), *Volunteering and communication volume 2: Studies in international and intercultural contexts* (pp. 3–24). New York, NY: Peter Lang.

Gouran, D. S., Hirokawa, R. Y., & Martz, A. E. (1986). A critical analysis of factors related to decisional processes involved in the Challenger disaster. *Central States Speech Journal, 37*, 118–135. doi:10.1080/10510978609368212

Graen, G. B. (2003). Interpersonal workplace theory at the crossroads. In G. B. Graen (Ed.), *Dealing with diversity: LMX Leadership: The Series* (Vol. 1, pp. 145–182). Greenwich, CT: Information Age.

Graen, G. B., & Uhl-Bien, M. (1995). Relationship-based approach to leadership: Development of leader-member exchange (LMX) theory of leadership over 25 years: Applying a multi-level multi-domain perspective. *The Leadership Quarterly, 6*, 219–247. doi:org/10.1016/1048-9843(95)90036-5

Graham, C. R. (2003). A model of norm development for computer-mediated teamwork. *Small Group Research, 34*, 322–352. doi:10.1177/1046496403034003003

Gramsci, A. (1973). *Letters from prison*. New York, NY: Harper & Row.

Granholm, A. R. (1991). *Handbook of employee termination*. New York, NY: Wiley.

Granovetter, M. S. (1973). The strength of weak ties. *American Journal of Sociology, 78*, 1360–1380. doi:10.2307/2776392

Greenhalgh, L., & Jick, T. D. (1989). Survivor sense making and reactions to organizational decline: Effects of individual differences. *Management Communication Quarterly, 2*, 305–327. doi:10.1177/0893318989002003002

Greenhaus, J. H., & Beutell, N. J. (1985). Sources of conflict between work and family roles. *Academy of Management Review, 10,* 76–88. doi:10.5465/amr.1985.4277352

Greenhaus, J. H., & Kopelman, R. E. (1981). Conflict between work and nonwork roles: Implications for the career planning process. *Human Resource Planning, 4,* 1–10.

Griffeth, R. W., Hom, P. W., & Gaertner, S. (2000). A meta-analysis of antecedents and correlates of employee turnover: Update, moderator tests, and research implications for the next millennium. *Journal of Management, 26,* 463–488. doi:10.1177/014920630002600305

Griffin, R. W. (1988). Consequences of quality circles in an industrial setting: A longitudinal assessment. *Academy of Management Journal, 31,* 338–358. doi:10.2307/256551

Griffin, R. W., & Wayne, S. J. (1984). A field study of effective and less-effective quality circles. *Academy of Management Proceedings,* 217–221. doi:10.5465/ambpp.1984.4979005

Guerrero, L. K., & La Valley, A. G. (2006). Conflict, emotion, and communication. In J. G. Oetzel & S. Ting-Toomey (Eds.), *The Sage handbook of conflict communication: Integrating theory, research, and practice* (pp. 69–96). Thousand Oaks, CA: Sage.

Guo, C., & Acar, M. (2005). Understanding collaboration among nonprofit organizations: Combining resource dependency, institutional, and network perspectives. *Nonprofit and Voluntary Sector Quarterly, 34,* 340–361. doi:10.1177/0899764005275411

Gutek, B. A., Cohen, A. G., & Konrad, A. M. (1990). Predicting social-sexual behavior at work: A contact hypothesis. *Academy of Management Journal, 33,* 560–577. doi:10.2307/256581

Hackman, M. Z., & Johnson, C. E. (2000). *Leadership: A communication perspective* (3rd ed.). Prospect Heights, IL: Waveland.

Hale, C. L., & James, A. C. (2013). The sisterhood of the hammer: Women organizing for community and self. In M. W. Kramer, L. K. Lewis, & L. M. Gossett (Eds.), *Volunteering and communication: Studies from multiple contexts* (pp. 131–148). New York, NY: Peter Lang.

Hall, B. J., & Valde, K. (1995). "Brown nosing" as a cultural resource in American organizational speech. *Research on Language and Social Interaction, 28,* 131–150.

Hall, D. T., & Gordon, F. E. (1973). Career choices of married women: Effects on conflict, role behavior, and satisfaction. *Journal of Applied Psychology, 58,* 42–48. doi:10.1037/h0035404

Hall, J. (1973). *Conflict management survey: A survey of one's characteristic reaction to and handling of conflicts between himself and others.* Woodlands, TX: Teleometrics Int'l.

Hanchey, J. N. (2015). Constructing "American exceptionalism": Peace Corps volunteer discourses of race gender and empowerment In M. W. Kramer, L. K. Lewis, & L. M. Gossett (Eds.), *Volunteering and communication volume 2: Studies in international and intercultural contexts* (pp. 233–250). New York, NY: Peter Lang.

Harris, D. H. (2000). The benefits of exit interviews. *Information Systems Management, 17,* 17–20. doi:10.1201/1078/43192.17.3.20000601/31236.3

Harris, M. M. (1989). Reconsidering the employment interview: A review of recent literature and suggestions for future research. *Personnel Psychology, 42,* 691–726. doi:10.1111/j.1744-6570.1989.tb00673.x

Hart, Z. P., & Miller, V. D. (2005). Context and message content during organizational socialization. *Human Communication Research, 31,* 295–309. doi:10.1111/j.1468-2958.2005.tb00873.x

Harvey, M. G., Heames, J. T., Richey, R. G., & Leonard, N. (2006). Bullying: From the playground to the boardroom. *Journal of Leadership & Organizational Studies, 12,* 1–11. doi:10.1177/107179190601200401

Hellweg, S. A. (1987). Organizational grapevines. *Progress in Communication Sciences, 8,* 213–230.

Hersey, P., & Blanchard, K. H. (1993). *Management of organizational behavior: Utilizing human resources.* Englewood Cliffs, NJ: Prentice-Hall.

Hirokawa, R. Y., & Rost, K. M. (1992). Effective group decision making in organizations: Field test of the vigilant interaction theory. *Management Communication Quarterly, 5,* 267–288. doi:10.1177/0893318992005003001

Hochschild, A. R. (1983). *The managed heart.* Berkeley, CA: University of California Press.

Hoffman, M. F., & Cowan, R. L. (2008). The meaning of work/life: A corporate ideology of work/life balance. *Communication Quarterly, 56,* 227–246. doi:10.1080/01463370802251053

Hoffner, C. A., Levine, K. J., & Toohey, R. A. (2008). Socialization to work in late adolescence: The role of television and family. *Journal of Broadcasting & Electronic Media, 52,* 282–302. doi:10.1080/08838150801992086

Hofstede, G. (1980). *Culture's consequences: International differences in work-related values.* Beverly Hills, CA: Sage.

Hofstede, G. (1997). *From fad to management tool.* In G. Hofstede, G. J. Hofstede, & M. Minkov (Eds.), *Cultures and organizations: Software of the mind* (pp. 178–204). New York, NY: McGraw-Hill.

Hooghe, M. (2003). Participation in voluntary associations and value indicators: The effect of current and previous participation experiences. *Nonprofit and Voluntary Sector Quarterly, 32,* 47–69. doi:10.1177/0899764003251198

House, R. J. (1971). A path goal theory of leader effectiveness. *Administrative Science Quarterly, 16,* 321–339.

House, R. J. (1996). Path-goal theory of leadership: Lessons, legacy, and a reformulated theory. *The Leadership Quarterly, 7,* 323–352. Retrieved from http://dx.doi.org/10.1016/S1048-9843(96)90024-7

House, R. J., Filley, A. C., & Gujarati, D. N. (1971). Leadership style, hierarchical influence, and the satisfaction of subordinate role expectations: A test of Likert's influence proposition. *Journal of Applied Psychology, 55,* 422–432. doi:10.1037/h0031775

Hylmö, A., & Buzzanell, P. (2002). Telecommuting as viewed through cultural lenses: An empirical investigation of the discourses of utopia, identity, and mystery. *Communication Monographs, 69,* 329–356. doi:10.1080/03637750216547

Ingersoll, V. H., & Adams, G. B. (1992). The child is 'father' to the manager: Images of organizations in U.S. children's literature. *Organization Studies, 13,* 497–519. doi:10.1177/017084069201300401

Iverson, J. O. (2013). Communicating belonging: Building communities of expert volunteers. In M. W. Kramer, L. K. Lewis, & L. M. Gossett (Eds.), *Volunteering and communication: Studies from multiple contexts* (pp. 45–64). New York, NY: Peter Lang.

Jablin, F. M. (1979). Superior-subordinate communication: The state of the art. *Psychological Bulletin, 86,* 1201–1222. doi:10.1037/0033-2909.86.6.1201

Jablin, F. M. (1980). Superior's upward influence, satisfaction, and openness in superior-subordinate communication: A reexamination of the "Pelz effect." *Human Communication Research, 6,* 210–220. doi:10.1111/j.1468-2958.1980.tb00141.x

Jablin, F. M. (1985). An exploratory study of vocational organizational communication socialization. *Southern Speech Communication Journal, 50,* 261–282.

Jablin, F. M. (1987). Organizational entry, assimilation, and exit. In F. M. Jablin, L. L. Putnam, K. H. Roberts, & L. W. Porter (Eds.), *Handbook of organizational communication: An interdisciplinary perspective* (pp. 679–740). Thousand Oaks, CA: Sage.

Jablin, F. M. (2001). Organizational entry, assimilation, and disengagement/exit. In F. M. Jablin & L. L. Putnam (Eds.), *The new handbook of organizational communication: Advances in theory, research, and methods* (pp. 732–818). Thousand Oaks, CA: Sage.

Jablin, F. M., & Kramer, M. W. (1998). Communication-related sense-making and adjustment during job transfers. *Management Communication Quarterly, 12,* 155–182. doi:10.1177/0893318998122001

Janis, I. L. (1972). *Victims of groupthink: A psychological study of foreign policy decisions and fiascos.* Boston, MA: Houghton Mifflin.

Janis, I. L. (1982). *Groupthink: Psychological studies of policy decisions and fiascoes* (2nd ed.). Boston, MA: Houghton Mifflin.

Jehn, K. A. (1995). A multimethod examination of the benefits and detriments of intragroup conflict. *Administrative Science Quarterly, 40,* 256–282. doi:10.2307/2393638

Johnson, J. R., Bernhagen, M. J., Miller, V., & Allen, M. (1996). The role of communication in managing reductions in work force. *Journal of Applied Communication Research, 24,* 139–164. doi:10.1080/00909889609365448

Jones, G. R. (1986). Socialization tactics, self-efficacy, and newcomers' adjustments to organizations. *The Academy of Management Journal, 29,* 262–279. doi:10.2307/256188

Joos, J. G. (2008). Social media: New frontiers in hiring and recruiting. *Employment Relations Today, 35,* 51–59. doi:10.1002/ert.20188

Kassing, J. W. (2005). Speaking up competently: A comparison of perceived competence in upward dissent strategies. *Communication Research Reports, 22,* 227–234. doi:10.1080/00036810500230651

Kassing, J. W. (2009). Breaking the chain of command: Making sense of employee circumvention. *Journal of Business Communication, 46,* 311–334. doi:10.1177/0021943609333521

Kassing, J. W. (2011). *Dissent in organizations.* Malden, MA: Polity.

Kassing, J. W., & Waldron, V. R. (2014). Incivility, destructive workplace behavior, and bullying. In L. L. Putnam & D. K. Mumby (Eds.), *The Sage handbook of organizational communication* (pp. 643–664). Thousand Oaks, CA: Sage.

Kast, F. E., & Rosenzweig, J. E. (1972). General systems theory: Applications for organization and management. *Academy of Management Journal, 15,* 447–465.

Katz, D., & Kahn, R. L. (1978). *The social psychology of organizations.* New York, NY: Wiley.

Katz, R. L. (1974). Skills of an effective administrator. *Harvard Business Review, 52,* 90–102.

Kelley, K. M., & Bisel, R. S. (2014). Leaders' narrative sensemaking during LMX role negotiations: Explaining how leaders make sense of who to trust and when. *The Leadership Quarterly, 25,* 433–448. Retrieved from http://dx.doi.org/10.1016/j.leaqua.2013.10.011

Keyton, J. (2005). *Communication and organizational culture.* Thousand Oaks, CA: Sage.

Keyton, J. (2014). Organization culture: Creating meaning and influence. In L. L. Putnam & D. K. Mumby (Eds.), *The Sage handbook of organizational communication: Advances in theory, research, and methods* (pp. 549–568). Thousand Oaks, CA: Sage.

Keyton, J., & Stallworth, V. (2003). On the verge of collaboration: Interaction processes versus group outcomes. In L. R. Frey (Ed.), *Group communication in context: Studies of bona fide groups* (pp. 235–260). Mahwah, NJ: Lawrence Erlbaum.

Kirby, E. L., & Krone, K. J. (2002). "The policy exists but you can't really use it": Communication and the structuration of work-family policies. *Journal of Applied Communication Research, 30,* 50–77. doi:10.1080/00909880216577

Kirby, E. L., Wieland, S. M., & McBride, M. C. (2006). Work/life conflict. In J. G. Oetzel & S. Ting-Toomey (Eds.), *The Sage handbook of conflict communication: Integrating theory, research, and practice* (pp. 327–357). Thousand Oaks, CA: Sage.

Kirkman, B. L., & Rosen, B. (1999). Beyond self-management: Antecedents and consequence of team empowerment. *Academy of Management Journal, 42,* 58–74. doi:10.2307/256874

Kirkpatick, S. A., & Locke, E. A. (1991). Leadership: Do traits matter? *The Executive, 5,* 48–60. doi:10.5465/ame.1991.4274679

Klatzke, S. R. (2008). *Communication and sensemaking during the exit phase of socialization* (Unpublished doctoral dissertation). University of Missouri, Columbia, MO.

Knouse, S. (1994). Impressions of the resume: The effects of applicant education, experience, and impression management. *Journal of Business and Psychology, 9,* 33–45. doi:10.1007/BF02230985

Kossek, E. E., & Ozeki, C. (1998). Work–family conflict, policies, and the job–life satisfaction relationship: A review and directions for organizational behavior–human resources research. *Journal of Applied Psychology, 83,* 139–149. doi:10.1037/0021-9010.83.2.139

Kostova, T., & Roth, K. (2003). Social capital in multinational corporations and a micro-macro model of its formation. *Academy of Management Review, 28,* 297–317.

Kraimer, M. L., Shaffer, M. A., & Bolino, M. C. (2009). The influence of expatriate and repatriate experiences on career advancement and repatriate retention. *Human Resource Management, 48,* 27–47.

Kram, K. E., & Isabella, L. A. (1985). Mentoring alternatives: The role of peer relationships in career development. *Academy of Management Journal, 28,* 110–132.

Kramer, M. W. (1989). Communication during intraorganization job transfers. *Management Communication Quarterly, 3,* 219–248. doi:10.1177/0893318989003002004

Kramer, M. W. (1995). A longitudinal study of superior-subordinate communication during job transfers. *Human Communication Research, 22,* 39–64. doi:10.1111/j.1468-2958.1995 .tb00361.x

Kramer, M. W. (1996). A longitudinal study of peer communication during job transfers: The impact of frequency, quality, and network multiplexity on adjustment. *Human Communication Research, 23,* 59–86. doi:10.1111/j.1468-2958.1996.tb00387.x

Kramer, M. W. (2002). Communication in a community theater group: Managing multiple group roles. *Communication Studies, 53,* 151–170. doi:10.1080/10510970209388582

Kramer, M. W. (2004a). *Managing uncertainty in organizational communication.* Mahwah, NJ: Lawrence Erlbaum.

Kramer, M. W. (2004b). Toward a communication theory of group dialectics: An ethnographic study of a community theater group. *Communication Monographs, 71,* 311–332. doi:10.1080/0363452042000288292

Kramer, M. W. (2005). Communication and social exchange processes in community theater groups. *Journal of Applied Communication Research, 33,* 159–182. doi:10.1080/00909880500045049

Kramer, M. W. (2006a). Communication strategies for sharing leadership within a creative team: LMX in theater groups. In G. B. Graen (Ed.), *LMX leadership: The series: Sharing network leadership* (Vol. 4, pp. 1–24). Greenwich, CT: Information Age.

Kramer, M. W. (2006b). Shared leadership in a community theater group: Filling the leadership role. *Journal of Applied Communication Research, 34,* 141–162. doi:10.1080/ 00909880600574039

Kramer, M. W. (2010). *Organizational socialization: Joining and leaving organizations.* Cambridge, UK: Polity.

Kramer, M. W. (2011a). A study of voluntary organizational membership: The assimilation process in a community choir. *Western Journal of Communication, 75,* 52–74. doi:10.1080/105 70314.2010.536962

Kramer, M. W. (2011b). Toward a communication model for the socialization of voluntary members. *Communication Monographs, 78,* 233–255. doi:10.1080/03637751.2011.564640

Kramer, M. W., & Berman, J. E. (2001). Making sense of a university's culture: An examination of undergraduate students' stories. *Southern Communication Journal, 66,* 297–311. doi:10.1080/10417940109373209

Kramer, M. W., Callister, R. R., & Turban, D. B. (1995). Information-receiving and information-giving during job transitions. *Western Journal of Communication, 59,* 151–170.

Kramer, M. W., & Crespy, D. A. (2011). Communicating collaborative leadership. *Leadership Quarterly, 22,* 1024–1037. doi:10.1016/j.leaqua.2011.07.021

Kramer, M. W., & Danielson, M. A. (2016). Developing and re-developing volunteer roles: The case of ongoing assimilation of docent zoo volunteers. *Management Communication Quarterly, 30,* 103–120. doi:10.1177/0893318915612551

Kramer, M. W., & Hess, J. A. (2002). Communication rules for the display of emotions in organizational settings. *Management Communication Quarterly, 16,* 66–80. doi:10.1177/0893318902161003

Kramer, M. W., & Noland, T. L. (1999). Communication during job promotions: A case of ongoing assimilation. *Journal of Applied Communication Research, 27,* 335–355. doi:10.1080/00909889909365544

Kreiner, G. E., Hollensbe, E. C., & Sheep, M. L. (2009). Balancing borders and bridges: Negotiating the work-home interface via boundary work tactics. *Academy of Management Journal, 52,* 704–730. doi:10.5465/amj.2009.43669916

Krone, K. J., Jablin, F. M., & Putnam, L. L. (1987). Communication theory and organizational communication: Multiple perspectives. In F. M. Jablin, L. L. Putnam, K. H. Roberts, & L. W. Porter (Eds.), *Handbook of organizational communication: An interdisciplinary perspective* (pp. 18–40). Thousand Oaks, CA: Sage.

Kübler-Ross, E., & Kessler, D. (2008). *On grief & grieving: Finding the meaning of grief through the five stages of loss.* New York, NY: Scribner.

Kumar, R., & Dutta, M. J. (2015). Organizing for social justice: Serving the needs of Bhutanese refugees in Atlanta, Georgia. In M. W. Kramer, L. K. Lewis & L. M. Gossett (Eds.), *Volunteering and communication volume 2: Studies in international and intercultural contexts* (pp. 273–291). New York, NY: Peter Lang.

Langellier, K. M., & Peterson, E. E. (2006). "Somebody's got to pick eggs": Family storytelling about work. *Communication Monographs, 73,* 468–473. doi:10.1080/03637750601061190

Larkey, L. K. (1996). Toward a theory of communicative interactions in culturally diverse workgroups. *Academy of Management Review, 21,* 463–491. doi:10.5465/amr.1996.9605060219

Larwood, L., Falbe, C. M., Kriger, M. P., & Miesing, P. (1995). Structure and meaning of organizational vision. *Academy of Management Journal, 38,* 740–769. doi:10.2307/256744

Latane, B., Williams, K., & Harkins, S. (1979). Many hands make light the work: The causes and consequences of social loafing. *Journal of Personality and Social Psychology, 37,* 822–832. doi:10.1037/0022-3514.37.6.822

Lauver, K. J., & Kristof-Brown, A. (2001). Distinguishing between employees' perceptions of person–job and person–organization fit. *Journal of Vocational Behavior, 59,* 454–470. doi:10.1006/jvbe.2001.1807

Lee, S. K. (2014). The impact of social capital in ethnic religious communication networks on Korean immigrant's intercultural development. *International Journal of Intercultural Relations, 43,* 289–303.

Lee, T. W., Mitchell, T. R., Wise, L., & Fireman, S. (1996). An unfolding model of voluntary employee turnover. *Academy of Management Journal, 39,* 5–36. doi:10.2307/256629

Lefkowitz, J., & Katz, M. L. (1969). Validity of exit interviews. *Personnel Psychology, 22*, 445–455.

Leonardi, P. M., Huysman, M., & Steinfield, C. (2013). Enterprise social media: Definition, history, and prospects for the study of social technologies in organizations. *Journal of Computer-Mediated Communication, 19*, 1–19. doi:10.1111/jcc4.12029

Leonardi, P. M., & Treem, J. W. (2012). Social media use in organizations: Exploring the affordances of visibility, editability, and association. In C. T. Salmon (Ed.), *Communication Yearbook 36* (pp. 143–189). New York, NY: Oxford University Press.

Levine, K. J., & Hoffner, C. A. (2006). Adolescents' conceptions of work. *Journal of Adolescent Research, 21*, 647–669. doi:10.1177/0743558406293963

Levinson, H., & Rosenthal, S. (1986). *CEO: Corporate leadership in action*. New York, NY: Basic Books.

Lewin, K., & Lippett, R. (1953). Leader behavior and member reaction in three social climates. In D. Cartwright & A. Zander (Eds.), *Group dynamics: Research and theory* (pp. 585–611). Evanston, IL: Row, Peterson, and Co.

Lewis, L. K. (2011). *Organizational change: Creating change through strategic communication*. West Sussex, UK: Wiley.

Lewis, L. K. (2013). An introduction to volunteers. In M. W. Kramer, L. K. Lewis, & L. M. Gossett (Eds.), *Volunteers and communication: Studies in multiple contexts* (pp. 1–22). New York, NY: Peter Lang.

Li, J., Karakowsky, L., & Siegel, J. P. (1999). The effects of proportional representation on intragroup behavior in mixed-race decision-making groups. *Small Group Research, 30*, 259–279. doi:10.1177/104649649903000301

Lipsky, D. B., & Seeber, R. L. (2006). Managing organizational conflicts. In J. G. Oetzel & S. Ting-Toomey (Eds.), *The Sage handbook of conflict communication: Integrating theory, research, and practice* (pp. 359–390). Thousand Oaks, CA: Sage.

Lois, J. (1999). Socialization to heroism: Individualism and collectivism in a voluntary search and rescue group. *Social Psychology Quarterly, 62*, 117–135. doi:10.2307/2695853

Louis, M. R. (1980). Surprise and sense making: What newcomers experience in entering unfamiliar organizational settings. *Administrative Science Quarterly, 25*, 226–251. doi:10.2307/2392453

Lucas, K. (2011a). Socializing messages in blue-collar families: Communicative pathways to social mobility and reproduction. *Western Journal of Communication, 75*, 95–121. doi:10.1080/10570314.2010.536964

Lucas, K. (2011b). The working class promise: A communicative account of mobility-based ambivalences. *Communication Monographs, 78*, 347–369. doi:10.1080/03637751.2011.589461

Lutgen-Sandvik, P. (2008). Intensive remedial identity work: Responses to workplace bullying trauma and stigmatization. *Organization, 15*, 97–119. doi:10.1177/1350508407084487

Lutgen-Sandvik, P., Tracy, S. J., & Alberts, J. K. (2007). Burned by bullying in the American workplace: Prevalence, perception, degree and impact. *Journal of Management Studies, 44*, 837–862. doi:10.1111/j.1467-6486.2007.00715.x

Malgwi, C. A., Howe, M. A., & Burnaby, P. A. (2005). Influences on students' choice of college major. *Journal of Education for Business, 80,* 275–282. doi:10.3200/JOEB.80.5.275-282

Marcketti, S. B., & Kozar, J. M. (2007). Leading with relationships: A small firm example. *The Learning Organization, 14,* 142–154. doi:10.1108/09696470710727005

Marks, M. L., & Mirvis, P. H. (2001). Making mergers and acquisitions work: Strategic and psychological preparation. *Academy of Management Executive, 15,* 80–92. doi:10.5465/ame.2001.4614947

Marshall, A. A., & Stohl, C. (1993). Participating as participation: A network approach. *Communication Monographs, 60,* 137–157. doi:10.1080/03637759309376305

Martin, J. (1992). *Cultures in organizations: Three perspectives.* New York, NY: Oxford University Press.

Martin, J., Feldman, M. S., Hatch, M. J., & Sitkin, S. B. (1983). The uniqueness paradox in organizational stories. *Administrative Science Quarterly, 28,* 438–453.

Maslach, C., & Jackson, S. E. (1981). The measurement of experienced burnout. *Journal of Occupational Behavior, 2,* 99–113.

Maslow, A. H. (1954). *Motivation and personality.* New York, NY: Harper Row.

Mayo, E. (1946). *The human problems of industrial civiliations.* Boston, MA: Harvard.

McAllum, K. (2013). Challenging nonprofit praxis: Organizational volunteers and the expression of dissent. In M. W. Kramer, L. K. Lewis, & L. M. Gossett (Eds.), *Volunteering and communication: Studies from multiple contexts* (pp. 383–404). New York, NY: Peter Lang.

McAllum, K., & Zahra, A. (2015). Constructing "them" and "us": Host communities' perspectives of voluntourists identities. In M. W. Kramer, L. K. Lewis, & L. M. Gossett (Eds.), *Volunteering and communication volume 2: Studies in international and intercultural contexts* (pp. 109–128). New York, NY: Peter Lang.

McComb, M. (1995). Becoming a travelers aid volunteer: Communication in socialization and training. *Communication Studies, 46,* 297–316. doi:10.1080/10510979509368458

McCulloch, M. C., & Turban, D. B. (2007). Using person–organization fit to select employees for high-turnover jobs. *International Journal of Selection and Assessment, 15,* 63–71. doi:10.1111/j.1468-2389.2007.00368.x

McDonald, L. M., Creber, M., Sun, H., & Sonn, L. (2015). Developing public disaster communication for volunteer recruitment: Understanding volunteer motivations. In M. W. Kramer, L. K. Lewis, & L. M. Gossett (Eds.), *Volunteering and communication Volume 2: Studies in intercultural and international contexts* (pp. 27–47). New York, NY: Peter Lang.

McGregor, D. M. (1957). The human side of enterprise. Reprinted in J. M. Shafritz, J. S. Ott & Y. S. Jang (Eds.), *Classics of organizational theory* (6th ed. 2005), pp. 179–184). Belmont, CA: Wadsworth.

McLaughlin, M., & Cheatham, T. R. (1977). Effects of communication isolation on job satisfaction of bank tellers: A research note. *Human Communication Research, 3,* 171–175. doi:10.1111/j.1468-2958.1977.tb00515.x

McLeod, P. L., Lobel, S. A., & Cox, T. H. (1996). Ethnic diversity and creativity in small groups. *Small Group Research, 27,* 248–264. doi:10.1177/1046496496272003

McNamee, L. G., & Peterson, B. L. (2014). Reconciling "third space/place": Toward a complementary dialectical understanding of volunteer management. *Management Communication Quarterly, 28,* 214–243. doi:10.1177/0893318914525472

McPhee, R. D., & Zaug, P. (2000). The communicative constitution of organizations: A framework for explanation. *The Electronic Journal of Communication, 10.* http://www.cios.org/EJCPUBLIC/010/1/01017.html

Meares, M. M., Oetzel, J. G., Torres, A., Derkacs, D., & Ginossar, T. (2004). Employee mistreatment and muted voices in the culturally diverse workplace. *Journal of Applied Communication Research, 32,* 4–27. doi:10.1080/0090988042000178121

Meglich-Sespico, P., Faley, R., & Knapp, D. (2007). Relief and redress for targets of workplace bullying. *Employee Responsibilities and Rights Journal, 19,* 31–43. doi:10.1007/s10672-006-9030-y

Mendenhall, M. E., Dunbar, E., & Oddou, G. R. (1987). Expatriate selection, training and career-pathing: A review and critique. *Human Resource Management, 26,* 331–345. doi:10.1002/hrm.3930260303

Meyer, A. (1987). *Environmental jolts, industrial metamorphosis, and organizational adaptation.* Paper presented at the Second Annual Texas Conference on Organizations, Austin, TX.

Meyer, J. C. (1995). Tell me a story: Eliciting organizational values from narratives. *Communication Quarterly, 43,* 210–224. doi:10.1080/01463379509369970

Mignerey, J. T., Rubin, R. B., & Gorden, W. I. (1995). Organizational entry: An investigation of newcomer communication behavior and uncertainty. *Communication Research, 22,* 54–85. doi:10.1177/009365095022001003

Miller, K. I. (2000). Common ground from the post-positivist perspective: From "straw person" argument to collaborative coexistance. In S. R. Corman & M. S. Poole (Eds.), *Perspectives on organizational communication: Finding common ground* (pp. 46–67). New York: NY: Guilford Press.

Miller, K. I., Considine, J., & Garner, J. (2007). "Let me tell you about my job": Exploring the terrain of emotion in the workplace. *Management Communication Quarterly, 20,* 231–260. doi:10.1177/0893318906293589

Miller, K. I., Ellis, B. H., Zook, E. G., & Lyles, J. S. (1990). An integrated model of communication, stress, and burnout in the workplace. *Communication Research, 17,* 300–326. doi:10.1177/009365090017003002

Miller, V. D., & Buzzanell, P. M. (1996). Toward a research agenda for the second employment interview. *Journal of Applied Communication Research, 24,* 165–180. doi:10.1080/00909889609365449

Miller, V. D., & Jablin, F. M. (1991). Information seeking during organizational entry: Influences, tactics, and a model of the process. *Academy of Management Review, 16,* 92–120. doi:10.2307/258608

Miller, V. D., Jablin, F. M., Casey, M. K., Lamphear-Van Horn, M., & Ethington, C. (1996). The maternity leave as a role negotiation process. *Journal of Managerial Issues, 8,* 286–309. Retrieved from http://www.jstor.org/stable/40604108

Minei, E., & Bisel, R. (2013). Negotiating the meaning of team expertise: A firefighter team's epistemic denial. *Small Group Research, 44,* 7–32. doi:10.1177/1046496412467830

Mizruchi, M. S. (1996). What do interlocks do? An analysis, critique, and assessment of research on interlocking directorates. *Annual Review of Sociology, 22,* 271–298. doi:10.2307/2083432

Mohn, T. (2013). Vacation deprivation: Americans have twice as many unused days off as last year, new survey finds. Retrieved September 16, 2015, from http://www.forbes.com/sites/tanyamohn/2013/11/30/vacation-deprivation-americans-have-twice-as-many-unused-days-off-as-last-year-new-survey-finds/

Monge, P., & Eisenberg, E. M. (1987). Emergent communication networks. In F. M. Jablin, L. L. Putnam, K. H. Roberts, & L. W. Porter (Eds.), *Handbook of organizational communication* (pp. 304–342). Newbury Park, CA: Sage.

Moore, W. E. (1969). Occupational socialization. In D. A. Goslin (Ed.), *Handbook of socialization theory and research* (pp. 861–883). Chicago, IL: Rand McNally.

Moreland, R. L., & Levine, J. M. (1982). Socialization in small groups: Temporal changes in individual-group relations. In B. Leonard (Ed.), *Advances in experimental social psychology* (Vol. 15, pp. 137–192). New York, NY: Academic Press.

Morrison, E. W. (1993). Longitudinal study of the effects of information seeking on newcomer socialization. *Journal of Applied Psychology, 78,* 173–183. doi:10.1037/0021-9010.78.2.173

Muchinsky, P. M., & Harris, S. L. (1977). The effect of applicant sex and scholastic standing on the evaluation of job applicant resumes in sex-typed occupations. *Journal of Vocational Behavior, 11,* 95–108. Retrieved from http://dx.doi.org/10.1016/0001-8791(77)90020-3

Mumby, D. K. (1987). The political function of narrative in organizations. *Communication Monographs, 54,* 113–127. doi:10.1080/03637758709390221

Mumby, D. K. (2000). Common ground from the critical perspective. In S. R. Corman & M. S. Poole (Eds.), *Perspectives on organizational communication* (pp. 68–86). New York, NY: Guilford Press.

Mumby, D. K. (2001). Power and politics. In F. M. Jablin & L. L. Putnam (Eds.), *The new handbook of organizational communication: Advances in theory, research, and methods* (pp. 585–623). Thousand Oaks, CA: Sage.

Mumby, D. K. (2013). *Organizational communication: A critical approach.* Los Angeles, CA: Sage.

Myers, K. K., Jahn, J. L. S., Gailliard, B. M., & Stoltzfus, K. (2011). Vocational anticipatory socialization (VAS): A communicative model of adolescents' interests in STEM. *Management Communication Quarterly, 25,* 87–120. doi:10.1177/0893318910377068

Namie, G. (2014). *Believe it or not: Impugning the integrity of targets of workplace bullying.* Wellington, WA: Workplace Bullying Institute. Retrieved from http://www.workplacebullying.org/multi/pdf/WBI-2014-IP-F.pdf

Namie, G., & Lutgen-Sandvik, P. E. (2010). Active and passive accomplices: The communal character of workplace bullying. *International Journal of Communication, 4,* 343–373. doi:1932-8036/20100343

Napier, N. K., Simmons, G., & Stratton, K. (1989). Communication during a merger: The experience of two banks. *Human Resource Planning, 12,* 105–122.

Nathanson, A. I., Wilson, B. J., McGee, J., & Sebastian, M. (2002). Counteracting the effects of female stereotypes on television via active mediation. *Journal of Communication, 52,* 922–937. doi:10.1111/j.1460-2466.2002.tb02581.x

National Center for Disease Control and Prevention. (2011). Life expectancy at birth, at age 65, and at age 75, by sex, race, and Hispanic origin: United States, selected years 1900–2010. (Table 22). Atlanta, GA: Center for Disease Control. Retrieved from www.cdc.gov/nchs/data/hus/2011/022.pdf.

Nicholson, N., & West, M. A. (1988). *Managerial job change: Men and women in transition.* New York, NY: Cambridge University Press.

Nicotera, A. M. (1993). Beyond two dimensions: A grounded theory model of conflict-handling behavior. *Management Communication Quarterly, 6,* 282–306. doi:10.1177/0893318993006003003

O'Connell, S. E. (1988). Human communication in the high tech office. In G. M. Goldhaber & G. A. Barnett (Eds.), *Handbook of organizational communication* (pp. 473–482). Norwood, NJ: Ablex.

Oliphant, V. N., & Alexander, E. R. (1982). Reactions to resumes as a function of resume determinateness, applicant characteristics, and sex of raters. *Personnel Psychology, 35,* 829–842. doi:10.1111/j.1744-6570.1982.tb02225.x

Onyx, J. (2013). Breaking the rules: The secret to successful volunteering in a caring role. In M. W. Kramer, L. K. Lewis, & L. M. Gossett (Eds.), *Volunteering and communication: Studies in multiple contexts* (pp. 343–364). New York, NY: Peter Lang.

Oreg, S. (2003). Resistance to change: Developing an individual differences measure. *Journal of Applied Psychology, 88,* 680–693. doi:10.1037/0021-9010.88.4.680

Orlitzky, M., & Hirokawa, R. Y. (2001). To err is human, to correct for it divine: A meta-analysis of research testing the functional theory of group decision-making effectiveness. *Small Group Research, 32,* 313–341. doi:10.1177/104649640103200303

Osborn, A. F. (1957). *Applied imagination.* New York, NY: Schribners.

Ouchi, W. G., & Price, R. L. (1978). Hierarchies, clans, and theory Z: A new perspective on organization development. *Organizational Dynamics, 7,* 25–44. doi:10.1016/0090-2616(78)90036-0

Pacanowsky, M. E., & O'Donnell-Trujillo, N. (1983). Organizational communication as cultural performance. *Communication Monographs, 50,* 126–147. doi:10.1080/03637758309390158

Papa, M. J., Auwal, M. A., & Singhal, A. (1997). Organizing for social change within concertive control systems: Member identification, empowerment, and the masking of discipline. *Communication Monographs, 64,* 219–249. doi:10.1080/03637759709376418

Papa, M. J., Daniels, T. D., & Spiker, B. K. (2008). *Organizational communication: Perspectives and trends.* Los Angeles, CA: Sage.

Parker, P. S. (2001). African American women executives' leadership communication within dominant-culture organizations. *Management Communication Quarterly, 15,* 42–82. doi:10.1177/0893318901151002

Pearce, C. L., & Conger, J. A. (2003). All those years ago: The historical underpinning of shared leadership. In C. L. Pearce & J. A. Conger (Eds.), *Shared leadership: Reframing the hows and whys of leadership* (pp. 1–18). Thousand Oaks, CA: Sage.

Perry, M. L., Pearce, C. L., & Sims, H. P. (1999). Empowered selling teams: How shared leadership can contribute to selling team outcomes. *Journal of Personal Selling & Sales Management, 19,* 35–51. doi:10.1080/08853134.1999.10754180

Peters, T., J., & Waterman, R. H. J. (1982). *In search of excellence: Lessons from America's best run companies.* New York, NY: Harper & Row.

Peterson, G. W., & Peters, D. F. (1983). Adolescents' construction of social reality: The impact of television and peers. *Youth and Society, 15,* 67–85. doi:10.1177/0044118X83015001005

Pfeffer, J. (2009). Understanding power in organizations. In D. Tjosvold & B. Wisse (Eds.), *Power and interdependence in organizations* (pp. 17–32). New York, NY: Cambridge University Press.

Phillips, J. M. (1998). Effects of realistic job previews on multiple organizational outcomes: A meta-analysis. *Academy of Management Journal, 41,* 673–690. doi:10.2307/256964

Pierce, T., & Dougherty, D. S. (2002). The construction, enactment, and maintenance of power-as-domination through an acquisition. *Management Communication Quarterly, 16,* 129–164. doi:10.1177/089331802237232

Pinder, C. C. (1977). Multiple predictors of post-transfer satisfaction: The role of urban factors. *Personnel Psychology, 30,* 543–556. doi:10.1111/j.1744-6570.1977.tb02326.x

Planalp, S., & Honeycutt, J. M. (1985). Events that increase uncertainty in personal relationships. *Human Communication Research, 11,* 593–604. doi:10.1111/j.1468-2958.1985.tb00062.x

Ploeger, N. A., Kelley, K. M., & Bisel, R. S. (2011). Hierarchical mum effect: A new investigation of organizational ethics. *Southern Communication Journal, 76,* 465–481. doi:10.1080/10417 94x.2010.500343

Poggi, G. (1965). A main theme of contemporary sociological analysis: Its achievements and limitations. *British Journal of Sociology, 16,* 283–294.

Pomerol, J.-C. (2013). *Decision-making and action.* New York, NY: Wiley.

Pompper, D. (2013). Volunteerism and corporate social responsibility: Definitions, measurements, roles, and commitment. In M. W. Kramer, L. K. Lewis, & L. M. Gossett (Eds.), *Volunteers and communication: Studies in multiple contexts* (pp. 273–295): New York, NY: Peter Lange.

Pondy, L. R. (1967). Organizational conflict: Concepts and models. *Administrative Science Quarterly, 12,* 296–320. doi:10.2307/2391553

Poole, M. S. (1981). Decision development in small groups I: A comparison of two models. *Communication Monographs, 48,* 1–24. doi:10.1080/03637758109376044

Poole, M. S. (1983a). Decision development in small groups II: A study of multiple sequences in decision making. *Communication Monographs, 50,* 206–232. doi:10.1080/03637758309390165

Poole, M. S. (1983b). Decision development in small groups, III: A multiple sequence model of group decision development. *Communication Monographs, 50,* 321–341. doi:10.1080/03637758309390173

Poole, M. S., DeSanctis, G., Kirsh, L., & Jackson, M. (1995). Group decision support systems as facilitators of quality team efforts. In L. R. Frey (Ed.), *Innovations in group facilitation techniques: Applications in natural settings* (pp. 299–321). Cresskill, NJ: Hampton Press.

Poole, M. S., Seibold, D. R., & McPhee, R. D. (1985). Group decision-making as a structurational process. *Quarterly Journal of Speech, 71,* 74–102. doi:10.1080/00335638509383719

Powell, T. C. (1995). Total quality management as competitive advantage: A review and empirical study. *Strategic Management Journal, 16,* 15–37. doi:10.1002/smj.4250160105

Pratt, M. G. (2000). The good, the bad, and the ambivalent: Managing identification among Amway distributors. *Administrative Science Quarterly, 45,* 456–493. doi:10.2307/2667106

Premack, S. L., & Wanous, J. P. (1985). A meta-analysis of realistic job preview experiments. *Journal of Applied Psychology, 70,* 706–719. doi:10.1037/0021-9010.70.4.706

Putnam, L. L. (1982). Paradigms for organizational communication research: An overview and synthesis. *Western Journal of Speech Communication: WJSC, 46,* 192–206.

Putnam, L. L. (2006). Definitions and approaches to conflict and communication. In J. G. Oetzel & S. Ting-Toomey (Eds.), *The Sage handbook of conflict communication: Integrating theory, research, and practice* (pp. 1–32). Thousand Oaks, CA: Sage.

Putnam, L. L., & Jones, T. S. (1982). Reciprocity in negotiations: An analysis of bargaining interaction. *Communication Monographs, 49,* 171–191. doi:10.1080/03637758209376080

Putnam, L. L., & Poole, M. S. (1987). Conflict and negotiation. In F. M. Jablin, L. L. Putnam, K. H. Roberts, & L. W. Porter (Eds.), *Handbook of organizational communication* (pp. 549–599). Newbury Park, CA: Sage.

Putnam, R. D. (1995). Bowling alone: America's declining social capital. *Journal of Democracy, 6,* 65–78.

Rafaeli, A., & Sutton, R. I. (1991). Emotional contrast strategies as means of social influence: Lessons from criminal interrogators and bill collectors. *Academy of Management Journal, 34,* 749–775. doi:10.2307/256388

Ragins, B. R., Townsend, B., & Mattis, M. (1998). Gender gap in the executive suite: CEOs and female executives report on breaking the glass ceiling. *The Academy of Management Executive, 12,* 28–42. doi:10.5465/ame.1998.254976

Rahim, M. A. (2015). *Managing conflict in organizations* (4th ed.). New Brunswick, NJ: Aldine Transaction.

Rahim, M. A., Antonioni, D., & Psenicka, C. (2001). A structural equations model of leader power, subordinates' styles of handling conflict, and job performance. *International Journal of Conflict Management, 12,* 191–211.

Redding, W. C. (1985). Rocking boats, blowing whistles, and teaching speech communication. *Communication Education, 34,* 245–258. doi:10.1080/03634528509378613

Reichers, A. E. (1987). An interactionist perspective on newcomer socialization rates. *The Academy of Management Review, 12,* 278–287.

Reutter, L., Field, P. A., Campbell, I. E., & Day, R. (1997). Socialization into nursing: Nursing students as learners. *The Journal of Nursing Education, 36,* 149–155.

Riggio, R. E., Bass, B. M., & Orr, S. S. (2004). Transformational leadership in nonprofit organizations. In R. E. Riggio & S. S. Orr (Eds.), *Improving leadership in nonprofit organizations* (pp. 49–64). San Francisco, CA: Jossey-Bass.

Robinson, R. J., Lewicki, R. J., & Donahue, E. M. (2000). Extending and testing a five factor model of ethical and unethical bargaining tactics: Introducing the SINS scale. *Journal of Organizational Behavior, 21,* 649–664.

Robinson, R. K., Franklin, G. M., Tinney, C. H., Crow, S. M., & Hartman, S. J. (2005). Sexual harassment in the workplace: Guidelines for educating healthcare managers. *Journal of Health and Human Services Administration, 27,* 501–530.

Rodgers, W. (1969). *Think: A biography of the Watsons and IBM.* New York, NY: Stern & Day.

Roethlisberger, F. J. (1947). *Management and morale.* Cambridge, MA: Harvard University Press.

Rogers, E. M. (1995). *Diffusion of innovations.* New York, NY: The Free Press.

Roloff, M. E. (1981). *Social exchange: Key concepts.* Beverly Hills, CA: Sage.

Roth, L. M. (2004). The social psychology of tokenism: Status and homophily processes on Wall Street. *Sociological Perspectives, 47,* 189–214.

Rotondo, D. M., & Perrewé, P. L. (2000). Coping with a career plateau: An empirical examination of what works and what doesn't. *Journal of Applied Social Psychology, 30,* 2622–2646. doi:10.1111/j.1559-1816.2000.tb02453.x

Ruppel, C. P., Gong, B., & Tworoger, L. C. (2013). Using communication choices as a boundary-management strategy: How choices of communication media affect the work–life balance of teleworkers in a global virtual team. *Journal of Business and Technical Communication, 27,* 436–471. doi:10.1177/1050651913490941

Russell, B. (1938). *Power: A new social analysis.* New York, NY: Norton.

Ryan, A. M., & Tippins, N. T. (2004). Attracting and selecting: What psychological research tells us. *Human Resource Management, 43,* 305–318. doi:10.1002/hrm.20026

Salamon, L. M., & Abramson, A. J. (1982). *The federal budget and the nonprofit sector.* Washington, DC: Urban Institute.

Salas, E., Sims, D. E., & Burke, C. S. (2005). Is there a "Big Five" in teamwork? *Small Group Research, 36,* 555–599. doi:10.1177/1046496405277134

Salin, D. (2003). Ways of explaining workplace bullying: A review of enabling, motivating and precipitating structures and processes in the work environment. *Human Relations, 56,* 1213–1232. doi:10.1177/00187267035610003

Sand, G., & Miyazaki, A. D. (2000). The impact of social support on salesperson burnout and burnout components. *Psychology and Marketing, 17,* 13–26. doi:10.1002/(SICI)1520-6793(200001)17:1<13::AID-MAR2>3.0.CO;2-S

Scheidel, T. M., & Crowell, L. (1964). Idea development in small discussion groups. *Quarterly Journal of Speech, 50,* 140–145. doi:10.1080/00335636409382654

Schein, E. H. (1968). Organizational socialization and the profession of management. *Industrial Management Review, 9,* 1–16.

Schneider, K. T., Swan, S., & Fitzgerald, L. F. (1997). Job-related and psychological effects of sexual harassment in the workplace: Empirical evidence from two organizations. *Journal of Applied Psychology, 82,* 401–415. doi:10.1037/0021-9010.82.3.401

Schramm, W. (1954). The nature of communication between humans. In W. Schramm (Ed.), *The process and effects of mass communication* (pp. 3–53). Urbana, IL: University of Illinois Press.

Schweiger, D. M., & Denisi, A. S. (1991). Communication with employees following a merger: A longitudinal field experiment. *Academy of Management Journal, 34,* 110–135. doi:10.2307/256304

Scott, C., & Myers, K. K. (2005). The socialization of emotion: Learning emotion management at the fire station. *Journal of Applied Communication Research, 33,* 67–92. doi:10.1080/0090988042000318521

Scott, C. R. (2007). Communication and social identity theory: Existing and potential connections in organizational identification research. *Communication Studies, 58,* 123–138. doi:10.1080/10510970701341063

Shannon, C., & Weaver, W. (1949). *The mathematical theory of communication.* Urbana, IL: University of Illinois Press.

Sharma, G., & Good, D. (2013). The work of middle managers: Sensemaking and sensegiving for creating positive social change. *The Journal of Applied Behavioral Science, 49,* 95–122. doi:10.1177/0021886312471375

Shaw, M. W. (1981). *Group dynamics: The psychology of small group behavior* (3rd ed.). New York, NY: McGraw-Hill.

Shen, W., & Cannella, A. A. J. (2002). Revisiting the performance consequences of CEO succession: The impacts of successor type, postsuccession senior executive turnover, and departing CEO tenure. *Academy of Management Journal, 45,* 717–733. doi:10.2307/3069306

Shimanoff, S. B. (1980). *Communication rules: Theory and research.* Beverly Hills, CA: Sage.

Shimanoff, S. B. (1992). Group interaction via communication rules. In R. S. Cathcart & L. A. Samovar (Eds.), *Small group communication: A reader* (6th ed., pp. 250–262). Dubuque, IA: Wm. C. Brown.

Shockley-Zalabak, P. (1988). Assessing the Hall Conflict Management Survey. *Management Communication Quarterly, 1,* 302–320. doi:10.1177/0893318988001003003

Shuler, S., & Sypher, B. D. (2000). Seeking emotional labor: When managing the heart enhances the work experience. *Management Communication Quarterly, 14,* 50–89. doi:10.1177/0893318900141003

Shumate, M., & Contactor, N. S. (2014). Emergence of multidimensional social networks. In L. L. Putnam & D. K. Mumby (Eds.), *The SAGE handbook of organizational communication: Advances in theory, research, and methods* (3rd ed., pp. 449–474). Los Angeles, CA: Sage.

Sias, P. M. (2005). Workplace relationship quality and employee information experiences. *Communication Studies, 56,* 375–395. doi:10.1080/10510970500319450

Sias, P. M. (2009). *Organizing relationships: Tradition and emerging perspectives on workplace relationships.* Thousand Oaks, CA: Sage.

Sias, P. M. (2014). Workplace relationships. In L. L. Putnam & D. K. Mumby (Eds.), *The Sage handbook of organizational communication* (pp. 375–399). Thousand Oaks, CA: Sage.

Sias, P. M., & Cahill, D. J. (1998). From coworkers to friends: The development of peer friendships in the workplace. *Western Journal of Communication, 62,* 273–299. doi:10.1080/10570319809374611

Sias, P. M., & Jablin, F. M. (1995). Differential superior-subordinate relations, perceptions of fairness, and coworker communication. *Human Communication Research, 22,* 5–38. doi:10.1111/j.1468-2958.1995.tb00360.x

Signorielli, N. (2009). Race and sex in prime time: A look at occupations and occupational prestige. *Mass Communication & Society, 12,* 332–352. doi:10.1080/15205430802478693

Simon, H. A. (1972). Theories of bounded rationality. In C. B. McGuire & R. Radner (Eds.), *Decision and organization* (pp. 161–176). Amsterdam, Netherlands: North-Holland.

Sitkin, S. B., Sutcliffe, K. M., & Barrios-Choplin, J. R. (1992). A dual-capacity model of communication media choice in organizations. *Human Communication Research, 18,* 563–598. doi:10.1111/j.1468-2958.1992.tb00572.x

Smith, F. L., & Dougherty, D. S. (2012). Revealing a master narrative discourses of retirement throughout the working life cycle. *Management Communication Quarterly, 26,* 453–478.

Smith, R. C., & Eisenberg, E. M. (1987). Conflict at Disneyland: A root-metaphor analysis. *Communication Monographs, 54,* 367–380. doi:10.1080/03637758709390239

Smith, R. C., & Turner, P. K. (1995). A social constructionist reconfiguration of metaphor analysis: An application of "SCMA" to organizational socialization theorizing. *Communication Monographs, 62,* 152–181. doi:10.1080/03637759509376354

Smith, W. P., & Kidder, D. L. (2010). You've been tagged! (Then again, maybe not): Employers and Facebook. *Business Horizons, 53,* 491–499. Retrieved from http://dx.doi.org/10.1016/j.bushor.2010.04.004

Solomon, D. H., & Williams, M. L. M. (1997). Perceptions of social-sexual communication at work as sexually harassing. *Management Communication Quarterly, 11,* 147–184. doi:10.1177/0893318997112001

Sowa, J. E. (2008). The collaboration decision in nonprofit organizations: Views from the front line. *Nonprofit and Voluntary Sector Quarterly, 38,* 1003–1025. doi:10.1177/0899764008325247

Stahl, G. K., Maznevski, M. L., Voigt, A., & Jonsen, K. (2010). Unraveling the effects of cultural diversity in teams: A meta-analysis of research on multicultural work groups. *Journal of International Business Studies, 41,* 690–709.

Steele, F. I. (1973). *Physical settings and organization development.* Reading, MA: Addison-Wesley.

Steingard, D. S., & Fitzgibbons, D. E. (1995). Challenging the juggernaut of globalization. *Journal of Organizational Change Management, 8,* 30–54. doi:10.1108/09534819510090204

Stephens, K. K., & Davis, J. (2009). The social influences on electronic multitasking in organizational meetings. *Management Communication Quarterly, 23,* 63–83. doi:10.1177/0893318909335417

Stewart, L. P. (1980). "Whistle blowing": Implications for organizational communication. *Journal of Communication, 30,* 90–101. doi:10.1111/j.1460-2466.1980.tb02020.x

Stogdill, R. M. (1948). Personal factors associated with leadership: A survey of the literature. *The Journal of Psychology, 25,* 35–71.

Stohl, C. (2001). Globalizing organizational communication. In F. M. Jablin & L. Putnam (Eds.), *The new handbook of organizational communication: Advances in theory, research, and methods* (pp. 323–375). Thousand Oaks, CA: Sage.

Stohl, C., & Cheney, G. (2001). Participatory processes/paradoxical practices: Communication and the dilemmas of organizational democracy. *Management Communication Quarterly, 14,* 349–407. doi:10.1177/0893318901143001

Street, M. D. (1997). Groupthink: An examination of theoretical issues, implications, and future research suggestions. *Small Group Research, 28,* 72–93. doi:10.1177/1046496497281003

Stroh, L. K. (1999). Does relocation still benefit corporations and employees?: An overview of the literature. *Human Resource Management Review, 9,* 279–308. Retrieved from http://dx.doi.org/10.1016/S1053-4822(99)00022-4

Sypher, B. D., & Zorn, T. E. (1986). Communication-related abilities and upward mobility. *Human Communication Research, 12,* 420–431. doi:10.1111/j.1468-2958.1986.tb00085.x

Tan, C. L., & Kramer, M. W. (2012). Communication and voluntary downward career changes. *Journal of Applied Communication Research, 40,* 87–106. doi:10.1080/00909882.2011.634429

Taylor, F. W. (1923). *The principles of scientific management.* New York, NY: Harper & Brothers.

Taylor, J. R., Cooren, F., Giroux, N., & Robichaud, D. (1996). The communicational basis of organization: Between the conversation and the text. *Communication Theory, 6,* 1–39. doi:10.1111/j.1468-2885.1996.tb00118.x

Thibaut, J. W., & Kelley, H. H. (1959). *The social psychology of groups.* New York: Wiley.

Thomas, D. C. (1999). Cultural diversity and work group effectiveness: An experimental study. *Journal of Cross-Cultural Psychology, 30,* 242–263. doi:10.1177/0022022199030002006

Thomas, K. W. (1974). *Thomas-Kilmann conflict mode instrument.* Tuxedo, NY: Xicom.

Thomas, K. W., & Kilmann, R. H. (1978). Comparison of four instruments measuring conflict behavior. *Psychological reports, 42,* 1139–1145.

Thoms, P., McMasters, R., Roberts, M., & Dombkowski, D. (1999). Resume characteristics as predictors of an invitation to interview. *Journal of Business and Psychology, 13,* 339–356. doi:10.1023/A:1022974232557

Tichy, N. M. (1981). Networks in organizations. In P. C. Nystsrom & W. H. Starbuck (Eds.), *Handbook of organizational design* (Vol. 2, pp. 225–248). London: Oxford University Press.

Tichy, N. M., & Ulrich, D. O. (1984). SMR forum: The leadership challenge—A call for the transformational leader. *Sloan Management Review, 26,* 59.

Timmerman, C. E., & Scott, C. R. (2006). Virtually working: Communicative and structural predictors of media use and key outcomes in virtual work teams. *Communication Monographs, 73,* 108–136. doi:10.1080/03637750500534396

Tourish, D., Paulsen, N., Hobman, E., & Bordia, P. (2004). The downsides of downsizing communication processes information needs in the aftermath of a workforce reduction strategy. *Management Communication Quarterly, 17,* 485–516.

Tracy, S. J. (2000). Becoming a character for commerce: Emotion labor, self-subordination, and discursive construction of identity in a total institution. *Management Communication Quarterly, 14,* 90–128. doi:10.1177/0893318900141004

Tracy, S. J., Myers, K. K., & Scott, C. W. (2006). Cracking jokes and crafting selves: Sensemaking and identity management among human service workers. *Communication Monographs, 73,* 283–308. doi:10.1080/03637750600889500

Tremblay, M., Roger, A., & Toulouse, J. M. (1995). Career plateau and work attitudes: An empirical study of managers. *Human Relations, 48,* 221–237. doi:10.1177/001872679504800301

Trice, H. M., & Beyer, J. M. (1984). Studying organizational cultures through rites and ceremonials. *Academy of Management Review, 9,* 653–669. doi:10.5465/amr.1984.4277391

Trice, H. M., & Beyer, J. M. (1986). Charisma and its routinization in two social movement organizations. *Research in Organizational Behavior, 8,* 113–164.

Trice, H. M., & Beyer, J. M. (1991). Cultural leadership in organizations. *Organization Science, 2,* 149–169.

Trice, H. M., & Beyer, J. M. (1993). *The cultures of work organizations.* Englewood Cliffs, NJ: Prentice-Hall, Inc.

Tuckman, B. W., & Jensen, M. A. C. (1977). Stages of small-group development revisited. *Group & Organization Management, 2,* 419–427. doi:10.1177/105960117700200404

Tuffrey, M. (1997). Employees and the community: How successful companies meet human resource needs through community involvement. *Career Development International, 2,* 33–35. doi:10.1108/13620439710157470

Turnage, A. (2013). Technological resistance: A metaphor analysis of Enron e-mail messages. *Communication Quarterly, 61,* 519–538. doi:10.1080/01463373.2013.803995

U.S. Bureau of Labor Statistics. (2010). *Women in the labor force: A databook.* (Report 1049). Retrieved from www.bls.gov/cps/wlf-databook-2013.pdf.

U.S. Census Bureau. (2014). *Family and living arrangements.* Retrieved from http://www.census.gov/hhes/families/.

U.S. Department of Labor Women's Bureau. (2015). *Data & statistics.* Retrieved from http://www.dol.gov/wb/stats/stats_data.htm.

U.S. Equal Employment Opportunity Commission. (1990). *Policy guidance on current issues of sexual harassment.* Retrieved from http://www.eeoc.gov/laws/types/sexual_harassment_guidance.cfm.

U.S. Equal Employment Opportunity Commission. (2015). *Prohibited employment policies/practices.* Retrieved June 4, 2015, from http://www.eeoc.gov/laws/practices/index.cfm

Van Dijk, C., & Van Den Ende, J. (2002). Suggestion systems: Transferring employee creativity into practicable ideas. *R&D Management, 32,* 387–395. doi:10.1111/1467-9310.00270

Van Maanen, J., & Kunda, G. (1989). "Real feelings": Emotional expression and organizational culture. *Research in Organizational Behavior, 11,* 43–103.

Van Maanen, J., & Schein, E. G. (1979). Toward a theory of organizational socialization. In B. M. Staw (Ed.), *Research in Organizational Behavior* (pp. 209–264). Greenwich, CT: JAI Press.

Viswesvaran, C., Sanchez, J. I., & Fisher, J. (1999). The role of social support in the process of work stress: A meta-analysis. *Journal of Vocational Behavior, 54,* 314–334. Retrieved from http://dx.doi.org/10.1006/jvbe.1998.1661

Waldeck, J. H., Seibold, D. R., & Flanagin, A. J. (2004). Organizational assimilation and communication technology use. *Communication Monographs, 71,* 161–183. doi:10.1080/0363775042331302497

Waldron, V. R. (2012). *Communicating emotion at work.* Malden, MA: Polity.

Wanous, J. P., Poland, T. D., Premack, S. L., & Davis, K. S. (1992). The effects of met expectations on newcomer attitudes and behaviors: A review and meta-analysis. *Journal of Applied Psychology, 77,* 288–297. doi:10.1037/0021-9010.77.3.288

Waters, R. K. (2001). *An investigation of faculty socialization into advising role.* Unpublished dissertation at the University of Missouri. Columbia, MO.

Watson, W. E., Kumar, K., & Michaelsen, L. K. (1993). Cultural diversity's impact on interaction process and performance: Comparing homogeneous and diverse task groups. *Academy of Management Journal, 36,* 590–602. doi:10.2307/256593

Wayne, S. J., Liden, R. C., Graf, I. K., & Ferris, G. R. (1997). The role of upward influence tactics in human resource decisions. *Personnel Psychology, 50,* 979–1006. doi:10.1111/j.1744-6570.1997.tb01491.x

Weber, M. (1924/1978). *Economy and society: An outline of interpretive sociology: Vol. 1.* Berkeley, CA University of California Press.

The Wedding Report Incorporated. (2015). *Cost of wedding.* Retrieved September 11, 2015, from http://www.costofwedding.com/

Weick, K. E. (1995). *Sensemaking in organizations.* Thousand Oaks, CA: Sage.

Weick, K. E., Sutcliffe, K. M., & Obstfeld, D. (2005). Organizing and the process of sensemaking. *Organization Science, 16,* 409–421. doi:10.1287/orsc.1050.0133

Wentzel, K. R., & Looney, L. (2007). Socialization in school settings. In J. E. Grusec & P. D. Hastings (Eds.), *Handbook of socialization: Theory and research* (pp. 382–403). New York, NY: Guilford Press.

Willems, J., Huybrechts, G., Jegers, M., Vantilborgh, T., Bidee, J., & Pepermans, R. (2012). Volunteer decisions (not) to leave: Reasons to quit versus functional motives to stay. *Human Relations, 65,* 883–900. doi:10.1177/0018726712442554

Wojno, A. E. (2013). "You just gotta be careful about those boundaries": Managing risk in a volunteer-based organization In M. W. Kramer, L. K. Lewis, & L. M. Gossett (Eds.), *Volunteering and communication: Studies from multiple contexts* (pp. 213–228). New York, NY: Peter Lang.

Wood, J. T. (1992). Telling our stories: Narratives as a basis for theorizing sexual harassment. *Journal of Applied Communication Research, 20,* 349–362.

Worldwide ERC. (2014). *U.S. domestic transfers: Relocation statistics.* Retrieved from http://www.worldwideerc.org/Resources/Research/Pages/Facts-and-Statistics.aspx

Wrigley, B. J. (2002). Glass ceiling? What glass ceiling? A qualitative study of how women view the glass ceiling in public relations and communications management. *Journal of Public Relations Research, 14,* 27–55. doi:10.1207/S1532754XJPRR1401_2

Zanin, A. C., Bisel, R. S., & Adame, E. A. (2016). Supervisor moral talk contagion and trust-in-supervisor: Mitigating the workplace moral mum effect. *Management Communication Quarterly, 30,* 147–163. doi:10.1177/0893318915619755

Zey, M. (1992). Criticisms of rational choice models. In M. Zey (Ed.), *Decision making: Alternative to rational choice models* (pp. 9–31). Newbury Park, CA: Sage.

Zhu, Y., May, S. K., & Rosenfeld, L. B. (2004). Information adequacy and job satisfaction during merger and acquisition. *Management Communication Quarterly, 18,* 241–270.

Zoller, H. M. (2003). Working out: Managerialism in workplace health promotion. *Management Communication Quarterly, 17,* 171–205. doi:10.1177/0893318903253003

Zoller, H. M. (2014). Power and resistance in organizational communication. In L. L. Putnam & D. K. Mumby (Eds.), *The SAGE handbook of organizational communication: Advances in theory, research, and methods* (3rd ed., pp. 595–618). Los Angeles, CA: Sage.

Zoller, H. M., & Fairhurst, G. T. (2007). Resistance leadership: The overlooked potential in critical organization and leadership studies. *Human Relations, 60,* 1331–1360. doi: 10.1177/0018726707082850

CREDITS

Photo 8.2: Photo by Colin McConnell/Toronto Star via Getty Images

Photo 8.3: © Richard T. Nowitz/CORBIS

Photo 9.1: © iStock/Jacob Ammentorp Lund

Photo 9.3: © iStock/tstajduhar

Photo 10:1: © Florian Franke/Corbis

Photo 11:1: HBO/Allstar picture library

Photo 11.2: Dreamworks/Andrew Cooper/The Kobal Collection at Art Resource, NY

Photo 11.3: Dreamworks/Allstar picture library

Photo 11.4: Dreamworks/Allstar picture library

Photo 12.1: © iStock/Steve Debenport

Photo 12.2: www.CartoonStock.com

Photo 13.1: Patrick T. Fallon/Bloomberg via Getty Images

Photo 14.1: © iStock/leolintang

Photo 14.2: © Helen King/Corbis

Photo 15.1: © iStock/iNueng

Photo 15.2: AP Photo/Sue Ogrocki

INDEX

cultural diversity and, 359–64, 359t, 366, 367–68
decision making expectations and, 354–55
diffusion of innovation and, 344–46, 345f
emotion and, 346–47
expectations and, 353
globalization and, 364–66, 368
grieving process and, 347
and how meaning is established, 353
of interpersonal communication interactions, 356–58
media richness theory and, 351–53
for NPOs, 366–68
resistance to, 347–49
charismatic leadership
Ash and, 225–26
characteristics of, 224–25
framing and, 234
circumvention, 309
CITs. *See* communication and information technologies
classical management theory
in *Amazon Rising*, 95–96
centralization in, 91
context in, 87
economic rewards in, 102
Fayol general management theory and, 87–90
focus of, 117
Hawthorne studies challenging, 96
management approach as, 86
McGregor theory X and, 94, 101
Taylor and, 87–90, 93
transmission model of communication in, 92
Weber bureaucratic theory as, 87, 92–94
coercive power, 295, 297
cognitive differentiation, 300
committees, 136
communication. *See* specific topics
communication and information technologies (CITs), 352–53
communication challenges
comparing workplaces as, 39
exit interviews as, 408
framing theory and, 234
groupthink in, 259
happiness and productivity in, 98
hegemony in, 304

internet usage policies as, 355
leading group decisions in, 248
motivation at Despair, Inc., 105, *105*
network density in, 145
new technology of the job search in, 54
new values as, 159
open door policy as, 188
Pelz effect in, 187
personal power in, 298
realistic expectations in, 36
reducing volunteer turnover and, 113
resisting change as, 349
rumors and sensemaking in, 388
span of control as, 92
suggestion box as, 128
trusted colleague in, 71
underrepresented groups in, 222
upward communication and, 129
work-life boundaries and, 324
communication exchange 71–74
communicative definition, of organizations 8, 26
community stakeholders, 9
community theater
ethnography study of, 178–79
power and, 311–12
conceptual skills, 377
concertive control, 110–11
conflict, 255, 316; *See also* Chapter 10
abuse as, 277–78
bargaining in, 275–76
bullying as, 278–83, 288
defining, 265–66
dysfunctional, 270–71
emotion and, 266
functional, 265, 270–71
groupthink reduced through, 270
incompatible goals defining, 266
internal, 287
levels of, 267–68
and nonprofits, 287
in NPOs, 287
resolution of, 266
retreat planning committee scenario and, 264–65
scarce resources impacting, 273
sexual harassment and, 283–86, 288
third parties in, 276–77
typologies of, 267–70

conflict styles, 271–72, 272f
gender dynamics in, 273–74
situational appropriateness of, 274t
connectedness, 143f, 146–47
Connolly, T., 252, 262
Conrad, Charles, 100
consumerism norm, 321–22
contender successions, 376
content innovators, 67
contingency model of leadership
Hersey and Blanchard model as, 218–19, 218f
path-goal model in, 217
for volunteers, 223
corporate social responsibility, 9, 334
cost–benefit ratio, 402, 406, 417
country club management, 214, 215f
cover letters, 48–49
Covey, Steven, 40
critical perspective, 20, 23
criticisms of, 21
feminist perspective as, 24–25
management theories in, 115–16
on organizational culture, 181
cross-cultural training, 383–84
Crowell, L., 247, 249t, 262
cultural diversity, 364
changing demographics of, 359, 359t
group performance and, 362, 363
homogeneous groups opposed to, 362–63
intercultural communication and, 360
minority participation and, 361–62
NPOs and, 366, 367–68
cultural feminism, 24
culture, of organizations, 60, 421. *See* Chapter 6
artifacts in, 154–55, 181
assumptions of, 155
comparing methods of analyzing, 179–80, 179t
critical perspective on, 180–81
differentiated perspective on, 165, 166
ethnography and, 177, 178–79
fragmented perspective on, 165, 166–68
institutional leadership and, 231
integrated perspective on, 164–65, 166

culture, of organizations (*Continued*)
  interpretive perspective on, 180–81
  M&As and, 390–91
  member interactions and, 156
  metaphor analysis and, 173–76
  norms in, 159, 160–64
  permission in analyzing, 180
  post-positivist perspective on, 180
  reflective comment analysis and, 176–77
  ritual analysis on, 172–73
  script analysis and, 169–71
  structuration theory and, 156–58, *158*, 168
  in teamwork management, 107
  values of, 155
Cushman, P., 420
custodial roles, 67, 302

Deal, Terrance, 346–47, 350
decaf resistance, 306–8
decision making, *See* Chapter 9, 262
  alternative descriptive models of, 246–49
  assumptions in, 250–51
  bait boxes scenario and, 253
  brainstorming in, 242
  changing expectations in, 354–55
  comparing models of, 249*t*
  descriptive models of, 243–46
  faulty, 255–60
  garbage can model and, 252–53, 254
  groupthink in, 256–58, 259
  in NPOs, 260–61
  phases of, 246*t*
  prescriptive model of, 241–43
  retrospective rationality and, 254–55
  satisficing, 251–52, 254
decision-making groups, 147
deep structure power, 295, 313
  assumptions and, 301
  contradictions transmuted in, 302–3
  IBM example of, 301–5
  sectional interests in, 302
  systematic distortion in, 303
democratic manager, 214
density, 143*f*, 146–47
descriptive model
  alternative, 246–49
  of decision making, 243–46

phase model as, 243–46
prescriptive model compared to, 243
Despair, Inc., 105, *105*
Dewey, John, 241–43, 249*t*
dialectical theory, 220–23, 221*t*
dialogic perspective, 25
differentiated supervisor-subordinate relationships
  LMX in, 189–92
  middle-group relationships in, 191
  overseer relationships in, 190
  partnership relationships in, 189–90
diffusion of innovation theory
  change adoption and, 345–46, 345*f*
  principles of, 344
  Rogers developing, 344
direct-factual appeal, 309, 310*t*
directive leadership, 217
direct observation, 141
discrimination, 384–85
discursive changes, 343
disjunctive socialization, 64
dismissal meeting, 413, 414
Disney World
  emotion management at, 205
  metaphor analysis of, 174–76
dissent
  boat rocking as, 310
  strategies in voicing, 309, 310*t*
  upward, 308, 310
  whistleblowing as, 310–11
divestiture socialization, 65, *65*
downward communication, 126
  issues with, 124–25
  nature of feedback in, 125
  types of, 124
  for volunteers, 149
downward remediation plan, 412
Drago, R. W., 320
dual-career households, 321–22

EAGR approach, 412
education system 35–37
EEOC. *See* Equal Employment Opportunity Commission, U.S.
effective communication, 6–7, 15
Eisenberg, E. M.,
  metaphor analysis, 174–75
  strategic ambiguity, 10–12
emotional labor, 203–4
emotion at work, 204–5

emotion management
  change and, 346–47
  conflict and, 266
  expectations in, 202
  neutrality in, 201–2
  peer communication and, 206
  professionalism in, 205–6
  types of, 203–5
  for volunteers, 207–8
emotion toward work, 205
emotion with work, 204
emotion work, 204
empowerment, 293
encounter outcomes
  boundary passages in, 74–78, 75*f*, 76*f*, 78*f*
  expectations and experiences in, 78–81
  general newcomer adaptation in, 81–82
Enron, 9
  as faulty decision making, 255
  Lay at, 236
  metaphor analysis of, 175
Equal Employment Opportunity Commission, U.S. (EEOC)
  illegal interview questions and, 53
  on sexual harassment, 286
equifinality, 342
Erosion Model of Employee Turnover, 145, 414
ethical issues
  bargaining as, 275
  bullying as, 279
  in deconstructing labels, 42
  disingenuous volunteering and, 336
  dual-career households as, 321
  in Enron metaphors, 175
  ethical bargaining as, 275
  gossip as, 135
  humans as resources as, 100
  in inappropriate interview questions, 52
  mixed messages as, 66
  promotion bias as, 376
  retrospective rationality and, 254
  salary for segmenters as, 326
  sexual harassment as, 283
  "signaling function" and, 203
  social media use as, 354, 357, 411
  of strategic ambiguity, 12
  team diversity as, 361

top-level management and, 106
in upward communication, 129–30
vocabulary of hierarchy as, 77
ethical leadership behavior, 236–37
ethnography, 177–79
exit, *See* Chapter 15
bullying and, 400, 415
involuntary, 398, 399, 410–14,
416–17
SET and, 398–99, 417
third form of, 415–16
voluntary exit, 398, 400–09
exit interviews, 408–10
expectations and experiences, 78
changes as objective in, 79
contrasts as subjective in, 79–80
positive differences in, 80–81
for students, 79
surprises as subjective in, 80
expert power
in *Catch Me If You Can*, 296–97
as personal power, 297
external communication, 219–20, 364

face-to-face communication (FtF),
352–53
technology impacting, 356
volunteers and, 367
Fairhurst, Gail, 232, 233–34, 307
family-friendly policies, 327, *332*
career repercussions from, 329–30
negotiation leave in, 330
peer pressure and, 330–31
"third-place" roles in, 332–33
work-family conflict and, 332–33
work-life balance and, 328, 331–32
family influence, 32–35, 34*f*
Family Medical Care Act, 331
family-to-work conflict, 323
faulty decision making
cognitive influence in, 258–59
Enron and, 255
groupthink as, 256–58
ineffective persuasion in, 260
psychological influence in,
259–60
social influence in, 260
Volkswagen and, 255
Fayol, Henri
classical management and, 92
general management theory of,
90–92

organizational structure and
management for, 90
Taylor compared to, 93
transmission model for, 92
Weber compared to, 93
feedback, 125, 178,188, 382
Feeley, Thomas, 145, 414
feminism, 24–25
"fired at will," 410
Fisher, B. A., 244
fixed socialization, 64
Florida A&M, 257
follow-up interviews, 51
illegal questions in, 53
pitfalls of, 53
screening interview compared
to, 52
food bank example, 26–27
formal communication channels,
120, 418
downward communication as,
124–26
horizontal communication as,
131–33
informal communication, 133–36 in
information transfer in, 137
integrative structures in, 136–37,
138*f*
limitations of, 137–39
organizational chart in, 122, 123*f*
upward communication as,
126–29, *127*
formal socialization, 62*t*, 63
framing theory
devices in, 233
leadership framing in, 232
in managerial leadership, 234
French, J. R. P., 295–96, 299
friendship development model,
195–96
FtF. *See* face-to-face communication
Fulghum, R., 35
Fuller, Linda and Millard, 235
functional boundaries, 74, 75, 75*f*

Game of Thrones, 290–91
garbage can model, 252–53, 254
GDSS. *See* group decision support
systems
gender stereotypes
families reinforcing, 33
in media, 41

general management theory, 90–92
general newcomer adaptation, 81–82
Gibson, M. K., 34–35
Giddens, Anthony, 156, 157
glassdoor.com, 54
globalization
convergence and divergence
in, 365
external communication and, 364
interdependence in, 366
multinational corporations
and, 264
volunteers and, 368
Google
human resource approach of,
104–5
as investiture socialization, 65, *65*
Gossett, Loril, 411
gossip, 135
Gouran, D. S., 258, 262
gradual disenchantment, 401
role stress and burnout in, 402
social support and, 403
Graen, George, 189
Grameen bank, in Bangladesh, 111
"grapevine" communication. *See*
informal communication
Greenhaus, J. H., 317–19
Greyston Bakery, 228
group decision support systems
(GDSS), 354
group restricted codes, 132
group socialization, 62*t*, 63
groupthink, 256–58, 261, 420
guard role, 220

Hall, D. T., 271, 272*f*
Hawthorne effect, 97, 136
Hawthorne studies
Bank Wiring Room Experiments
in, 98, 110
classical management theory
challenged by, 96
Human Relations Management
developed from, 99
Illumination Studies of, 96–97
Relay Assembly Experiments in,
97–98
of Roethlisberger, 96
hazing, 257, 378
headhunting, 404
Healy, Bernadine, 236

laggards, 345, 346, 347
laissez-faire management, 214, 216, 218–19
late majority, 345
latent conflict, 269
lateral communication. *See* horizontal communication
Lay, Kenneth, 236
leader–member exchange theory (LMX)
　high LMX relationships in, 189, 197, 379
　low LMX relationships in, 190, 197
leadership. *See* Chapter 8, managerial leadership; organizational leadership
leadership traits, 212
legal definition, of organizations, 7–8, 26
legitimate power, 295–96
　as positional power, 297
Levy, Jan, 235
Lewis, L. K., 333, 335
　change classified by, 343–44
　on communication strategies for change acceptance, 349–50
　on resistance behaviors, 348
liaisons, 144, 145
liberal feminism, 24
life satisfaction, 323
lifetime employment, 28–29, 39
linkage characteristics
　intensity as, 142, 144
　reciprocity as, 142
　uniplexity and multiplexity in, 144
LMX. *See* leader–member exchange theory
loyal followers, 225
Lucas, K., 33, 34*f*
Lutgen-Sandvik, P., 278

Machiavelli, Niccolo, 301
Machiavellianism, 301
maintenance communication, 121
Malden Mills company, 171
"malicious compliance," 306
management approach, 86
management theory *See* Chapter 4
　classical management 87–96
　critical perspective on, 115–16

human relations approach to, 96–100
human resource approach to, 100–103
interpretive perspective on, 115
post-positivist perspective on, 114–15
summary of, 117
teamwork approach to, 106–12
for volunteers, 112–13
managerial leadership
　contingency model of, 217–19, 218*f*
　dialectical theory and, 220–22, 221*t*, 223
　ethical behavior in, 235–36
　external communication in, 219–20
　framing theory in, 234
　leading groups in, 213
　models of, 213–16, 215*f*
　organizational leadership compared to, 211, 223–24, 236–37, 237*t*
　situational model of, 216–17
　social inequities in, 213
　traits of, 212–13, 237
　volunteers and, 222–23
manifest conflict, 269
Martin, Joann
　critique of perspectives of, 168–69
　perspectives on organizational culture of, 164–68
Marx, Karl, 294
Mary Kay Cosmetics, 225–26
M&As. *See* mergers and acquisitions
Maslow's hierarchy of needs, 101–2, 299
McGregor, Douglas
　Theory X of, 87, 94, 101
　Theory Y of, 101–2
media influence, 40–41
media richness theory
　FtF and CTIs in, 352–53
　information-carrying capacities in, 351–52
　symbol carrying capacity in, 352
mediator, 276–277
membership negotiation, 8
mentoring
　changing models of, 199
　formal and informal, 200

international job transfers and, 384
multiple goals of, 198–99
upside down, 201
for volunteers, 207
mergers and acquisitions (M&As)
　conglomerate strategy in, 386–87
　culture and, 390–91
　failure in, 387, 391
　horizontal and vertical integration in, 386
　in-play phase in, 387–89
　NPOs and, 395
　pre-merger phase in, 387
　RIFs and, 391
　stabilization phase in, 391
　strategic organizational communication plan for, 389
　transition phase in, 389–90
metamorphosis phase, 28
metaphor analysis, 173–76
　of Disney World, 174–76
　of Enron, 175
Microsoft, 346
middle-group relationships, 191
middle-of-the-road management, 214–15, 215*f*
mid-level employees, 135
Miller, V. D., 68–70
mission statement
　artifacts in, 154
　strategic ambiguity in, 11–12
monochronic cultures, 365
monolithic organizations, 360
monster.com, 54
motherhood norm, 320–323
Mouton, Jane, 214, 215*f*, 271, 272*f*
multiple sequence model, 249*t*
　breakpoint in, 247–48
multiplexity, 144
Mumby, D. K., 292, 301–2
mutual performance monitoring, 109

Nanus, Burt, 226
National Cash Register. *See* NCR.
National Security Agency, 140–41
naturalistic observation. *See* direct observation
NCR, 230, 347, 349
　M&A of, 386–87
nepotism, 159–60

pivotal norms, 161
P-J. *See* person-job fit
planned exits, 400
    career change and, 405
    preannouncement phase for, 406
plausible deniability, 12
plural organizations, 360
P-O. *See* person-organization fit
policy responses and feedback, 127
political influence network, 144
polychronic cultures, 365
Pondy, L. R., 269
Poole, M. S., 247–48, 249t
    on structuration theory, 156
post-positivist perspective, 16–18,
        102–3
    management theories from,
        114–15
    on organizational culture, 180
power *See* Chapter 11
    as attributed, 291, 305
    deep structure, 295
    dominance and, 293
    exercise of, 291–92
    expert, 296–97
    in *Game of Thrones*, 290–91
    ideologies and, 293–94
    influence and, 292
    Machiavellianism and, 301
    in NPOs, 310–11
    personal characteristics and,
        300–301
    resistance to, 305–8
    resource dependency and,
        298–99
    as social exchange, 299–300
    surface level, 294–95
    typology of, 295–98
pre-promotion phase, 377
prescriptive model of decision
        making 241–43
previous experience
    full-time employment as, 39
    part-time employment as, 38–39
    volunteering as, 40
The Prince (Machiavelli), 231
problem reports, 127
process conflict, 269
production communication, 121
progressive discipline, 410
    attribution theory in, 412–13
    dismissal meeting in, 413

problem-solving breakpoint in,
        411, 413
    termination breakpoint in, 412–13
project teams, 137, 138f
promotions, 395
    bias in, 376
    hierarchical boundaries and, 76
    pre-promotion phase of, 377
    selection context in, 375–76
    sensemaking and, 374–75
    shifting phase in, 377–78
    skill set for, 376–77
    stabilization phase of, 378–79
Putnam, L. L., 265, 275

quality circles, 136, 137
"quid pro quo" requests, 284, 401

random socialization, 64
rational models, 249t, 250–51
Raven, B., 295–96, 299
reachability, 147
realistic job previews (RJPs), 53–55
realistic merger preview, 389
"real job" colloquialism
    anticipatory role socialization in,
        42–43
    ethical issue in, 42
    volunteering and, 44
rebels, 67
recall method, 140
reciprocity
    isolates and, 145
    as linkage characteristic, 142
recruitment process. *See also* selection
        process, in recruitment
    in anticipatory organizational
        socialization, 46–48
    improving, 46
    P-J and P-O in, 45, 46, 53, 404
    RJPs in, 53–54
    strategies in, 46–47
    for volunteers, 56
reductions-in-force (RIFs), 386
    announcement phase for, 392–93
    hiring freeze and, 392
    M&As and, 391
    post-layoff phase in, 393–94
    pre-announcement phase in, 392
    sensemaking in, 394
    survivors of, 393–94
referent power, 296, 297

reflective comment analysis 176–77
    decision-making comments in,
        176–77
    psychiatric healthcare
        organization study of, 177
    steps of, 176
reflective thinking model, 241–43,
        249t
    NGT in, 242
    VIT compared to, 249
relational communication. *See* social
        communication
relational conflict, 269, 270
relational uncertainties, 59–60
relationship development, 191–92
Relay Assembly Experiments, in
        Hawthorne studies, 97–98
relevant norms, 161
reputational networks, 141
research perspectives, 29
    critical perspective as, 20–25, 27,
        115–16
    dialogic approach to, 25
    feminist perspectives as, 24–25
    interpretive perspective as, 18–20,
        27, 115
    post-positivist perspective as,
        16–18, 22, 27, 102–3, 114–15
resistance, to power, 313
    covert, 306
    decaf resistance as, 306–8
    forms of, 307–8
    "malicious compliance" as, 306
    at NPOs, 312
    voicing dissent as, 308
resistance behaviors, 348
resource dependency
    NPOs and, 310
    organizational and group, 299
    in surface power relationships, 298
résumés, 48–49
retirement
    cost–benefit ratio ~~ ·~~
    exit ph~~ase~~

464

sequ~~···~~
serial s~~···~~
service-b~~···~~
service lea~~···~~
SET. *See* soci~~···~~